About the Author

LITA-ROSE BETCHERMAN received a doctorate in Tudor and Stuart history from the University of Toronto and was the Women's Bureau director for the province of Ontario. She is the author of three books on Canadian history. She lives in Toronto.

HARPER ⬤ PERENNIAL

NEW YORK • LONDON • TORONTO • SYDNEY

COURT LADY

COUNTRY WIFE

Two Noble Sisters in

Seventeenth-Century England

LITA-ROSE BETCHERMAN

To the memory of my daughter
Barbara Betcherman (1948–1983),
author, lawyer, feminist

HARPER ● PERENNIAL

FIRST HARPER PERENNIAL EDITION PUBLISHED 2006.

Designed by Judith Abbate/Abbate Design

The Library of Congress has catalogued the hardcover edition as follows:

Betcherman, Lita-Rose.
    Court lady and country wife / Lita-Rose Betcherman.—1st ed.
      p. cm.
    ISBN-10: 0-06-076288-8 (acid-free paper)
    ISBN-13: 978-0-06-076288-9
      1. Carlisle, Lucy Hay, Countess of, 1599–1660.   2. Leicester, Dorothy Sidney, Countess of, 1958?–1659.   3. Carlisle, James Hay, Earl of, 1580–1636—Marriage. 4. Leicester, Robert Sidney, Earl of, 1595–1677—Marriage.   5. Great Britain—Court and courtiers—History—17th Century.   6. Women in politics—Great Britain—History—17th century.   7. Great Britain—History—Stuarts, 1603–1714—Biography.   8. Country life—England—History—17th century. 9. Women—Great Britain—History—17th century.   10. Nobility—Great Britain—Biography.   11. Sisters—Great Britain—Biography.   12. Penshurst Place (England) 13. Percy family.   I. Title.

    DA 378.C27B48   2005
    941.06'092'2—dc22
    [B]   2005041548

ISBN-10: 0-06-076289-6 (pbk.)
ISBN-13: 978-0-06-076289-6 (pbk.)

06 07 08 09 10 ❖/RRD 10 9 8 7 6 5 4 3 2 1

Contents

Acknowledgments

I AM DEEPLY GRATEFUL to my Canadian editor, Phyllis Bruce, for her masterly editing of the manuscript, which infinitely improved it, and to my American editor, Carolyn Marino, for her expertise and her confidence in the project. I also wish to thank Jennifer Civiletto, who oversaw production of the book, and Noelle Zitzer along with Katie Hearn on the Canadian side. My thanks to Barbara Czarnecki for her painstaking copyediting. I cannot sufficiently express my gratitude to my agent, Beverley Slopen, for her unfailing support and sage advice. Special thanks to my husband, Irving Betcherman, for his constant encouragement in this, as in all my ventures.

I wish to acknowledge permission received for access to their family papers from the tenth Duke of Northumberland, the first Viscount De L'Isle, and the tenth Earl Fitzwilliam.

Note on Names

IN SEVENTEENTH-CENTURY BRITAIN, influential men vied with one another for titles that would elevate them to the peerage. The king could grant five titles. In ascending order, these were baron (whose wife would be baroness); viscount (viscountess); earl (countess); marquess or marquis (marchioness); and duke (duchess). The titles were hereditary, passing in most cases to the peer's eldest son or closest male heir, though some ancient peerages allowed for the title to pass to a daughter in the absence of a male descendant. Knights and baronets, who are not in the peerage, were customarily addressed as "Lord" in the seventeenth century, a usage that would be considered incorrect today.

Here is a list of principal characters and the date of their new titles:

Lucy Percy—Lady Hay (1617), Viscountess Doncaster (1618), Countess of Carlisle (1622)

Dorothy Percy—Lady Sidney (1616), Viscountess Lisle (1618), Countess of Leicester (1626)

Sisters' father—Henry Percy, ninth Earl of Northumberland (1585)

Sisters' mother—Dorothy Devereux, Countess of Northumberland (ca.1594)

Sisters' brothers—Sir Algernon Percy, tenth Earl of Northumberland (1632)

— Henry Percy (Harry), Baron Percy of Alnwick (1643)

Lucy's husband—Sir James Hay, Viscount Doncaster (1618), first Earl of Carlisle (1622)

Lucy's stepson—James Hay, Viscount Doncaster (1623)

Dorothy's husband—Sir Robert Sidney, Viscount Lisle (1618), second Earl of Leicester (1626)

Dorothy's elder sons—Philip Sidney, Viscount Lisle (1626)

— Algernon Sidney

Dorothy's father-in-law—Sir Robert Sidney, Viscount Lisle (1605), first Earl of Leicester (1618)*

Dorothy's son-in-law—Henry Spencer, Baron Spencer (1636), first Earl of Sunderland (1642)

Sisters' uncle—Robert Devereux, second Earl of Essex (1576)

Cousins—Robert Devereux, third Earl of Essex (1601)

— Sir Henry Rich, Viscount Kensington (1623), first Earl of Holland (1624)

Friends—Sir George Goring, Baron Goring (1628), Earl of Norwich (1644)

— Edward Montagu, Viscount Mandeville (1626), second Earl of Manchester (1642)

—William Cecil, second Earl of Salisbury (1614)

—Thomas Howard, Earl of Berkshire (1626)

—Thomas Wentworth, first Earl of Strafford (1640)

Royal favorite—George Villiers, Viscount Villiers (1616), Earl of Buckingham (1617), Marquess of Buckingham (1618), first Duke of Buckingham (1623)

---

*Not to be confused with Queen Elizabeth's Earl of Leicester, Robert Dudley, who had died in 1588 without leaving a legitimate heir. King James conferred the extinct title on the Sidney family.

COURT LADY

COUNTRY WIFE

Percy Family

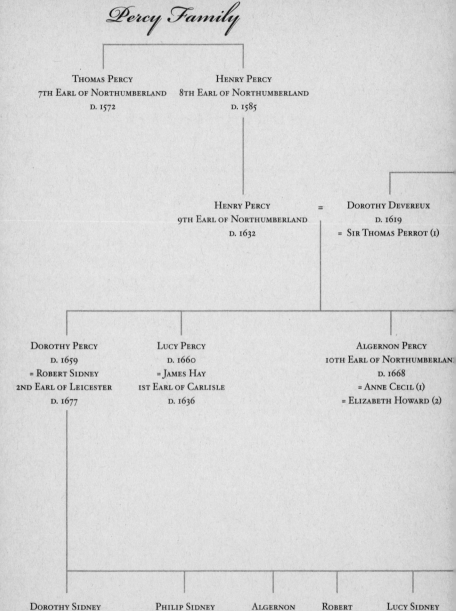

THOMAS PERCY
7TH EARL OF NORTHUMBERLAND
D. 1572

HENRY PERCY
8TH EARL OF NORTHUMBERLAND
D. 1585

HENRY PERCY
9TH EARL OF NORTHUMBERLAND
D. 1632

=

DOROTHY DEVEREUX
D. 1619
= SIR THOMAS PERROT (1)

DOROTHY PERCY
D. 1659
= ROBERT SIDNEY
2ND EARL OF LEICESTER
D. 1677

LUCY PERCY
D. 1660
= JAMES HAY
1ST EARL OF CARLISLE
D. 1636

ALGERNON PERCY
10TH EARL OF NORTHUMBERLAN
D. 1668
= ANNE CECIL (1)
= ELIZABETH HOWARD (2)

DOROTHY SIDNEY
= HENRY SPENCER
1ST EARL OF SUNDERLAND (1)
D. 1643
= ROBERT SMYTHE (2)

PHILIP SIDNEY
3RD EARL OF LEICESTER
= CATHERINE CECIL

**ALGERNON
SIDNEY**

**ROBERT
SIDNEY**

LUCY SIDNEY
= SIR JOHN PELHAM

Devereux Family

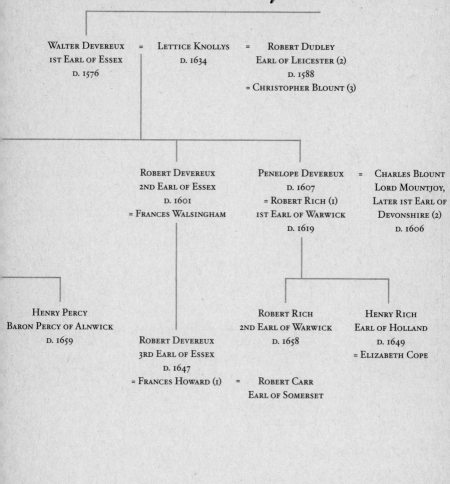

WALTER DEVEREUX
1ST EARL OF ESSEX
D. 1576

=

LETTICE KNOLLYS
D. 1634

=

ROBERT DUDLEY
EARL OF LEICESTER (2)
D. 1588
= CHRISTOPHER BLOUNT (3)

ROBERT DEVEREUX
2ND EARL OF ESSEX
D. 1601
= FRANCES WALSINGHAM

PENELOPE DEVEREUX
D. 1607
= ROBERT RICH (1)
1ST EARL OF WARWICK
D. 1619

=

CHARLES BLOUNT
LORD MOUNTJOY,
LATER 1ST EARL OF
DEVONSHIRE (2)
D. 1606

HENRY PERCY
BARON PERCY OF ALNWICK
D. 1659

ROBERT DEVEREUX
3RD EARL OF ESSEX
D. 1647
= FRANCES HOWARD (1)

=

ROBERT CARR
EARL OF SOMERSET

ROBERT RICH
2ND EARL OF WARWICK
D. 1658

HENRY RICH
EARL OF HOLLAND
D. 1649
= ELIZABETH COPE

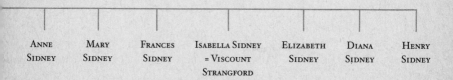

ANNE
SIDNEY

MARY
SIDNEY

FRANCES
SIDNEY

ISABELLA SIDNEY
= VISCOUNT
STRANGFORD

ELIZABETH
SIDNEY

DIANA
SIDNEY

HENRY
SIDNEY

ON A RAINY FEBRUARY DAY in 1617, a barge drew up
to Tower Wharf on the River Thames and two young women disem-
barked. From their dress and from the barge bearing a coat of arms, it
was obvious that these young women were members of the nobility.
Dismissing the oarsmen, they crossed the drawbridge over the moat
and entered the confines of the Tower of London as the great iron
gates clanged shut behind them. Escorted by a pair of oafish guards,
they circled the inner wall, carefully averting their eyes from Tower
Hill, where their uncle not so many years before had been beheaded,
and continued on to the Martin Tower in the northeast corner of the
bastion wall. Dorothy and Lucy Percy had come to visit their father.

Henry Percy, ninth Earl of Northumberland, had been a prisoner
in the Tower during the years when the sisters were growing up. In
1606 he had been found guilty of complicity in the failed Gunpowder
Plot to blow up Westminster Hall at the very moment King James I,
having ascended to the throne just three years earlier, was opening
Parliament. The case against the Earl had, in fact, never been proven.
His conviction rested on guilt by association; during the investigation it came out that the day before the plot was discovered, one of

the chief plotters, a distant relative employed by the Earl to collect the rents from his northern estates, had dropped in on him at his country house. Whether guilty or not, the ninth earl was following in the family tradition. His grandfather Sir Thomas Percy had been attainted and executed for his part in the revolt against Henry VIII, known as the Pilgrimage of Grace. His uncle, the seventh earl, had been beheaded in the Tower for treason, and his father, the eighth earl, committed suicide when he was sent to the Tower a third time for plotting against Queen Elizabeth I.

Yet the room the sisters entered was no dank prison cell. It was the withdrawing room in a suite of six luxuriously furnished rooms. The Earl had brought the finest tables, chairs, and chests from his castles throughout England. The stone walls were hung with tapestries, and Turkey carpets warmed the floors. Even in prison the Earl remained a great noble, living in style as if the Tower were his private castle. Through well-placed bribes, particularly to the Lieutenant of the Tower, he had appropriated the Martin Tower for himself and converted it into this comfortable habitation. As well, he had set up a laboratory for his scientific experiments. Several of his protégés— mathematicians and astronomers—stayed with him in the Tower, and he kept twenty servants, renting a house on Tower Hill for the overflow. With the cooperation of the Lieutenant of the Tower, he acquired the use of Tower grounds for a bowling alley, an archery range, and stables for his horses, which were regularly exercised by his Master of the Horse.

An irritable and overbearing man, Northumberland was as arrogant in prison as out. When a fellow prisoner wandered onto the gravel path where he took his daily walks, he beat the unfortunate interloper with his cane. It was said of the Earl of Northumberland that were it not for the blot on his escutcheon, he would have been perfectly content with his incarceration.[1]

If the Earl had paid attention to his pretty daughters on this particular visit in 1617, he might have noticed that they were somewhat subdued. Dorothy was always reserved, but Lucy, the younger sister, was ebullient by nature. This day her contagious laughter was not to be heard by the guards and prisoners. The truth was that the sisters had come with news they knew would make their father exceedingly angry. They had decided their future on their own, in defiance of his plans for them. Each in her own way was looking forward to living happily ever after with a wealthy, well-placed husband. But in their youthful self-confidence, they could not know all that the future held for them or for England itself. As fate would have it, one of them would also end up in the Tower of London and in very different circumstances from those of their father.

PART ONE

MONEY

AND

MARRIAGE

TWO PRETTY SISTERS

DOROTHY WAS SEVEN and Lucy six when their father, Henry Percy, ninth Earl of Northumberland, was sent to the Tower. On November 4, 1605, he set out by water from Syon House, his country home on the banks of the Thames just west of London, to attend the opening of Parliament the following day. Six months later he was found guilty of treason. It would be sixteen years before he returned.

The sisters' lives, however, hardly changed as a result of their father's imprisonment. Like all children of the nobility, they saw little enough of their mother and even less of their father. Theirs was a world of nurses and maids, grooms and gardeners. In truth, they were better acquainted with the seventy blue-liveried servants at Syon than they were with their father. Nor was the Earl a fond parent to be missed. When he came upon them at play, he would not stop to talk: the conversation of children "is unsuitable to my humour," he was wont to say.[1] For their part, the sisters shed few tears at his absence. With their father gone they no longer had to listen to their parents' squabbles. How it had made their hearts pound to hear their hot-tempered mother shouting at their father and his cold, low-spoken replies goading her into wild sobbing.

The little girls would have had no recollection of it, but their parents had separated when Lucy was an infant and Dorothy just a toddler. In October 1599, the Countess left her husband. Her side of the story was that the Earl had thrown her out for no reason: "It was his Lordship's pleasure upon no cause given by me to have me keep house by myself," she wrote her brother, Essex.[2] It may have been no coincidence that at this very time the Earl of Essex, formerly Queen Elizabeth's pampered favorite, was under house arrest for disobeying the Queen. The ambitious Northumberland had married the sister, Dorothy Devereux, because of the brother: a family connection with the fallen favorite now was politically unwise.

Forced to live on her own, Lady Northumberland rented a modest house in Putney, leaving the baby girls with their father. It was not that she did not love her daughters; she simply did not have the wherewithal to provide for them in a manner suitable to an earl's children. Because the land and goods she had brought into the marriage had automatically become her husband's property, she was left with a very small allowance. Nevertheless, several months later when she heard that her daughters were not thriving, she insisted that they live with her. Perhaps Lucy was rejecting the wet nurse's milk, or perhaps the two-year-old was pining away. Lord Northumberland allowed the girls to go to their mother but provided no increase in her allowance to care for them.

In December 1601, Lady Northumberland returned to her husband. Again, the fate of her brother may have determined her own. Essex had recently been beheaded for an abortive insurrection against the Queen. Without a powerful male relative, Lady Northumberland took the most prudent course for her little girls. The resumption of their parents' stormy marriage produced two brothers: Algernon in 1602 and Henry, called Harry, in 1604.

Two years after Lady Northumberland went home, Queen Elizabeth died in her seventieth year. It had been a pathetic death. Word seeped out of the palace of Her Majesty sitting on a pile of cushions on the floor, unable to sleep and eating nothing, her finger in her mouth like a child.[3] At last, she allowed the doctors to carry her to bed, where on March 23, 1603, she passed away.

She had reigned for almost forty-five years and few could remember an England without her. She had remained unmarried, to be, in her own words, "king as well as queen" of her realm. A very visible monarch, while on progress (as royal visits to the country homes of the nobility were called) she would stop at hamlets and villages to show herself in all her glory to her subjects, dazzling them with her jewel-bedecked gowns and winning their hearts with flattering speeches. Everywhere the Virgin Queen went, she was greeted with aves as if she were the Virgin herself.

Elizabeth was a true daughter of the formidable Henry VIII. Along with his red hair she had inherited his domineering personality and his charisma. Her father had broken with Rome and declared himself head of the Church of England for no other reason than that he had lusted after her mother, Anne Boleyn, and the Pope would not grant him a divorce from his Spanish queen, Catherine of Aragon. After the short reign of the sickly boy king Edward VI, Roman Catholicism had enjoyed a brief revival under Catherine's daughter Mary, known to history as Bloody Mary for the hundreds of Protestants she burned for heresy. When Elizabeth came to the throne in 1558, she completed her father's reformation, establishing the Anglican Church and effectively outlawing Catholicism.

But the Old Faith died hard in England. These were the days of the "priest's holes," where the Catholic nobility hid their chaplains. Indeed, during her reign, Elizabeth had to put down a Catholic rebellion (led by the seventh Earl of Northumberland) and an assassination plot, both of which were aimed at replacing her with her cousin, Mary Queen of Scots. Having fled from her hostile barons in Scotland to save her life, Mary Stuart lived as a prisoner in England. Ultimately, Elizabeth had to execute this royal troublemaker.

Almost as troublesome to Elizabeth as the Anglo-Catholics were the Puritans who wanted to import the strict Protestantism that John Calvin had introduced in Geneva. Calvinists wanted no bishops, no ritual or music in church, sermons by a lay preacher rather than the parson, and a Sabbath without festivals or saints' days. Elizabeth, who favored moderation in religion, regarded the Puritans as zealots.

Anglicanism, as she conceived it, was a broad, shallow faith that could encompass all Englishmen.

Elizabeth's state Protestantism earned her dangerous enemies abroad. The papacy, still hoping to bring England back into the fold, connived with the Anglo-Catholics, and in 1570 the Pope excommunicated her. A more dangerous enemy was the Spanish king, Philip II. After failing to acquire England through marriage—his wife, Queen Mary, had died and Elizabeth would not have him—Philip resolved to take it by conquest. Elizabeth's wise rule was rewarded in 1588 when her valiant seamen repulsed the Spanish Armada, and Catholic, Puritan, and Protestant Englishmen rejoiced as one nation in Spain's defeat.

To the end, the old queen had maintained the illusion of an ageless Gloriana, masking her wrinkled face with white lead, covering her thin, graying hair with a flaming red wig, and encasing her shrunken body in rich gowns stiffened with buckram. However, the execution of the Earl of Essex, a hero to the common people for his dash and derring-do, had diminished her popularity, and her last public appearances met with little enthusiasm.

Elizabeth had died without leaving an heir. Ironically, her legitimate successor was James VI of Scotland, the son of Mary Queen of Scots whom she had executed. News of Queen Elizabeth's death sent the English courtiers galloping up to Edinburgh to swear allegiance to the Scottish king who was now King James I of England.

THE FACT THAT the English and the Scots had the same king did not result in a union of the two countries. Scotland continued to have its own parliament, its own laws, and its own version of the Reformed Church: Presbyterianism.

If, as James believed, he was God's anointed on earth, the Almighty had not chosen a very attractive vessel. He wore thickly padded vests and breeches stuffed with wool (to protect himself, some said, from assassination), giving him a top-heavy appearance. His tongue was seemingly too large for his mouth and he dribbled when he spoke; he had a habit of scratching himself in embarrassing places. He never washed and he drank too much.[4] Yet with all his repellent personal habits, he was a highly intelligent man, a scholar who could argue cogently with theologians and lawyers, and his sobriquet "the British Solomon" was not undeserved. Vastly preferring Anglicanism to the severe Presbyterianism he had left behind in Scotland, he worried that the Bible most commonly used in England was the radical Geneva Bible, which, among other tenets, approved of regicide. One of his first acts as King of England was to commission the Authorized Version, also called the King James Bible and still in use today. As well as intelligence, James possessed a quick wit, and his thick Scottish burr added flavor to his puns and jests. Like a good humorist, he never laughed at his own jokes. His queen, Anne of Denmark, had provided him with two sons and a daughter. Thus he had the advantage over Elizabeth of giving England a royal family.

James's court proved to be very different from Elizabeth's. Hers had been refined and elegant, though never lacking in pleasurable festivities. Elizabeth regaled her courtiers with masques and feasts and plays—Shakespeare's *Twelfth Night* was performed at court by royal command—and there was constant dancing, for she herself was a high-stepping dancer. The Queen was very strict about morals, demanding chastity of her young maids-in-waiting—if she must remain a virgin, so must they. Indeed, she preferred her courtiers to stay unmarried, and when they did not, she sulked, or even banished them. Her attendants were, of course, female, and it seemed to visitors that her court was overrun with women. For his part, James held women in contempt, and his inner circle was exclusively male.

While Elizabeth thrived on the love of her people—they were the jewel in her crown, she liked to say—James shunned the adulation of the crowd. "What do they want from me?" he once inquired of a courtier. "They want to see you," he was told. "Then I'll pull down my pants and show them my arse."[5] As this uncouth remark indicates, the prevailing coarseness and rowdiness in James's court reflected the tastelessness of the sovereign.

Elizabeth was parsimonious to a fault, even underprovisioning her armies serving abroad. James was lavish with gifts of money, grants, and pensions to his favorites so that his coffers were always depleted. Whereas Queen Elizabeth kept the reins of state in her own hands—it must be said that her indecision nearly drove her counselors mad—James had no patience for the business of governing. At most, he made snap decisions, but as a rule he left state affairs to his overworked and underappreciated Lord Treasurer and Secretary of State, Robert Cecil, Earl of Salisbury, while he himself went hunting or hawking with his cronies. In actual fact, James was seldom at his palace of Whitehall in London. Hunting was a passion with him, and most of the time he was at his hunting lodges at Royston or Newmarket.

It appeared as if the Earl of Northumberland would fare very well under the new regime. He had been among the many English nobles who had offered his allegiance to James in Elizabeth's dying hours. For currying favor at the right moment, he was appointed to the Privy Council—the King's body of advisers composed of the great officers of state and some of the nobility. Moreover, Northumberland had the expensive honor of a royal visit to Syon House, and Lady Northumberland was chosen to assist at the baptism of a royal baby.

Then came the discovery of the horrendous Gunpowder Plot. Believing that James had broken his promise of tolerance, four English Catholics, among them a soldier named Guy Fawkes, had planted twenty barrels of gunpowder in the cellar under Westminster Hall, where both the upper and lower houses of Parliament met. The conspirators' plan was to explode the gunpowder when Parliament opened on November 5, 1605. The resulting inferno would have destroyed the royal family, the bishops, and the assembled Lords and Commons—in short, the entire government of the realm. Fortunately, the scheme was discovered in time.

One of the conspirators captured was Thomas Percy. The very name of Percy being associated with rebellion against the sovereign, Thomas's involvement raised suspicion about his kinsman and employer the Earl of Northumberland, who, though brought up as a Protestant, was a strong advocate of clemency for Catholics.

Northumberland was sent to the Tower, and on June 26, 1606, his case came up before the Star Chamber. Glancing around at his judges, Northumberland saw the same men who had been his colleagues on the Privy Council.

The Star Chamber was simply the Privy Council sitting in judgment. Unlike the common law courts, which were bound by statute and precedent and trial by jury, the Star Chamber had total discretion. Its primary purpose was to deal with matters of sedition and treason, yet their Lordships heard private disputes about adultery, inheritance, property, and money. Although unable to order capital punishment, they had a range of corporal punishment at their disposal, including nose slitting and the chopping off of ears and hands. Sending convicted men and women to stand in the pillory with papers on their head spelling out their offenses was an oft-used penalty for minor offenders. Proud Northumberland was humiliated to be judged by his peers, especially since he regarded each man as inferior to himself in intellect and position. The judgment would have wiped the sneer off his face. He was deprived of all honors, fined £30,000, and sentenced to life in the Tower.

The Percys were great landowners in Northumberland, Westmorland, and Cumberland—"the North knows no prince but a Percy" was the common saying. They also had estates in the warmer and more civilized south of England—the Earl's favorite seat was the mansion of Petworth House in Sussex. From the Tower, Northumberland directed his empire with ruthless efficiency. To be fair to him, his hard dealings with his tenants were partly due to a need to raise cash to pay off the enormous fine levied upon him when he was sent to the Tower—"the greatest fine that was ever got on any subject in this realm," he complained to King James with good reason.[6]

But while the change of regime from Elizabeth Tudor to James Stuart in 1603 had once more tainted the Percys with treason, it had removed the stigma of treason from Lady Northumberland's own family, the Devereux. Indeed, the reputation of her brother was being rehabilitated posthumously. In Elizabeth's last years, the Earl of Essex had secretly corresponded with the Scottish king to bring about his accession to the English throne. Now James, as King of England, was showing marked favor to the Essex circle.

The sisters' relatives on their mother's side provided enough drama for a Shakespearean play. Lady Northumberland's mother, Lettice Knollys, had created a sensation in her young days with a secret marriage to the Earl of Leicester, the love of Queen Elizabeth's life. When the marriage came to light, the Queen exhibited all the fury of a woman scorned. Then there was Lady Northumberland's sister, Penelope, Lady Rich, who abandoned her husband and children to live in open adultery, producing five children, until her divorce in 1605 permitted her to marry her lover. Lady Northumberland herself had a romantic past, having first married the man of her choice against the Queen's wishes. Her runaway marriage had not proved a success, but her husband had released her from it by dying. Her second marriage, to Henry Percy, was arranged to seal a political alliance between Northumberland and her brother, Essex. With all the second and third marriages in their mother's family, the Percy children were related to half the aristocracy of England.

As they had before the Earl's imprisonment, the Countess and her children lived most of the time at Syon House. Lady Northumberland had inherited the lease from her first husband and brought it to Northumberland as part of her dowry. In 1604 King James, then full of gratitude to the Earl for supporting his ascension to the English throne, granted the house to Northumberland in fee simple.[7] Once he owned it, the Earl made extensive renovations that continued even after his imprisonment. Today, the low, battlemented Bath stone building looks much as it did in the early seventeenth century. But the White House, as it was known, was disfigured by unsightly red brick wings that time has happily demolished. Vanished too are the walled formal gardens, transformed into an English park by Capability Brown in the following century. The interior of the house has changed beyond all recognition. Reflecting the neoclassical taste of its eighteenth-century owners, the oak-beamed great hall and wainscoted long gallery have been replaced by the marble and gilded decor of Robert Adam.

Life at Syon House was pleasant for Dorothy and Lucy, despite their mother's fits of depression, which cast a pall over the household. And they missed their brother Algernon. When he turned seven his father took him to live in the Tower "to wean him from his nursery company and his mother's wings."[8] Until he went to Cambridge in his early teens, the boy lived and studied in the Tower under the noted scientists and scholars who received the Earl's generous patronage. The Earl took less interest in his younger son. Harry was sent at five years of age to the common school in the village of Islesworth near Syon House.

So the sisters were the only children at home. Having been born just eleven months apart in 1598 and 1599, the "young ladies" (as they were respectfully referred to by the servants) were inseparable. The delights of growing up in a country house were doubled because they discovered them together. For their playground they had acres of gardens and orchards stretching down to the river. They skipped along the shaded walks of sycamores and elms, plucked succulent grapes from the vine wall, and watched the gardeners prune the masses of rosebushes. The kitchen gardens were full of strange-tasting pot herbs and salad greens; stomachaches taught the girls the consequences of overindulgence in apples and cherries. Then there were the stables ringing with the clatter of hoofs; Lucy, already a keen rider, was particularly bold in patting the high shiny rumps of the horses. But above all there was the Thames, the main highway of the day, which brought the world to their doorstep. The little girls would sit on the banks of the river, watching the river craft glide past: market barges laden with stacks of wood, bags of grain, piles of coal, and all the products of the farm necessary to feed the two hundred thousand Londoners; and private barges, painted and gilded like the one rocking at their own wharf. Often a bargeman or some gorgeously garbed lady would wave to the children on the riverbank.

Inside the house were many things of splendor and beauty to attract the sisters: floral tapestries, Turkey carpets, cavernous fireplaces, high bedsteads richly curtained in velvets and silks. But nothing fascinated them so much as the new "bathing house" and "cabinet" their mother had recently built into the nooks and crannies in her bedchamber. Although the Earl paid for this indoor plumbing from his countinghouse in the Tower, he dismissed it with disgust as a fanciful thing "which this fifteen years before was never missed nor wanting."[9]

In the landscape of their childhood, another house loomed almost as large as Syon. This was Essex House in London. One of the venerable mansions on the Strand between the City and Westminster, Essex House belonged to their maternal grandmother, the Countess of Leicester. She did not occupy it herself at this stage of her life—perhaps the house was too full of memories of her husband, the magnificent Leicester, and of her son, the dashing Essex. After Essex's execution in 1601, she leased the rambling, gabled building to her son-in-law Northumberland.[10] To travel to their town house from Syon, the Countess of Northumberland and her children went by water on their private barge, disembarking at Essex Stairs, or climbed into their large, cumbersome coach and jolted along the deeply rutted London Road.

Although the sisters' life in town was still bounded by garden walls and the river, it was more exciting than the country because of the visitors. The most frequent caller was their mother's best friend, Lucy Russell, Countess of Bedford—Lucy may have been named after her. Her husband, the third Earl of Bedford, had followed Essex in his failed rebellion against Queen Elizabeth and had saved his own neck only by paying a large fine to the Crown. The Essex connection served Lady Bedford well under the new regime. She was Queen Anne's First Lady of the Bedchamber, and her court gossip fascinated the little girls, particularly her young namesake. A beautiful, intelligent woman in her late twenties, as Queen Anne's favorite lady she was an influential courtier.[11] In the Countess of Bedford, we discover a role model for young Lucy Percy.

The King and Queen lived amicably but separately. Anne of Denmark's official residence was Greenwich Palace, some twenty miles downriver from London. Possibly influenced by Lady Bedford, Queen Anne remained a staunch friend to Lady Northumberland while the Earl was in the Tower of London. Lady Northumberland would often make the journey by water to Greenwich, dressed in the monstrous farthingale then in fashion, with powdered and frizzed hair and heavily painted face. In the annals of fashion, Queen Anne is famous for taking the farthingale, a cagelike construction of whalebone worn under voluminous skirts, to its most exaggerated proportions. She herself was "never seen without a farthingale as large as a tea-table." She even wore it for hunting. A painting by Paul Van Somer shows Anne about to mount her horse. Her riding habit is described with great glee by her nineteenth-century biographer Mrs. Strickland: "a farthingale of dark green velvet, made with a long tight-waisted boddice, a very queer grey beaver hat, of the clerical shape, called a shovel, with a gold band and a profusion of fire-coloured plumes, and this formidable head-tire is mounted on a high head of hair, like a periwig, elaborately curled and frizzed."[12] As Mrs. Strickland would have written these lines sitting in a crinoline, she was in no position to criticize the farthingale.

Queen Anne was passionately fond of masquing. Designed to glorify the monarchy, the masque was a dramatic entertainment combining music, poetry, and dance, using lavish sets and costumes. With scripts by the poet Ben Jonson and sets designed by Inigo Jones, Queen Anne attempted to evoke the golden age of antiquity. Amusingly, Inigo Jones's drawings for the nymphs and dryads show filmy gossamer costumes ballooning out over farthingales. Breaking the tradition of using male courtiers, Queen Anne established the custom of a ladies' masque presented at Whitehall or Hampton Court on Twelfth Night, and this evening had become the highlight of the Christmas revels. The Queen and her chosen ladies (twelve in all, including herself) began practicing their dances for the Christmas masque in early November. Lady Bedford was a regular performer, but from the records we see that Lady Northumberland was not a masquer, although her sister, Penelope, was one of the favored dozen until her death in 1607.[13]

From time to time Lady Northumberland would also go to the King's palace of Whitehall to plead for her husband's release. On July 16, 1606, shortly after the Earl's trial and conviction in the Star Chamber, it was reported that she waylaid the King as he went to chapel.[14] James was accustomed to the tearful pleadings of noble-women on behalf of their disgraced husbands. He gave them "gracious audience," raised their hopes, and sent them away well pleased but no further ahead. A better route (and one pursued by Lady Northumberland) was to work through the Queen, who sometimes brought the King around by such marital discomforts as prolonged sulking or a show of temper. The Queen did what she could to console Lady Northumberland. In the summer of 1607, she honored her with a visit to Syon House.

The sisters must have wondered why their mother was so eager to have their father back, considering how unhappy he made her. They were too young to understand that their world turned on royal favor, indeed that their own future could be put in jeopardy if their father remained in the Tower.

GROWING UP, Dorothy and Lucy saw nothing of London beyond the gates of Essex House. With a population rising toward a quarter of a million, London was dirty, noisy, smelly, overcrowded, and dangerous—no place for well-brought-up daughters of the nobility, their mother told them. However, the sisters were able to hear some of the sounds of London. If they stood near the gatehouse that fronted on the Strand, they could listen to the cries of the street hawkers: "Cheese and cream... Knives to grind... Chimney sweep... What d'ye lack." At night, lying in their trundle bed, they heard the reassuring sound of the night watchman ringing his bell and calling out, "Eight o' the clock and all's well." By the time he passed again at nine o'clock, the little girls were sound asleep. Night and day there was the tolling of the bells of dozens of London's churches.

Lady Northumberland took full advantage of city life. Accompanied by her maid, she drove into town to shop, pay visits, go to a playhouse, or attend church. Her coach, drawn by four matched bays, made slow progress through the narrow, crowded streets. Drivers of interlocked coaches and farm carts shouted abuse at one another.

Dreadful specimens of humanity trundled wheeled barrows of eels and fruit and hot spiced gingerbread. In front of the taverns and ale-houses, drunken men and women sprawled in the gutters. The diversity of the crowd was a feature of London streets. On Cheapside, the main street, aldermen in scarlet velvet rubbed shoulders with ragged beggars, and fashionable young blades elbowed the dowdy wives of decent citizens out of their way.

More often than not, Lady Northumberland's destination was the Royal Exchange in Cornhill. Built in Elizabeth's time by the banker and philanthropist Sir Richard Gresham, this was London's financial and commercial center. Merchants conducted their business affairs on the ground floor, while on the second floor, rows of shops offered fine goods of all descriptions. The New Exchange on the Strand, a business venture of the Earl of Salisbury, also offered a tempting selection of goods. As well as shopping, churchgoing was a popular activity of noblewomen. Lady Northumberland attended many of London's churches, but most frequently the footman would hand her down at the steps of St. Paul's Cathedral,[15] the home church of the Archbishop of Canterbury, to hear a sermon by some famous Protestant theologian.

Should her Ladyship be on her way to the Globe Theatre or to the Bear-Baiting Hall (women as well as men enjoyed this gruesome spectator sport), the coachman would have to cross London Bridge, as it was the only bridge connecting the north and south shores of the Thames. Rows of tall houses lined the bridge so that it looked like any other street to the passenger inside the coach. Pedestrians, however, could see the heads of criminals displayed over the gateways.

Lady Northumberland's pleasure outings were restricted to central London and the west end, as the east end was the district of the dockyards and the Tower of London. She always turned for home at nightfall, before the footpads and cutpurses came out like an insect infestation.

London's air was fetid, pungent with garbage and urine, and no doubt helped breed the plague that came upon the city every few years. Slops, tossed out the windows, ran freely down the gutters, not only in the streets of tenements that housed the poor but also on the Strand, where the wealthy resided. Disease struck rich and poor equally.

THE ONLY TIME THE SISTERS left Essex House was when their mother took them to visit their father. How they must have dreaded these visits! The time was passed in listening to their parents arguing. Besides, their father was a frightening figure. Wreathed in smoke, he sat glowering at a table covered with the diabolical-looking instruments he used for his experiments. To the little girls he was a being straight out of their nurse's tales of wizards and hobgoblins. The one bright spot was the chance to see their brother Algernon—if their father would let him off from his studies. Algernon was tutored daily by the scholars and scientists in residence. But for the really important training of an aristocrat—how to make a marriage that would increase his landholdings or bring influence at court (and how to handle his wife thereafter)—the Earl undertook to tutor Algernon himself. His views can be read in a long letter entitled "Advice to My Son," which was printed after his death.[16]

The Earl of Northumberland was a man of his time in his attitude toward women and their place in society. In the early seventeenth century, women were regarded as intellectually inferior, slaves of fashion, scolds, and gossips, whose only function was breeding: a desirable wife was a fecund and malleable creature who brought a good dowry. Their education was designed to give them social graces such as a smattering of French and Italian, needlework, dancing, and playing the lute or virginal, but to provide nothing for the mind. A woman intellectual, indeed, was a figure of fun. The London letter writer John Chamberlain heaped scorn on "compleat women for learning, language and all other rare qualities" and fled them like the plague. In law, women were consigned to the status of children and imbeciles. The use of the property that a woman brought with her in marriage passed entirely into her husband's hands. "That which the husband hath is his own; that which the wife hath is the husband's," commented a bitter proponent of women's rights.[17] A wife could not make a contract or a will without her husband's permission. The only way a married woman could own property was through the establishment of a trust in the name of a male relative or retainer. It was rare for a widow to gain the wardship of her own eldest son. The Court of Wards either made the grandfather the legal guardian or sold the wardship (with the use of the estate) to the highest bidder.

Male bias aside, there was some substance to the stereotype of the shrewish wife. Given the poor education and childlike dependence of women and their constant pregnancies, it is not surprising that many acted like undisciplined children. The bad-tempered, highly emotional woman is a recurring figure in the diaries and letters of the period. Chamberlain's letters (a principal source of Early Stuart social history) are full of anecdotes of upper-class shrewishness. Still, it was an emotional age for men as well as women. They were forever quarreling and dueling, and immaturity and instability were condoned as manly behavior.

Most noblemen spent their days hawking, hunting, bearbaiting, betting on cockfights, jousting, or running at the ring in the tiltyard. Both men and women attended the playhouses, particularly the Globe, where Shakespeare's company performed, and both sexes were addicted to card games and dicing. Backgammon, called "tables," was a favorite pastime.

Filled with the general prejudice against women, the Earl's view was further jaundiced by his own experience of an unhappy conjugal life. Lady Northumberland was a highly emotional woman given to depression. In his long letter of advice to his son, Northumberland wrote that "women are as wise at fifteen as at fifty." They have no moral sense and guide themselves only by the dictates of worldly fashion. Their learning is limited to "love, a little craft, and a little thriftiness, if they are so addicted out of disposition; handsomeness and trimness being the idol of their hearts till time write deep wrinkles on their forehead." In choosing a wife he advised his son to select one who is not ugly in mind or body, but above all with wealth and powerful friends who can aid in his advancement. He admitted that it did not work out that way in his own case, because he and his wife's powerful brother, Essex, were "at war." He counseled his son "never to suffer your wife to have power in the management of your affairs," and never to let her keep the coffers. As for the duties of women, they are to look after children, manage the household servants, "and to have a care when great personages shall visit to sit at one end of the table, and to carve handsomely." He allowed that they could amuse themselves with needlework and female society. Drawing on his own experience, he warned his son to stay calm in the face of feminine tantrums. "Will you be angry at a poor woman that understands little?" Indeed, the whole sex is foolish and must not be taken seriously. "Treat their extravagant words with silent railery: if they threaten to kill themselves, give them a knife; if to hang themselves, lend them your garter; if to cast themselves headlong out of windows, open the casement; and if to swound and die, let them be till they come to themselves again." With more justice than many of his contemporaries, he acknowledged that the fault lay largely in female education. Yet despite this insight, the Earl did nothing about his own daughters but left their upbringing entirely to their mother, whom he regarded as a hysteric. It was Lady Northumberland who hired their teachers and determined what they should study. The sisters received no more than the superficial education of a gentlewoman: Lucy learned to be a beautiful dancer, while Dorothy took to feminine skills such as needlework. As the letters they wrote in later life show, they were never taught to spell.

Still, the very fact that their father was in the Tower gave the Percy sisters an advantage over their female contemporaries when it came to self-assurance. Their mother was not only the chatelaine but also the acting head of the household. It was she who made all decisions regarding the girls and Harry. The periodic blasts of orders from the Martin Tower were ignored. In spite of living in a highly patriarchal society, the Percy sisters grew up in a household where male authority was peculiarly absent. Unhampered by their father's restrictive view of women's place and by the tradition of male superiority, Lucy and Dorothy developed strong personalities of their own, personalities that would enable them to thrive in the tumultuous period in English history that lay ahead.

DOROTHY'S CHOICE

WHEN DOROTHY TURNED FOURTEEN, finding a suitable husband for her was very much on Lady Northumberland's mind. Having her father in the Tower made her a less desirable catch than other noble young ladies such as Elizabeth Cecil, Lord Burleigh's eldest daughter. Still, Lady Northumberland consoled herself with the thought that the Percys were an ancient line (not like the come-lately Cecils, who first appeared at Henry VIII's court) and possessed vast property holdings. Moreover, she was as much in Queen Anne's graces as ever before. The Queen now spent much of her time at Somerset House in London, which King James had remodeled and renamed Denmark House in honor of his Danish queen. Denmark House was just a short distance up the Thames from Essex House, and Lady Northumberland paid court sedulously at this more convenient royal residence, sometimes bringing her daughters.

At fourteen, Dorothy was more than old enough to marry. For that matter, so was Lucy at thirteen. Among the nobility and the gentry, the parental search for a good match began as soon as the child entered puberty. Twelve-year-old brides were not uncommon, but if one spouse or both were very young, the marriage was not consummated for several years. The groom was usually sent to tour the Continent while the bride remained in her parents' home. As these very early marriages indicate, the selection of a spouse was not a matter of personal inclination but a parental decision imposed on the children. Although the occasional marriage was contracted "without the privity" of the parents, it was always a cause for scandal. Arranged marriages among the nobility were the norm because marriage was determined by political and economic considerations. Sometimes these amalgamations were carried out in the teeth of a violent aversion. Frances Coke, the daughter of the Chief Justice of the King's Bench, and just Dorothy's age, was forcibly married to the unbalanced brother of the King's favorite to shore up her father's shaky position at court. Predictably, the marriage proved a disaster. While Sir Edward Coke's harshness was unusual, few parents permitted their children to choose their own spouse. At best they gave them a veto. Only the most progressive allowed for the vagaries of personal selection.

We can be sure that marriage was the chief topic of conversation between the sisters. They had no doubt that they would soon be betrothed; the only uncertainty was the bridegrooms. Like all the daughters of the nobility, Dorothy and Lucy idolized the heir to the throne, the eighteen-year-old Prince of Wales—he was, of course, beyond their dreams, as he would certainly marry a foreign princess. Prince Henry was a good-looking, well-built youth with a natural authority beyond his years, who surrounded himself with writers, poets, artists, and architects. To redesign his palace at Richmond and to create Italianate gardens with grottoes and waterworks, he brought over the Florentine Constantino de Servi and the Frenchman Isaac de Caus.[1] They were to work with (and also instruct) his surveyor, Inigo Jones, who as yet was limited to designing sets for the masques. Henry also patronized Dutch and English portrait painters, and he was beginning to collect art. The Prince of Wales's cultured milieu was the antithesis of his father's court.

The Prince was extremely skilled in the martial arts, and if the sisters saw him at all, it would have been at the palace tiltyard. Taking its name from tilting—charging one's opponent with a lance—the tilt-yard was a long field on the grounds of Whitehall where armor-clad noblemen on horseback competed in the medieval games of jousting, running at the ring, and fighting at the barrier. Prince Henry was known to spend six hours a day in armor, practicing at the tiltyard.

As it happened, the perfect occasion for Dorothy's debut presented itself in 1612. Elizabeth, the Princess Royal, was to be married to Frederick V, Prince Elector of the Palatinate. The religious wars of the sixteenth century had left Germany a patchwork of Catholic and Protestant principalities, and the Elector Palatine was, by inheritance, the head of the Union of Protestant Princes. The Prince of Wales had pressed his father to make this marriage. Young Henry had dreams of leading a military campaign to unite Germany as a Protestant nation.

In England great plans were afoot for the wedding. On October 16, the groom arrived, accompanied by his uncle Count Henry of Nassau. The aristocracy had come out in full force to welcome him. A flotilla of 150 boats, decorated with flags and banners, escorted him and his suite up the Thames from Gravesend to Whitehall, with cheering crowds all the way and a deafening salute of cannon at the Tower of London.[2] Dorothy and Lucy would have seen it passing by Essex House. To add to their excitement, when he first arrived in England, the prospective bridegroom was lodged in an apartment in Essex House, affording them numerous opportunities to see him. He was far from an imposing figure. "Young and small-timbered," he would not have been the man of their dreams. But from what they heard, the Princess was very satisfied with her suitor; the arranged marriage had turned into a love match. Leaving his uncle to play tennis with the Prince of Wales and joust with the courtiers, the Elector Palatine could not tear himself away from his intended bride.[3]

This happy state of affairs was not to last. From whispered conversations between their mother and Lady Bedford, the sisters heard the disturbing news circulating around the court that the Prince of Wales was seriously ill. Although he forced himself to continue entertaining the visitors (even including a hectic tennis match with the Elector Palatine), he had a persistent cough and his pallor was becoming more marked every day. At the beginning of November he took to his bed. Rumors were flying as to the nature of his illness, and to the doctors' desperate attempts to save him, the most bizarre being the application of newly killed cocks and pigeons to his shaven head. On November 12, 1612, he died, as we now know, of typhoid fever.

A deep sense of loss was felt throughout the country. Prince Henry had been the only popular member of the new Stuart dynasty. His spindle-shanked, stuttering twelve-year-old brother, Charles, was now the heir apparent. Although King James and Queen Anne were devastated, they cast off their mourning and prepared to stage a spectacular wedding for their daughter. Under the tragic circumstances, it was not for the love of display—that lingering medieval impulse that accounted for the jewel-spangled costumes and lavish feasts of James and his courtiers—but for sound reasons of state. The English people had been rabidly anti-Catholic since Elizabeth's time, and this Protestant marriage was greatly desired. Given the death of the promising Prince Henry, it was astute politics not to delay any further. The marriage ceremony was announced for February 14, 1613. From the Tower came the edict that Dorothy was not to attend the marriage festivities. Lady Northumberland was deaf to her lord's commands.

The days before the wedding were busy ones for Dorothy, as she was instructed in protocol and fitted for the magnificent and costly gown she was to wear to the wedding feast. The skirt—hanging straight down—was an innovation. King James had banned the wearing of farthingales at the wedding feast because they would create congestion. It seemed that at a recent masque at the Banqueting House, the passageway to the gallery had become blocked when several farthingales got wedged together at the entrance, causing a pileup of ladies in a rush to get seats.[4]

Standing on the terrace of Essex House, the sisters could watch the preparations on the river. Thirty-six gaily painted pinnaces, galleys, and carracks were lying at anchor, rigged and ready to stage a mock sea battle between Turks and Christians, and four floating castles on barges were hung with fireworks. Across the river, on the south bank, a huge model of the fort of Algiers was rising; this was also to burst into light. During the actual entertainment, some of the fireworks fizzled and the mock battle resulted in real casualties: one sailor lost his eyes, two others lost their hands, and many were maimed.[5]

On the great day, a crowd of cheering Londoners watched the wedding procession enter the Chapel Royal at Whitehall. The groom entered first, wearing a white suit embroidered with pearls and gold. He was attended by a corps of young Englishmen, Scots, and Hollanders. Then came the bride in cloth of silver, with thirteen bridesmaids carrying her long train. Her "amber coloured hair" hung down to her waist and was crowned by a gold coronet studded with enormous diamonds that was said to be worth millions of pounds. The bridal couple were followed by the bridesmen, Prince Charles and the Earl of Northampton. Then came the royal parents. Queen Anne, mourning her son, had abandoned her usual gaudy dress for a simple white gown, relieved only by a few jewels. King James, eccentric as ever, was "strangely attired in a cap and a feather, with a Spanish cape and a long stocking."

In the center of the chapel a stage had been erected for the ceremony, with stalls on either side for the nobility, men to the right, women to the left. The walls were colorful with banners and tapestries, and the chapel resounded with organ music and choral singing by the Gentlemen of the Chapel. The Bishop of Bath and Wells preached a sermon on the theme of the wedding feast at Cana in Galilee; then the Archbishop of Canterbury performed the marriage ceremony. The King gave away the bride. To the sound of blaring trumpets and the crowd shouting, "God give them joy," the newly married couple led the procession to the Banqueting House for the wedding feast.[6]

Stationing herself modestly toward the back of the hall, Dorothy watched the bridal party make its entrance. She was pleasurably excited but more than a little nervous. Would she be able to handle this most important social event? Though she did not have the breezy self-confidence of her younger sister, Dorothy was a self-possessed, dignified girl, and there can be no doubt that throughout the festivities she was a credit to the Percys and the Devereux. A fortune had been spent on dress for this social event of the season. The men's doublets and breeches and the women's gowns were embroidered with jewels, silver, and gold. The court dandies, Sir James Hay and the Earl of Dorset, outdid themselves with their rich outfits. One lord was said to have spent £1,500 dressing his two daughters, and Lady Northumberland was not far behind with Dorothy's finery. "I hear the Earl of Northumberland's daughter was very gallant," John Chamberlain wrote his friend Sir Dudley Carleton, the ambassador at Venice, who had been Northumberland's secretary when the sisters were little.

The masque by Thomas Campion was judged "long and tedious" by the blasé courtiers, but it would have enchanted Dorothy since it was the first of these extravaganzas she had seen. Court masques were presented on a proscenium, or picture-frame, stage, and in this shallow space Inigo Jones devised astonishing effects with movable sets. On this evening, the guests beheld not only moving clouds and stars but artificial fires with rotating circles of lights. A cloud descending from the upper stage parted to reveal masked courtiers in cloth of silver embroidered with a design of flames, each wearing a flamelike crown topped with a silk feather like a wisp of smoke. From revolving golden niches, silver statues stepped down to partner the "Star Lords" in an elegant dance. The masque concluded with a sibyl drawing a silver obelisk by a golden cord to the royal dais and pronouncing a blessing in Latin upon the bridal couple.

The following day the bridegroom gave a much-applauded demonstration of the art of manège, taking the trained "high bounding horse" through its paces, backward and forward and sideways, in figure eights and crosses, and onto its hind legs like an equine ballet dancer. In the evening, lawyers from Lincoln's Inn and the Middle Temple rode to the palace in a colorful cavalcade. With trumpets blaring from open chariots, they circled the tiltyard several times at the King's request. The ladies in the gallery exclaimed with delight over the dozen little boys costumed as baboons, who performed the ante-masque. On the third day, the gentlemen from the other two Inns of Court, Gray's Inn and the Inner Temple, came by water. Their barges, strung with lamps in fantastic shapes, sparkled on the slate-gray Thames like jeweled brooches. Every day the younger or more sporting courtiers displayed their athletic prowess at the tiltyard and the tennis court. The local champions, Sir James Hay and Sir Henry Rich, were outplayed by Count Henry of Nassau, the bridegroom's uncle. A sophisticated, amiable man of thirty or so, Count Henry had been trained in a French academy and possessed the elegant French manners that impressed the insular English.

Dorothy found herself sought after by this distinguished visitor. Perhaps he had first seen her at Essex House and had been taken with her. The courtiers were soon gossiping about Count Henry's obvious interest in Dorothy Percy. In a tournament at the tiltyard, the Count declared himself her champion and wore her ribbons on his armor. In the banqueting hall he led her onto the floor for a saraband or a galliard. His attentions continued after the wedding. "Here is whispering," Chamberlain wrote Carleton on March 25, "that the Count Henry of Nassau hath a month's mind to my Lord of Northumberland's daughter, which if it should fall right might prove a great match for her." Indeed it would have. Count Henry was destined to become a famous general and to succeed his brother as Prince of Orange. Even in 1613 he was akin to royalty, and any noble Protestant family would have grasped at an alliance with him. Just how serious his intentions were toward Dorothy remains unknown. Whatever they were, Count Henry went home to Holland unbetrothed after the departure of his nephew and his bride at the end of April.

And how did Dorothy feel about her princely admirer? She made no reference to this extraordinary chapter in her life in any letters now extant. We can safely conjecture that she was flattered, but did she regret that the affair had petered out? Or did she think the Count too old at twice her age? Probably not, because girls her age were married off to men old enough to be their grandfathers. (In the case of the Earl of Nottingham, the Lord High Admiral, a great-grandfather!) Or did she not want to leave her family and go to live in a foreign country? Or was Dorothy already in love?

Northumberland was shrewdly aware that his daughters had reached marriageable age. Shortly after Dorothy began going to court, he used their need for dowries to plead for a settlement of his fine. "The time of their preferments for all their lives is at hand and will not admit long delay," he petitioned King James.[7] Whether this argument helped or not, the fine was reduced from £30,000 to £11,000, and Northumberland paid it all off in 1613. Still, he did nothing about a husband for Dorothy.

Offers for her began to come in. In the autumn of 1614, she had a suitor in the eminently suitable person of Walter, second Lord Scott of Buccleuch. His family was influential at court, and Chamberlain wrote Carleton that "some think [the marriage] may be a means of her father's delivery." But despite any political advantages it may have promised for the Percys, by Christmas it was clear that the marriage would not take place. Had Dorothy used her veto? More to the point, was she pressing for another match?

In March 1615, Northumberland began negotiating a marriage for his elder daughter with Robert Sidney, the son of Viscount Lisle. Although nineteen-year-old Robert paid a visit to the Earl of Northumberland and was received amicably enough, the negotiations foundered almost immediately over the always contentious issue of the dowry. Lady Northumberland was extremely upset that the negotiations had broken down between the two fathers over money when "the world had taken so much notice of the young couple's affection." It would be a disgrace to her daughter, she berated her husband, "if a money matter should break off so fit a match."[8]

True to form, Lady Northumberland did not hesitate to reopen negotiations on her own initiative, without telling her husband. She was closely connected with the Sidney family through her mother, who was Viscount Lisle's aunt by marriage. Not only that, but Sir Philip Sidney, Lisle's elder brother, had addressed his finest love poems to her sister, Penelope, and her brother, Essex, had married Sir Philip's widow. The closeness had continued into the present generation. Dorothy and Robert Sidney had known each other from childhood. Lady Northumberland's eagerness to promote this particular match rather than the Buccleuch one indicates that Dorothy had set her heart on Robert Sidney.

THE SIDNEYS LIVED at Penshurst Place in Kent, where they had been Lords of the Manor since 1552. They also owned lands in Sussex, Wales, Warwickshire, and Norfolk. But though land rich, they were cash poor. Even Viscount Lisle's marriage to an heiress had not substantially improved the family fortunes, and he was dependent on royal patronage to supplement his income from land. Under Queen Elizabeth he had been Governor of Flushing in the Low Countries, and he was sufficiently in favor with James to be appointed Lord Chamberlain to Queen Anne. Following the restless queen was, however, no sinecure. Judging from his letters, Lisle seems to have found it more tiring and demanding than his youthful soldiering in the Netherlands. As he shuttled between Oatlands, Queen Anne's favorite country residence, and Denmark House in London, he often stopped to rest for a day at a neighbor's manor at Brentford near Syon House.

It was this neighbor, Sir Francis Darcy, whom Lady Northumberland employed to conduct the marriage negotiations. Darcy knew that Lisle was now free to entertain a proposal for his son. He had recently been disappointed in his hopes of marrying Robert to the sought-after Elizabeth Cecil. Although the Cecil family had lost its primacy at court since the death of the first Earl of Salisbury in 1612, it still retained the wealth engendered by his influence. Elizabeth Cecil was outstanding among girls of her age. Lovely, with a pleasant dignity, she was deemed "the finest gentlewoman about the court." To add to her charms, she came with an £8,000 dowry. The matchmaking was going very well when suddenly her family broke it off. A week later the Cecils announced Elizabeth's betrothal to Sir Thomas Howard, second son of the powerful Earl of Suffolk. Obviously the Cecils preferred an alliance with the Howards to one with the Sidneys, and on May 24, 1614, Elizabeth Cecil married Thomas Howard.

Viscount Lisle swallowed his keen disappointment like a gentleman and began looking for another bride for Robert. Like other peers, he regarded his son as a negotiable asset. In 1612 his first-born boy, William, had died of smallpox. From then on the Viscount's hopes centered on Robert, and he was indefatigable in seeking a good match for him. Robert was not handsome; he had a long, narrow, pockmarked face; nevertheless, he was a personable enough young man. Educated at Oxford and well traveled, he was chiefly interested in books and study. Sir Henry Savile, the erudite provost of Eton, described him as "a very proper gentleman and exceedingly well given in every way."[9] Well bred and endowed with a well-stocked mind, Robert was a strong candidate for the hand of an heiress.

When Sir Francis Darcy approached him on behalf of Lady Northumberland, Lisle was of two minds.[10] On the one hand, the Percys were the old aristocracy and immensely rich; on the other, they were in disgrace. And Lady Northumberland was asking Lisle to use his influence at court to obtain her husband's release. As for the monetary settlement, she was offering a respectable, but not exceptional, portion of £5,000 and land worth £350 a year, which Dorothy would inherit on her mother's death. This was little or no improvement over the dowry proposed by the Earl, which Lisle had refused. Ambivalent toward the match, Lisle drove a hard bargain, insisting that the dowry be raised to £6,000. At this Darcy confessed the difficulties facing Lady Northumberland. In fact she had not informed her husband of her matchmaking. Like all wives, she could not transfer her own property without her husband's consent; moreover, Northumberland was determined not to have any land alienated from the estate that would ultimately be passed to his elder son. Lisle's response was to make Darcy promise that Northumberland would be spoken to immediately, and that he, Lisle, should be advised how matters stood within eight days.

It is obvious from the frank correspondence between Lisle and Darcy that, before long, Lisle would be looking to break off negotiations with the Percy family. He was afraid the King would disapprove of the marriage; he did not want to use his credit at court pleading Northumberland's case; but the prime drawback was uncertainty over the dowry. Without a word to Darcy, Lisle started negotiating for another bride for his son. This time the girl was the daughter of a rich but low-born official named Thomas Watson. A teller in the Exchequer (it was these officers who issued tallies for payment from the royal coffers), Master Watson was a useful person to have as a family connection. Lady Lisle was particularly "earnest," even "rather violent" for this match. But the way was not all clear for the capture of this desirable plebeian. Another aspirant for Watson's daughter had brought suit in the ecclesiastical court, claiming that she was already contracted to him. According to the marriage laws, when a man and woman had contracted themselves to each other, neither was free to marry another person.

When Lady Northumberland heard that Lisle was treating for another match, she was outraged. Although their negotiations had not reached the stage of a marriage contract, she had believed matters sufficiently advanced to "reserve herself very honourably" or, to put it bluntly, to pull Dorothy off the marriage market. Reflecting her anger, Sir Francis Darcy wrote a strongly worded letter to Lisle: "It is told my Lady of Northumberland that your Lordship should entertain conference, and that in great forwardness, in a far meaner place, and of much less reputation, which is very distasteful unto her, and very unkindly taken." At least, Darcy admonished, she should have been informed of "your resolution to surcease" negotiations for her daughter "before you would have entered conference with any other." The letter ended with a reminder of the advantages of marrying into one's own class: "I confess I know not where your lordship should have matched so happily." But Lisle was hot on the trail of a middle-class fortune. He reminded Darcy that he had warned him that Lady Northumberland "should not for me forsake any other good match should such be offered unto her." Having thus exculpated himself, Lisle continued his courtship of Master Watson and his wife. In August the Watsons were invited to Penshurst. Evidently the Watsons were favorably disposed to the match, but nothing could be done until the judgment came down on the other suitor's claim. The case was long drawn out and caused a good deal of talk. Although in the end the ecclesiastical court found that no prior marriage contract existed, the evidence was enough to soil the young woman's reputation.

Writing to Ambassador Carleton in February 1615 about the Watson court case and the stalled match with young Sidney, Chamberlain remarked, "It is thought the young gentleman inclines to a daughter of the Earl of Northumberland, and grows weary of hunting in a foiled scent, that hath been haunted by so many suitors."[11] When the Sidneys broke off the Watson match, the girl's irate father pursued the perfidious aristocrats with threats of a lawsuit.

Although the unsentimental negotiations between their parents had broken down, Dorothy and Robert had taken matters into their own hands by falling in love. As Lady Northumberland had informed her husband, the romance was no secret. Beyond a doubt, theirs was a love match. The lovers met no opposition from Lady Northumberland or the Lisles—it was, after all, a suitable match. Dorothy and Robert were married early in 1616, even though the dowry question had not been resolved. The Earl of Northumberland was not informed of his daughter's marriage.[12]

Since her father had not been told, Dorothy's mother decided that the marriage should be kept secret. It seems to have leaked out, however. The Countess of Dorset, a neighbor at Knole House and a friend of the Penshurst ladies, recorded in her diary in March 1616 that now "the marriage between Sr Robert Sidney and my Lady Dorothy Percy was openly knowne."[13] As there is no mention of the marriage in the newsletters, diaries, or correspondence of the time, knowledge of it probably did not go beyond the great houses in the vicinity of Penshurst. In any event, it did not penetrate the fastness of the Martin Tower.

In May Robert accompanied his father to the Netherlands. Since the days of Queen Elizabeth, England had held the three towns of Flushing, Brille, and Rammekens as pledges for loans made to the Dutch during their war of independence from Spain. In the sixteenth century the Netherlands, composed of seventeen states, formed part of the Spanish empire. The predominantly Protestant northern provinces rebelled against the heavy hand of their Spanish overlords, declaring themselves the United Provinces of the Netherlands, or the Dutch Republic. Spain sent in an army to quell the rebellion and the Dutch turned to England for help. Elizabeth sent troops and money, receiving the so-called cautionary towns as collateral. After trying in vain for years to recapture the northern provinces, in 1612 Spain signed a truce with the triumphant Dutchmen. The southern provinces had joined in the revolt initially, but they were reconquered and continued as the Spanish Netherlands, also known as Flanders.

In 1617 the de facto Dutch Republic redeemed the cautionary towns from England, and Viscount Lisle was sent over to formally render them. This transaction was personally advantageous to him. As a former governor of Flushing, he was granted an annuity of £1,200 from the proceeds, and, under the terms of the settlement, his son Robert was given a regiment of English troops in the Dutch service with the rank of colonel.[14]

When father and son set out, it had been agreed that Robert would stay on and travel through France and Germany to improve his languages. Although he had already taken the customary continental tour of the young aristocrat, his family wished to give him every opportunity to prepare himself for a brilliant career in the royal service. Despite all the interest travel offered, the young man seems to have been thinking more of the joys of marriage awaiting him. From France his mother received instructions "to have a lodging ready for him and his wife against winter," and she was reminded of her promise to give them a particular bed.[15] All that summer Robert traveled on the Continent and kept Dorothy informed of his whereabouts and his homecoming plans. Sadly, his letters have been lost. They must have been beautiful, for Robert was a sensitive, well-educated young man and very much in love. "Other news I cannot learn out of France," Lisle wrote his wife in September, "but such as my daughter and my Lady Lucy brought with them to Penshurst." Robert was expected back at the end of September. Dorothy had come to Penshurst with her sister to wait for his return. It is most unlikely that the marriage had been consummated before Robert left. Dorothy was to prove so fecund that had they lived together as man and wife she would undoubtedly have been pregnant already. As it was, when Dorothy visited Penshurst with her sister, Lucy, in September 1616, she was still a carefree, laughing girl.

Penshurst looks now much as the sisters saw it in the autumn of 1616. In a vast rambling manor house of old-gold stone, the fourteenth-century great hall is still intact and the paneled long gallery has been restored to its original proportions. But the garden wall is just a token of the crenellated curtain wall that enclosed the house and gardens and the famous orchards in the seventeenth century. A Tudor village with its ancient church nestles nearby, and both village and great house gaze eternally on the sweep of the Kentish weald. This smiling countryside made a perfect setting for the lovely Percy sisters. Their gaiety and charm delighted their hosts. Back on duty at Oatlands, the Queen's country house, Viscount Lisle wrote his wife: "I trust they continue merry there still, which I was very glad to see, and I pray you tell them." With what regret he tore himself away from the company of the adorable sisters is evident: "I take it exceeding kindly that they should like so well of their entertainment, and was very sorry that I was forced to come so soon from them."[16]

In October Robert at last returned from abroad and Dorothy's married life finally began. Although she was passionately in love with her new husband, she found that marriage brought many problems.

three

LUCY'S CHOICE

DURING THE MONTHS of Dorothy's courtship and marriage, Lady Northumberland began taking Lucy to the King's palace of Whitehall. She was an immediate success at court. While Dorothy was a handsome young woman, the younger sister had grown into a beauty. Her oval face with its ivory complexion and perfect features was like an exquisite cameo framed by lustrous, wavy brown hair. She had a voluptuous figure and carried herself like a princess. The consensus of the courtiers was that she was "the most lovely damsel in all England."[1] Her gaiety and girlish laughter added to the charm of her person. Basking in admiration, Lucy was utterly dazzled by court life: the masques and feasts, the pomp and ceremony, the gay bravado of the tiltyard, the swooping players on the tennis court, the gambling until the candles guttered.

Whitehall, located in London itself, was the principal royal residence and the official court of English monarchs since Henry VIII. A sprawling complex on the Thames, it housed fifteen hundred servants of the King, ranging from the Lord Chamberlain, who was in charge of the palace, down to the rat catcher and the chimney sweep.

The King's private apartments, known as the Bedchamber, and

the adjacent state apartments occupied the upper floor of the palace. In the Presence Chamber, James, seated on his throne, received arriving and departing ambassadors or gave audiences on special occasions. Next to this room was the Privy Chamber, always filled with courtiers waiting for the King or a privy councillor to appear. For less official meetings with foreign envoys and for reports from his officers of state, James used the Withdrawing Room. The gallery, stretching the length of the facade, served as the meeting place for the court: here, officials, courtiers, and suitors paced up and down, holding confidential discussions, gawked at by ordinary folk, for Whitehall was open to the King's subjects.

As well as the Great Hall, dating back to Henry VIII, a Banqueting House had been built in 1606 for masques and other royal entertainments.[2] Indeed, the palace provided a veritable recreation center for the courtiers, with the tiltyard, tennis courts, bowling alleys, a cockpit, and the Privy Garden for strolling in good weather. For religious ceremonies and great events, such as weddings and funerals, there was the Chapel Royal. Entrance to the royal compound was either by Whitehall Stairs or through the gatehouse on King Street.

Scattered around the palace grounds were the lodgings of the officials of the royal Household—the Lord Chamberlain, the Gentlemen of the Bedchamber, the Grooms of the Privy and Presence Chambers, the Master of the Horse. As well, there were cubbyholes for the carvers, cupbearers, sewers, Clerks of the Closet, pages, and messengers. Owing to James's laxity and extravagance, their numbers— and their expensive upkeep—had more than doubled since Elizabeth's day.

Commodious lodgings were also provided for the great officers of state: the Lord Treasurer, the Lord Chancellor and Keeper of the Great Seal, the Lord Privy Seal, the Lord High Admiral, the two Secretaries of State, the Chancellor of the Exchequer. Some of these officials conducted their business at Whitehall, but the law courts, including the Star Chamber that derived its name from the gilt stars on its ceiling, were located at Westminster Hall, where Parliament sat, a short distance by water from Whitehall.

Lucy was a quick study in the ways of the court. She saw that it was the Howards—great magnates like her family—who held the important posts. Thomas Howard, Earl of Suffolk, had become Lord Treasurer upon the Earl of Salisbury's death, and Charles Howard, Earl of Nottingham, was the Lord High Admiral. The Howard family had recently consolidated its position by marrying the Earl of Suffolk's daughter, Frances Howard, to the King's favorite, the Earl of Somerset.

Suitors flocked around Somerset and the Howards. For a price these grandees would use their influence with the King to obtain grants of land, patents, or other rewards for their clients. Like all royal officials, they traded in offices shamelessly, selling them to the highest bidder. Indeed, bribery greased the wheels of the administrative machine. Salaries and fees for service were a mere pittance; officials received their payment in the form of "gifts" or bribes. Lucy would see courtiers bearing massive silver salvers, entering the apartments of the officers of state or the household. Less flagrant were the cash gifts that passed from hand to hand. Some officials used their wives and daughters as surrogates to receive the money. Lucy was never approached because her imprisoned father could not oblige anyone. Lucy took the general corruption at court for granted. At church on Sunday, she would hear the minister preach respect for the nobility and unquestioning allegiance to the King.

Although Lucy took great interest in the court's favorite game of who's in and who's out, she cared not a whit about the truly important issue of the reign: King James's growing conflict with Parliament. James met little opposition from the House of Lords, but the House of Commons no longer accepted without question the divine right of kings to rule. These knights and squires—sheriffs or justices of the peace in their own counties—came to Westminster as the elected representatives of their constituents. Their dogged defense of their "privileges" clashed with the King's insistence on the royal "prerogative." Both antagonists had their strengths. Parliament could not meet unless called by the King, but, compelled by his penury, James had to call it. Unless Parliament passed votes of supply for him, he did not have the right to levy taxes.

In the distant past, a king of England had been able to be financially independent. Enough income had been generated from customs duties (also known as tonnage and poundage, and granted by Parliament for an entire reign), rent or sale of royal lands, wardship, occasional "gifts" from the nobility, and the fees from the Crown's feudal rights to pay for the upkeep of the household, the state departments, and the navy. There was no government payroll to speak of because civil servants supplemented their nominal salaries by accepting bribes. But the traditional sources of revenue were totally inadequate by Queen Elizabeth's time. The war with Spain had been extremely costly. To raise money by taxation was essential. Thus the monarch had to go, cap in hand, to Parliament annually for permission to levy taxes. Elizabeth had used her charm and awe of her person to extract enough votes of supply to keep her government functioning. James, on the other hand, was inept in handling the members of Parliament. Increasingly, they would not grant supply before the King satisfied their grievances, the most complained of being his wholesale granting of monopolies to favored courtiers. The last parliament, in 1614, had ended with rancor on both sides.

Lucy had expected the heir to the throne, Prince Charles—a shy youth of her own age—to be surrounded by servile flatterers; instead, it was George Villiers, King James's new favorite, who was fawned over by all the courtiers. Villiers, a younger son of a Leicestershire knight, was born without money or prospects; however, he was stunningly good-looking and his widowed mother groomed him for a career at court as a page. With this modest ambition in mind, she stretched her finances to send him to France for "finishing" at a French academy. At an academy at Blois in the Loire country he learned to sit a horse well, dance and fence gracefully, and speak a passable French. George was to far exceed his mother's fond hope. On his return to England in 1614, he was taken up by a cabal determined to oust the current favorite, the Earl of Somerset. Knowing the King's weakness for beautiful young men, this cabal, headed by the Archbishop of Canterbury, paraded Villiers before the monarch like a prize stallion. James was immediately smitten, and Villiers's rise began. When Lucy started coming to court in 1614, he had just been knighted and made a Gentleman of the Bedchamber. After Somerset's fall some months later, the King appointed Villiers his Master of the Horse and named him to the elite Order of the Garter. In August 1616, he made him a baron and a viscount, with a gift of £80,000 in land to boot. Then in January 1617, the doting King created his new favorite Earl of Buckingham.

King James was very often away from court, either hunting or on a progress, but when he was at Whitehall, Lucy would see him leaning on young Villiers, pawing him and kissing him on the mouth. Homosexuality, or more precisely bisexuality, was common at James's court. Not only the King but many of the married lords had their minions—pretty young men who warmed their beds, or more, for them. The Lord Keeper, Sir Francis Bacon, had a stable of such favorites, and his brother, Sir Anthony, who worked for English intelligence abroad, had been charged with sodomy in France. Lucy would also have heard whispers about the passionate "friendships" among the Essex set that had clustered around her late uncle.

Whitehall saw something of Queen Anne. James's consort appeared dutifully with him at all formal events, but, sadly, her Christmas masques were a thing of the past. Since her son's death in 1612, she had given up masquing though not the farthingale.

HANDSOME YOUNG MEN from the best families were swarming around beautiful Lucy Percy, but before long she was swept off her feet by a dandy and royal favorite, Sir James Hay, a recent widower more than twice her age, with two children. A Scot from a modest family of gentry, James had come to England with King James in 1603. Unique among the King's rowdy early favorites, he was sophisticated and polished, the result of several years traveling in Italy and France. The King heaped grants upon him, and James lived extravagantly on the royal bounty. In 1613 he was given the office of Master of the Wardrobe.[3] As this entailed purchasing supplies for the royal household, the emoluments were far in excess of the token salary. A fine house on Upper Thames Street in the Blackfriars neighborhood went along with this lucrative office, and the Master's entertainments there were famous for their showy display. At court Sir James was always on hand to dance in a masque or run at the ring.

A magnifico in his dress, for a ceremonial visit to the French court in the summer of 1616 he ordered twenty suits for a stay of twenty days. This entailed weeks of work for his tailor. A suit consisted of doublet and hose—a close-fitting vest with a short skirt of overlapping tabs and above-the-knee breeches with a cloak to be thrown casually over the shoulders. The long stockings were held up by sewing them to the breeches or by strings that went under the doublet and were tied to loops at the waist. A pleated ruff circled the straight collar of the doublet—instead of an uncomfortable metal frame, the ruff was now stiffened by the new invention of starch. A hat with a plume and shoes adorned with large rosettes completed the outfit. Just after James's tailor had made up all the suits, news came out of France that fashions had changed. This had put James "out of countenance," Chamberlain gleefully wrote Carleton, because he always had to be "set out after the last edition."[4]

Physically, Sir James Hay was slim and of middle height. His features were finely drawn and aristocratic, but pouches under his eyes and a sagging of the cheeks spoke eloquently of too much food, drink and keeping late hours. By the time Lucy met him, he was no longer as young as he liked to appear, and the odd attack of gout foreshadowed middle age.

Hay's clique was the other free-spending, high-living courtiers, notably his late wife's cousin Sir George Goring and Lucy's first cousin Sir Henry Rich. Both looked up to Hay as a greater favorite than themselves. Goring had soldiered in the Low Countries, fighting for the Dutch in their revolt against their Spanish overlords, and he retained the bluff manner of the military caste. An inveterate partygoer, he arranged tasteless foolery and practical jokes to amuse the monarch—he and two other jokesters were known around the court as the King's "chief and master fools."

Sir Henry Rich was some seven or eight years younger than his cronies. He was the second son of the Earl of Warwick, and his mother was that aunt of the sisters whose mother had abandoned her children to run away with her lover. Rich had also done a stint in the Dutch wars but was far better suited to the court than to the camp. Although a fop, he was extremely good-looking and, gradually, by his friend James's example, was acquiring savoir faire and courtly graces. While Goring was good-natured and took the world as it came, Rich had a hair-trigger temper and was quick to call out other nobles to the dueling field. He had married Betty Cope, the colorless daughter of one of the Earl of Salisbury's right-hand men, only to have the all-powerful Lord Treasurer die, taking with him the worldly influence of his new father-in-law. However, Rich was compensated for bestowing his handsome person on Betty Cope when his father-in-law died in 1614 and a fine country estate at Kensington passed into his hands. Rich neglected "his poor Lady" shamefully and had one affair after another.[5] Hay was much superior to his two sidemen. Though reckoned "a cunning observer" and a "bell-wether of court favour," he was invariably courteous and full of civilities to everyone.[6]

In spite of his sophistication, his age, and much experience with women, Sir James Hay fell madly in love with Lucy Percy. As only an older lover could be, he was totally bemused by this enchanting girl. At the same time, it is easy to see what attracted Lucy to him. In her eyes he personified the exciting court life. His lavishness, his gorgeous clothes, his prowess at sports impressed her still-adolescent mind. In her fancy she saw him as the godlike Jove of the masques. (And—no small thing in an age that set little store by personal hygiene—he was sweet-smelling. The royal physician, Theodore de Mayerne, has left a list in Latin of the "scents and emollients" he prepared for Hay. These included hair powder, toothpaste, mouthwash, and a lotion to keep the hands soft and white. Lucy would not yet have benefited from the lozenges he took "to keep the breath sweet in the bedchamber.")[7] James was a past master of the flattering phrase, and for a young girl his exquisite compliments were heady stuff indeed. Nor were they without effect on her mother. Encouraged by the Countess of Bedford (who floated like a fairy godmother over this whole affair), Lady Northumberland allowed Hay to pay court to her younger daughter. Before long Lucy and James reached an understanding.

While the sisters were disposing of themselves without their father's knowledge, the Earl began to show a sudden interest in them. Deciding that they were now ready for marriage, he determined to take charge and arrange suitable matches. Unlike Viscount Lisle, who was primarily interested in money, Northumberland was looking for powerful alliances to dispel the cloud hovering over the House of Percy. Regarding his lovely daughters through a haze of tobacco smoke, he had no doubt that, with a sweetening of generous dowries, they could make the most brilliant marriages in England. To bring them under his influence, he commanded them to visit him daily.

For an entirely different reason their mother was also urging them to visit him. In the spring of 1616, the Tower had received two more illustrious residents, the Earl and Countess of Somerset. Two years earlier, after her divorce from the third Earl of Essex (whom she had publicly and falsely branded as impotent), Frances Howard had married the favorite Somerset in the King's presence and with his enthusiastic consent. However, the couple did not enjoy their felicity long. Within little more than a year they were tried and found guilty of murdering Sir Thomas Overbury, a former friend of Somerset's. Whereas a poor man in Stuart England was hanged for stealing a sheep, the Somersets were merely established in a comfortable suite in the Tower. From the day this Jezebel arrived, the Earl of Northumberland was totally spellbound. Casting aside his usual irascibility, he set out to make himself "friendly and sociable." Visitors to the Tower observed him strolling in the garden with the Somersets, dancing attendance upon the young, pretty countess. Wounded by her husband's notorious infatuation with Lady Somerset, Lady Northumberland stopped her visits to the Tower, sending her daughters in her place.[8]

BY FEBRUARY 1617, both sisters realized that they must inform their father of their respective matches. Dorothy was pregnant, and

Lucy had contracted herself: there was no time for delay. The prospect of such an interview would have terrified most young women, but Lucy and Dorothy were not the ordinary dutiful daughters. Conditioned by their upbringing to be independent, they were further fortified by their united front. Since the spankings of childhood, the sisters had stood together against all threats. Now grown up, they were mutually supportive, come what may. Their father's long imprisonment had both removed paternal authority and created problems for them—witness Viscount Lisle's initial lack of enthusiasm for Dorothy as a daughter-in-law. Beleaguered by the world, the sisters had learned to face it shoulder to shoulder.

When they went to the Tower to break the news to their father of Dorothy's marriage and Lucy's betrothal, he was sitting at his usual place at his writing table, wearing a black velvet gown trimmed with gold braid and wreathed in smoke from his habitual pipe. Other than offering them some sweetmeats—the Earl had a very special Genoa paste of quinces, spices, and sugar that he kept in a little cupboard—he showed little interest in his daughters' arrival. His thoughts were clearly on the tubular instrument with glass ends that he was fingering—it was called a telescope, he told the girls, and looking through it one could see the stars clearly.[9]

Dorothy spoke up first and told her father of her secret marriage. Despite the deceit of his womenfolk and his dislike of the Sidneys, he took it calmly. The Sidneys, after all, were members of the peerage, and Robert, with his bookish habits, promised to be a congenial companion for his father-in-law. The Earl was sufficiently brought round to provide a dowry of £6,000 for Dorothy.[10] Though not extraordinary, it was somewhat more than the £3,000 to £5,000 with which most aristocrats endowed their daughters.

If Northumberland grudgingly accepted Dorothy's choice, he was adamantly opposed to Lucy's. He hated the courtiers who had come from Scotland with the King, displacing the old English families. He was a Percy, he stormed, "and could not endure that his daughter should dance any Scottish jigs."[11] He had no use for Sir James Hay in particular. It is not difficult to understand why. James's lifestyle appeared utterly frivolous to the serious-minded earl and a special affront to him in his captivity. Moreover, James had no land but lived on royal gifts and offices. Not only that, but as the son of an obscure Scottish knight he had no lineage, according to the standards of a Percy. Hoping to dissuade Lucy from marrying this man of whom he was so contemptuous, Northumberland promised her an extraordinary dowry of £20,000 if she would let him choose a husband for her.[12]

Angrily, she told her father that nothing he could offer would make her give up James. He was her chosen husband and she would have no other. Taken aback by his daughter's spirited response, the Earl said no more that day. After Lucy flounced out, the Earl began to plot a diabolical scheme.

On the sisters' next visit to the Tower, they found their father extraordinarily benign. He kissed them both and acted quite out of character in a new role of loving father. After they had been there some time, he dismissed Dorothy, telling her to go home to her husband and to send Lucy's maids to attend her, "for that he meant not to part with her but that she should keep him company."[13] Lucy suddenly found herself a prisoner in the Tower for the crime of choosing her own husband.

Lucy's restraint could not have come at a worse time. That evening James was throwing a feast the likes of which London had seldom seen, ostensibly for a visiting French diplomat. But the real guest of honor was the host's intended bride. This was subtly broadcast by his choice of the Countess of Bedford as mistress of the feast; Lady Bedford, as all the court knew, was managing his campaign to marry Lucy Percy. When Dorothy arrived with the news that Lucy was confined in the Tower, James was distraught. The supper and masque (in which Goring and Rich were the principal dancers) cost several thousand pounds, and without Lucy it was all gall and wormwood to him.[14]

The great romance was the talk of the court. When the King set out on a progress to Scotland in April, James forsook his duty and stayed behind, "his vain hope in obtaining my Lord of Northumberland's daughter being the chief cause of his stay," gossiped one courtier.[15] The same source observed that Hay "prosecutes" his suit "with all violence." He besieged Northumberland with letters and visits from his friends. But while the Earl remained deaf to these appeals, the Tower failed to keep his daughter from her ardent suitor. Unknown to the Earl, Lucy and James were meeting secretly with the help of Lady Somerset. Encouraged by her father to visit this lady of whom he was so enamored, Lucy was soon running in and out of her apartment on a familiar basis. At the same time, James was often at the Tower, carrying royal messages to the Somersets. It was an easy matter for the sly Lady Somerset to arrange a rendezvous for the lovers; her purpose in doing so may have been to oblige an influential courtier or it may simply have been mischief making.

When Northumberland discovered what had been going on under his nose, he threw Lucy out unceremoniously. He ranted to all around him that his ungrateful daughter had betrayed him and that she and her Scot would not see a penny of his money. His wrath was so monumental that, for once, Lady Northumberland was intimidated, and when Lucy came to her at Essex House, she was afraid to take her in. Not so Dorothy, who was staying at the London town house of Robert's cousin. She welcomed her sister with open arms. Lucy's sojourn at Baynard's Castle in 1617 marks the beginning of a recurring pattern: Dorothy providing a refuge for Lucy to recover her health or spirits, and Lucy, for her part, bringing to her sister's uneventful life all the excitement and color of her own. Though they were as close as ever, their relationship was changing to one where Lucy was the star and Dorothy the sympathetic audience. Some weeks later, when Sir James could no longer put off going to Scotland, it was decided that Lucy would move into his house at Blackfriars during his absence. To make sure that she lacked for nothing, he gave her £2,000.[16] Another theme was emerging to change the familiar sisterly equality: Lucy luxuriating in money, Dorothy having difficulty making ends meet.

By the time of the summer exodus from London, Lady Northumberland had recovered her spirit and took Lucy with her to Syon

House. In July Sir James posted back from Scotland at record-breaking speed. Nevertheless, while the marriage was a foregone conclusion, it did not take place immediately. King James was still in Scotland, and as he had promised to give the bride away, they had to wait for his return. "Lord Hay thinks long till the King's coming that he may consummate his marriage," Chamberlain wrote Carleton. Waiting for the King was only part of the reason for the delay. Lucy's suitor was still trying to win over Northumberland and some, at least, of the £20,000 dowry. His chances were poor, for the Earl was very bitter. Not only was he angry at his disobedient daughter, but he was deeply hurt by Lady Somerset's perfidy. He was aware that he had made a fool of himself over her, and his anger was mixed with shame. Proud Northumberland was in no mood for conciliation. To be near Lucy, James rented Sir Francis Darcy's house at Brentford. From there he visited Syon House every day and was "wonderful observant and obsequious" to both mother and daughter.[17] At least twice a week, he feasted them at his rented house at such expense that Lady Northumberland claimed she could not hope to reciprocate; poor James had to interrupt his daily visit to return to his own house for dinner. The delightful summer afternoons usually found the trio driving in his coach and six, and so Viscount Lisle encountered them one day on his way to Oatlands.

MEANWHILE, AT PENSHURST, Dorothy was getting ready for the birth of her first child—"I hope you and the greate belly and all the rest came well to Penshurst," her jovial father-in-law wrote his wife in July.[18] Robert was abroad on summer maneuvers with his regiment, and Dorothy was lonely and bored, despite her mother-in-law's daily lessons in housewifery and the great number of visitors. How happy she was when Lucy arrived with their cousin Isabella Rich.[19] Isabella was several years older than the sisters. A short childhood marriage had given her the freedom of a widow, and she was pleasure-loving and worldly. The house party was further enlivened when Viscount Lisle arrived with James. The two men were old friends and associates, bound together in service to the royal family. It would not have been James's first visit to Penshurst. Seeing the sisters together at Penshurst, James understood how deep the attachment was between them. To entrench himself still further in Lucy's affections, he suggested that Dorothy come to his house at the Wardrobe to have her baby, assuring everyone that he and Lucy would be married by that time. On their return to Syon House, Lady Northumberland was enlisted in the scheme. She wrote Dorothy that she liked the idea of her lying-in at the Wardrobe since "my Lord was making so earnest request for it." But James's plan had to be discarded when Dorothy entered her final month of pregnancy and he and Lucy were still not wed. From London Lisle wrote anxiously to his wife: "My daughter's time draws on and some place for her must be thought of."[20]

Lying-in was no simple matter for a noblewoman. Nor was it cheap, what with the childbed linen and elaborate hangings for the bedchamber, to say nothing of providing a fine and impressive bed. Lisle was clearly afraid of the expense, and Dorothy herself wished to be with her mother. Thus in late August, very pregnant, she set out for Syon House accompanied by her mother-in-law. Lucy and her somewhat discomfited fiancé met them halfway at Bromley in Kent. In September, Dorothy gave birth to a girl. Robert was back from the Continent and by her side. A week later the peripatetic grandfather stopped in at Syon and reported to his wife that he found the new mother well "and the little one also, who is a very pretty one, God bless it."[21] The baby was christened Dorothy after her mother and her maternal grandmother.

Lisle also reported that James and Lucy's wedding date remained uncertain. Actually, the famous love match had been put off so long that the gossips were at work. "For so hot love," wrote Chamberlain, "they have a great deal of patience, but the world suspects it begins to cool and if matters go not forward, we might chance hear no further of it." Aside from Chamberlain's remark, there is no evidence that James or Lucy wished to break the engagement. Certainly there is no hint of such a thing in Lisle's letters to his wife. From his correspondence it appears that the couple were still trying to get Lucy's father's consent and, with it, a dowry. On October 25, Lisle was able to inform his wife that James had seen Northumberland and finally obtained his consent. The wedding was now expected to take place "very speedily." Nothing was said about a dowry. Northumberland had evidently washed his hands of the whole affair.

At the end of September, when King James returned from Scotland, there was no further need to wait.

On November 6, 1617, Lucy Percy and Sir James Hay were married at the Wardrobe, the groom's fine house at Blackfriars, in the presence of King James, the Prince of Wales, the favorite, Buckingham, and a host of lords and ladies. King James gave the bride away—a signal honor bestowed upon the couple. All those at the ceremony exclaimed that the new Lady Hay was the most radiant and beautiful bride they had ever seen. After the ceremony the groom provided a splendid wedding supper. King James was in a convivial mood, struggling to his feet to toast the bride and groom a dozen times and downing one cup of wine after another until he was plainly inebriated. During the evening he kept wandering into the bedchamber to chatter with Lucy's handsome gentlewoman, Mistress Washington. Lucy charmed King James. One wedding guest has left a description of the bride kneeling beside the seated king while they toasted each other's health.[22] The only thing that dampened Lucy's happiness was that neither her sister nor her mother was at the wedding: Dorothy was resting after giving birth, and Lady Northumberland did not want to vex her irate husband any further over this marriage that he so disliked.

Immediately after the wedding, Lucy's training for court life began. It was obviously James's desire to shape his young wife into a courtier in his own image. To dress fashionably, entertain opulently, amuse the royal couple: these were the requirements of a favorite at the Jacobean court. During the hectic days leading up to the Christmas festivities, Lucy organized a masque of ladies (at their own expense) to entertain the King and Queen on Twelfth Night. Dorothy, slim once more, was among the masquers, as were Isabella Rich, the wives of Sir Henry and Sir Robert Rich, and Dorothy's sister-in-law, Barbara Sidney. Lucy was to play the stellar role as Queen of the Amazons. The ladies practiced every day and were "almost perfect" when the royal couple put a stop to the masque.[23] The King had had his fill of Amazons. He was so disgusted with strong-minded women who were rocking the court with scandal that the masque's subject matter alone was enough to disqualify it. But Queen Anne felt even more strongly, regarding it as pure presumption for young Lady Hay to appropriate her own discontinued Christmas masque. This initial setback seems to have discouraged Lucy from similar endeavors; henceforth masque playing was never one of her favorite pastimes.

James had no difficulty turning Lucy into a clotheshorse like himself. As soberly dressed Puritans were never tired of declaiming, feminine interest in fashion was excessive, and young Lady Hay was no exception. During Lent in 1618, it was remarked that she wore a new dress to church every Sunday. Like the rest of the upper class, Lucy had her own tailor who came to the house with his fabrics and patterns. Her gowns would have had a very daring décolleté, a tightly laced bodice, and, we must assume, the farthingale. Queen Anne's undeviating devotion to that tablelike skirt continued until her death in 1619, and Lucy was under instructions from her husband to dress in a manner to please the Queen. In these years, if a lady went out without the farthingale it was thought worthy of mention. The Countess of Dorset noted in her diary on November 2, 1617, that she went to church, to a dinner party, and to court in a green damask gown "without a farthingale." Before long, Lucy Hay would set the style rather than follow it.

We can be sure that the fashionable Hays enjoyed many a shopping spree. There was no limit to the luxury goods available at the two Exchanges: muffs of Russian sable, Persian silks, Indian jewels, richly colored cloth from Venice, lace from France, leather gloves from Spain. Sir James Hay was an incorrigible spendthrift. His contemporary the historian Lord Clarendon said of him (in a coarse idiom of the day) that "he had no Bowels in the Point of running in Debt or borrowing all he could." To bedeck his beautiful young wife, money would have been no object with Hay. Perhaps Lucy's valuable pearl necklace, which was to play a part in the English Civil War, was a honeymoon gift.

By spring Lucy knew that she was pregnant. James was delighted and began to think dynastically. Although he had a son and a daughter by his first marriage, he took little interest in them. In the early days of his second marriage, they lived with their maternal grandparents. Now that he was about to have a child by Lucy, he decided to invest in land and establish a country seat. He entered into negotiations to purchase a large landed estate in Essex called Copt Hall. Ultimately the owner refused to sell. In the meantime, however, James had taken over the lease of Essex House from Lady Northumberland and was spending a fortune renovating the old mansion and improving the garden.[24]

The fact was that James needed a town house because he was giving up the Wardrobe and, with it, the luxurious dwelling on Upper Thames Street that he had occupied free of charge. Why did he resign the office? Though the King paid him the large sum of £20,000 for surrendering it, the money would not have compensated him for the handsome kickbacks from suppliers that went with the post. His own explanation was that his lack of experience in purchasing might have bred corrupt practices among the officers under him. Many suspected that it was Sir James himself who could not stand an investigation.

Reforms were under way. Lionel Cranfield, a City merchant coopted by the King and Buckingham, was applying businesslike methods to combat the waste and corruption in government departments, both in and out of the royal household. Cranfield's reforms had already brought down the Lord Treasurer, the Earl of Suffolk. James probably feared the same fate. This was the opinion of various astute court watchers like the Venetian ambassador. That James exploited his office shamelessly is indicated by a petition to Parliament from tradesmen who had done work for the palace. The petitioners charged that Lord Hay had defrauded them of their payments. Although the morality of public office sanctioned such practices as taking bribes, using cash balances for private moneylending, and selling inferior offices, to put money in one's pocket in lieu of paying poor tradesmen was not permissible.[25] That James saw the light in time undoubtedly owed something to Cranfield's friendly advice. With a further payment of £9,000 or £10,000 to James, Cranfield himself took over the Wardrobe.

This same summer saw James elevated to the peerage as Viscount Doncaster, an honor that may have been part payment for relinquishing the Wardrobe. By coincidence, Dorothy's husband, Robert Sidney, became a viscount at the same time, the result of his father becoming the Earl of Leicester. As a reward for all his shuttling between Oatlands and London, Queen Anne had prevailed upon the King to revive the earldom and to bestow it upon her loyal, if bibulous, servant. Thus Lucy and Dorothy became viscountesses at the same time.

Dorothy's husband may have become Viscount Lisle, but the couple could not compete financially with Viscount Doncaster. In 1618 the Earl of Leicester settled £200 annually upon the young couple, derived from rents in Sussex and Kent; he promised to raise the amount to £400 when Robert gave up his regiment.[26] This was undoubtedly the best he could do. The only way Robert and Dorothy could subsist at all on their niggardly income was by living with his parents. In the summer they stayed at Penshurst. During the winter, then becoming the social season in London, they lived at Baynard's Castle. This venerable mansion belonged not to the Earl of Leicester but to his sister, the Dowager Countess of Pembroke, and her stepson, the present Earl of Pembroke, who was a boon companion and favorite drinking partner of Leicester's. So it was as perennial houseguests that Dorothy and Robert wintered in London.

By the time of her confinement, Lucy at the age of nineteen was the Viscountess Doncaster and the mistress of her childhood home, Essex House. Toward the end of November 1618, she gave birth to a son. A week later the baby was christened with nobody present but his godparents: the new Viscount Lisle, Isabella Rich (who had just remarried), and Doncaster's cousin Sir George Hay. The private christening surprised the court; it was not the Doncasters' style at all. "The

World thinks it a great change," observed Chamberlain, "and contrary to both their brave spirits, to huddle up things thus in secret, but it seems they grow wise, and see that such a place as the Wardrobe is not easily found again." Despite Chamberlain's usually well-informed opinion, belt-tightening had nothing to do with it. The truth was that the infant was sickly and not expected to live. Two weeks after the christening it was dead, following a fit of convulsions.[27]

Infant mortality was so taken for granted that Lucy probably regarded the loss as simply a disappointment, to be quickly remedied by another pregnancy. She was young and healthy. She could be expected to follow her sister's example—Dorothy was expecting her second child imminently. The nobility did not practice birth control, and since the women of Dorothy's and Lucy's class did not nurse their babies, a birth every twelve or thirteen months was the norm. Families of a dozen children (of which perhaps three would grow to adulthood) were common. Although inept deliveries and childbed fever decimated the ranks of new mothers, such was the social pressure that women entered upon the annual contest with death eagerly and proudly.

In mid-January 1619, there was "much joy" at Baynard's Castle when Dorothy gave birth to a son. She had an easy delivery and was feeling well; everyone was congratulating her for having produced "a brave boy" for her husband. But the rejoicing among the family turned to grief a few days later when Dorothy took sick with smallpox. Fear of this disease hung over all classes, "for it was very common among great ladies as inferior ones."[28] It was particularly dreaded by upper-class women because good looks were so important to them. At the same time as Dorothy was struck by smallpox, another victim was Isabella Rich's new bridegroom, Sir John Smythe, "and she forgetting her late promise of better or worse in sickness and in health," snorted Chamberlain, "is fled to save her fair skin." Dorothy was so ill that her life was despaired of, yet she managed to survive and so did the infant who, in due course, was christened Philip after his famous great-uncle, the poet-soldier Sir Philip Sidney.

Both sisters had suffered and worried about each other's suffering: trouble had only brought them closer together. But unfortunately a coolness had developed between their husbands. For some time, Lisle had not visited the other's home. Lisle complained of Doncaster treating him with neglect or coldly with much ceremony, as if he were a stranger. "I often asked him what was the reason for his strangeness towards me," Lisle would later say.[29] The likely reason is that Doncaster was resentful and jealous of Lisle because of their father-in-law's obvious preference for him. On Lisle's part there was bound to be jealousy when Doncaster spent ten times Lisle's annual income on a single banquet. Moreover, Lisle resented Doncaster's failure to help him get royal patronage. Eager to give up his army commission in the Low Countries, he could not do so until he had some other employment. What particularly galled him was that his influential brother-in-law could so easily have helped him if he chose.

IN JANUARY 1619, King James appointed Doncaster to undertake a very sensitive embassy involving the King's daughter and her husband, the Elector Palatine. Since the end of the religious wars in the sixteenth century and the truce between the Dutch states and Spain, a shaky peace had prevailed in Europe. Under the august title of the Holy Roman Empire, the Austrian Hapsburgs ruled most of central Europe, including Bohemia. In 1619 the Bohemian Protestant majority rejected the Emperor's appointed king, Ferdinand of Styria, threw the imperial envoys out of the windows of Prague Castle, and offered the crown of Bohemia to the Elector Palatine, James's son-in-law, Frederick. From Vienna, the Emperor denounced the action of the Bohemians as a rebellion against his authority. If the Elector Palatine accepted the Bohemian crown, it could lead to war with the imperial power. Moreover, if the Union of Protestant Princes supported the Elector Palatine, the league of Catholic princes and bishops would probably support the Emperor, and Germany would erupt in flames. The domino effect did not stop there. The Spanish kings were Hapsburgs, and Philip III would no doubt take the side of his imperial cousin the Holy Roman Emperor.

James hated war; he could not afford it, and he had no stomach for it. He reveled in his self-bestowed title of Peacemaker of Christendom. One of his first acts on coming to England had been to sign a peace treaty with Spain. Indeed, his foreign policy was based on good relations with Spain, and his dynastic plan was to marry Prince Charles to a Spanish infanta. Now, the nice boy whom he had come to like so much during his six months' stay in England, and to whom he had given his daughter, was threatening to shatter the peace of Europe and possibly drag his father-in-law into war with Spain. Doncaster was being sent to mediate the dispute between Frederick and the Emperor's designated King of Bohemia, Ferdinand.

Notwithstanding the strained relations between them, Doncaster invited Lisle, as well as another brother-in-law, young Algernon Percy, to travel with his suite to Germany.[30] But Doncaster's departure was delayed by the death of Queen Anne. Lisle and Algernon went ahead to do some traveling before Lisle had to go to Holland to take his regiment on summer maneuvers.

The Queen's death was not unexpected. She had been lying ill all winter at Hampton Court with what her physicians, for want of a better diagnosis, called dropsy. Three times a week King James visited her from London until he himself became ill with an attack of "the stone" (gallstones). On March 2, 1619, the Queen passed away. She had not believed that she was dying and had refused to make a will. At the last moment, she made an oral will, leaving everything to Prince Charles. She had intended a casket of jewels for her daughter, Princess Elizabeth, but it was filched by her closest personal servant, Danish Anna.[31]

Like a royal marriage, a royal funeral required much planning. It was not until May that the corpse was transported by water to Denmark House, where it lay in state until the thirteenth of the month, when the burial took place. The King did not attend the funeral.[32] Although he had recovered from the stone, his legs were so weak that he had to be carried in a chair. James remained at Theobalds palace in Hertfordshire, and many of the courtiers judged it more rewarding to be with a live king than a dead queen, and they too missed the funeral.

Rigid rules of protocol determined the order of the cortège that accompanied the coffin from Denmark House to Westminster Abbey, where the Queen was to be buried. Leading the procession were a phalanx of barons, bishops, eldest sons, viscounts, earls, the Lord Chancellor, the Archbishop of Canterbury, and the late queen's Lord Chamberlain, the Earl of Leicester. Prince Charles walked directly in front of the coffin that was borne by eight earls and marquesses. (Buckingham was at Theobalds with the King and had another peer stand in for him as pallbearer.)

Next came the chief mourner, the Countess of Arundel, whose train was carried by the Countesses of Derby and Sussex. The choice of trainbearers had been the subject of gossip in the weeks before the funeral. It seemed that Lady Northumberland and Lady Shrewsbury had been asked first but had refused the honor, saying they would not stoop to bear the train of a woman of their own rank.

Lady Northumberland's daughters, however, accepted the invitation to take part in the cortège. Dorothy and Lucy were among the second tier of noblewomen following the coffin. (Dorothy's mother-in-law, the Countess of Leicester, and the Countess of Bedford were in the group ahead of them.) Walking with the sisters was their cousin Isabella Smythe. We can imagine the glances (and possibly giggles) the three young women exchanged as they dragged themselves along in the heavy black robes that were issued to the mourners. There may have been some flirting, for each lady had a gentleman to lean upon.

Spectators lining the road thought the ladies made a poor show of it. Chamberlain wrote Carleton that they came "laggering along, apparelled all alike, tired with the length of the way and the weight of their clothes, every Lady having twelve yards of broad cloth about her and the Countesses, sixteen." The whole funeral march, he said, was "a drawling, tedious sight."[33]

TWO WEEKS BEFORE the funeral, Doncaster had finally set out for Germany with twenty-four carriages and his entire entourage of hundreds, including the poet John Donne as chaplain, all clothed in mourning for the late Queen Anne. Before his departure, Doncaster and Lucy had made a great show of their sorrow at being parted. There were "long congés and leave-takings" in public. On the day he left, weeping Lucy lamented that she could not live without him for so long; kissing away her tears, Doncaster promised that he would be faithful and would bring her lovely presents from Heidelberg and Vienna. When Doncaster was delayed at the coast by foul weather, it was the talk of the court how his devoted wife followed him to Gravesend and "would not forsake him" until he sailed.[34] Waving until the ship was out of sight, Lucy, now a grass widow, journeyed to Syon House.

That summer Lucy stayed in the country with her mother, her two stepchildren, her gentlewoman, Mistress Washington, and William Woodforde, the family chaplain, whose letters to Doncaster are the source of our information. Lady Doncaster, he wrote, "received content in nothing more than to hear of you and from you."[35] The children were well, he assured their father. Ten-year-old James was working conscientiously on his lessons, but Woodforde hoped the French tutor would arrive soon, because the boy had the bad habit of "frenchifizing" English when he did not know the French word. The greatest excitement for the household, Woodforde wrote, was the arrival of Sir Robert Killegrew from Germany with Lord Doncaster's commands for his family. Dorothy was living an identical life at Penshurst, with two babies and an absent husband.

The tedium of country living was shattered for both sisters in August when their mother took a sudden fever and died at Syon House. Lucy, of course, was with her when it happened and mourned the best of mothers, but we do not hear that her grief was immoderate. Dorothy, on the other hand, went to pieces. She and her mother had always been particularly close. Feeling like a stranger in her mother-in-law's house, Dorothy was inconsolable. "Lady Lisle is at Penshurst and much bemoans her mother," one family friend wrote another.[36] Coming on top of two babies in two years, an almost fatal attack of smallpox, loneliness for her husband, and the boredom of country life, Dorothy found this blow just too much to bear.

That Dorothy took Lady Northumberland's death to heart was to be expected. But the Earl of Northumberland's excessive grief surprised everyone. All his arrogance, contempt for women, and rivalry with his dead wife dissolved into self-recrimination. He condemned himself for his ingratitude, citing her unceasing efforts to have him freed. Obviously his unspoken guilt over the Lady Somerset interlude was torturing him. Determined to accord his late wife all honor in death, at least, he planned an impressive funeral for her. The dead woman was floated down the river by barge from Syon House to Petworth House in Sussex, where she was interred with great pomp in the Percy crypt.

ONCE FINISHED WITH his regiment's summer maneuvers, Lisle joined Doncaster's embassy for a short time before returning to England. In a dispatch dated July 9, 1619, Doncaster informed Secretary of State Sir Robert Naunton that Lisle would explain to him and the King why the mission was taking so long. Indeed, the mission had turned into a fool's journey, with Doncaster chasing up and down the rivers and byways after the elusive King Ferdinand and just missing him. When he finally caught up with Ferdinand, he was treated to a polite but unproductive audience. Apparently, Lisle was in no hurry to get home because Naunton scribbled in the margin of Doncaster's dispatch: "I have not heard of my Lord Lisle's arrival."[37]

Meanwhile, the Bohemian situation had evolved past the point of no return. In the late summer, the Elector Palatine accepted the crown of Bohemia, and he was asking for King James's assistance against the Hapsburgs. Doncaster was all in favor of supporting him. His dispatches left no doubt that it was too late for diplomacy. Prophetically, Chamberlain wrote to Carleton: "There is now no place left for deliberation, nor for mediation of peace till one side be utterly ruined."[38]

Once back at Penshurst, Lisle found himself unable to alleviate Dorothy's grief over her mother. She longed for her sister's company, so in October they went to stay with Lucy at Syon House. Immediately after Doncaster's return in January 1620, Lisle wrote to him in the hope of healing the breach between them—considering Lisle's habitual reserve, the letter probably did not appear as conciliatory as he intended. Doncaster's answer was, in Lisle's opinion, unsatisfactory. Nevertheless, "desiring only an outward familiarity," Lisle began visiting Doncaster's house once more "because of the love between our wives."[39]

BUCKINGHAM'S CHARMS

WHEN DONCASTER RETURNED from Germany in the winter of 1620, little did he suspect that George Villiers, now Marquess of Buckingham, had turned his attentions to Lucy.

Villiers's power and physical charms would have made him irresistible to a young woman of twenty-one. He was extraordinarily handsome, with that natural grace that is equally attractive to men as well as women. A Gentleman of the Bedchamber noted that Buckingham's "hands and face seemed especially effeminate and curious." The celibate Bishop William Laud of London confessed in his diary that he dreamed Buckingham got into bed with him.[1] Whether dancing or riding at the ring or playing tennis, he was an Adonis in motion. King James adored him—a combination of homosexual yearning and paternal pride. When first introduced at court in 1614, George Villiers had been the most agreeable of young men, radiating good humor and making himself generally well-liked. Six years later he was still as charming when he chose to be, but he had become increasingly arrogant and overbearing.

No longer simply the favorite, he had become James's chief minister and the Lord High Admiral, though he knew nothing of the sea.

Most important, he was the sole channel of patronage. Buckingham carried the burden of office obtrusively. The ready smile that had once enchanted the court was replaced by a preoccupied frown. Holding himself above the crowd, he insisted that the shoals of suitors approach him through one or other of his intimates or retainers. In spite of the signs of corrupting power, Buckingham retained his amazing personal magnetism. King James was as doting as ever, and the heir to the throne, Prince Charles, was equally attached to him. Buckingham and the Prince were constant companions, hunting and playing tennis together or indulging their shared interest in art collecting. To his political role Buckingham brought abundant energy and some administrative ability. But he was too impressionable, too easily influenced by suave ambassadors, so that his foreign policies were impulsive and even whimsical.

Buckingham was a notorious womanizer. As demonstrated by his later attempts on the virtue of the Spanish prime minister's wife and even the Queen of France, no woman was safe from his desires. His tactics were crude. When he saw a woman he desired, his friends would lure her to a respectable house where he would then turn up "as by accident" and debauch her, "while all his Train attended at the door as if it were an honourable visit."[2] Inevitably, he would set his sights on the most beautiful woman at court. Lecher that he was, he would have insisted upon a physical relationship. It is unlikely that the impressionable and ambitious Lucy put up much resistance.

Doncaster had been married to his adored Lucy for just over two years. It was only six months since she had made her romantic journey to Gravesend to spend every last moment with him. He had received reports that all summer she had been the picture of the devoted wife. Now he was back, and instead of a happy reunion he found a disgruntled wife who did not appear at all glad to see him. When he tried to tell her of his embassy (though he had accomplished nothing, he had been treated royally), Lucy's response was to raise her eyebrows and gaze out the window. He even made a bid for sympathy, turning a mild attack of purple fever at Montauban into a life-threatening illness. The warm, soft arms that had once embraced him remained folded severely across her chest. Doncaster had to demand his marital rights.

They were soon quarreling openly. Tobie Mathew, the apostate son of the Archbishop of York, heard while traveling on the Continent the rumors that the famous love match had soured: "It hath been written hither," he informed Doncaster, "that there is some little disgust between thy noble lady and thyself (saving that no disgust can be little between such a couple of creatures as you two)."³ What caused the quarrel?

The French ambassador's correspondence reveals what Doncaster soon found out: his wife was having an affair with the King's favorite. Indeed, the Comte de Tillières, the French ambassador, believed that Buckingham had deliberately delayed Doncaster's return in order to complete his conquest. "They say that it is not the King's business that necessitates the ambassador's return visit to the Emperor," he reported to Paris in November, "but to consummate a love that the Marquis of Buckingham has for someone very close to him."⁴ A few years later Lucy was widely known to be Buckingham's mistress. An extramarital affair would explain why the passionate romance that had so titillated the court in 1617 had suddenly ended. No doubt it would have provided grim satisfaction for Lucy's father and a vindication of the practice of properly arranged marriages.

Adultery was commonplace in James's court, especially after Queen Anne's death. As well, Doncaster was bound to suffer by comparison with the youthful favorite in Lucy's eyes. He was now forty years old and showing his age; he had given up masquing and the tiltyard. All his feasting had caught up with him, lending him a decidedly dissipated appearance. The bags under his eyes, combined with his sloping forehead and sandy hair and beard, had inspired the playful Princess Elizabeth to dub him "camel face" during his recent visit to Germany. Lucy was quickly losing the girlish admiration that had formed the basis of her side of the love affair. His self-esteem crushed, he began to complain to his crony Sir George Goring about his wife's treatment of him. Lucy's relationship with the favorite undoubtedly was the cause of the quarrels that marked their marriage until Buckingham's death.

Whatever his personal feelings, Doncaster had little choice but to accept the situation. A court lord without an acre of land, he was dependent on royal patronage, and Buckingham controlled its dispensation. Not only that, but the costly diplomatic missions that he so much enjoyed would cease if he broke with the favorite. So Doncaster in effect swore fealty to his wife's lover. During a public quarrel with Lisle in 1622, he declared, "I am so much this noble lord's servant [indicating Buckingham] that I will perform whatsoever he commands me."[5] Always the politician, he became the most reliable of Buckingham's intimates. In the Privy Council, he followed the favorite's shifts and turns faultlessly, most notably over the Palatinate issue.

IN OCTOBER 1619, James's son-in-law had moved his family to Prague and assumed the title of King of Bohemia, notwithstanding the fact that imperial forces were massing at the border, ready to oust him as soon as the snow was off the ground. At the Battle of the White Mountain, Frederick was decisively defeated. Meanwhile, the Spanish general Ambrogio Spinola had invaded the Palatinate and taken Frederick's hereditary lands away from him. Having no home either in Germany or in Bohemia, Frederick fled with his family, seeking refuge.

They had left everything behind them and were virtually penniless. Elizabeth was in the last stages of a pregnancy. From Silesia, King James received a heartbreaking letter from his daughter. Describing their misfortunes, Elizabeth pleaded with her father to have pity on them and not to abandon her husband. She herself was resolved never to leave him, she wrote. If he perished, she would perish with him.[6] King James wept when he read her letter. But then he comforted himself with the thought that he had warned Frederick not to assume the Bohemian crown. Frederick had preferred to listen to the advice of his uncle Prince Maurice of Orange, who approved of the venture. Well then, James said to himself, let Prince Maurice look after him. As it happened, Maurice did so, inviting the couple to Holland, where he supported them in decent fashion at The Hague. Prince Maurice was in complete sympathy with the exiles. The truce with Spain had broken down, and the Dutch states were once again fighting the Spanish Hapsburgs in the Netherlands.

The English people were outraged by the treatment of their beloved Princess Elizabeth at the hands of the Catholic Hapsburgs and demanded that England send military help. It had all unfolded just as James had predicted. Although he bemoaned his beloved daughter's sad situation, James refused to send over troops. Any that went would have to go as volunteers. Buckingham had initially supported the war party, donating £20,000 to the war chest, and in the Privy Council he had sided with the pro-war councillors, boasting that he would bring the King around. But under the influence of the Spanish ambassador, the Conde Gondomar, Buckingham changed his mind; he now agreed with King James that England should not become involved militarily in Frederick's plight.

Doncaster had returned from Germany advocating war in support of the Elector Palatine's claim to the Bohemian throne, but when Buckingham dropped his war policy, Doncaster unhesitatingly concurred. In return, Buckingham encouraged the King's generosity to the older favorite. Doncaster's intimacy with Buckingham reinforced his position at court, to the point where he became one of James's chief diplomats in the last years of the reign.

In due course, the Doncasters' quarrel was resolved, but the marriage took on a brittleness, a stylish superficiality. As a couple they enjoyed tremendous social success: he, the essence of courtliness, and she, the most elegant woman at court. To be in fashion had become Lucy's absorbing passion. We can picture her in the provocatively masculine styles of 1620 (the "manlike and unseemly apparel"[7] inveighed against from the pulpit) that had women wearing pointed doublets and broad-brimmed hats: some went so far as to stick a stiletto in their belt and bob their hair. Lord and Lady Doncaster's continual entertaining on a gargantuan scale provided the London news-writers who congregated at St. Paul's churchyard with perpetual subject matter for their provincial readers. Essex House was the scene of suppers, balls, musical soirées, masques.

Her husband's new alliance with the favorite meant that Lucy had to associate with the Buckingham women—a dubious pleasure on both sides. First and foremost was his mother, the domineering Countess of Buckingham, who shouldered her way into the void created by the death of the royal consort and queened it over the court. Then there was her daughter, the Countess of Denbigh, a younger version of herself. She, in turn, had produced a daughter who, though barely at puberty, had been married to the great Scottish lord the Marquess of Hamilton. Then there were the countless cousins and nieces of the favorite who came in from the country to find a husband. One by one, Buckingham married them into the best families in order to form a solid power base for himself.

But Lucy could hold her own with these women. She was indisputably the most beautiful woman at court, and the Buckingham ladies had to listen to their husbands lavishing praise upon her. She was the wife of a leading courtier and, if the rumor was true, the mistress of the Marquess of Buckingham, to whom they owed their good fortune. Lady Doncaster was certainly not a person to be cowed by feminine cattiness. Even as a child she had been self-confident, riding spirited horses and daring Dorothy to do the same. While other girls were brought up in homes where obedience to the father was the law, Lucy had received little discipline from her indulgent mother and at eighteen had defied her father by marrying against his wishes. Behind her smiles and compliments, there was the hidden dagger of a sharp wit. The rather plain ladies of the Buckingham connection did not tangle with the exquisite Lady Doncaster.

In the spring of 1620, Buckingham himself got married, predictably to a wealthy heiress, Katherine Manners, the Earl of Rutland's daughter. The Earl was adamantly opposed to the marriage, in part because of Buckingham's reputation as a libertine. Relentless as always in his pursuit of women, Buckingham, with the collusion of his mother, abducted the girl and kept her a willing captive overnight under the same roof as himself. Having ruined her marital chances, Buckingham then turned around and told the infuriated father that he could have her back.[8] Rutland had to practically beg the insolent favorite to marry Katherine. The marriage took place quietly in May.

The new Lady Buckingham—no beauty judging from her pictures—was passionately in love with her handsome husband. Sensible and undemanding, she soon realized that he was unfaithful. She once referred to his "one sin" of "loving women too well."[9] She cannot have been fond of Lady Doncaster. Nevertheless, they were thrown together constantly.

Lord and Lady Doncaster danced attendance upon Buckingham and his family. In September 1620, Chamberlain reported to Carleton that they gave "a great feast at Syon to the Lord Marquis, his Lady and the Countess his mother." Happily, it was all worthwhile. Grants poured in upon them. According to Chamberlain, the King was so generous to Doncaster at a time when royal finances were strained that it created considerable animosity toward him. Conceding that he was "a very sufficient, bountiful, complete, and complimental gentleman," Chamberlain goes on to say of the Scottish Doncaster, "yet I have heard divers wise and judicious men wish (for more respects than one) that he had never seen England, or England never seen him."

One royal grant was particularly pleasing to Lucy. In May 1620, Doncaster received the keepership of Nonsuch Palace "and the gardens and parks thereof for life."[10] About twenty miles out of London in Surrey, Nonsuch had been built by Italian and Flemish craftsmen for King Henry VIII to rival Fontainebleau and the Loire castles. To the visitor arriving by coach along the road from London, the palace rose up from the rolling countryside like a fantastic mirage. Flanked by octagonal corner towers five stories high, its exterior walls were completely covered with plaster bas-reliefs and life-size statues in niches. The garden was as fanciful as the building, with animal topiary and an elaborate stone fountain of an antlered Acteon and three naked goddesses. The palace was surrounded by miles of parks and salubrious springs, providing all the healthful amenities of a spa. Lucy loved her country retreat and spent much time there. The air and water agreed with her, and no doubt she thought a fairy-tale castle a suitable residence for her. Lucy's new status was beginning to go to her head.

Having a suite of rooms at Nonsuch Palace did not interfere with Lucy's summer visits to Penshurst to be with Dorothy. In September 1620, she was there as usual (as we know because the Earl of Leicester sent his best regards to her through his wife), and the devoted sisters spent a great deal of time in each other's company. For part of each winter, Dorothy and Robert were in London, and there were daily visits back and forth between Essex House and Baynard's Castle. Dorothy put off returning to the country as long as possible. In 1621 she extended her stay throughout the spring, with no plans for returning to Penshurst until June.

Much of Lucy's time in London was taken up with the family of the French ambassador, the Comte de Tillières. Doncaster was the resident expert on France; he spoke the language perfectly, knew the country, and had many contacts at the French court. In fact, he was under instructions from the King to sound out de Tillières on a possible French marriage for Prince Charles, should the negotiations for a Spanish princess fall through. Doncaster could be said to have a vested interest in a French match, so he and Lucy cultivated the French diplomats.

The Comte de Tillières, his wife the Comtesse, and her niece, Mademoiselle Saint-Luc, were a great addition to the social life of the court circle. Among other French fashions, they introduced the "running masque"—a movable version of the courtly theatricals, which played each night at a different house. Enthusiasm over this new craze was so high that the aristocratic masquers happily turned themselves into strolling players. But Buckingham, Goring, and Rich were upstaged by "the great porter at court" who played the part of a giant and came on holding the Earl of Montgomery's diminutive page like a falcon on his fist. After a first performance at the ambassador's residence, the players moved on to Essex House, where the Doncasters improved upon the occasion by offering their guests a banquet and a ball attended by the King and the Prince of Wales.[11]

At the same time as Doncaster was conducting serious business with the Comte de Tillières, according to a Venetian envoy he was "very intimate" with Madame de Tillières.[12] A sophisticated *parisienne* of his own age, she was the sister of a French marshal and very knowledgeable about politics. The Venetian claimed that she even influenced Doncaster's views on Anglo-French relations. Lucy could not have been unaware of her husband's liaison and seemingly accepted it just as he accepted hers.

Monsieur de Tillières and his family were frequently entertained at Essex House; but none of these lavish functions compared to the feast that the Doncasters gave in January 1621 in honor of a special French envoy, the Maréchal de Cadenet. Even in an age of ostentatious display the feast shocked contemporaries with its "sumptuous superfluity."[13] For weeks the Essex House "cater" had been buying up the choicest meats and fowl in such quantities as to create a shortage. There were 240 pheasants alone, dozens of partridges and larks, fresh salmon from the Thames, and huge Muscovy salmon purchased at the London docks. As well there were the "grosser meats"—swans, chines of beef, and two whole suckling pigs. Eight days before the event, a brigade of a hundred cooks, forty of them master chefs, marched into the kitchens and baked, boiled, roasted, marinated, jellied, and concocted sixteen hundred dishes. They used £300 worth of precious ambergris (a perfume ingredient then used sparingly in cookery) and mounds of spices, such as mace, nutmeg, cloves, cinnamon, and ginger, as well as raisins and currants by the peck. Sweating porters carried casks of wine off the barges docked at Essex Stairs and rolled them into the cellar while the butler counted them off: a pipe of canary, a tun of claret, another of Rhenish, a butt of sack, and so on.

On the great night itself, liveried footmen ushered the guests to the lower gallery, where a long table was spread with the most luscious array of food. But this was a feast for the eyes only. It was all whisked away and replaced by a second feast, this one to be consumed! After supper the glutted guests were led upstairs to watch a masque and partake of sweetmeats piled on huge salvers almost too heavy for the footmen to carry: these alone were said to have set the host back £500. This Lucullan feast with the novelty of the antesupper—another French importation perhaps suggested by Madame de Tillières—further consolidated Doncaster's status. King James, seated at the head of the table with the Prince of Wales and the French ambassadors, was seen enjoying himself hugely. It was a triumph for Lord and Lady Doncaster, albeit a costly one, for estimates ran as high as £3,000. On the Maréchal de Cadenet's departure, Doncaster gave him some horses and Lucy presented him with two waistcoats and petticoats for his wife, "all of an extraordinary richness."

LUCY APPEARED TO have achieved her mother's ambitions for her: a wealthy, titled husband and a high position at court. Yet from time to time Lucy's hectic social life was interrupted by bouts of stomach disorders that may have been psychosomatic in origin. There were no more babies to replace her dead infant son, and at this stage of her life she perhaps regretted it. Fecundity was a woman's greatest glory; the barren woman was an object of pity, second only to the spinster. Like most young women of her time, Lucy accepted these values. Her childlessness would have aggravated her dissatisfaction with her marriage. Since she had no history of organic disease, her ailments were possibly a sign of nervous tension.

The beginning of this hypochondria is indicated by a journey abroad to Spa in the summer of 1621. For years the English nobility had been traveling to this little village near Liège in the Low Countries to drink the healthful waters. Doncaster probably advised Lucy to go since he had been there himself in the summer of 1619. On the first of June, Lucy set out with the faithful William Woodforde and a suite of servants. She was accompanied by her cousin Isabella Smythe. This social butterfly was in a pitiable situation as her new husband had deserted her, fleeing to the Continent with his cousin Tom Smythe. Isabella's second marriage was a casualty of town life in the upper circles. Writing to his father to explain his bunk, young John Smythe blamed "the clamour of creditors, the high state of expense he was fallen into and the avoidance of some company unfit for him." In his rake's progress he was aided and abetted by his cousin Tom, a nineteen-year-old homosexual far gone in debauchery. Two years before, Tom Smythe had eloped with Barbara Sidney, Dorothy's sister-in-law, and married her without the knowledge of either family. Tom's clandestine marriage had amazed Chamberlain, for, as he told

Carleton at the time, "he is known to have no more mind to her than to any other woman, and perhaps not so much."[14]

The journey was arduous: to Gravesend by the river, across the Channel to Flushing (contrary winds could hold travelers up for a week), then days of uncomfortable coach travel, culminating in twelve hours in a bone-shaking wagon on the rutted road from Liège to Spa. Also, the continental inns were unsanitary, bed linen was never changed, and the traveler arose in the morning, after a sleepless night, covered with flea bites. Considering the hardships of travel, many travelers must have thought the cure worse than the disease.

Lucy and Isabella either rented a house for the season or stayed at the comfortable Golden Fleece Inn. They then entered upon the strict regimen of the cure. On the first day the *curiste* drank ten to twelve ounces of the acidic water, increasing it to as much as fifty or even seventy ounces, tapering off to a daily dose of a glass or two. The waters were of four strengths. The strongest, often causing vomiting, was taken only by those most dedicated to the cure; those less Spartan mixed the water with wine to make it more palatable. Lucy and Isabella would have soon fallen into the routine of rising at four, drinking the waters, and strolling or visiting with the other aristocratic visitors.[15] The constant wet dampened their spirits, however. The place had "a habit of raining," Lucy complained to Woodforde, "that would not be easily removed."

Lucy's journey to Spa was timed to coincide with another of Doncaster's missions. In July he was sent to France to remonstrate with Louis XIII over his treatment of the Huguenots. The Huguenots, as the French Protestants were known, had been granted toleration and a number of fortified towns in southwest France by the Edict of Nantes of 1598, which ended fifty years of religious wars. Nevertheless, the struggle between the monarchy and the Huguenots continued into the next century. Around 1620 a wily cleric, Armand du Plessis de Richelieu, bishop of a backwater diocese, insinuated himself into the position of Louis XIII's principal adviser. Soon to become the all-powerful Cardinal Richelieu, he aimed to create a strong central monarchy, not only for domestic reasons but ultimately to

challenge the territorial ambitions of the Austrian and Spanish Hapsburgs. Regarding the Huguenot fortified towns as a state within a
state, Richelieu moved King Louis to systematically retake them.
Doncaster's impossible assignment was to make peace between the
King of France and the Huguenots.

Before Lucy left for the Continent, Doncaster gave her the enormous sum of £5,000 for her expenses, half the amount the King had
given him for his embassy.[16] This generous sharing indicates the nature
of their relationship. Although both went their separate ways roman-
tically, a partnership had evolved between husband and wife. Doncaster respected Lucy's intelligence and ability, as yet confined to the
conventional feminine sphere. She had proved an apt pupil in the social arts and an extraordinary helpmate in his lavish entertaining. Although not a happy marriage, it was successful in a worldly sense. In
contrast to the Earl of Northumberland's low opinion of women,
Doncaster's admiration for his wife can be seen as a rare tribute to her.

While Lucy was at Spa, her father at long last was released from
prison. Like all other favors, his freedom came through the grace and
favor of the Marquess of Buckingham, although Doncaster was behind it. Actually, Northumberland could have got out of the Tower
much sooner had he not scorned his son-in-law's good offices. Now,
however, he condescended to leave, and on a fine July day Doncaster
drove up to the Tower in his magnificent coach and six and carried
the Earl to Essex House. Buckingham and all the great lords rushed
to pay their respects, and Northumberland, looking not a day older
after fifteen years in prison, was immediately reinstated in his preem-
inent position in the social hierarchy. A few days later, Doncaster set
out for France, and Northumberland retired to the country. After
spending ten days at Syon and a few weeks at Petworth in Sussex, he
went to visit Dorothy at Penshurst. He had long since forgiven her
for marrying without his permission and, despite his misogynist personality, was devoted to her and her family.

Lucy returned from the Low Countries still unwell. Unfortunately, taking the laxative waters had addicted her to purgatives, and
she was swallowing stronger and stronger dosages. Purging and blood-

letting (using leeches) were the popular remedies of the day for everything from cholera to typhoid to cancer. The fashionable court physician, Monsieur de Mayerne, was a great believer in both, so much so that when Prince Henry died of typhoid fever in 1612, Mayerne was severely criticized for excessive purging of the hopelessly ill boy. The criticism had blown over, and Mayerne continued to minister to the royal family and the nobility. The purgatives used were of extraordinary strength. After "glisters" and "purging syrup" taken orally (with what damage to the digestive system can only be imagined), the patient was confined to the bedchamber for days. All autumn and into the winter of 1622, Lucy dosed herself in this fashion, no doubt under Mayerne's prescription, and when Doncaster returned to England for fresh instructions in February, he found her extremely ill. She had so weakened her body through overdoses of physic that she was thought to be "at the last cast."[17] A worried Doncaster remained with her until mid-March, when she was sufficiently out of danger for him to return to France.

As soon as she was fit to travel, Lucy went to Penshurst. During her husband's long absences, and particularly when she was not well, she always turned to Dorothy. An additional reason for retiring to Kent this time was that her father had reclaimed Syon for his own use, and when he was in London, he treated Essex House as if he were still paying the rent. Undoubtedly Lucy showed him the outward deference of a dutiful daughter, but too much unpleasantness had passed between them to be forgotten. Not only had he imprisoned her against her will to stop her marriage, but she resented the scant respect he showed her husband. That Northumberland was equally uncomfortable under the same roof as his younger daughter can be inferred from his renting a town house the following season.

LIFE IN THE COUNTRY
AND LIFE AT COURT

WITH THE DEATH of her mother-in-law in June 1621, the running of the great house at Penshurst became Dorothy's responsibility. She quickly proved herself an excellent manager, not only of the manor house but of the entire estate. Her father-in-law was usually away in London, and her husband was only too happy to leave the practical concerns of household and estate management to her. Lisle was at his happiest in his study, reading or scribbling down his thoughts, and it was with a sense of relief that he handed over as many of his responsibilities as possible to his capable wife.

Dorothy, always pregnant, found running the estate exhausting. There were bad days when the manager would come to the great house with his ledger in hand to report that some of the tenants were in arrears with their rent, or the gamekeeper would stomp in in his heavy boots and, in his strong country accent, complain that poachers were killing all the deer, or the bad-tempered cook would threaten to leave if the housekeeper did not stay out of her kitchen. Trained by her mother-in-law, Dorothy had acquired the necessary skills of a good housewife: distilling, pickling, preserving, smoking and curing bacon, salting fish, drying herbs and lavender (the latter to keep the sheets sweet-smelling), storing apples and roots over the winter away from marauding mice and rats. She was also well versed in the medicinal use of herbs, cordials, and physics, because the lady of the manor was the doctor for house and village, dressing wounds and even setting bones. Dorothy was responsible for the family, and in the seventeenth century that included all the servants as well as her children.[1]

Her new obligations as mistress of Penshurst ruled out long winter visits to London, and it was at this time that Dorothy's complaints about the boredom of life in the country began seriously. She had inherited her mother's tendency to melancholy, and Penshurst brought out the worst in her. (Even her more cheerful mother-in-law had grown melancholy there, as the first earl's correspondence reveals.) By nature Dorothy loved society and its excitements as much as Lucy, but through force of circumstance she found herself living in the country and tied down with a growing family. Her youthful gaiety became inverted and a somberness took its place. As she went about her rounds, her chatelaine's keys jangling at her waist, the outwardly sober young matron longed for the delights of London and the court. The contrast of her life with her sister's unsettled her, particularly since she would have submerged such thoughts. With every visit or letter from Lucy, describing the festivals and weddings at court, Dorothy's feelings of discontent were heightened and found expression in complaining to her husband. Still, Dorothy was deeply in love with her husband, and he reciprocated her feelings as much as his narrow, introspective nature would allow.

Like all couples, they had their areas of conflict. Dorothy was often impatient with Lisle for spending his time reading, and her complaints in turn drove him back to his books behind the closed door of his study. Nevertheless, there was a strong current of passion between them, which Lucy was never to know in or out of marriage.

For the first summer since his marriage, Lisle did not go abroad in 1622. With no preferment in sight, he had given up his regiment in the Dutch service. He had last spoken to Doncaster in February when the latter came over briefly from France, but his brother-in-law's vague promises had so far yielded no result. Lisle was extremely depressed about his future. Dorothy was pregnant again. He was becoming desperate for some employment to subsidize this burgeoning family, and perhaps also to escape from the heavy family responsibilities that weighed upon his slim scholar's shoulders. In July 1622, when Doncaster returned from France in even greater favor with the King and Buckingham, Lisle decided to try again to obtain his help. Putting aside his pride, when both were at Petworth in early August, he went to Doncaster to reopen the subject of his preferment. He found Doncaster sitting in the withdrawing chamber near the parlor "with his men pulling on his breeches and stockings being sewed together." On seeing him, Lisle said, Doncaster "stood up on one leg and saluted me only with a strange look." Deeply offended by what he regarded as a snub (could Doncaster have simply been embarrassed to be caught in such an undignified posture?), Lisle grew angry and some hot words passed between them.

A month later, both were at Syon House, where their father-in-law was entertaining Buckingham and other nobility. According to Lisle's account, Doncaster was frankly insulting to him in front of the guests. Humiliated by such treatment, Lisle sought out his brother-in-law to remonstrate with him in private. Finding him surrounded by his hangers-on, he tried to talk calmly but in a matter of moments the two were exchanging blows. The news of their fight spread through the house. Summoned to their father-in-law's bedside, they stood before him in the presence of Buckingham and the Duke of Richmond like sheepish schoolboys. For the sake of his daughters, Northumberland commanded them, they must reconcile their differences because continuing this feud would be "a great grief" to their wives, who would be unable to "enjoy one another's company so much as they had."[2] It was only a sham reconciliation. Both men were burning with indignation, the more so because they had forsworn any further action.

It is Lisle's version of the quarrel that has come down to us, and his self-portrayal as the innocent party must be heavily discounted. The sensitive youth of courtship days had matured into an overly sensitive man who took offense easily. He often imagined slights where none were intended; he may well have done so here. Moreover, it is difficult to reconcile Lisle's picture of Doncaster with "the complete and complimental" gentleman others saw. Doncaster was known for his unfailing courtesy. It would have been more characteristic of him to turn Lisle away with a polite word, if such was his intention. On the other hand, Lisle was undoubtedly correct that Doncaster was jealous of him because of Northumberland's patent preference for him. Granting that he had offended Lisle, Lisle had also offended him, and Doncaster made a point of calling upon Lisle's father to tell him so. In a letter to his son, who was now licking his wounds at Penshurst, the Earl of Leicester reported on the visit. Though Doncaster had been as friendly as ever to him, he was obviously angry over something that Lisle had said or done after leaving Petworth. This could explain his coldness at Syon. "He told me," Leicester wrote, "that he retained very much estimation of you but protested not to love you."[3] The old earl was clearly upset by the quarrel. Far from exonerating his son, he urged him to patch it up without delay. Of course Leicester was a wily old courtier and would not have wished to offend his influential colleague.

In September 1622, Doncaster was created Earl of Carlisle and shortly afterward was granted an annual pension of £2,000 for twenty-one years to help maintain his new honor. He and Lucy, now the Countess of Carlisle, threw themselves into the social life of the Buckingham set with renewed vigor. That Christmas they were all caught up in a hectic round of feasting and dancing, "somewhat like fiddlers," remarked Chamberlain wryly. The Comtesse de Tillières and her niece were returning to France, and there were numerous farewell parties for them. The court was sorry to part with the adorable Mademoiselle Saint-Luc. King James offered her a choice of young lords if she would stay in England. Among those proffered with such careless royal largesse was the sisters' twenty-year-old brother, Algernon, who promptly left for the Continent. On his own account, Carlisle was sorry to part with Madame de Tillières, and, according to embassy gossip, he began looking out for a mission to France.[4]

Naturally, the Carlisles entertained for the departing ladies. But on this occasion the court's most notable party givers suffered an acute embarrassment. Buckingham took so sick at supper that he had to be put to bed at Essex House. Lord and Lady Carlisle undoubtedly berated the kitchen staff, from the master cook to the scullery maid who washed the dishes. However embarrassing for the hosts, Buckingham's illness was not serious, and the next day he was able to rejoin the festivities. When Mademoiselle Saint-Luc finally tore herself away from her English admirers, the Buckinghams and the Carlisles jointly presented her with some costly jewelry.

EARLY IN 1623, news broke that Prince Charles, accompanied by Buckingham, had traveled incognito to Madrid to woo the Infanta in person. Carlisle was one of the few people Buckingham had confided in beforehand.[5] Knowing that Lucy could not keep a secret (as we too shall see), Carlisle would not have told her.

Negotiations for a marriage between the English and Spanish Crowns had been dragging on for some time. King James was especially anxious at this time for the Spanish match, hoping that in this way he could recover the Palatinate for his son-in-law without going to war. Some towns in the Lower Palatinate were in Spanish hands, and handing them back to Frederick would make a nice wedding gift for Prince Charles. James was encouraged to believe in this happy ending by the Spanish ambassador, Gondomar, and it was this suave diplomat who planted the idea in Buckingham's head that the marriage could be expedited if he and Prince Charles went to fetch the Infanta themselves. Masquerading as simple Tom and John, the two young men paid a quick visit to Paris, then galloped south into Spain, staying at hostelries like any ordinary travelers. This required some explaining at the French court, and Carlisle was sent to the Louvre Palace to smooth over the Prince's precipitous dash through French territory. That mission completed, he was dispatched to Madrid to lend some dignity to the unseemly proceedings. He was also to teach the King's "sweet boys" some of the finer graces. James had written a letter of thanks to King Philip for the good reception accorded his son. Buckingham was to deliver it. King James advised him to do it with the "best compliments thou can, and Carlisle can best instruct thee in that art."[6]

Just before Carlisle left for the Continent, his son and heir, fifteen-year-old James Hay, came to stay at Essex House. Carlisle had never liked this child of his first marriage. Perhaps his attitude reflected his feeling for his first wife, or perhaps he still hoped to have a son with Lucy and resented the fact that his first-born would inherit his title. As a result of this parental indifference, young James lived for long periods with his grandparents, Sir Edward Denny and Lady Mary. He was the apple of their eye, and they parted with him so reluctantly that we wonder why he went to live at all at Essex House. "I have at length sent you your jewel, Donna Maria's darling and my best beloved," the grandfather wrote Carlisle in January, "not doubting that with Lady Carlisle's help, with over-making of him, and very often fetching him as we have done from school, we shall make him in the end a most learned clerk without book."[7] The jocular tone does not conceal the grandfather's worry that the boy would be left unwanted at school over holidays.

For some time Sir Edward had been pressing Carlisle to obtain a knighthood for James. The doting grandfather wished to leave his estate to the boy but was held back by fears of wardship. If Carlisle should die while his son was a minor, Denny claimed that one-third of any inheritance James received during his minority would be forfeited. (Indeed Denny never ceased to raise the specter of wardship with his former son-in-law. While Carlisle was in Spain, he received the following parental advice: "As for you, dear son, though I am not wise enough to advise you, yet I find love to admonish you to have a care in your feasts, a fig too much mean ruin to me and mine."[8] Such a reminder of his own mortality would have taken the joy out of that night's feasting!) According to Denny, if the youth were knighted, the estate would not be subject to the Master of the Wards. At his age Denny did not feel that he could gamble on staying alive until James reached his majority. He warned Carlisle that if no knighthood for James was forthcoming, he would be forced to leave the estate to an adult male relative, adding that "whenever the deed is signed it will be sealed with tears."

Carlisle was constitutionally unable to refuse outright to do a favor. He promised to speak to the King, but a year went by and nothing happened. Denny finally realized that Carlisle would never act, and while the latter was in Spain, Denny personally solicited the Privy Council for the knighthood. Of course it was assumed that he acted with Carlisle's knowledge and approval, and Cranfield, the Lord Treasurer, eager to oblige Buckingham's close friend, went out of his way to accomplish it. On March 30, 1623, he wrote triumphantly to Carlisle:

> My Lord Denny your lordship's father-in-law did lately make a
> suit for the knighting the Lord Viscount Doncaster your hope-
> ful son; wherewithall though you were not pleased to acquaint
> me, yet well knowing your lordship's design went with it, as
> matter of much importance to your lordship howsoever the
> precedent might produce some ill consequence, yet I dealt
> therein for your lordship as for my most esteemed friend and
> so that business is despatched.[9]

When Carlisle returned from Spain in April, he found his son had already been knighted. He was doubtless better pleased with a warrant from the Lord Treasurer for "a good round sum" for himself.

Lucy did not become a dutiful stepmother, "over-making" young James as Sir Edward had hoped. But the very fact that he had looked to her for this is significant. An admirer would later say that Lady Carlisle's salon was an academy superior to those in Italy and France. Denny's remark indicates that at twenty-four Lucy already enjoyed a reputation for great savoir faire. Certainly she could not have had a better teacher in the art of compliment than her husband—witness King James's advice to Buckingham in Spain. And tiresome as it was, her attendance upon the Buckingham women was proving an excellent training in the courtier's craft of ingratiating oneself with the powerful.

While Lucy was gaining in admiration, Carlisle's ever-increasing ostentation was causing some snickering behind his back. Even by the standards of an age that loved finery, his costumes verged on fancy dress. By now the ruff had given way to a falling collar, but Carlisle continued to affect that strange piece of neckwear that made the head look as if it were sitting on a platter. "But for the Earl of Carlisle, wearing of ruffs and gartering of silk stockings would be forgotten," sniffed Secretary of State Sir Edward Conway, himself a bon vivant and man of fashion. And although Carlisle adopted the black suit that became the rage when the English courtiers returned from Spain, his was embroidered all over with gold pearls. A constant belittler of the new earl was his father-in-law. Northumberland told people that the only reason he kept a coach with eight horses was to surpass his son Carlisle and the Spanish ambassador with their "six carrion mules."

Despite these sour notes, Carlisle enjoyed great prestige. His diplomatic career was flourishing. His newest assignment was a joint embassy with Henry Rich, now Baron Kensington, to arrange a marriage between Prince Charles and King Louis XIII's youngest sister, Henrietta Maria. The Spanish match had failed. The Prince and Buckingham had returned to England without the Infanta, and Buckingham (consoled with a dukedom) was now in pursuit of a French match. As a matter of course, Carlisle supported Buckingham's anti-Spanish policy in the Privy Council.

With Carlisle in France, Lucy took the opportunity to stay with Dorothy at Penshurst. The continuing bad feeling between their husbands made life difficult for the devoted sisters, but Carlisle was away so often that they had plenty of time to be together. Once again Lucy's health was not good, as we learn from a letter of Sir George Goring to Carlisle:

> Yesterday I fetched my sweet dear mistress from Penshurst to Hansworth where she intended to make but short stay, and so back again. I thank my God she hath much more quickness in her face though not more flesh than when your lordship left her, in so much as I am now undertaking [?] her with a rule of diet from my own experience which if she observe carefully [illegible]. Tomorrow I am to kiss her hands again.[10]

Goring's solicitude for Lucy went beyond simple friendship for Carlisle. He clearly exhibits the idolatry that she inspired in men—

her "slaves," Dorothy called them. We can only imagine what Lady Goring made of such knight errantry.

At Penshurst the atmosphere was somber. Family finances were in a deplorable state. To help pay his debts, which included arrears to the Crown going back to his father's lifetime, the Earl of Leicester had been forced to mortgage the Sidney estates in Wales. He had now mortgaged the Warwickshire lands as well. Lord Lisle was despondent. His patrimony was being "eaten out with interest," and he was much pressed by his own debts. He had received no preferment and had only his classical philosophers for consolation. His letters to his father at court were unremittingly bleak. One letter was so despairing that the poor earl was alarmed. "It was small comfort that you write that you sometimes wished yourself out of England, nay out of the world, in regard of your wants," he replied to his son. With her husband in such a state, Dorothy, who was melancholy in the country at the best of times, also fell into the depths of depression. In the spring of 1625, Leicester wrote his son that he would like to retire to Penshurst to escape from the expenses of court for a time, "if the state my daughter is in will permit it."[11] It is unlikely that he was simply referring to Dorothy's latest pregnancy.

THE LAST DAYS of King James were filled with sadness. His favorite and his son had come back from their foolish knight errantry, bent on war with Spain. King Philip and his chief minister, the Conde Olivarez, had duped the two inexperienced negotiators. Although Buckingham and Charles had made concession after concession, the Spaniards continually demanded new terms in the marriage contract, blaming it on the papacy. For six months the English contingent, which had swollen to several hundred, lingered on because Charles was enamored of the blond princess; he thought her beautiful in spite of her projecting lower lip—a physical trait of the Hapsburgs. For his entire stay he was never allowed to be alone with her; indeed, it seems they never exchanged two words—so much for courting her in person.

Furious with their reception in Spain, on their return to England, Buckingham and Charles informed James brusquely that his pro-Spanish policy, which had given England peace and a flourishing trade for twenty years, was obsolete. England must return to the heroic days of Queen Elizabeth, when Spain was recognized as the enemy. The new anti-Spanish policy that Charles and Buckingham forced on King James was enthusiastically seconded by the members of the Commons who equated Spaniards with Catholicism: when one member cried out that the hearts of the English papists were "knit with the Spaniards," with one voice the other members shouted, "Hear, hear." On the eve of his reign, Charles had the support of the Commons for his foreign policy and no significant opposition from the Lords, who felt they had better go along with Buckingham if they wanted any patronage. But by lifting the ban on discussion of foreign affairs, Charles and Buckingham were buying present favor at the cost of future opposition from Parliament.

Almost as if he were playing King Lear at the Globe Theatre, James was shunted aside by his favorite and his son. He put up little resistance. Judging by his erratic behavior, his babbling speeches to Parliament, and his pathetic letters to his "sweet boys" begging for their love, it is apparent that he was slipping into a second childhood.

His physical health was also deteriorating. Crippling arthritis kept him in his bedchamber over the Christmas revels at Whitehall. Then at Theobalds, in March, he came down with an intermittent fever, diagnosed as tertian ague (probably a form of malaria). Soon he was having convulsions. The end came with a stroke on March 27, 1625.

With the death of King James, a new era began at court. Gone was the flamboyant, free-spending society where Carlisle had shone. The new king was a highly refined individual with a reserved, even introvertive, personality. From the first, Charles was burdened by his royal duties. Perhaps because of a stammer, he preferred to leave the onstage role to Buckingham. A man of great taste, for some years he had been collecting art (particularly the Venetians, after seeing the glorious Titians and Tintorettos at Madrid). He was as knowledgeable about art as the Earl of Arundel, the greatest collector in England, and certainly more so than Buckingham, who relied on expert advice in the assembling of his famous art collection at York House. Only in his love of hunting was Charles his father's son.

Shortly before James's death, Carlisle and Henry Rich (who had bounded up from Baron Kensington to Earl of Holland) had concluded the negotiations for Charles's marriage with the French princess. The ambassadors were far from pleased with the terms of the marriage treaty. They had been bested at every turn by Cardinal Richelieu, the new power behind the French king, but with war with Spain imminent, Buckingham was set on a French alliance. The English had to be content with Richelieu's vague assurances that France would help Charles's sister and brother-in-law, the so-called King and Queen of Bohemia, living in exile in Holland with their children. Frederick had never recovered his hereditary German lands seized by the Spanish Hapsburgs, and although the recovery of the Palatinate was held to be the principal object of English diplomacy, the marriage treaty was concluded without any military commitment from the French. On the other hand, the English had given in to French demands for guarantees of religious toleration for English Catholics. In the end, England had got nothing out of the treaty but a wife for Charles.

In May the wedding took place by proxy on the porch of Notre Dame cathedral. As King Charles was in mourning for his father, he could not be present in person. Two weeks later, Buckingham arrived in France to bring Henrietta Maria to England. His nine days in Paris were a sojourn Parisians would never forget. He caused a sensation wherever he went: he was so handsome, so magnificently accoutered— one white velvet suit was embroidered with pearls loosely sewn on, so that he literally shed jewels in his wake. His French counterpart, Cardinal Richelieu, gave a lavish fête champêtre in his honor in the beautiful gardens of his country house, and King Louis and his queen, Anne of Austria, tendered him a sumptuous banquet.

Buckingham took full advantage of his Parisian holiday to give vent to his sexual appetites. But it was not his adventures with court ladies that astounded *le tout Paris,* it was his scandalous pursuit of the

French queen. The courtiers looked on in amazement while the two danced English country dances, which permitted close contact between the dancers, for all the world like a couple in love. But Anne of Austria's timorous personality preserved her honor and the honor of France, and she repulsed Buckingham when he exceeded the bounds of propriety. Buckingham had come with hopes of obtaining French support for a war against Spain. Instead, he made himself persona non grata in France for the rest of his life. Tales of his extravagant behavior at the French court preceded his arrival at Dover with the new queen of England.

While Buckingham's wife displayed her usual patience with his infidelity, his mistress was less forgiving—if the Duc de La Rochefoucauld is to be believed.[12] In his memoirs La Rochefoucauld recounts that in a fit of pique over her lover's public passion for Anne of Austria, Lady Carlisle conspired with his archenemy Cardinal Richelieu to take revenge on Buckingham. From a woman he had placed around Anne of Austria, Richelieu learned that on the eve of Buckingham's departure, the Queen had sent him a gift of a dozen diamond pendants from a necklace recently given her by the King. Anxious to destroy what little influence Anne had over Louis, Richelieu saw a golden opportunity to show the King that his consort was unfaithful.

When gossip reached the French court that the Countess of Carlisle was furious with Buckingham, Richelieu secretly sent her a note asking her to make up with Buckingham and, if the occasion arose, to steal the diamonds and send them over to him. Lady Carlisle went along with the plan, made herself agreeable to Buckingham, and, while dancing with him at a masked ball at Windsor Castle, snipped off two of the diamond pendants, which Buckingham was wearing as a shoulder knot to hold his sword belt in place. After the ball, his valet drew his attention to the missing jewels. Buckingham immediately guessed that Lady Carlisle was the culprit and realized at once the purpose of the theft. In his capacity as Lord High Admiral, he ordered all Channel ports closed, ostensibly for reasons of state but really to give his jeweler time to cut stones to match the remaining ten. A trusted courier was then dispatched to Paris with all twelve diamonds and given instructions to deliver them to the Duchesse de Chevreuse. This incorrigible troublemaker had been Buckingham's hostess in Paris and had tried her best to bring the French queen into his bed. As Anne of Austria's dearest friend, she was able to carry the diamonds into the Louvre without exciting Richelieu's suspicions. Anne got the replicas just in time before Richelieu received the originals from Lady Carlisle. Confident that his scheme had succeeded, the Cardinal hurried to the King. He told Louis that he had secret information that the Queen had given away a dozen diamonds from the gift necklace, and that he himself had been offered two of them by an English jeweler, insinuating that the jeweler had purchased them from the Duke of Buckingham. King Louis commanded the Queen to produce the necklace at once. Expecting to find the diamonds missing, he opened the jewel box to see the complete necklace sparkling up at him. The Queen smiled as the royal wrath descended upon the red hat of the shamefaced cardinal.

This story reads like the plot of a cloak-and-dagger novel, and indeed it inspired Alexandre Dumas's *The Three Musketeers,* but it may be true. The Duc de La Rochefoucauld was one of Madame de Chevreuse's legion of lovers; he could have heard it from her as a bedtime story.[13]

Lucy's affair with Buckingham survived this betrayal (if indeed it occurred) and became even more notorious under the new reign. Surprisingly, her husband's relationship with the favorite was closer than ever. Carlisle's biographer Roy Schreiber describes him at this period as the Duke's most trusted confidant. Thus if it was true, as Henrietta Maria's chaplain claimed, that Buckingham planned to make Lady Carlisle the King's mistress, it must be understood that he hatched this plan not only with her consent but with her husband's full knowledge.

HENRIETTA MARIA ARRIVED in England in May 1625 an underdeveloped adolescent, at sixteen still tied to her French governess. Charles had first seen her in Paris practicing a masque with Queen

Anne and a group of ladies, when he and Buckingham had gone to the French court incognito on their way to Spain in 1623. She had seemed little more than a child to him. Besides, he had had eyes only for Queen Anne, whose beauty, he wrote his father from Paris, had made him even more eager to see her sister, the Infanta.

While the Infanta had flaxen hair and a pink and white complexion, Henrietta Maria was a brunette with dark brown hair and large eyes almost as black as jet. She was somewhat buck-toothed, but then the Infanta had had the projecting Hapsburg jaw. She was pert and quick, as Charles had discovered when he went to welcome her at Dover. The ambassadors at Paris had referred to her small stature, and Charles, having little recollection of her appearance, had feared she might be almost a midget. As if reading his thoughts, Henrietta Maria had pointed to her feet and said in French: "Sire, I stand upon mine own feet; I have no help from art; thus high am I, neither higher than lower."[14] Charles was short, just five feet, four inches. He found his bride just the right size for him.

The marriage was consummated satisfactorily at Canterbury the night after her arrival. Determined to avoid the traditional invasion of the newlyweds' bedchamber by boisterous well-wishers that his sister, Elizabeth, had endured, Charles locked all the doors of the bridal suite. The next morning he slept late, and when he arose was very "jocund" with his courtiers, who had been deprived of their fun.

Normally the King would have ridden through the streets of London to show the new queen to the people, but plague had broken out for the first time since the epidemic of 1605. Carried in by flea-bearing rats on the ships in the port of London, it made swift headway through the dirty streets of old wooden houses whose floors were strewn with straw—an excellent incubator for the rat population. Bills of mortality were starting to alarm Londoners; those who could left for the country. (The death toll from the plague in Greater London would rise to thirty-five thousand before the plague of 1625 blew itself out.)[15]

To avoid the plague, the King and Queen traveled to Gravesend and from there by water to Hampton Court. Hundreds of decorated boats followed in their wake. Although it was raining hard, the King and Queen, both dressed in green, opened the barge windows to wave at the cheering crowds on either side of the river. One onlooker commented that he had "never beheld the King to look so merrily."

Delighted with his bride at first, Charles was unprepared for her immaturity, which made itself apparent at Hampton Court. If he attempted to take her away from her priests and her French ladies to have some time alone with her, she sulked or threw a tantrum. The courtiers soon learned that although she was "little of stature, she was of more than ordinary resolution." One day, irritated by an overheated and overcrowded room, she scowled so fiercely that, as one courtier present wrote a friend, "she drove us all out of the chamber."

For the first year of her marriage she would have nothing to do with the English, including her husband, but like the spoiled, immature child she was, withdrew to her private apartments in the company of her priests and French attendants. The most notable example of her withdrawal was her refusal to participate in her husband's coronation. Not without justification, Charles blamed her French suite for her obstinate refusal to assume her duties as wife and queen. Buckingham and Carlisle encouraged him in this belief. The new queen's principal advisers were her chaplain, the Bishop de Mende, and the Comte de Tillières. The Comte had been recalled to France in 1624, but in 1625 he was back in England as Henrietta Maria's chamberlain. Gone were the days when he and his wife were part of the Buckingham set. The intimacy between Madame de Tillières and Carlisle was also a thing of the past. Now de Tillières could not be critical enough of his former friends. He loudly proclaimed that Buckingham and Carlisle were responsible for turning the King against the Queen.[16]

As the King's favorite, Buckingham had two options: either to attain influence over the Queen or to make sure that she had no influence over the King. The former looked more unlikely every day. Henrietta Maria detested Buckingham, who showed little patience with her childish petulance. She lived more like "a petite demoiselle" than a queen, he told her, with a scornful glance at her priests. And he once warned her to behave herself because English queens had had their heads cut off before. When she refused her marital duties by pleading a headache, he told Charles that if she were his wife, he would impose his husband's rights more often.

Six months after the Queen's arrival, Charles was already talking of sending her French entourage home "for fomenting discontentments in my wife."[17] It was an easy matter for Buckingham to convince Charles that the Queen should have English ladies around her to counter the bad influence of the French. In July 1626, Charles formally requested Henrietta Maria to accept Buckingham's wife, his sister the Countess of Denbigh, his niece the Marchioness of Hamilton, and the Countess of Carlisle as Ladies of the Bedchamber. The Queen initially refused. However, when Charles insisted, she agreed to accept Buckingham's relatives but not Lady Carlisle. She had "a great aversion" to that lady, she told him: "It would be very difficult to accommodate herself to the humours of the Countess of Carlisle."[18]

There is no doubt that Lucy was an intimidating personality. Dorothy, who knew her best and loved her, described her as conceited and even "insufferable." Buckingham's favor fed these character traits. Lucy disdained the company of women. For their part, the court ladies envied her beauty and feared her wit. Even in the self-imposed convent in which Henrietta Maria lived, tales of Lady Carlisle's overbearing behavior toward other women would have reached her ears.

But was this the only reason for her aversion? The Bishop de Mende provides another explanation. In his dispatch of July 24, 1626, the bishop informed Richelieu that for two months the Queen had been getting along quite well with the King, and this had made the favorite very jealous. "His principal aim now was to give his master new affections" by introducing the beautiful Countess of Carlisle into the royal household.[19] Since this was what her chaplain believed, it is a fair assumption that Henrietta Maria believed it too.

It is doubtful that Charles heard about Buckingham's scheme. Straitlaced as he was, he would not have countenanced it. In the end, overriding his wife's objections, Charles named Lucy a Lady of the Queen's Bedchamber, along with Buckingham's relatives. Shortly afterward, the Countess of Holland was also appointed. "Thus gradually," remarked the Venetian ambassador, "they place the ladies most in the Duke's confidence." The ambassador advised the Doge that to be a Lady of the Queen's Bedchamber was "an honour very highly esteemed at the court." For Lucy her appointment opened up a fascinating prospect of a career in her own right. No longer would she be a mere appendage to her husband or her lover.

At the same time, Carlisle was appointed a Gentleman of the King's Bedchamber. While Lucy exulted over her appointment, her husband was disgruntled with his. He had hoped to be Lord Chamberlain, but Buckingham had given that office to the Earl of Montgomery. The upstart duke wanted an alliance with the wealthy and aristocratic Herbert family. The price for affiancing his little daughter to the scion of the Herberts was the appointment of Lord Montgomery to the most coveted post in the royal household.

The Earl of Holland was also named a Gentleman of the Bedchamber, putting a further damper on Carlisle's enthusiasm over his appointment. He had become jealous and resentful of his former protégé. It was Holland, not Carlisle, whom Buckingham sent back to France on a joint embassy with Sir Dudley Carleton, and it was Holland who accompanied Buckingham on a flying mission to The Hague. Henry Rich had advanced from Carlisle's faithful follower to his equal (as the Bedchamber appointments confirmed), and Carlisle feared that he might soon outpace him at court.

Lucy's introduction to the Queen's service began with a ludicrous incident. When she and the Buckingham women attempted to enter the Queen's quarters, they found their way physically barred by Henrietta Maria's French ladies.[20] This was a last-ditch stand. Shortly after the new appointments were made, Charles expelled his wife's French attendants. From now on, Henrietta Maria was thrown upon the companionship of her English ladies.

Within a short time, Lucy became her favorite. Daily contact overcame the Queen's aversion to this beautiful woman ten years her senior. (Besides, nothing had come of Buckingham's plan.) Lucy was famous for her outrageously malicious wit. Time and again we read that Lady Carlisle "made sport of" or "game of" her acquaintances without respect for rank or office. This type of wit, so characteristic of French salon society, delighted Henrietta Maria. A French visitor commented on the Queen's favor to the Countess of Carlisle. Henrietta Maria had taken to having small private suppers with her most charming and amusing ladies. The visitor reported that Lady Carlisle was a regular at these suppers, along with the young and attractive Countesses of Exeter, Oxford, and Bourchier. The table talk sparkled with gossip and witticism—except on one occasion when Charles attended and "behaved with a gravity which spoiled the conversation." The Duke of Buckingham was reported to be most offended that his wife was never invited to "these little festivities."[21]

For some months after his disappointment over the Lord Chamberlain's post, Carlisle managed to conceal his growing disaffection from Buckingham. As late as September 1626, Dorothy's husband was advised by his London agent that "two words" from his brother-in-law to Buckingham would elicit immediate payment from the foot-dragging Exchequer. In November, however, Carlisle finally had a falling-out with Buckingham. He was not alone. The Marquess of Hamilton was also estranged from his wife's powerful relative. But by and large it was Carlisle's palace revolution and there was no secret about it. Word reached into Wales and as far as Venice. Despite an apparent reconciliation, Carlisle's relationship with Buckingham worsened steadily during 1627.

THE MOST NOTABLE consequence of Charles's French marriage was that it contributed to Parliament's growing alienation from the monarchy. Having only a rudimentary understanding of foreign affairs, the Commons could not appreciate the role of Catholic France in the "Protestant Cause"—an alliance with the Dutch and the Danes to recover the Palatinate from the Catholic Hapsburgs. (They need not have worried; Richelieu was not prepared to contribute one soldier to England's war against Spain.) At the same time, the Commons was losing confidence in Charles and Buckingham as war leaders. An attack on the Spanish coast, the Cadiz expedition, planned by Buckingham in his capacity as Lord High Admiral, totally miscarried. The 1626 session of Parliament opened with impeachment proceedings against the Duke in the House of Commons, charging him with mismanagement of the war and with engrossing all the lucrative posts and sinecures. To save his friend, Charles dissolved Parliament without having obtained a single subsidy.

Perhaps to regain popularity with the Puritan majority in the Commons, Buckingham now decided to go to the relief of the Huguenots. In the interest of French national unity, Cardinal Richelieu had set out to destroy the autonomy of the Huguenots once and for all, and government forces were besieging the Protestant stronghold of La Rochelle. With characteristic recklessness, Buckingham launched England into a war with France while she was still fighting Spain. (Richelieu's refusal to let him back into France to continue his seduction of the French queen may have played a part as well, for the personal element as a casus belli should not be overlooked.) A less self-serving explanation for the war with France, put about by Buckingham's supporters, was that saving the Huguenots from extinction would weaken French unity and thereby increase King Louis's dependence on English friendship—and his readiness to join England's war against Spain.

Wearing his Lord High Admiral's hat, Buckingham was engaged all the summer of 1627 in a futile attempt to overcome a French garrison on the island of Rhé near La Rochelle. During his absence, Carlisle worked openly to undermine him with King Charles. After Buckingham's return in October, he and Carlisle were veiled enemies. Carlisle was soon relieved of his duties with the King and assigned to attend upon the Queen like one of her pet spaniels. ("He has to accompany the Queen everywhere," the Venetian ambassador reported, "which he much dislikes.") Worse still, the stately earl found himself in a situation where he had to play second fiddle to his wife.

Queen Henrietta Maria idolized the sophisticated Lucy. Magnificently attired for all occasions, Lucy taught the young queen much about fashion. Styles had changed: the farthingale had died with Queen Anne, and skirts moved gracefully with the body. Actually, there were two skirts, an overskirt usually of damask or cut velvet that was drawn back to reveal a silk or satin petticoat. The very low-cut bodice had puffed sleeves and a falling lace collar worn off the shoulder. Lucy also taught the Queen to paint her face with rouge and powder—"an ignominious thing" in that era. And gossip had it that, in time, she would lead her royal mistress into even "more debaucheries," for Lady Carlisle's continuing affair with Buckingham provided much gossip. The liaison was talked about at the Royal Exchange and reported in the newsletters that reached the country houses and the diplomatic legations abroad. Buckingham's female relatives were her sworn enemies. "The Duke's mother, wife and sister hate her," an observer commented, "not only for the Duke's intimacy with her, but also that she has the Queen's heart above them."[22]

Apart from her manifest physical attractions, Lucy's position as confidante to Henrietta Maria made her indispensable to Buckingham. During the expedition to the Isle of Rhé, he relied on her to mend his quarrel with the Queen, and she relayed encouraging messages about Henrietta Maria's more friendly attitude toward him. Her powerful position at court was making her even more "insufferable" in the eyes of the Buckingham women. Here was one rival who the patient Kate could not stomach. "Your great Lady that you believe is so much your friend," she wrote her husband, "uses your friends something worse than when you were here, and your favour has made her so great as now she cares for nobody."[23]

In 1627 the Countess of Carlisle wrote to an unnamed correspondent. It is a fair conjecture that the recipient was the Duke of Buckingham, while he was fighting in France. Lady Carlisle "hopes he will not regret the favours he has done her. She cannot doubt anything he says, and does not feel herself absolutely unworthy, being his humblest and faithfullest servant." Far from sharing her husband's quarrel with Buckingham, Lucy continued her liaison with the man who her own brother Harry called "the desirer and plotter of [Carlisle's] ruin and destruction."[24]

Carlisle was generally regarded as a complaisant husband and, seeing his own influence wane, on the surface he condoned his wife's friendship with the favorite. Royal patronage continued to come his way, which would have been impossible without Buckingham's approval. In 1627 Charles granted Carlisle the patent for the island of the Barbados and the Leeward Islands.[25] He also increased Carlisle's Irish holdings. And in the winter of 1628, "to content them both the better" (in the words of a news-writer), Lucy was given a sizable pension of £2,000 a year. These emoluments bought Carlisle's silence; yet he was sorely humiliated to be cuckolded and overshadowed by his wife. His quarrels with Lucy increased, and so did his complaints about her to his old crony Sir George Goring.

To beat "an honourable retreat from court," Carlisle was pressing for an overseas mission. Buckingham also wanted to get him away, and the desired appointment was shortly announced. According to gossip at the Exchange, the affair with Lucy was not the main factor in Buckingham's decision to send Carlisle abroad. "For putting him off for the better access to his lady," said one news-writer, "it needed not, for he was quiet enough with all that was done by her."[26]

THE QUEEN'S FAVORITE

IN APRIL 1628, Carlisle set out with pomp and ceremony on an embassy said by King Charles to be of "the greatest importance." Yet nobody seemed to know whether it was to enlist allies against France or against Spain or both. The Florentine agent predicted that its results would be "more showy than substantial," and the Venetian ambassador remarked that the purpose was simply "to gratify private passion." The Prince of Orange told the Venetian ambassador at The Hague that Carlisle's mission had "no real motive beyond some affection of Buckingham for Carlisle's wife."[1]

Traveling in Carlisle's entourage were his son, James, and Goring's twenty-year-old son, George.[2] For both young men this was the first stage of their grand tour, the period of continental travel that capped the spotty education of aristocratic youths. James was to stay away a year to improve his French and to learn Italian. As was customary, he was put in the charge of a tutor, one James Traill. These traveling tutors were usually impoverished clerics or pedagogues not much older than their charges, with whom they had discipline problems from the first footfall on the Continent. But Carlisle's son James was a dutiful sightseer and diligent linguist, judging by the lack of tutorial complaints in the many letters Traill wrote to the Earl after the men set off on their own.

During Carlisle's absence, Lucy was left with the sole responsibility for his daughter by his first marriage. A girl about the Queen's age, Anne Hay had been living with her father and stepmother for some time. Shy by nature and sickly, she stayed in the shadow of her brilliant stepmother. Few at court had ever spoken with her, yet this self-effacing young woman had quite unwittingly aggravated the ill will between her father and Buckingham the year before. Neglected by her father, she had become involved with one of the Queen's court musicians, a fleshily handsome, profligate French lute player named Gautier. No harm would have come of it had Gautier not got in trouble by boasting that "by the dulcet tones of the lute he could make his way even into the royal bed and had been urged to do so." As a result of his loose talk, he was imprisoned in the Tower. Under torture he spilled forth a stream of confessions, including the admission of "a close intimacy with a daughter of the Earl of Carlisle." Among the charges brought against him was an allegation that he had planned to murder Buckingham; poor Anne came under suspicion briefly as an accomplice. Buckingham vindictively broadcast the story of Anne's involvement with the lute player. Naturally, the Venetian ambassador reported to the Doge, her father "would have preferred silence."[3] Henceforth, Carlisle disliked the sight of his daughter.

While Carlisle was making his ceremonial progress through Europe's capitals, Lucy and her stepdaughter passed the early summer of 1628 at Nonsuch Palace with the King and Queen. Lucy never felt better than she did at Nonsuch, where she spent long hours on horseback. In June the court physician, now Sir Theodore Mayerne, wrote Carlisle that his wife and daughter were well, and that he would continue to watch over their health. Lucy was still the uncontested favorite, according to the Queen's secretary.[4] Like the other courtiers, she rejoiced to see the royal marriage improving day by day. (Charles's relations with Parliament had soured to the point where he had been presented with the Petition of Right, a serious attack on the royal prerogative; this was an unpleasant subject avoided in the royal circle.) Henrietta Maria had matured into a vivacious, pretty young woman, although somewhat dark-complexioned by English standards. Charles was falling more and more in love with her, and she visibly reciprocated his affection. During Buckingham's absence fighting the French the previous summer, their mutual attraction had had a chance to take root. With Buckingham about to take out the fleet again this summer, there would be no impediment to the flowering of the royal romance.

In July Lucy and Anne accompanied the Queen to Northamptonshire, where she went to take the waters at Wellingborough. With the Dutch and the Spanish fighting in the Low Countries, Spa was inaccessible, so English watering places had come into their own. Bath, of course, with its sulfurous waters for drinking and bathing, was an old established resort, but newer ones such as Tunbridge Wells in Kent, only a few miles from Penshurst, and Knaresborough in Yorkshire, whose waters were said to be similar to those at Spa, were "much frequented" of recent years. Wellingborough was one of the newest. This was Henrietta Maria's second summer there. During the royal sojourn, Lucy and Anne stayed nearby at Holdenby, a country house built by an ambitious peer to entertain Queen Elizabeth.

Thus Lucy was at Holdenby House when the shocking news arrived that the Duke of Buckingham had been assassinated at Portsmouth. He was on the point of taking out a huge fleet in a second attempt to relieve the Huguenot city of La Rochelle, still under siege by French government forces. The expedition the previous year had ended in humiliating defeat. After a day and a half of fighting on the Isle of Rhé, Richelieu's superior force had slaughtered hundreds of Buckingham's soldiers and sailors, including many colonels and captains. Buckingham had returned to Plymouth a disgraced Lord High Admiral. He had become the most hated man in England. His retainers were carrying pistols when they went into the town, and his astrologer, Dr. Lamb, was torn to pieces by a mob. Desperate to repair his reputation, Buckingham had prevailed upon King Charles to give him a second chance, and somehow Charles had found the money to outfit the fleet. Sailors were rounded up by press gangs.

One lovely June day, Charles and Buckingham had visited the shipyards at Deptford to view ten fine new fully rigged fighting ships. "George," Charles had said gravely, "there are some that wish that both these and thou mightest both perish. But care not for them. We will both perish together, if thou doest."[5] It would be twenty years before the King's part of the pact would be carried out.

Strangely enough, just before leaving for Portsmouth, Buckingham had commanded the actors at the Globe to perform Shakespeare's *Henry VIII*. It was remarked that he and his party had left right after the death scene of the sixteenth-century Duke of Buckingham.[6]

Buckingham was assassinated at a house in Portsmouth in full sight of his army commanders and the usual swarm of servants and suitors. He had just finished breakfast and was moving into the next room. Waiting for him in the passageway, the assassin struck a knife deep into his victim's left side. With blood gushing from his wound, Buckingham pulled out the knife, stumbled into the hall, and expired. At the hubbub, the Duchess of Buckingham and her sister-in-law, the Countess of Anglesey, came out on the gallery overlooking the hall and, seeing the Duke in a pool of blood, began weeping and screaming. Witnesses to the dreadful scene said they had never in their life heard such "screechings, tears, and distractions."

The assassin made no attempt to flee but lingered in the kitchen. With everyone shouting, "Where is the villain?" he stepped forward boldly and declared, "I am the man. Here I am." He gave his name as John Felton and said he was a former lieutenant in an infantry regiment. He freely described how he had bought a cheap knife in a shop on Tower Hill in London and had made his way to Portsmouth, partly on foot and partly on horseback. Under interrogation he offered a mixed bag of motives, one of them being that after reading of the Duke's abuses in Parliament's Remonstrance against him, he thought that he would do his country good service by killing him. Taken to the Tower by water, he was cheered by crowds shouting, "The Lord be merciful unto thee." Puritanism was spreading among the common people, and it sanctioned tyrannicide. Felton's execution was relatively merciful. Instead of being drawn and quartered while still breathing, he was simply hanged.[7]

The death of the Duke of Buckingham was greeted with relief and joy all over England. One Englishman spoke for the country when he called him "a monster not to be endured." Under Charles, Buckingham had become the effective ruler of England. He controlled all patronage, creating lucrative monopolies for his brothers and his sycophants while selling government posts for enormous sums. He himself held a plurality of lucrative offices. It was no secret that he had bought the office of Lord High Admiral from the incumbent in 1619 with £3,000 from King James, and popular opinion blamed his mismanagement for the navy's decay. He had led the country into two expensive wars, with one military disaster following another. In the Remonstrance that had inspired Felton to kill him, Parliament had named the Duke "the cause of all misfortunes." Yet, sustained by royal favor, he was unassailable until an assassin's knife felled him.

King Charles was heartbroken and planned a funeral for his best friend even more sumptuous than King James's funeral. The projected cost, to be borne by the Crown, was estimated at £40,000. But Charles's advisers argued that the Duke was so unpopular that a state funeral would undoubtedly be disrupted by a mob. The grandiose plans were laid aside. Instead, six men carried an empty coffin through darkened streets to Westminster Abbey, followed by no more than a hundred mourners. The corpse had been buried the day before at the Abbey, as it was feared "the people in their madness" might have broken open the coffin.[8]

Whether Lucy would have shared in the general rejoicing or mourned a personal loss there is no way of knowing, because at that very time she fell ill with smallpox. It was a bad case, but Mayerne and the other royal physician, Matthew Lister, gave her a favorable prognosis. Their treatment was to let blood under her tongue; since she did not die, it was regarded as highly effective. The disease ran its course and, in spite of the medical care, by the beginning of September, Harry Percy was able to reassure Carlisle that Lucy was out of danger, except for her own "unruliness." Evidently, she was not a model patient.

The Queen's devotion to the Countess of Carlisle in her illness was the talk of the courtiers. On first hearing that Lucy was smitten by the feared disease, Henrietta Maria could only "with much ado" be constrained from rushing to her side. As soon as the danger of contagion was past, she hurried over to Holdenby House from nearby Wellingborough. "The Queen was the first creature I saw after my recovery," Lucy wrote Carlisle. Henrietta Maria was so tender and caring during her visit that Lucy was touched. "I did not think the heart of a Queen could have been so sensible to the loss of a servant."[9] At their parting, Henrietta Maria wept uncontrollably.

Once out of danger, did Lucy mourn for Buckingham? She had been his mistress for years. He was handsome, presumably a good lover, and a patron to whom she owed her enviable position at court. All her life Lucy sought out powerful men. As a girl, she thought she had found such a man in James Hay; however, he had turned out to be a hero for the masques only. Buckingham had been a truly powerful man, and she had been attracted to him for that reason. But as his power died with him, she soon forgot him. Besides, she had found a new patron, no less than the Queen herself.

For any woman, and particularly a beauty, the first glance in a mirror after a bout of smallpox could be traumatic. Lucy had seen what the ravages of smallpox could do to a beautiful woman. Some years before her death in 1627, the Countess of Bedford, Lucy's patron and a friend of her family, had been stricken. The disease had been so "full and foul" that not only was Lady Bedford left horribly pockmarked, but she had lost an eye.[10]

From the moment of her recovery Lucy took to wearing the fashionable half-mask indoors that court ladies wore when they went out in public. A month later she wrote Carlisle that the mask had never been off her face since her sickness, and that she had made the wearing of it a condition for her return to court. Does this mean that Lucy's exquisite face was scarred? Letters from friends assured Carlisle that his wife's beauty was unblemished. But how could these well-meaning people see behind the mask? The truth of the matter was revealed by Mayerne, who informed the Earl of Carlisle that the disease "has scarcely left a mark." The few pockmarks dismissed so lightly by her doctor would nevertheless have been agonizing for Lucy. She had the vanity of a spoiled beauty. Her refusal to remove the concealing mask suggests the extent of that vanity.

By mid-September Goring (now Baron Goring) was writing Carlisle in glowing terms of Lucy's return to health. "Your Lady, my mistress, is recovered miraculously, and not a whit marked with that venomous beast," he reassured his friend. As for her plans, he reported that "this week she intends to be at London, and the next with the Countess of Berkshire to air herself there a while before returning to her sacred mistress."[11] Lady Berkshire was that same Elizabeth Cecil who had married Tom Howard in preference to Robert Sidney, thus clearing the way for Dorothy. She and her husband were close friends of the Carlisles, who frequently visited them at Charlton Park, their estate in Wiltshire. Unpredictable always, Lucy changed her mind at the last minute and, taking Anne Hay with her, went instead to Dorothy at Penshurst. Robert and Dorothy were now the Earl and Countess of Leicester; the genial old earl had died in 1626.

On October 3, Leicester wrote Carlisle from the "solitude" of Penshurst that "Lady Carlisle is here, perfectly recovered and unblemished by her great sickness." He described the effect in England of Buckingham's death. "The fall of the great tree planted by your old master has made such a percussion in the air as I doubt not but the noise has far outgone the place where you heard it. In these nearer parts it has caused such a brawl in divers things (as they say) that to right and quiet them your presence is wished by many."[12] The brothers-in-law had become reconciled. Although Leicester would later say sourly that they were never friends again, their correspondence from 1628 on was unreservedly friendly. Carlisle even revived his old affectionate nickname for Robert—"Noks"—and Robert responded warmly. With what joy the sisters would have welcomed the end of hostilities between their husbands.

A few months before his death the old earl had taken out insurance in the form of a second marriage to a wealthy widow, and life at Penshurst was more agreeable with the improvement in the family's finances. Under Dorothy's careful management, the houseful of servants carried out their appointed tasks like clockwork. The principal rooms, filled with tapestries and paintings, chairs and stools upholstered in needlework and cloth of gold, were kept "clean and sweet-smelling" by the Groom of the Chamber. When the Earl and Countess dined in the medieval great hall on formal occasions, the usher saw to it that those at the second table sat "orderly, civilly and quietly." This sharp-eyed upper servant also took care that "broken meats" (partially carved roasts and fowl) were put in the tub for the poor. In the buttery the butler kept regular hours like a publican, dispensing bread and beer to all comers through the hatch. The master cook presided over the vast kitchen, chasing out scroungers and scolding his helpers if they forgot to wear their caps while dressing the meat.

At the main gates the porter was on duty around the clock. Promptly at ten o'clock, he shut up for the night, and any stragglers who returned later than "that lawful hour of reposing themselves" were reported. To make doubly sure that the house was fast for the night, the housekeeper checked the gate, as well as all doors and passageways. Women servants working in the nursery, laundry, or dairy were forbidden to receive their swains while on duty. And to keep order among the unruly band of grooms and stable hands, the coachman slept in the stable. For all servants there were rules against blasphemy, fighting, or urinating in the passages "where the same may be offensive."[13]

After a dozen years of marriage, Dorothy had filled the nursery to overflowing. Young Dorothy, or Doll, as they called her, was now a beautiful, sweet-natured eleven-year-old. Philip and Algernon were eight and six, respectively. Toddling around the nursery were three-year-old Lucy and two-year-old Robert. A sign of Dorothy's love for her sister, when the first baby Lucy died in 1624, was that the next girl, born the following year, was given the same name. The never-empty cradle was now occupied by infant Anne. Dorothy had not fattened on childbearing. Energetic to a fault, she was always hurrying to attend to one matter or another. Her good works extended beyond the walls surrounding the great house to the little village of Penshurst, where they centered upon the ancient parish church. The cycle of birth and death, the seasonal celebrations, and religious observances claimed much of Dorothy's time. She also had her duties as a hostess. Although Penshurst under the second earl was not the scene of lavish hospitality as in the days of his father and grandfather, once again, after the lean years, friends and relations came to visit. Particularly welcome were Viscount Mandeville and his second wife, a cousin of Dorothy's, who often stopped to visit on their way to Kimbolton, the country house of Mandeville's father, the Earl of Manchester.

But Dorothy's melancholy spirits had not lifted with the improved finances, her busyness, or the visits of friends. The loneliness of country living had become her constant complaint, unmitigated by her husband's presence. Only the short parliamentary sessions took Robert away from Penshurst in these years. The older she got, the more Dorothy was becoming like her mother. At times she let herself go in fits of temper that illustrated only too well her father's uncomplimentary opinion of the female sex. By her own admission, Dorothy would fly into a passion and rail at everyone. Like most husbands of short-tempered women, Robert came in for much of this abuse. He met these outbursts with appeasement, and those close to the household regarded him as henpecked.[14] When Dorothy's sudden storms burst upon his head, he retreated without a word to his study, but Dorothy in her wifely wisdom knew that he went not out of meekness but glad of the excuse to retire to his books and shut out the cares of the household. Indeed, much of Dorothy's temper was provoked by Robert's scholarly detachment. Warm, passionate, and fiercely loyal, she sometimes feared that her husband did not sufficiently reciprocate her strong feelings — her "extraordinary passion," as she called it.

In spite of Dorothy's many responsibilities, during Lucy's convalescence the entire household revolved around her. Even in the best of health Lucy was self-centered. Several years later Dorothy spoke of her sister's conceit as a confirmed personality trait. Lucy's present situation certainly was such as to flatter her vanity. Goring had always been her "slave"—that was an old story—but now other lords were her courtiers, eager for the latest health bulletin. Above all, there was Queen Henrietta Maria herself "sending day and night to her."[15] Lord and Lady Leicester could not help but see that their familiar house-guest had become a very important personage.

Dorothy was not envious of Lucy's career. She had no desire to play the courtier. But she was ambitious for Robert. She viewed the hours he spent poring over his books as time wasted. Still, he continued in his study, not averse to receiving a call from King Charles but doing nothing to elicit it. Observing Lucy's growing influence, both husband and wife hoped that she would be able to assist his as yet unlaunched career. For the moment, however, Dorothy's concern was simply to cater to her sister and watch over her recovery.

Dorothy was also very hospitable to Lucy's stepdaughter. Anne was not well. Sir Theodore Mayerne acquainted her father with her poor state of health but did not say what ailed her. Probably nobody had ever been as kind to the lonely young woman as Dorothy was, for in Anne's stilted letters to her father, only her gratitude to Lord and Lady Leicester emerges as anything more than a copybook exercise. Poor Anne penned beautiful letters in both French and English to her absent parent, but she was never able to win his approval. In all her letters there is a note of contrition, as if she was always conscious that she had not been forgiven for her involvement with the French lute player. From Essex House she wrote that she continually did those things she thought would please her father. From Penshurst she gladly undertook to obey his commands; another letter, in French, assured him of her humble duty.[16] Carlisle supported the daughter of his first marriage not ungenerously—from abroad he arranged with a London banker to send £100 to the Earl of Leicester for her keep—but he did not love her.[17]

Relaxing in her sister's company, Lucy had little urge to take up her life at court. In mid-October, however, she went back to London, accompanied by Anne, for whom Mayerne had prescribed a course of physic. Shortly afterward, Dorothy arrived at Essex House to keep her sister company, but she could not stay long and after a few weeks returned to Penshurst, taking Anne with her.

Commanded by the King and Queen to come back to court as soon as possible ("with leave to keep on my mask," she wrote Carlisle), Lucy put in an appearance at the end of November. Still listless from her illness, she was seized by a nostalgia for the days when her husband and Buckingham had been the peacocks of the garish, colorful court of the old king. Plaintively, she told Carlisle that if he saw the little gallantry there was at court, he would believe it no great adventure for her to go there after her bout with smallpox. "It was most desolate," she reported, and she had "no great desire to return till she was made happy with his company." This sentiment is characteristic of her letters to Carlisle during her convalescence. There was in Lucy at this period a retrospective yearning for her husband's protection. It was years since she had turned to him with such words as these, written from Penshurst: "I wish you would speedily return for I have been in great danger."[18] Still, as her strength revived, so did her independent spirit and her zest for court life. That was her milieu. She had striven to earn a place for herself. She was not likely to give it up on the whim of a moment. She had become the confidante of queens.

seven

COURT POLITICS

IN THE VACUUM created by Buckingham's death, two factions at court were jockeying for power: one favored a French alliance, the other, alliance with Spain. The French party, Puritan to a man, supported the cause of the exiled King and Queen of Bohemia and the treaty with the Dutch that Charles had signed in 1625. Among the French faction were Puritan lords like the Leicesters' good friend Viscount Mandeville and the sisters' cousin the Earl of Holland. The strong anti-Spanish sentiments of these lords could be accounted for only partly on religious grounds, since France was also a Catholic country. Closer to the mark was the fact that many of the French partisans at court had extensive interests in the West Indies that would not permit them to recognize the New World as a Spanish preserve. They had visions of reviving the privateering of Elizabeth's reign, when English ships plundered Spanish settlements in the Caribbean and captured Spanish galleons, and of profiting from the new concept of exploitive colonization. So long as England was at war with Spain, Charles assumed the right to plant colonies in the Indies and grant charters to his favorite courtiers. The Earl of Holland had just been appointed governor of the newly chartered Providence Island

Company, which planned to finance a Puritan colony in the West Indies that would yield a nice profit to its "adventurers," as the shareholders were called. King James's tacit observance of the Spanish monopoly in the Americas had left the English meager pickings, and they wanted to ensure that Charles did not return to the pro-Spanish policy of his father. As England's self-interest led them to advocate continued war with Spain, of necessity it made them proponents of peace with France.[1] As Buckingham had discovered, two wars were one too many. The French faction was considered to be the majority on the Privy Council, and, in fact, Mandeville was the council president.

Around King Charles, however, a new body of advisers was forming that reflected his undeclared leanings toward Spain. There was Sir Francis Cottington, who enjoyed a secret pension from the Spanish king. In November 1628, Cottington was appointed a privy councillor and soon after Chancellor of the Exchequer, making him one of the most powerful men in the kingdom. Politically, Cottington seconded his friend the Lord Treasurer, Sir Richard Weston, another "Spanish pensioner" and a closet Catholic. After Buckingham's death, Weston became Charles's principal minister. Secretive and wily, he kept his politics and his religion to himself, but he fooled nobody. His unpopularity with the growing number of Puritans throughout the country was matched only by that of the Bishop of London, William Laud, another new appointee to the Privy Council.

While the French party wanted peace with France only, the Spanish party wanted peace with everybody so that England could resume trade with Spain and the Spanish Netherlands. Contemporary opinion held that the Spanish trade was more profitable than the French. Spain bought what England had to sell—woolens, cotton, linen, hardware, leather, tin, butter, tobacco, and Newfoundland fish—and sold what England wanted to buy—wool from Segovia, Mexican dyes, olive oil, Spanish wines, and fruits. Moreover, the Anglo-Spanish war had a devastating effect on England's carrying trade since Spain, as an enemy, no longer used English ships to transport goods to and from the Spanish Netherlands.

The reopening of the lucrative Spanish trade and the end of expensive wars appealed to Charles, as it had to his father. After the tumultuous parliaments of 1628 and 1629, he had decided he would no longer humble himself by seeking parliamentary subsidies, which came at the expense of his royal prerogative. No doubt in retaliation for Charles's forced loans after the 1627 session, the parliament of 1628 presented him with the Petition of Right prohibiting "any gift, loan, benevolence or tax, without common consent by act of parliament." Initiated in the Commons, the bill had been passed by the House of Lords. Charles had signed it and proceeded to ignore it. In 1629 the Commons was even more unruly, refusing to allow the King's officers to collect custom duties called tonnage and poundage—a royal practice that had been rubber-stamped by parliaments for two centuries. When Charles attempted to adjourn Parliament, irate members held the Speaker in his chair by physical force. In a portentous speech to the House of Lords (he did not invite the Commons), Charles reasserted his divine right to rule but assured the Lords that he would "maintain the ancient and just rights and liberties of our subjects." It was a speech such as King John might have delivered to the barons when he signed the Magna Carta in 1215. Charles dissolved Parliament and was not to reconvene it for eleven years. During his Personal Rule (as historians have named this period), Charles levied taxes and forced loans as he pleased.

CARLISLE'S NATURAL PLACE was with the French party, particularly since he was the proprietor of the island of the Barbados and the Leeward Islands. Many members of this faction looked to him for leadership and urged him to return quickly from the Continent. However, Carlisle lingered abroad, and by default the leadership of the French party passed to his rival the Earl of Holland.

Once back at court, Lucy threw herself into promoting her absent husband's interests. She realized that in this war of factions she would stand or fall with her husband. All the Scottish courtiers adhered to the party that wanted peace with France, and they regarded Carlisle as their leader. Lucy's activities on her husband's behalf were greeted with warm approval by this group. At the end of December 1628, Sir David Murray wrote Carlisle of "a secret working for his continuance abroad by those who carry an outward show of friend-ship to him"—a patent reference to the Earl of Holland. The writer then went on to say that "Fair Lucibella, or rather Philocles, has played her true part, which more and more procures her the writer's love and respect."[2] From numerous sources Carlisle was informed of Lucy's devoted efforts for his good. Goring, as might be expected, rubbed it in. Lady Carlisle, he wrote on November 22, was her hus-band's "careful friend beyond that of ordinary in a wife." After all she was doing for him, Goring rebuked his friend gently, "let old Goring not hear one syllable of old quarrels." On December 22, he reported on "the great esteem for Lady Carlisle throughout the court." He ad-vised Carlisle to let her know "how heartily he takes her watchful and truly loving respects." (The good-natured Goring also tried to keep the peace between his cronies, assuring Carlisle of Holland's good-will, "much for my comfort, for so should old friends live.")[3]

Through this Venetian intrigue, the masked "Lucibella" (as Sir David Murray dubbed her) moved with confidence, her power base the Queen's affection. Pregnant with her first child, Henrietta Maria was becoming "a great courtier." Naturally all her efforts were bent toward promoting an accord between her husband and her brother Louis. On "the Queen's side"—the suite of rooms at Whitehall occu-pied by Henrietta Maria and her ladies—the Spaniard was very much the villain. The rivalry between Louis XIII and the Hapsburgs had flared into open conflict. Having subdued the Huguenots and the French nobility, Richelieu was ready to challenge Hapsburg hege-mony. French and Spanish troops were fighting in Mantua over the ducal succession. The Duke of Mantua had died, and each of the rival nations had its candidate to succeed him. Henrietta Maria was full of wrath against Spain and the Spanish party at court. In her heavily ac-cented English she vilified Weston, Cottington, and Laud.

While Lucy's influence increased with the Queen's participation in affairs of state, she was placed in a difficult position by persistent rumors that Carlisle inclined toward an alliance with Spain. She alerted her husband that he was thought "hugely Spanish." To her the rumors were ridiculous. It was not the Spanish but the French ambassadors they had been wining and dining through the years. She would need more than "a common report" to "believe him a Don Diego," she wrote, but in the meantime "the noise of it troubled some of his best friends."[4]

The truth of the matter was that Carlisle was abroad acting on secret instructions from King Charles. In the last months of his life, Buckingham had actively sought peace with Spain. With his death, it was generally felt that the peace talks would terminate. There was rejoicing in the Venetian and Dutch embassies and among the French party when Charles called the Spanish negotiations "cabals and things of no consequence."[5] But far from abandoning an Anglo-Spanish treaty, he was deeply committed to it. This meant reneging on his obligations. In 1625, when he had needed allies against Spain, he had signed a treaty of alliance with the Dutch against Spain for fifteen years. At the same time, he had solemnly promised his sister and her husband, the self-styled King and Queen of Bohemia living in exile at The Hague, that he would fight to recover their hereditary Palatinate. Since he was now proceeding unilaterally to make peace with Spain without his Dutch allies or his sister and her husband, Charles encouraged the belief that Carlisle had acted on his own initiative in visiting pro-Spanish powers.

Charles was eager to keep his spirited wife as uninformed of his peace feelers as his allies. All Henrietta Maria heard was the rumors of Carlisle's purported "leanings toward Spain." Lucy devoted much of her time and effort to convincing the Queen that the rumors were false. In February 1629, Carlisle came home from his thankless mission, and Lucy found that the rumors of his Spanish leanings were only too true. Since the King had not made his own position clear, Carlisle said little publicly, but he was known to have formed "a triumvirate" with Weston and Cottington. To the consternation of his erstwhile friends in the French party, he was frequently closeted with Charles. A worried Venetian ambassador reported that "Carlisle perseveres in his cabals" and expressed his fear that he "captivates the mind of a young king."[6]

Lucy soon learned that her husband's political change of heart had affected her own position with the Queen. Henrietta Maria was basking in her pregnancy, her only worry that her husband might not make peace with her brother. From various sources she heard that Carlisle was privately talking against the French, and this earned him her strong displeasure. "His wife has already begun to find this out," reported the Venetian ambassador with satisfaction. At times Henrietta Maria was almost cold to Lucy. The vivacious face no longer lit up automatically at her appearance. One day Lucy would find the Queen her old self, another day even her wittiest conversation could not draw forth a royal smile. Where previously the Queen had claimed to be bored by the Countess of Holland, she now sat stitching needlepoint and talking placidly with her by the hour. Lucy reacted to the Queen's indifferent treatment with superb composure. Every inch a Percy in her pride, she had the lèse-majesté of her forefathers ingrained in her. Not for her the chair in the anteroom. She simply ceased her daily court attendance and appeared when she felt like it.

Meanwhile, the magnificent Lord and Lady Carlisle were having money problems. Though their opulent lifestyle continued unabated, Carlisle was heavily in debt. There were no more royal gifts of thousands of pounds. As all the court knew, King Charles could barely find means to provide for himself and the Queen in the style to which they were accustomed. In March 1629, Charles dissolved the turbulent parliament without obtaining a subsidy, so there was little financial relief in sight for him or for his courtiers. Carlisle had always spent money as if the golden stream would never dry up. He had no savings and his assets were of a speculative kind. After several years "the island business" had not yielded him above £200.[7] And while prospects were good for the Irish wine customs and the Irish lands that King James had granted him, so far they were not very profitable either. His mainstay was his pension and the several thousand pounds that flowed from his influential position as First Gentleman of the Bedchamber. Carlisle's expenditures were so high and he was so negligent in his business affairs that he owed over £100,000 to London moneylenders on which he was paying interest at 20 to 30 percent. Only by pawning plate and jewels was he able to maintain the grand style.[8]

As if that weren't enough, the couple found themselves ousted from Essex House, the splendid if somewhat run-down mansion in the Strand that Carlisle leased from Lucy's grandmother, the aged Dowager Countess of Leicester. Out of the blue she wrote her "grandson" requesting him to leave the house he had "so long held" of her and to deliver up his leases so that she might dispose of the property. Moreover, Carlisle was two years in arrears with the rent and the old lady demanded immediate payment "in order to make repairs." The eviction notice closed with a grandmotherly blessing on the Earl and her "noble daughter."[9] This unpleasant letter was not to be dismissed as the whim of a relative in her dotage. At ninety years of age, the wealthy countess was in command of all her faculties, conducted her own business affairs (as this letter shows), and had the physical stamina to walk a mile every morning. In the end, she went to court to evict them.[10] The Carlisles had to go house hunting. From this time on, they were to move their costly possessions to a series of rented houses, like a general in the field who, wherever the battle takes him, sets up his tent with its silver-fitted folding camp furniture.

Moreover, Carlisle was having a bother with his children. Anne had been living at Penshurst ever since Lucy's recovery from smallpox the previous autumn, supposedly on a visit to improve her health in the country air. Her father and stepmother were quite satisfied to leave her there indefinitely. On Carlisle's return to England in February 1629, Dorothy had written him a little note excusing herself for not welcoming him in person and promising to come up to London soon with Anne to show him "how well she had grown."[11] At the end of May the young woman was still at Penshurst, and Leicester advised his brother-in-law that he would be "forced to part with Lady Anne." He explained that he and Dorothy were about to go to Petworth for a visit, and the Earl of Northumberland was restricting them to one child only and a small number of servants. He asked Carlisle to consider where Anne might best be placed. Thus Carlisle was squarely faced with his parental responsibility. He was far from pleased. Once again poor Anne was associated with something unpleasant in her father's mind. Northumberland's preference for Leicester still rankled with Carlisle. He would have liked to spend the month of June at Petworth; in fact, he had angled for an invitation. Early in May he wrote his father-in-law full of concern about his health. Northumberland replied civilly enough, complaining of the weather and a bad cold, but extending no invitation.

Over the years the old earl had become even testier, and he was a trial to his children. He was strongly opposed to Algernon's prospective marriage to Anne Cecil, the eldest daughter of the second Earl of Salisbury—the Salisbury Papers contain a series of very cranky letters from him on the subject. Northumberland was against this love match because he still harbored resentment against the first Earl of Salisbury for his imprisonment. However, he was somewhat mollified by the present earl's tact. At times his letters reveal a more amiable side, as, for instance, when he wrote that the young woman would be lucky to escape living under such an ill-natured person as himself. Like his sisters, Algernon went ahead and married the person of his choice, secure in the knowledge that his father had settled almost all his estate on him twelve years earlier. "I am simply a tenant for life," grumbled Northumberland to Salisbury.[12] Still, the old man had retained £200,000 in ready money, which he dangled before his children's noses. Except for Algernon, he was not very generous to any of them. Harry was about to set out on his grand tour, but the Earl told a family friend that "he will go as a younger son and not in pomp."

Elderly and sickly as he was, he had some woman living with him, and this caused his children concern. It would seem that Salisbury was also worried by this misalliance, with its prospect of additional heirs, because there is a letter from Algernon reassuring his father-in-law that his father had no intention of remarrying, "and his marrying that woman the most unlikely thing of anything that is not impossible."[13] In spite of everything, the old curmudgeon's word was his children's command. When he asked the Leicesters to hasten their coming to Petworth, they quickly altered their plans. As Leicester wrote Carlisle, "No kindness from him must be slighted."[14]

About the time that Anne came back to London, her brother, James, returned from the Continent. After parting from Carlisle in the Low Countries the previous autumn, he and his tutor, James Traill, had set out for Italy. At Turin the young tourist had fallen ill with smallpox. Traill reported that during his illness the English ambassador to the ducal court of Savoy, Sir Isaac Wake, had been "like a father to him." This was just as well since his own father appeared to be as unconcerned as a stranger. When James was well enough to travel in mid-December, he and his tutor continued to Genoa, and from then on they never heard from Carlisle. In March, which found them in Florence, Traill expressed his concern in a letter to Ambassador Wake: Lord Carlisle had not written a word and they needed instructions about going home. In April James wrote his father from Rome that since leaving Turin he had received no commands, and he feared his father had not got his letters. Meanwhile, Carlisle was being badgered by Edward Denny, now Earl of Norwich, to bring his grandson home. Still, Carlisle kept silent. Finally, in May, James announced flatly that he was returning to England. His traveling companion, another English youth, was going home, and as he did not want to travel on alone with his tutor, "in self defence" he too was leaving.[15] It is clear that as James grew up, Carlisle liked him even less than he had in his boyhood. It was a strong, unnatural antagonism. Carlisle no longer expected to have a second family with Lucy, and James was his only son. The boy had grown into a fine, upstanding young man, according to his proud grandfather. On James's return from his travels, Norwich told Carlisle he was "much affected with his manliness and all the good hopes which may well be entertained of him."[16]

NEITHER THE MOVE from Essex House nor the reappearance of the unwelcome Anne and James deflected Carlisle and Lucy from the courtier's life. In May the Queen had given birth prematurely and the baby boy had died. This called for constant attendance from Lucy, who had gone through the same sorrowful experience herself. Once again Henrietta Maria clung to Lucy, favoring her above all her ladies. Carlisle's tireless attendance at court was matched only by Holland's. In April an armistice was signed with France. This considerably enhanced Holland's prestige. But the French party's jubilation was premature. A French alliance alone would lead to an escalated war with Spain and the reconvening of a parliament to finance it. After the last obstreperous session of Parliament, Charles had no intention of ever calling another one. At the same time as he signed the armistice with France, he had Weston send word to Spain that he was ready to open peace negotiations. However, he did not make his views known; in fact, he played the factions against each other. To his courtiers he was a Delphic oracle whose every word or action had them cudgeling their brains to interpret it correctly.

In June 1629, there was great excitement at court over the arrival of diplomatic representatives from both France and Spain. Since the breaking off of diplomatic relations early in the reign, there had been no embassies from either country. The first to arrive was Peter Paul Rubens, the famous painter from the Spanish Netherlands, who had come to make preliminary arrangements for an Anglo-Spanish peace treaty. According to one observer, no one was happier to see him than the Earl of Carlisle, who "entertained him with great affection and invited him to dine with him." A few weeks later, it was Holland's turn to rejoice when the French ambassador, the Marquis de Châteauneuf, made his entry into London, accompanied by fourteen coaches. Châteauneuf was an impressive-looking man in his early fifties, tall and heavy with a luxuriant black beard. He had been sent on numerous diplomatic missions by Henrietta Maria's father, the great Henri IV, but of recent years he had not been much employed in this capacity. The Marquis exhibited all the arrogance and tactlessness that characterized most aristocratic legates, regardless of the country they represented. Standing on ceremony on all occasions, he would not take a step without an entourage. The first thing he did was to insist that the Master of Ceremonies, Sir John Finet, give him the use of the best royal coach while he was in England.

Despite his affiliation with the Spanish party, Carlisle could not resist an ambassador, and at the beginning, he and Lucy were on very friendly terms with the Marquis. They had him to dinner frequently and took him to visit their friends the Earl and Countess of Berkshire at their country house. Carlisle was appointed to escort the ambassador to Windsor Castle for the signing of the peace treaty on September 6. After the ceremony, he had to share him with Holland; the two rivals escorted him back to London, stopping over at Moor Park in Hertfordshire to show him the gardens and waterworks. Châteauneuf also went with the two lords to Cambridge (Holland had succeeded Buckingham as chancellor of the university), where he was awarded a master of arts degree and entertained royally.[17]

It was soon apparent that Châteauneuf intended to make use of the Queen in his negotiations. But he found her unresponsive. Henrietta Maria was "troubling her head very little with affairs of state." Satisfied that peace had been signed with her brother, she was more concerned with becoming pregnant again than with "playing the courtier." Nevertheless Châteauneuf persevered, confident of his ability to influence her and, through her, the King. As her countryman, Henrietta Maria had granted him the right to come to see her informally, without having the Master of Ceremonies arrange an audience. Châteauneuf took full advantage of this privilege and was a habitual visitor to the Queen and her ladies.

It was this self-important diplomat who was to bring the Queen's wrath down upon Lucy's head. While everyone was paying court to the new ambassador—her own husband attended upon him daily—Lucy could not resist mocking him in her inimitable fashion. By nature hypercritical and encouraged by her audience, the bored court circle, she had developed her satirical gifts into a minor art form. With a well-chosen phrase she would expose the personal foibles of the men and women around her. Dissecting one another was a favorite pastime at the Caroline court. It was the fashion to circulate anonymous word portraits, or "Characters," as they were called. Then there would be endless speculation about their authorship. Because of her talent for satire, Lady Carlisle was frequently hailed as the author. She always disclaimed them. But she could not deny her spoken character assassinations, which were quickly passed around the court. By this stage of her life she had added to her reputation as a beauty that of a "bright and sharp-witted" woman. She was serenely undisturbed that her sharp wit had earned her some enemies; it was not that she did not understand discretion but that she scorned it. This time, however, she had met a formidable adversary.

When the Marquis de Châteauneuf heard that Lady Carlisle had "made game of him," his dignity was outraged and he determined to pay her back. He informed the Queen "that Lady Carlisle abused her favour, and bore herself with little respect, going so far as to make sport of her actions." Henrietta Maria had heard Lucy's performance too many times not to find this report credible. Deeply hurt and angry, she wanted Lucy out of her sight at once. Without any investigation of the facts, she insisted that her husband remove Lady Carlisle from court. The King himself took Lucy aside and, as tactfully as possible, told her that "it would be advisable for her to abstain from coming to court until the Queen was appeased." Shocked beyond measure by this sudden disgrace, Lucy asked to know the accusation against her that she might defend herself. But Châteauneuf had no desire to prove his charges. He convinced the Queen that it was beneath her dignity to argue the matter with one of her husband's subjects.

Thus, in November 1629, Lucy found herself banished from court. Rumors were rife as to the cause. Many thought it was because of a quarrel with the Countess of Holland. It was true that Lucy had never liked her cousin's dull, prissy wife, and the Queen's sudden show of favor to Lady Holland had not improved their relationship. Undoubtedly, there was some strain between the Ladies of the Queen's Bedchamber at this time. But only the inquisitive Venetian ambassador sniffed out the true cause of Lady Carlisle's banishment—the malice of the French ambassador.[18]

Having ousted Lucy, Châteauneuf was trying to replace her permanently with another favorite. Although Lady Holland would have been the logical choice as the wife of the leader of the French party, he realized that she was too tedious for the Queen's taste after the scintillating Lucy. Instead, he was busily promoting another candidate in the person of the attractive Countess of Exeter. In seeking to ruin Lucy, the French ambassador had a political as well as a personal motive. He wanted the Earl of Holland to be appointed Lord High admiral to replace Buckingham, but Carlisle was effectively blocking the appointment. At the Privy Council, Carlisle argued reasonably enough that if his fellow councillors wanted a navy because of their mistrust of France, it was hardly good policy to leave the choice of admiral to the French ambassador. It was not difficult to see why Châteauneuf was striving to destroy the influence of Lord and Lady Carlisle.

The dispute over the admiralty brought out into the open the smoldering enmity between Carlisle and Holland. Although they had not been real friends for years, they had continued to march in tandem on the courtiers' daily rounds. They had been partnered so long in the sporting fields, in diplomatic missions, and in ceremonial and social life that they were usually spoken of in the same breath. Similar in their endowments and motivation, they responded to life in the same manner. Ambitious and spendthrift (Holland a younger son and Carlisle from the Scottish gentry), both were totally dependent on royal favor, either directly from the King or indirectly through the momentarily powerful. They were always the first to greet an ambassador and never more than two paces from their sovereign's elbow. Even when their quarrel had grown to some height, the Venetian ambassador paired them in his dispatches: "Carlisle and Holland dance attendance upon the Lord Treasurer . . . Carlisle and Holland live in great splendour and perpetually follow the court." Even in adversity they were twinned, the Venetian adding that "they are borne down by their great expenses."[19] In December came the break. Opposed politically, their ambitions clashing, Carlisle and Holland quarreled publicly.

Whereas this kind of disturbance had been endemic in his father's court, Charles would not tolerate it. After the last two sessions of Parliament, with the ferocious attacks on his prerogative, he had made up his mind to call no more parliaments and to finance his government through extraparliamentary measures. As Parliament receded like a bad dream, he envisaged his court as some private Elysium for himself and his queen, an elegant and cultured milieu free of jarring notes, the realization of the perfect court in Castiglione's *Il Cortegiano*. Two days before Christmas, when life at court was at its most delightful with revels and feasts in the best taste, of course, Charles summoned the two earls before him. Although he was soft-spoken, his was the voice of command. Their unseemly quarrels were disturbing the Queen's pleasure in the Christmas festivities, he told them sternly. They had better make peace between them or he would ban them both from court. With downcast eyes, the no-longer-young miscreants swore that they would quarrel no longer. Their stiffness and cold expressions belied their words, and it was a sham reconciliation. The event provided the day's news: "The two great lords reconciled yesterday," a letter writer reported on December 24, 1629, "but Lady Carlisle is still commanded from the court."[20]

All through the New Year's festivities and into the January season of masques and banquets, Lucy remained at home. When the newly arrived Spanish ambassador had his public audience in the Banqueting House, she was conspicuously absent from the assembly of "the noblest and fairest ladies of court and town." For her sake, Carlisle would have nothing further to do with the French ambassador. And out of the King's presence, he and Holland were not on speaking terms. At the end of the month, however, a second reconciliation took place and this one was effective. At the same time, Lady Carlisle was permitted to resume her duties around the Queen. The King had personally acted as peacemaker, persuading his wife to reinstate her suspended Lady of the Bedchamber. By February 1630, Lucy was back at court although, it was whispered, "not so much a favourite as she was wont to be." Châteauneuf predicted that she would never be prime favorite again. He was quite complacent that he had planted the seeds of distrust in the Queen's mind.[21]

DEATH OF CARLISLE

HENRIETTA MARIA WAS in her private chapel at St. James's Palace, praying that the baby she was carrying would survive. Her first baby, a son, had died the day of his birth. While telling her beads, she gazed around her. The April sunlight coming in through the three long windows over the high altar, gilding the statues of saints in the niches around the walls and the coffered vault of the ceiling, seemed to the Queen to be a benediction. She had chosen to give birth at St. James's Palace because of this beautiful chapel. Originally intended for the Infanta, it had remained partially constructed until 1627, when it had been completed for her own use. The Queen and the twenty or so priests and French attendants she had been permitted to keep with her in England were alone in the vast chapel. Because of the recusancy laws, English Catholics were not allowed to come for mass here; and to ensure that none entered, guards were posted outside the street door. With a final genuflexion to the statue of the Virgin Mary, Henrietta Maria raised her swollen body and, with her ladies hovering over her, withdrew from the chapel.

She repaired to a small room in her private apartments, where a woman was shortly brought to her. Her visitor had tight graying curls, a vague smile playing upon her lips, and pale blue eyes that seemed to be looking into some far-off place. This was Lady Eleanor Davies. She had made a reputation as a seeress by foretelling the death of Buckingham. She had also prophesied that the King's first-born would not live. For that, which had turned out to be only too true, Charles had banished her from the Queen's presence. If Charles knew she was consulting Lady Eleanor, the Queen thought, he would be angry, but she simply had to hear what the seeress was prophesizing for this baby. The answer was as vague as the lady's smile.

To add to Henrietta Maria's anxiety, the midwife dispatched by her mother from Paris had been captured at sea, along with Henrietta Maria's pet dwarf, who had been sent to fetch her. In her present state of mind, the Queen was a difficult mistress for all her Ladies of the Bedchamber. To Lucy she sometimes showed an edge of rancor, the indelible residue of the French ambassador's spiteful charges. But most days, the Queen welcomed Lucy warmly. Henrietta Maria delighted in frivolities. She loved masquing, clothes, and games of all sorts—indeed, she sent to France for the newest ones in vogue. Above all, she enjoyed having witty people around her. Consequently, she could not resist Lucy's charming company for long.

Although Henrietta Maria no longer gave Lady Carlisle the unquestioning love she had lavished upon her as a young girl, it was obvious to the courtiers that she still preferred her above all her other ladies. "It is more than I can hear," Tobie Mathew reported to Sir Henry Vane, another of Lucy's great admirers, "if there be at Court any other lady but she."[1]

At the end of May, the Queen was successfully delivered of a strong, healthy baby boy, an heir to the throne christened Charles after his father. As tradition required, certain nobles and officers of state were present at the last stages of her labor for the purpose of assuring the King that no other infant had been substituted for the royal infant. After giving birth, the Queen remained in her bedchamber for weeks. When she had "lain in" for the obligatory month, the Queen was taken to be churched, a celebratory occasion to give thanks for a successful delivery.

A few days later, the christening ceremony of the future Prince of Wales took place at St. James's Palace. The infant was brought on a velvet cushion to the Queen's Privy Chamber by the Countess of Denbigh, the appointed governess, who then passed the precious burden to her daughter, the Marchioness of Hamilton. Preceded by a procession of aldermen, judges, peers, great officers of state—all in full regalia—the young marchioness, supported by the Earl Marshal and the Lord Treasurer, carried the royal infant, under a canopy held by four lords, to the Chapel Royal (not the Queen's Catholic chapel, the palace was careful to point out). Behind her came the widowed Duchess of Richmond, whose train was borne by little Mary Villiers, the daughter of the late Duke of Buckingham. Then came countesses in pairs. The Master of Ceremonies, Sir John Finet, did not list the Countess of Carlisle among the countesses in the procession to the chapel, but in his notebook he recorded that "other ladies that should have preceded these had been invited, and were expected, but appeared not that day with apprehension, it was thought, that they might be called to lend a hand to the train of the duchess."[2] Lucy was probably one of these proud ladies who disdained to carry the duchess's train; we recall that her mother before her had done the same at Queen Anne's funeral.

Just past thirty, Lucy was at the zenith of her charms. Availing herself of the benefits of cosmetics, she glowed with the bloom of youth while other women of her age were already worn out with childbearing. As well, she was a fashion plate, favoring full skirts of a rich material, pulled back to display an embroidered petticoat, and a low-cut bodice edged with a wide collar of filmy muslin or lace. Fashion decreed that the perfect accessory for these silk and satin gowns was elbow-length leather gauntlets, so, however incongruous they looked, Lucy certainly added them to her costume. She wore her hair in the style of the day—flat on top of the head with frizzy curls on either side of the face. Tobie Mathew declared that other women learned how to dress merely by observing Lady Carlisle. She loved jewelry, in particular a magnificent pearl necklace that she is wearing in all her portraits. Her preoccupation with her appearance was frequently commented upon. In his 1636 "Character of the Countess of Carlisle," Mathew observed that "she takes the greatest joy in the perfections of her own person." Her narcissism is implicit in the flowery tributes of her admirers, who often portrayed her gazing in a mirror.

As one of the Queen's ladies, Lucy was assigned lodgings at court, and when she was in residence the great men flocked to her "chamber." The poet Edmund Waller has depicted her holding court at Whitehall, receiving tribute from the great men of the land like some wise and untouchable goddess:

> The gay, the wise, the gallant and the grave
> Subdued alike, all but one passion have.
> No worthy mind but finds in hers there is
> Something proportioned to the role of his;
> While she, with cheerful but impartial grace
> (Born for no one, but to delight the race
> Of men) like Phoebus so divides her light
> And warns us that she stoops not from her height.

Partly they came in tribute to her beauty and charm, but primarily they cultivated her because of her influence with the Queen. Reciprocally, Lucy chose as friends only those who were "of the most eminent condition, both for Power and Employment."[3] Thus her salon was an important element in the shifting political scene at court, and there she presided with all the finesse she had learned from Carlisle.

We see her through the eyes of the Earl of Exeter, a sixty-year-old member of the Cecil family, still very attracted by feminine beauty. Unable to come to court at the time, he sent her his homage, "which it would have been more pleasure to pay in her lodging at court, when she sees her perfections in the glass, adding perfection to perfection, approving the bon mots spoken in her presence, moderating the excess of compliments, passing over a dull jest with a sweet smile, giving a wise answer to an extravagant question."[4] Were he young again, he wrote gallantly, he would not go to Italy or France to attend an academy, but "would be a humble suitor that she would vouchsafe that her lodging might be his academy." It was springtime and he was looking forward to the violets that would be out in a few days, but her perfections outweighed all other delights.

Lucy's salon was almost exclusively male. She preferred the company of men, mainly because they were the movers and shakers in the political world that so attracted her; besides, women were jealous of her and fearful of her mocking wit. One who dauntlessly paid court was an unmarried gentlewoman, Marjorie Crofts. As worldly-wise as Lucy herself, Mistress Crofts was a habitué of the salon.

Sir Tobie Mathew was the majordomo of Lucy's salon. An aging homosexual with some literary reputation, he was possibly the papacy's most gratifying English convert—his father was a former Archbishop of York and his mother's four sisters had all married Anglican bishops. Because of his religion, Tobie Mathew had spent most of his adult life in exile on the Continent. With his inseparable companion, a younger man from an old Anglo-Catholic family, he had perambulated the courts of Catholic Europe, performing favors for English friends and patrons, for instance purchasing paintings for them by the great Flemish master Peter Paul Rubens. Following some undefined assignment at Madrid during the ill-fated visit of Charles and Buckingham in 1623, he was finally allowed to come home and even knighted, "for what services God knows," Chamberlain had written Carleton.

Sir Tobie had been a friend of Carlisle's for many years, but his friendship with Lucy did not flourish until her emergence as an influential courtier in her own right. For her part, she appreciated his knowledge of punctilio and protocol, acquired at European courts, and his finely tuned feeling for politics. Since his return to England, Sir Tobie had been the perennial houseguest of the Lord Treasurer. Soon to become the Earl of Portland, Sir Richard Weston was effectively the prime minister in Charles's nonparliamentary government. Naturally Lucy had enlisted him for her coterie of eminent friends. It may have been this connection that brought Tobie Mathew into her circle.

In any event, it was she, not Sir Tobie, to whom Portland imparted advance information about diplomatic and political appointments and other important news. Thus, Sir Tobie's power at the English court was at one remove. If people sought him out, it was because he was the confidant of the Countess of Carlisle. He admired her extravagantly. She was (he wrote Sir Henry Vane in 1632) "the highest creature" he had known, the possessor of "all kinds of excellencies," one whom other "woeful creatures" could not approach "in any other posture than that of doing her reverence."[5] He would not have been unhappy if these remarks had come back to Lucy. It was Sir Tobie's very real fear that one day Portland's enemies would triumph over him. In the Countess of Carlisle he found a second protector. In her case, everything depended upon her willingness to perform her court duties.

Lucy was a far cry from diligent servant of the Queen. Whether this sprang from a feeling that Henrietta Maria had not proved a constant friend to her, or from her own arrogance and conceit, the result was a sporadic attendance at court. The attendance record of the Countess of Carlisle was a matter of ongoing comment in court news. "My Lady Carlisle . . . is become a pretty diligent waiter," a courtier informed a friend abroad in November 1630, adding "but how long the humour will last in that course I know not."[6]

Carlisle was a much more reliable royal servant than his wife. No longer of any political importance, he still enjoyed considerable personal influence at court as First Gentleman of the Bedchamber, or Groom of the Stool. Charles was a stickler for observing ceremonial fine points, and he utilized Carlisle's exhaustive knowledge of protocol to deal with the constant flow of ambassadors to his court. Even Sir John Finet, the Master of Ceremonies, consulted him. We come upon Carlisle (in Finet's notebooks) conducting the French and Spanish ambassadors to their public audiences with the King to sign the peace treaties of 1630 and 1631. We see him in his magnificent coach and six, often assisted by his son, James, and Goring's son, George, driving the visiting diplomats hither and yon. The diplomats were always of ambassadorial rank, however, for an earl could attend only upon an ambassador; envoys of lower rank were squired by a baron.

Charles was comfortable having this urbane, faithful courtier around, so Carlisle hunted with him, viewed paintings with him, and accompanied him on all royal progresses. He carried messages to and from the King, interpreting Charles's Delphic utterances for the benefit of anxious suitors.

One suitor has described Carlisle's mediatory role. The King was at Newmarket; he had hunted all day and was tired and unapproachable. The suitor, who had come from London, sought out Lord Carlisle for assistance. Carlisle padded upstairs to see if the King would receive the visitor. As it turned out, he would not grant an audience, but Carlisle was happy to report that the King had read every word of the suit and the suitor left well pleased.[7]

It was observed by those around Carlisle at this stage of his life that he was utterly negligent of his own affairs and interested only "in doing civilities and courtesies to his friends." Gone were the days when Leicester could complain that his brother-in-law did not use his influence on his behalf. After a visit to the Carlisles in London in the autumn of 1630, Leicester was positively effusive in his thanks for some unidentified assistance: Carlisle was so "noble in his favours that if a man be not well provided of gratitude there is danger in making a request of him." In the high-flown metaphorical style of the day, Leicester indicated his own capacity for gratitude by likening his heart to a house: there was only one room in his heart and few guests were lodged there; but those that were entertained were so at home that they might, as the saying went, "throw the house out at the window."[8] Needless to say, Carlisle was an honored guest in Leicester's heart.

The metaphor of the house suggests that the favor on this occasion was Carlisle's promise to obtain the King's permission for Leicester to build a town house on property he owned in London. Unlike most of the nobility, the Sidneys did not have a London residence. When they came to town, they had to impose upon friends or family, as Leicester had just done. How Dorothy must have complained about the lack of a town house! No doubt to please her (or to quiet her complaints), Leicester now decided to build. But to do so required a royal license, and the King was strongly opposed to the nobility forsaking their country seats for life in the city: Charles believed that just as it was his duty to be a father to his people, the nobles had a paternalistic duty to their tenantry. Yet it was nothing for Carlisle to manage the matter, and on August 14, 1631, he was able to inform the Attorney General that it was "the King's pleasure" that a license be prepared for the Earl of Leicester "to build upon a piece of ground called Swan Close in St.-Martin-in-the-Fields, a house convenient for his habitation."[9] For some reason, probably financial, the house was not begun until 1636.

The same benignity pervaded Carlisle's relationship with his wife in these years. No longer was he jealous of Lucy's ascendancy nor of the swarm of admirers who crowded her Whitehall lodgings. At his own lodgings Carlisle still kept the best table at court. Thomas Raymond, the nephew of one of the Earl's retainers, recalled in his autobiography: "I have often seen his [Carlisle's] diet carried from his kitchen across the court at Whitehall, 20 or 25 dishes covered, most by gentlemen richly habited, with the steward marching before and the clerk of the kitchen bringing up the rear, all bareheaded. This for the first and as many more for the second course."[10]

When not on duty, the Carlisles entertained at their rented house on the Strand. But it was another age, and the fabulous feasts of their early married life were a thing of the past. Sir Tobie Mathew was, of course, a regular guest at their suppers. And so was Marjorie Crofts until she made the error of setting her cap for her courtly host. "Mistress Crofts is not so great a courtier at Lady Carlisle's," reported Tobie to Sir Henry Vane. Another observer remarked that the ladies were both so wise that they made it seem "the coolness in their friendship" was attributable to a drifting apart rather than to any malice. In any event, Mistress Crofts soon left England to become a lady-in-waiting to the Queen of Bohemia at The Hague, whence she wrote Carlisle letters of the most fulsome flattery and subtle encouragement.[11]

It was at this time that poor sickly Anne Hay passed away, in her early twenties. Had it not been for an elegiac poem by the courtier poet Thomas Carew, her early death might have gone unrecorded.

The poet admits that he never saw her, and the poem is more a tribute to her father's position than to Anne:

> But when I heard the noble Carlisle's gem,
> The fairest branch of Denny's ancient stem,
> Was from that casket stol'n, from this trunk torn,
> I found just cause why they, why I, should mourn.

Carew put more feeling into the New Year's poems he dedicated to Lucy, or "Lucinda," as he called her. In one poem he expressed the wish "that no access of years presume to abate / Your beauty's ever-flourishing estate." In another, he is more certain that her beauty is ageless:

> Give Lucinda pearl nor stone,
> Lend them light who else have none:
> Let her beauties shine alone.
> Gums nor spice bring from the East,
> For the phoenix in her breast
> Builds his funeral pile and nest.
> No tire thou canst invent
> Shall to grace her form be sent:
> She adorns all ornament.

In November 1631, the Queen gave birth to a daughter, Princess Mary, and this time she honored Lucy as well as Lady Denbigh, naming them both the infant's godparents along with the Lord Keeper, Lord Coventry.[12] In spite of Henrietta Maria's show of favor to Lucy, it was evident to the court that again there were strains between the two proud women. For those who depended on Lucy's influence with the Queen, this was a worrisome state of affairs, so when the Earl of Holland suddenly began paying court to Lucy, her friends were well pleased. In the circle around the Queen, Holland was the most influential male courtier as Lucy was the female—and more consistently in favor. He and Lucy were first cousins; in spite of the falling-out be-

tween Holland and Carlisle, they had remained friendly. As members
of the Queen's set, it was inevitable that the cousins would see much
of each other. The change was that a political alliance was forming
between them. "Lord Holland's friendship with Lady Carlisle is fully
perfected," a courtier wrote Sir Henry Vane in December 1631. "Her
friends hope his credit may restore her to the Queen's favour; his apprehend her pride may endanger him."[13]

What were Holland's reasons for this "sudden friendship"? No
doubt he realized that Lucy would soon swing back into favor—he
had seen the pattern repeat itself often enough. Some regarded it as a
sound move on Holland's part to strengthen the anti-Weston faction.
But his wooing of Lucy was not just political. He had become infatuated with her. How long he had harbored these feelings is not known,
but by the end of 1631 Holland had joined the ranks of those whom
Dorothy labeled drily Lucy's "slaves."

At forty, Holland cut as fine a figure as ever. Striding down the
palace halls, head thrown back, he attracted many admiring glances
(though those who knew him well were aware that there was not
much gray matter behind the handsome exterior). Like Lucy he was a
clotheshorse. A full-length portrait by Daniel Mytens, painted in
1632, shows him in a red and gold doublet and breeches, with slashed
sleeves over a white satin shirt, a lace collar and the blue ribbon of his
Order of the Garter, a stick in one hand and his plumed hat in the
other, scalloped hose tops turned down over high-heeled boots, and
the brown leather gauntlets that inspired the current female fashion.
He has a pointed beard and curly brown hair, and a lovelock (one long
lock worn over the shoulder). The cousins were mirror images of
each other in their good looks and elegance. In fact there was a family resemblance—the same oval faces with arched eyebrows, as if asking the world to state its business. Although a father of eight,
Holland had had many affairs. As the Venetian ambassador said of
him, he was "more given to amours than politics." Yet despite his infatuation with his beautiful cousin, their relationship was generally
understood to be a political alliance rather than a romantic liaison.

This would suggest that Lucy was a faithful wife at this stage.

Thomas Raymond, admiring her "excellent beauty and majestic person" from afar, certainly thought she was. He wrote in his autobiography that "notwithstanding the great disparity in years between her and the Earl (he growing old), she to his last breath approved herself (as I have often heard by those that know it) a most virtuous, tender and loving wife."[14] Obviously Raymond was unaware of Lucy's long affair with the Duke of Buckingham, so his testimony to Lady Carlisle's virtue must be given little weight, except as it presents an outsider's perception of the Countess.

A view from inside the court circle comes from the poet Sir John Suckling, who did not hesitate to write a scurrilous set of verses portraying her as no better than an elegant trollop. "Upon My Lady Carlisle's Walking in Hampton Court Garden" is in the form of a dialogue between Suckling and his fellow poet Thomas Carew. In parody of Carew's "Lucinda" poems, Suckling has Carew exalt Lady Carlisle as a deity whose passage through the garden makes the very flowers "start from their beds." Suckling's own responses are earthy, to say the least. Watching her stroll along in her fashionable mask and hood, he sees "no divinity" and is, in fact, mentally undressing her. Carew is shocked and warns his friend that at the sight of this goddess nude, he would be utterly lost. But Suckling sneers:

> What ever fool like me had been
> If I'd not done as well as seen?
> There to be lost why should I doubt,
> Where fools with ease go in and out?[15]

Was Lucy as promiscuous as Suckling claims? As a character witness he has low credibility. He was a libertine, a gambler who played with marked cards, and, above all, a cynic. In *Brief Lives,* John Aubrey dubbed him "the greatest gallant of his time" and told how he baited his hook with magnificent entertainments for "Ladies of Quality, all beauties and young, which cost him many hundreds of pounds, where were all the rarities that this part of the world could afford, and the last service of all was Silk stockings and Garters, and I think also Gloves."[16]

Against Suckling's besmirching we have Sir Tobie Mathew's word that Lady Carlisle had no inclination for the opposite sex and "no passion at all." In his 1636 "Character of the Countess of Carlisle," Mathew maintained that she "played with love, as with a child." She would "freely discourse of love, and hear both the fancies and powers of it"; but (he cautioned) let the listener "boldly direct it to herself" and she would quickly stifle the discussion. The passionless woman who turned aside any amorous remarks may well have been an attempt to whitewash Lucy's questionable reputation. Promiscuity was officially frowned upon at Charles's court. The royal couple set the example of monogamy. With evident surprise, a newly arrived Venetian ambassador reported to the Doge that the English king "loves his wife with remarkable affection, which keeps him from the slightest approach to anything that might give the Queen the slightest jealousy."[17]

With philandering out of place in Charles's Elysium, there was much discussion about the ideal of platonic love. "The Court affords little news at present," wrote a court watcher in 1634, "but that there is a love called Platonic Love, which much sways there of late; it is a Love abstracted from all corporeal gross Impressions and sensual Appetite, but consists in Contemplations and Ideas of the Mind, not in any carnal fruition."[18] Enjoying her own fruitful carnality in holy wedlock, Henrietta Maria encouraged the court poets and wits to versify in this vein; indeed she commanded a masque on the subject of platonic love. Since platonic love was the cult of the day, the ever-adaptable Lucy (with Sir Tobie's help) now presented herself as its high priestess. Seen in the context of the vogue for platonic love at the Caroline court, Sir Tobie's portrayal of Lucy as a woman cold to the point of frigidity (and therefore beyond any accusations of immorality) becomes less convincing. Suckling may have given us the real flesh-and-blood Lady Carlisle.

ALTHOUGH TURNING THIRTY heralded an even more brilliant career for Lucy as the reigning beauty of the court and a powerful courtier, for Dorothy it meant the approach of middle age. A sour note crept into the sisters' relationship. Isolated in the country while she longed for the city, Dorothy was growing envious of Lucy's exciting life and increasingly discontented with her own lot. Contrary to the Early Stuart ideal of womanhood, the fecund sister envied the childless one. Dorothy achieved some gratification, however, when in 1632 Leicester was appointed special envoy to the Danish king. At last he had commenced the career in the royal service for which he had been groomed and that Dorothy had so earnestly hoped for him. Since he had waited so long for preferment, it is probable that Carlisle had finally put in a good word for him with King Charles. On September 14, 1632, Dorothy saw her husband off at Penshurst. He was to be away at least several months.

Dorothy had achieved her vicarious ambition, but it meant even greater loneliness. Leicester was only too aware of the unhappiness he left behind him. From Denmark he wrote her brother Algernon, begging him to visit her at Penshurst. Her disposition was "apt enough to be melancholic," he wrote, "especially in that solitary place where, though it be the best I have, I must confess it was her ill fortune that placed her there." How often he must have listened to Dorothy's reproaches on this subject for, filled with guilt, he added: "In recompense whereof my greatest study is to procure comforts for her, which she shall never want of, if my life can serve her with any."[19] Compounding Dorothy's unhappiness, in November her father died. She had been the old earl's favorite daughter, and a few months before his death he had visited her at Penshurst. Although hardly as grief-stricken as when her mother died, she found that her father's passing increased her feelings of desolation.

Lucy's mourning was certainly very measured. There was no sisterly reunion to commiserate together. The younger sister was caught up in the life of the court. The Queen's on-again, off-again favor to the Countess of Carlisle continued to fascinate the courtiers, who had little else to occupy their minds. Henrietta Maria had long since learned that Lucy could not be relied upon to turn up for all her court functions. When the Queen presented her pre-Lenten masques at Somerset House, Lucy was seldom among "the divers great ladies" who acted with her. Lucy had a distaste for performing in the masques that were the Queen's chief delight and usually excused herself. She deigned to appear, however, in *Chlorida* in 1631 and Inigo Jones's *Tempe Restored* in 1632.[20] In 1632 the roving ambassador Sir Henry Vane was informed by a London correspondent that "Lady Carlisle was firm to her principles" and lived just as she had when Vane left England the year before: "If any change it is to less attendance."[21] Notwithstanding her spirit of independence, Lucy was a royal favorite and the recognized conduit to the Queen.

This is confirmed by the man who was to become the paramount figure in Lucy's life for the rest of the decade. In May 1633, Sir Thomas Wentworth came to London before taking up his appointment as Lord Deputy of Ireland. In a letter to Carlisle, who accompanied King Charles to Scotland for his long-deferred coronation (although Charles had succeeded his father as King of Scotland, in eight years he had not found time to go to his northern realm to be crowned before this), Wentworth wrote, "The Queen's favours to my Lady are apparent and much spoken of amongst us; and in good faith I persuade myself will continue so long as it shall please my Lady to set herself in the way to have them bestowed upon her."[22] Because of his leanings toward the Spanish party, Wentworth was in the Queen's bad books. Not the least of his motives in coming to London during the King's absence was the hope of finding someone who could ameliorate Henrietta Maria's opinion of him. Lady Carlisle was the obvious person.

A wealthy Yorkshire landowner, in the 1620s Wentworth had been one of the King's severest parliamentary critics. Charles had co-opted him by making him Lord President of the Council of the North. The northern council, an arm of the royal government in London, was established to quell the endemic disorder resulting from rivalry between "bullying magnates" and from festering family feuds. By bringing the magnates to heel, Wentworth had earned the reputation of an outstanding administrator—an ability rare, if not unique, under Charles's personal rule. Now he was being sent to Ireland to bring order out of the chaos that habitually reigned there. He would have much preferred a London appointment—he had his eye on the lord treasurership—but as the viceroy of Ireland he could look forward to holding one of the most important posts in the royal service. Wentworth was an old friend of Carlisle's. From Yorkshire he sent him a kennel of hounds, indicating that he would do more once he was in Ireland. Carlisle had extensive Irish interests and at the time was pressing a land claim.[23] In his letters, Wentworth always asked to be remembered to Carlisle's lady. It is doubtful that he had known her other than casually up to this time, but in 1633 they would see a great deal of each other.

At this stage of her life, Lucy was described by one besotted lord as "the killing beauty of the world,"[24] and Wentworth was clearly dazzled by her. Indeed his cousin Christopher Wandesford dared tease him about "my fair lady of Carlisle, your most sweet Egeria."[25] (Egeria was the fabled consort and counselor of Numa Pompilius, a legendary king of Rome.) The admiration was mutual. Lucy conceived an immense respect for the ungainly man with the beetling brows, whose simple dress made him look like one of the Puritans hauled up before the Star Chamber. Brusque and somewhat ill at ease in society, Wentworth had none of the smooth graces of a Holland or a Carlisle. Certainly he did not regard himself as an attractive man. "This bent and ill-favoured brow of mine was never prosperous in the favour of ladies," he responded to ragging (probably about Lucy) from the Earl of Exeter.[26] But Lucy knew a great man when she saw one, and in this admirer she found a person worthy of her admiration.

From all signs, Wentworth was content to keep the friendship on a high plane. In the first place, it would have been folly to risk alienating Carlisle, who was so close to the King. It is a fair conjecture that Wentworth and Lucy had many a discussion about platonic love, for a friend who was with him in Ireland said that the Lord Deputy often discoursed privately on the subject. Wentworth's love life was actually rather strange. The year before his close friendship with Lucy, he had married his third wife, the daughter of a Yorkshire neighbor, but for no apparent reason the marriage was kept secret until Wentworth arrived in Dublin. Clearly an undemanding young woman, his wife by satisfying his physical needs left his fancies free to dwell on Lady Carlisle's empyrean virtues.

A platonic friendship notwithstanding, during his stay in London that summer Wentworth displayed unmistakable signs of jealousy. The Earl of Holland was as enslaved as ever by Lucy. They spent much time together in the Queen's inner circle, and Wentworth glowered at reports of the "great courtesies" that passed between them. In a letter eloquent in its mixed motives, he warned the absent Carlisle that Holland and his clique were wooing Lucy frantically. Wentworth and Holland were members of opposing factions at court, and, seen in this light, an attempt to convert Lucy to the French party would run counter to Wentworth's political interests. But there was also the personal element. Holland was Carlisle's bête noire, as Wentworth well knew. An alarmed husband might be the best way of ridding himself of a rival. The letter ended with Wentworth's assurance that he had "no other interest" than the "honour and happiness of your Lordship and my Lady."[27]

At the end of July 1633, Wentworth left for Ireland, satisfied that in Lord and Lady Carlisle he had friends at court. (He had undoubtedly made known to Lucy his burning desire for an earldom.) Henrietta Maria was in the final months of another pregnancy, and Lucy was assiduous in attending her, as she always was at such times. On October 14, 1633, the Queen was delivered of a son. The christening of the baby James took place at St. James's Palace, as had that of his brother Charles. Once again, as at Charles's christening, Lucy had to take a back seat at the ceremony. The day belonged to her rivals the Buckingham women. The Countess of Denbigh, who as First Lady of the Queen's Bedchamber held the equivalent position to Carlisle's with the King, had the honor of carrying the royal infant in the august procession. Her daughter the Marchioness of Hamilton stood up as deputy godmother for King Charles's sister, the Queen of Bohemia. Her train was borne by Mary Villiers, Buckingham's ten-year-old daughter.[28] With Buckingham long gone, Henrietta Maria no longer disliked his female relatives. If anything, she showed more constant, if lukewarm, favor to them than she did to Lucy. As Lady

Denbigh remarked smugly to her son, there was nothing that could put her out of her place "but my want of health which thank God I now enjoy very well."[29] In January 1634, Lucy retired from the court, pleading illness. But it is more than possible that rancor against the Queen for her favoritism to Lady Denbigh and her family played a large part.

In the same month, the Reverend George Garrard, Wentworth's faithful correspondent, informed him that Lady Carlisle, although she looked well, had "utterly lost her stomach" and was staying at home in the Carlisles' rented house in the Strand to take physic and recover her health. Whether this was more hypochondria or whether she was genuinely ill we do not know. Wentworth wrote her, full of concern, and the indiscreet Lucy "showed his letters to everybody." This was reported to him by his horrified sister, who asked him what on earth he was doing writing to Lady Carlisle who, in her opinion, was simply "wild."[30] True, Lucy had a bad habit of sharing private letters. Dorothy once cautioned Leicester to be careful what he wrote to the Earl of Holland, as he would show the letters to Lucy, "and from thence it spreads all over England."[31] Wentworth thought none the less of Lucy for her indiscretion. He may have charged it to her "ingenuousness," which he found very appealing. He once remarked of Lady Carlisle that "she will not seem to be the person she is not, an ingenuity I have always observed and honoured her for."[32]

Lucy remained away from court for months, purportedly taking physic. Carlisle was also sick with an interminable cold. At the end of the year, however, Lucy returned to her duties, and in early January 1635, Garrard was able to report that "my Lady Carlisle lives now constantly in court again." She had given the Queen a very fine New Year's gift, which was graciously accepted. Viscount Conway, the son of the late secretary of state, a close friend and neighbor of Lucy's brother Algernon (who had become the tenth Earl of Northumberland on his father's death), wrote Wentworth that the real reason for her long absence was pique. Yes, Lady Carlisle was back at court, but there would never be "a perfect friendship" with the Queen. She and her sister-in-law, Lady Northumberland, were not in the Queen's pre-

Lenten masque. They had not offered, and the Queen and her ladies had not asked them, for fear of being refused.[33]

Lucy's influence over her aging husband was an accepted fact. The French ambassador reported in 1634 that the Earl of Carlisle "can only be reached through his wife who controls him absolutely." He added that she also controlled Sir Thomas Wentworth but went on to say that Lucy, in turn, was controlled by her brother, "who leans to the French side but has to be wooed with presents."[34] The ambassador was referring not to Northumberland, whose probity was above question, but to Lucy's younger brother, Henry Percy.

Harry had become a diligent courtier, making his addresses mainly to the Queen—he was her Master of the Horse. As a younger son with little money, he had remained a bachelor and was reputedly a rogue with women. Someone who clearly disliked him described him as a weak man but subtle and artful for his own ends—"bold and busy putting himself into every fiddling business." Dorothy saw her younger brother in much the same way. She was particularly scornful of him for making use of Lucy's influence, "yet when the Queen speaks of her with neglect he hears it with as much patience as if it did not concern him."[35] It is unlikely that Lucy allowed herself to be ruled by Harry, and in fact Conway reported to Wentworth in January 1635 that sister and brother had shocked the court by quarreling in public. At the same time, Harry had a falling-out with Lucy's husband, telling all who would listen that he would "rather be damned than receive a courtesy from my Lord of Carlisle." This did not stop him from freeloading at his brother-in-law's well-stocked table although, laughed Conway, "not being much bid welcome."

Viscount Conway's opinion of Lucy also belies the French ambassador's remark that she let Harry rule her. "Lady Carlisle," Conway wrote Wentworth, "will be respected and observed by her superiors, be feared by those that will make themselves her equals, and will not suffer herself to be beloved but of those that are her servants." Wentworth, in the throes of fighting corruption and mismanagement in Ireland, replied: "I admire and honour her, whatever be her position at court," and he asked Conway to relay a message. "You might tell her sometimes when she looks at herself at night in the glass that I have the ambition to be one of those servants she will suffer to honour her."[36]

By the summer of 1635, rumors were circulating that the Earl of Carlisle was seriously ill. He did not go on progress with the King, and, aside from a week's visit to the Earl of Northumberland at Petworth, the Carlisles remained in London. There, at the end of July, the Leicesters' agent found the Earl of Carlisle in good spirits and ready to expedite the recovery of some stolen plate if, he joked, his brother-in-law would return "the yellow book on the House of Austria" that he had misappropriated from him. Thomas Raymond has left us another, more somber picture of the ailing earl. Listening to a sentimental ballad of Elizabeth's reign, he was moved to tears by the words "his golden locks time hath to silver turned."[37] On July 30, 1635, Garrard wrote Wentworth that Carlisle had just settled an estate of £2,500 a year on his lady, to be held in trust by the Earl of Northumberland, who had come up from Petworth especially to sign the trusteeship document.[38]

Though Carlisle seemed to recover in the late summer, Lucy saw the end coming. On September 7, she sent a letter to Wentworth. After apologizing for engaging him in some unspecified "trouble" without his leave, she went on to ask for "the absolute security" of his protection. Wentworth's answer was the height of chivalry: "Surely Madame there are many of greater understanding and power you might have commanded, but not any that will more readily and cheerfully serve you than myself."[39] His fervor to serve his lady was no doubt sharpened by a letter from Conway in November, informing him that Lady Carlisle had a new admirer, the young Duke of Lennox. As a result, Conway gossiped, Holland hated Lennox and had formed a friendship with the Marquess of Hamilton against their common enemy. He had better end this letter, Conway said, "lest I write a libel."

By January 1636, Carlisle was plainly dying. "With much grief," Garrard reported to Wentworth that he "infinitely decays, his stomach gone." He could hardly walk but valiantly insisted that he would not yield to Goodman Death. At the end of February the Venetian ambassador reported that the Earl of Carlisle was in "an almost hopeless condition." By March he was having convulsions, and for a short time he lost his speech and recognized no one. He came out of the stroke, but, convinced now that he would die, he began to put his affairs in order. His debts were enormous, upward of £80,000.[40] To frustrate his creditors he put his estate in trust for Lucy. Everything was to go to her.

His son and daughter-in-law sat by his bedside faithfully, yet young Viscount Doncaster would get nothing but the title of Earl of Carlisle. Although his son had assisted him in his duties as First Gentleman of the King's Bedchamber, Carlisle still disliked him. James had aggravated this dislike by marrying the daughter of the Earl of Bedford in 1632 without his father's permission.[41] Also left out of the will was Carlisle's kinsman and faithful agent in Ireland, Sir James Hay. Carlisle had borrowed a great deal of money from him and his brother Archibald. This oversight was to cause Lucy considerable bother.

In the midst of his suffering, Carlisle was greatly comforted by several visits from King Charles, who stayed for hours and was demonstratively affectionate to his old favorite. Shortly before his death, Carlisle beseeched the King to confirm to Lucy for her lifetime all the benefits he himself had enjoyed. And to ensure that his creditors could not seize these grants legally, he asked Charles to accept their surrender on the understanding that they would be returned to Lucy after his death. Charles readily agreed to help Carlisle evade his debts.[42] Meanwhile from Ireland Wentworth assured Lucy that he was looking after the Carlisles' interests and that he would be leaving for England very soon. But delayed by a cruel attack of the stone that made him too weak to travel, he did not arrive before Carlisle died at the end of April. Clearly stricken by the "sad news," Wentworth wrote Lucy a tormented letter in which he cursed the ill health "that denied me the honour to kiss his hands before his departure and here detained me from the place where I might hope to be of some use in that trust whereby your Ladyship hath been pleased to dignify me."[43]

Sir James Hay, Viscount Doncaster, Earl of Carlisle—for nineteen years Lucy's husband—had been a faithful courtier to two kings. Contemporaries regarded him as "a gentleman every way complete," unaffected and courteous, whose "sweet and candid compliments" and "humbleness" warded off envy and left him without a single enemy.[44] (In reality, he quarreled with his brother-in-law, had a falling-out with Buckingham, and maintained a long-standing rivalry with Holland.) His missions to mediate conflicts abroad had met with no success, but he had carried them out with great finesse. A spendthrift and clotheshorse, his name was a byword for lavish display. In a society where land meant wealth and power, Carlisle was a landless peer, whose prestige rested upon his access to the Throne. "He left behind him," the historian the Earl of Clarendon writes, "the reputation of a very fine gentleman and a most accomplished courtier, and after having spent, in a very jovial life, above 400,000*l.*, which, upon a strict computation, he received from the Crown, he left not a house or acre of land to be remembered by."

Carlisle was, of course, embalmed while elaborate funeral arrangements were being made. We are told that the embalming of an earl required exceptional care. In the hands of a surgeon and an apothecary, the corpse was disemboweled (perhaps removing the heart to be kept in an urn by the bereaved) and the cavities filled with aromatic spices. The body was then sealed in wax and encased in lead, molded to its shape by a "plummer," and this served as the coffin. In this condition, the body could be kept above ground as long as required.[45] An unleaded body had to be buried at once, which was a disgrace to a noble family.

On the evening of May 6, 1636, the Earl of Carlisle was buried with full honors, the nobility turning out in force to pay its last respects. Starting from the Carlisles' house in the Strand, the cortège proceeded toward St. Paul's Cathedral, where the Earl was to be buried. Heading the procession were seventy poor men from an almshouse in black gowns provided for in Carlisle's will, and after them the Earl's thirteen watermen. Then a seemingly endless line of nobles and knights filed past, followed by a riderless horse in black velvet trappings with black plumes on its head. Officials representing the Wardrobe and the Bedchamber—the government departments Carlisle had headed—walked in front of the Earl's personal servants. Heralded by the somber strains of trumpets, the hearse carrying the black-draped coffin came in sight, drawn by six black horses. The Earl's coronet and his Order of the Garter lay upon a pillow on the hearse. Unfortunately, there was no family member walking in front of the coffin, because Carlisle's only son was ill and unable to attend the funeral. After the coffin passed, royal heralds hired for the funeral came bearing the achievements of the deceased: his banner, sword, spurs, gauntlets, his helmut with his crest, and silver and gold ceremonial ornaments presented to him in the course of his long diplomatic career. Bringing up the rear were the Earl's household servants, each carrying the white staff of his office. Arrived at the cathedral, the coffin was carried into the old Gothic building by the pallbearers to its final resting place.[46]

Carlisle's impressive funeral did not escape criticism. "Few bewail the Earl of Carlisle," one cynical observer wrote his son. "It is poor satisfaction to the Londoners, his creditors, to pay them with laying his bones in St. Paul's."[47]

Lucy found herself a wealthy widow: £5,000 a year, the Irish wine customs said to be worth £20,000, and a £2,000-a-year pension confirmed by the King. The Venetian ambassador reported, "It is reckoned that the Countess will have £5,000 for her life and more than £70,000 besides with jewels, furniture and plate, which will be at her free disposition."[48] Not only had she inherited her husband's estate (through conveyances that were possibly fraudulent), but as a widow she came into the large jointure he had settled upon her at the time of their marriage. (Though one letter writer hazards the opinion that Carlisle was "making her some repair from his personal estate . . . for his failings to her of late in his person,"[49] the fact is that both husband and wife had long found sex outside marriage.) Lucy had flouted all the rules for a good wife. Instead of wifely obedience and fidelity, she had established herself as her husband's equal and gone her own way. Yet Carlisle admired her and loved her to the end.

Apparently, Lucy did not spend much time mourning her departed lord. She did not attend the funeral (widows seldom did), and Edmund Waller poetizes that this was just as well because her beauty would have diverted the male mourners:

> We find not that the laughter-loving dame
> Mourned for Anchises; 'twas enough she came
> To grace the mortal with her deathless bed,
> And that his living eyes such beauty fed;
> Had she been there, untimely joy, through all
> Men's hearts diffused, had marred the funeral.[50]

At the age of thirty-seven, Lucy was finally free of an old husband, and she was rich.

PART TWO

AT THE

KING'S

COMMAND

nine

DOROTHY A GRASS WIDOW

THE DAY AFTER Carlisle's funeral, Leicester left for France to take up an appointment as ambassador to the court of Louis XIII. His mission to Denmark had been a failure, but he had conducted himself creditably (not least in walking away unassisted from the table after a marathon drinking bout with the Danish king)[1] and had thus placed himself in line for a promotion. With this high employment in the foreign service, Dorothy at last saw her ambitions for her husband achieved.

Charles's diplomacy in these years of nonparliamentary government centered on recovering the Palatinate for his sister's husband, and after 1632 for her son, at no cost to himself. With this objective he sent his envoys on contrary missions. Some were dispatched to the King of Spain to urge him to yield the garrisons he held in the Palatinate and to use his influence with the Holy Roman Emperor and the Duke of Bavaria for total restitution. Others, such as Leicester, were sent abroad to see what help they could get from France. Charles had a pet plan. It called for the French to cede Lorraine to the Hapsburgs in exchange for the Hapsburgs' returning the Palatinate to the Elector Palatine. Charles himself would give up nothing.

But Charles persuaded himself that because France was involved in a war with Spain, his brother-in-law, Louis XIII, could be induced to fall in with his plan in order to ensure English neutrality.[2] This was Leicester's task. As he would at length discover, the French would only help in the restitution of the Palatinate if England would join them in their war with Spain—the two superpowers had finally made their enmity official with a declaration of war on May 19, 1636. But Charles would not go to war under any circumstances, for fear of having to call a parliament.

Provided he stayed out of the continental wars and was very careful to cut down on domestic expenses, Charles could muster enough revenue to dispense with Parliament permanently. His extraparliamentary taxes and forced loans, however, were very unpopular. Ship money, a tax to raise money for the navy, which had been previously limited to the ports, was extended to the inland towns and cities. Customs duties were farmed out to favorites who paid the King an annual rent—merchants complained that the farmers were steadily increasing the rates. Similarly, the King granted monopolies of staples, even salt and soap, from which he received royalties. Long-disused feudal statutes were revived, and offenses under these new-old laws were heavily fined. In particular, the revival of the forest laws alienated the landed classes. Their ancestral holdings, which had been cultivated by tenant farmers for generations, were suddenly classified as forest, and heavy fines were imposed for trespassing on the King's property. Large landowners, who had enclosed the common land on their estates to raise sheep, were fined under ancient statutes for depopulating the area. Then there was the knighthood tax. Any landowner worth £40 a year or more had to pay a substantial fine for refusing the responsibilities of knighthood. Tame judges and intimidated juries legitimized the King's nonparliamentary money raising.

Leicester took his two older sons, Philip and Algernon, with him to Paris. Robin, the ten-year-old, was sent to board with his tutor. Dorothy, pregnant as usual, remained at Penshurst with her five girls, all under eleven except Doll. Before going abroad, Leicester put the entire management of his estate in Dorothy's capable hands. The rents from Penshurst and the landholdings in Wales and Warwickshire were to be paid to her. He himself planned to live on his "entertainment"—his allowances from the Exchequer. King Charles had assured him that he would not suffer from his employment abroad, and Leicester, who was still owed over £2,000 for his Danish embassy in 1632, believed him.

From the time Leicester's first bills began arriving from France, it was obvious that getting the Exchequer to pay up would be a major problem. Dorothy was in constant correspondence with Leicester's London agent, William Hawkins, who spent day after day at court waiting upon the Lord Treasurer, the two Secretaries of State, and numerous other officials, soliciting for his master's allowances. While Hawkins cooled his heels in the antechambers of Whitehall, from Penshurst Dorothy enlisted the help of the Earl of Holland, her cousin and Lucy's besotted admirer. Not only was he a favorite of Queen Henrietta Maria, but he had now stepped into Carlisle's boots as First Gentleman of the King's Bedchamber.[3] Initially, Holland lived up to his reputation as a very influential courtier, assuring Dorothy that a warrant would be issued to pay her husband's bills and his monthly allowance retroactive to his arrival in France. But as weeks went by and no money was forthcoming, Dorothy sent Holland a strong letter, impressing upon him that she had pawned her jewels and borrowed from her friends (including a loan of £500 from Lucy, although she did not mention this to Holland); she finished off by saying that her husband could hardly get any more credit in France. Lucy chided her sister that this far from tactful letter hurt Holland's feelings. Dorothy was unrepentant. "I did not say one syllable offensively or unkindly," she assured Leicester.[4]

With single-minded purpose, Dorothy now solicited help from Archbishop Laud—the former Bishop of London had risen to the highest ecclesiastical office, that of Archbishop of Canterbury. When Leicester's allowances were eventually paid, Dorothy believed it was thanks to Laud, for, as she informed her husband, Holland's influence was more apparent than real. For his part, Holland claimed the credit and was offended with Dorothy (as she heard from her brother Northumberland) "for doubting of his power and employing the little bishop."[5] Whoever it was that pried the payment out of the royal revenue, it simply marked the beginning of years of solicitation at court by Hawkins for "my lord's money business." While it was true that the Exchequer was a poor paymaster, Leicester lived in such state at Paris that he always exceeded his allowances anyway. Bills came for his lavish entertaining and for liveries of unnecessary servants. Then Hawkins had to scrounge around for lenders, or Dorothy had to put in rent money after all. The quiet scholar had turned into a big spender!

From Dorothy's letters it is clear that she took firm control of Leicester's financial affairs. She made all the decisions from felling timber to send to the ironmaster, to determining which creditors would be paid first. Not quite satisfied with a report she had from Hawkins, she summoned the agent to Penshurst to explain every detail to her. Hawkins learned to have the greatest respect for her business acumen. Unlike "many other noble ladies," he wrote Lord Leicester, she was careful to pay off debts as promptly as possible, which was necessary if they were to preserve the family's credit.[6]

Another responsibility that devolved upon Dorothy was overseeing the completion of Leicester House in London. It was almost ready for occupancy. A long, low building of red brick, it was built on the north side of a field known as Swan Close (today Leicester Square). The surrounding area was just beginning to be built up. Aside from a few other mansions, among them one belonging to Lord Goring, the house stood in open country. From Penshurst Dorothy arranged for the exterior woodwork to be painted and gilded and a balustrade erected on the roof. She had already seen to an impressive gate. A handsome chimneypiece was installed in the great chamber, and she ordered gilt leather for the walls of the stairway and the anteroom. Furniture was next.

Leicester had sent some pieces for the withdrawing room, but there remained the furnishing of the great chamber. It was all a tremendous expense, she sighed. The cost would go well beyond what they had allowed, but she assured her husband that she would make the money stretch as far as possible.

They missed each other sorely. Their correspondence reveals the extent to which Leicester was still passionate about his wife. He poured out his sexual frustrations in his letters, which Dorothy read "with a little shame but no dislike." She did not need to be persuaded, she said, to give him in her thoughts what he desired, "for had I the happiness to be with you, certainly nothing should be denied to you which is in my power to bestow." At one point he seems to have complained that she was not passionate enough, for she replied with spirit: "If there can be one in the world that can love above all others, I am deceived if I am not she." Leicester continued to vent his frustrations. After receiving some mirrors and pictures for Leicester House from Paris, Dorothy wrote: "If what you desire in return from me could be sent with as much case as these goods, it should not be denied."[7]

How incensed she would have been had she known that her good friends Will Crofts and "little Wat" Montagu were offering her sex-starved husband a mistress. From Tours in July 1637, Sir William Crofts wrote Leicester: "I have seen a lady here who thinks herself very happy in your Lordship's acquaintance although it be but small." It seems Walter Montagu had introduced the lady to Leicester, and Crofts told Leicester he was "sure" that if they met again "you would be yet more satisfied with one another . . . Your lordship could not choose but be with her."[8] In case Leicester took offense, Crofts covered himself by presenting the woman as a person interested in learning more about England. We do not know if Leicester availed himself of the opportunity to take a mistress.

Separation from Leicester would at least give Dorothy a respite from her chronic state of pregnancy. In the autumn she gave birth to another girl. Girl babies were hardly prized in Stuart England. Some weeks later, when her sister-in-law was delivered of a girl, Northumberland did not even bother to tell Dorothy. She must have taxed him with this neglect, because on December 5 he wrote from Syon House that "the having of another girl I thought so inconsiderable that I made no haste in acquainting you with it."[9] This was his fourth daughter in a row, and in light of his entailed estate, Northumberland was understandably eager for a male heir. The infant was christened Elizabeth after her maternal aunt, but Northumberland had named the last two girls after his sisters. Since the only quality that parents could hope for in a female child was beauty, when his daughter, born in 1635, was named Lucy, a well-wisher remarked: "Pray God it may prove as handsome, and as brave a Lady as her aunt that bears that name."[10]

Dorothy did not share the prevailing preference for boys. In fact, she favored her eldest daughter far above her sons. Doll was the apple of her eye. Next to Leicester himself, she loved her "above anything in this world." Doll's silent, retiring personality complemented her mother's bossiness and kept the mother-daughter relationship running smoothly. Doll resembled her aunt Lucy except that she was fairer, and her beauty inspired the poet Edmund Waller to write a series of sonnets to her under the name of "Sacharissa," which circulated in manuscript around the court. A recent widower, Waller harbored some hope that Doll might have him. But as a simple country gentleman, he did not meet the Countess of Leicester's requirements for her eldest daughter's husband, although she was pleased enough to have him broadcast Doll's beauty far and wide. She may have agreed with her husband that Waller could have one of the younger girls, but nothing came of that. Poor Waller was said to have suffered a nervous breakdown over the unattainable mistress of his verse.[11]

Doll was nineteen now. She had been in the market for a husband for well over a year. In January 1635, the Reverend George Garrard, writing to Wentworth, mentioned Dorothy Sidney as one of three daughters of the nobility "ripe of marriage." Her mother was beginning to worry that she would be called "a stale maid." The problem was the limited number of prospective bridegrooms for a girl of Doll's "quality."[12] The best prospect, and certainly Dorothy's first choice, was William Cavendish, the third Earl of Devonshire. He had all the requisites of rank, wealth, and good looks. And he and Doll had a bond between them because his sister Anne, Lady Rich, was

Doll's best friend. Although his tutor, Thomas Hobbes, had not made a philosopher of him, Devonshire was reasonably intelligent. He had recently returned from his grand tour of Europe with Hobbes and was presumably ready to settle down. Just with whom, however, would be the decision of his widowed mother, a strong-willed Scottish lady who was said to rule him absolutely. The Dowager Countess of Devonshire was a great friend of the Earl of Holland. In fact, she was one of the ladies the court laughingly referred to as his petticoat cabinet.[13] Once again Holland was sanguine that he could oblige Dorothy, and she lived in hopes that he would bring in a proposal.

In the meantime, her letters to Leicester were full of her habitual complaints about "the solitariness I suffer in this place." Writing to him on November 10, she complained that her brothers and sister, engrossed in their busy lives, were ignoring her. Northumberland, whom the King had appointed admiral of the ship-money fleet, was long back from summer maneuvers in the Channel but had not come to see her. She had offered to visit him (if he would pay for her journey), but no invitation had followed. There was a "coldness" in her brother, she told her husband. And Lucy was at Nonsuch Palace, basking in the admiration of the Lord Deputy, who had been in England since June. Until he returned to Ireland, Dorothy said, she had little hope of seeing her sister. Brother Harry, as usual, was dancing attendance upon the Queen. Thoroughly sorry for herself, Dorothy wrote Leicester that she would "content myself the best I can with this lonely life, without envying their greatness, their plenty or their jollity." Dorothy was probably suffering from postpartum depression, because she was certainly not as neglected by her kinsfolk as this depressing letter indicated. After all her complaints about her brother, an affectionate letter arrived from the usually aloof, self-contained Northumberland, explaining that problems in the navy were keeping him from coming to Penshurst: "Believe me, I long for nothing more than to see you," he wrote. And no doubt at Lucy's behest, Sir Thomas Wentworth sent her a kind note from Nonsuch, offering his services for anything that lay in his power. Dorothy seized the occasion to ask him to put in a good word for Leicester with the Archbishop of Canterbury.[14]

Wentworth had come over to England to seek reassurance that his enemies in Dublin were not undermining him with the King through their friends at Whitehall. To his intense satisfaction he received a wonderful reception. Charles commended him on his good work in Ireland before the entire Privy Council. The Queen was gracious, and even the Earl of Holland was civil—surely Wentworth had Lucy to thank for these courtesies. He was particularly gratified by her own warm welcome. "My Lady of Carlisle never used me with so much respect," he wrote Wandesford.[15] At Hampton Court, where the King and Queen were in residence in June, Wentworth saw a good deal of the widowed Lady Carlisle. Later in the summer, when she was staying at Penshurst, he traveled down to Kent to see her. Then, after spending some weeks on his Yorkshire estates, he joined her at Nonsuch Palace. Lucy still enjoyed the use of the palace as she had when Carlisle was alive. To ensure this, in July the Queen had appointed Northumberland and Holland the keepers of Nonsuch during her own lifetime and that of Lady Carlisle.[16]

It was a glorious rendezvous, much of it spent galloping over the countryside in the golden English autumn. Both were enthusiastic equestrians. "Much in love I am with riding which this place is not improper for, having very good Downs," Lucy told Wentworth. For his part, gout made walking torture; the only way he could take exercise was on horseback. Returning from their rides, there were long conversations in their private apartments when her witty sallies would make him burst out laughing. To sweeten the occasion still further, Wentworth had brought her £3,500 out of her Irish profits. They seem to have had the palace to themselves—the Queen and her suite were at Hampton Court. Did they become lovers? Carlisle was gone and the circumstances were ideal for romance. Yet the chivalric tone of Wentworth's letters argues convincingly for a continuation of a platonic relationship. In any case, they delighted in each other's company. Two years later, Lucy was back at Nonsuch for the first time since they were there together. "I cannot like it so well as I then did," she wrote Wentworth.[17] Wentworth dallied at Nonsuch longer than he had intended. On October 25, Dorothy wrote Leicester that the Lord Deputy was leaving that week for Ireland; however, on November 10, he was "still thereabouts," and she was still waiting for Lucy.

The Lord Deputy went back to Ireland in mid-November, and Lucy arrived at Penshurst, followed by cartloads of baggage containing gowns and petticoats of velvet, satin, and silk, collars of the finest Brussels lace, silk ribbons for lacing bodices, a mink stole (called a tippet), fur muffs, leather gloves (short, midlength, and long), embroidered slippers, and a pair of wooden clogs for wet weather; one case was reserved for an array of face paint and powder. Lucy did not travel lightly. As always, she was full of herself, recounting all her triumphs to her sister. Dorothy was shown all the verses by the court poets extolling Lucy's beauty in her mourning garb. To Waller she was no less than "a Venus rising from a sea of jet." Robert Herrick waxed poetic about the black mourning twist around her arm. After a week of her company, Dorothy told Leicester that she found her sister "greater in her own conceit than ever she was, for her two gallants are more her slaves than I think ever men were to any woman." Dorothy was of course speaking of Holland and Wentworth. She had observed how the Lord Deputy was under Lucy's spell when he came to see her at Penshurst during the summer: "She has more power with him than any creature,"[18] Dorothy told Leicester. Holland was an abject slave. As well as these two, the Duke of Lennox, twelve years Lucy's junior, was so smitten with her that he was evading the King's orders to marry the young widow Mary Villiers Herbert, the daughter of the late Duke of Buckingham. Young Lennox's infatuation was much remarked upon in court circles. "It seems that his affections rather lead him towards the widowed Countess of Carlisle," the Venetian ambassador reported.[19]

"Her great fortune, the observations of powerful men and the flatteries of some mean ones doth make her less sufferable than ever she was," Dorothy complained to Leicester, her patience clearly running out. Indeed, the sisters were not getting along at all well. "It is impossible for me to stoop to her as I believe she expects," Dorothy wrote in exasperation. There can be little doubt that Dorothy was resentful of Lucy at this point in their lives. While she was having difficulty making ends meet, her wealthy sister's talk was all about jewelry purchases and the investments Wentworth was making for her. In a letter to her husband during Lucy's stay, Dorothy apologized for dwelling so long on "money discourses," remarking sarcastically that she had learned it from the rich among whom "it is the fashion." Not only was Dorothy more than a little jealous of Lucy's money, but she was also bitter because she felt her sister was not exercising her influence sufficiently on her family's behalf. "I believe she might do us many courtesies," Dorothy told Leicester, but she was not doing so.[20]

At the beginning of December the sisters had a great quarrel. It had been brewing since Lucy arrived. A small incident had been the last straw for Dorothy. Lucy showed off an expensive brooch that one of her admirers had given her. Dorothy's resentment welled up and she accused Lucy of neglecting her duty to the family. What good was her prominence at court if she did not use it to advance her own flesh and blood? She was giddy and selfish, Dorothy charged. Lucy responded with fury. What gave Dorothy the right to criticize her? Dorothy was sour, hard on her family, and always complaining. Robert was fortunate to have escaped from her bossiness. The upshot of this ugly quarrel was that Lucy announced she was leaving.

That Lady Carlisle was "ill-satisfied" with her sister reached the ears of Viscount Conway in London, who reported to Wentworth that "the carts were sent for to carry away her stuff." But while there was no tearful reconciliation, the sisters made up to some extent. The following week, Dorothy wrote Leicester that Lucy's "humour is a little amended" and she was not speaking of leaving any more.[21] However, added Dorothy sourly, her sister was not staying on out of any love for her. In mid-December the sisters were diverted from their quarreling by the pleasure of a four-day visit from their brother Algernon. At thirty-four he was greatly looked up to by his older sisters, not only because he was the head of their house but because his personality commanded respect. Northumberland was one of those people who are born old, just as Harry, the younger brother, with his combustible temper that earned him the nickname Hotspur after an impetuous ancestor, was an eternal adolescent. Carlisle had called Northumberland "one of the honestest, discreetist and ablest young lords about the court," and this was the general opinion.[22] He impressed everyone as "a wise and able man," though the great contemporary historian Lord Clarendon would say that Northumberland got his reputation for sagacity because he was wise enough to speak very little.

Dorothy enjoyed her brother's brief visit to the full. They were continually together so that she had no time even to write her weekly letter to her husband. But apart from this minor lapse, Dorothy was the most faithful of correspondents. For that reason she felt a burning resentment when she did not get any letters from Leicester. On December 19, she complained of receiving only one letter in six weeks, and she resented it as "a great unkindness." In a revealing sentence she wrote: "Quarrels of any sort are troublesome though they proceed from an abundant affection which you know by experience, for most of my exception to you has ever been on that subject." Within the next week two letters arrived, and Dorothy was in heaven: "Your letters did not only give me satisfaction in my exceptions, but delivered also such inexpressible contentments as nothing but seeing you can go beyond what I did enjoy." Then followed two weeks without a letter. "Your letters come so rarely to me," she wrote sadly, "that I begin to think myself faulty in writing so often." If it was his duties that kept him from writing she had no complaint, but if it was his "old inclination to reading" she would not forgive it. Her complaints continued throughout January 1637 although she acknowledged receipt of two letters and mentioned that there had been no post from France for two weeks.

On his side Leicester was also experiencing delays in the delivery of her letters, and he was understandably annoyed with Dorothy's harping on the subject. Apparently he let her know it. "Though you reproach me for chiding," she wrote in a happy mood after receiving three letters in a row, "I hope consideration of the cause shall free me from any further punishment than that gentle rebuke you have given me." The letter ended with a beautiful expression of her wifely devotion:

> It is suppertime or else I should bestow one side of this paper in making love to you; and since I may with modesty express it, I will say that if it be love to think on you sleeping and waking, to discourse of nothing with pleasure but what concerns you, to wish myself every hour with you and to pray for you with as much devotion as my own soul; then certainly it may be said that I am in love.[23]

Lucy had gone at the beginning of January, and with her the flow of visitors and daily news from the court. Despite everything, Dorothy missed her. "Since my sister left Penshurst I have been lonely as you can imagine." As it happened, Leicester could not imagine; in fact he was worried that his wife's falling-out with her influential sister could harm his chances of royal favor. Dorothy reassured him. She had no more cause to fear Lucy's ill offices than formerly. He should know that her sister was "not affectionate to me or mine." For all she knew, she told Leicester, she and Lucy were on the same terms as when he left England.[24]

Husband and wife were now engaged in a new project. The French were stalling on the treaty with England; there was talk that Leicester would be recalled. In that case he would need another appointment. The new plan was for him to succeed Wentworth as Lord Deputy of Ireland. Lucy had confided to Dorothy that Wentworth would not stay in Ireland longer than another year. Dorothy was dubious. With her own ears she had heard Wentworth tell her sister at Penshurst that the post was worth £22,000 a year to him. Her own good sense told her that "the Deputy finds so much sweetness in Ireland that he will not hastily leave it."[25] Nevertheless, it was a possibility worth pursuing. Not that Lucy would help, Dorothy told her husband. "She will do nothing for our good."

Although Leicester House was not finished—work was still in progress on the upper story—early in March 1637, Dorothy went to

London, taking Doll with her. Leicester had urged her to go, because he wanted to get her away from the loneliness of the countryside. And Dorothy felt that in London she could better promote her husband's interests with the King, while Doll would have a better chance to catch Lord Devonshire. Word that the Countess of Leicester was in residence at her fine new town house brought a flock of company. Despite the plague, which had flared up in the late winter, London was full of society because the royal family was at Whitehall. The Queen was about to give birth and planned to lie in as usual at St. James's Palace. Lucy was in town, attending diligently on the Queen, and was obviously glad to see her sister. Dorothy found her "very jolly," abusing most of her friends behind their backs, including the devoted Holland. He was more her slave than ever and had taken to writing poetry to her—"the worst that was ever seen," Dorothy told Leicester. In fact, Holland was making himself a laughingstock over Lucy. Lord Conway reported to Wentworth with amusement that "her Dog hath lately written a sonnet in her praise, which Harry Percy burnt, or you had now had it." It is unlikely that Wentworth was as amused as Conway. Both Harry and Lucy were regular dinner guests at Leicester House, drinking up the fine burgundy that Northumberland's butler had selected from the wine cellar. Dorothy found the two closer than she had ever seen them. Harry was paying court to his wealthy, childless sister so shamelessly that Dorothy said she could not do it "for the best reversion in England."[26]

Dorothy lost no time in going to court to pay her respects to the King. Charles was clearly eager to show her some special attention but seemed at a loss for something to say. At last he remarked that he thought her fatter than she used to be. "You must have been too kind to your husband when he was with you, and that was what kept you lean," he told Dorothy. Where Lucy would have laughed this off, Dorothy—a prim and proper country lady—blushed to the roots of her hair. Indeed, as she admitted to Leicester, she was "so extremely out of countenance that all the company laughed at me."

Though Charles's embarrassing kindness to her augured well for Leicester's future, Doll's future was less encouraging. Dorothy was incensed to learn from Lucy that Lady Devonshire had asked Holland to make an overture for her son to a French heiress. Not only would this end Dorothy's hopes for Doll, but she had also had the young Frenchwoman in mind for Philip, who was now a handsome boy of fifteen. Dorothy gave Leicester some shrewd advice on how to quash the French match for the Devonshires. He should let it be known in Paris that Lord Devonshire's income would be only £3,000 a year during his mother's lifetime and that the heiress was still a young woman.

While Dorothy was worrying about losing Devonshire, an offer came in for Doll from the Earl of Danby on behalf of John Lovelace, a baron. Two years earlier, this young noble had inherited an estate worth £7,000 a year. Dorothy responded with alacrity, assuring Danby that her daughter was "in no way engaged," and that if the young people liked each other, she would be happy for a match. In her husband's absence, her brother Northumberland would treat with Danby. In due course, the suitor presented himself at Leicester House. Good-looking and well-spoken, he made a favorable first impression on Dorothy. Although Lord Danby reported that the young man had liked Doll very well, they saw little more of him. But Dorothy heard plenty, and what she heard made her afraid to give Doll to him. From all accounts, she reported to Leicester, Lovelace was "idle, addicted to mean company, and easily drawn to debauchery." She wanted to end negotiations, but she had to make sure that "it appears to the world that we refused him."[27]

Meanwhile the Devonshire match was still alive—but barely. Holland was once again an enthusiastic matchmaker and had presented Lady Devonshire with a proposition from the Leicesters. When her answer came, Dorothy found it "full of civility, craft and coldness." She pretended that her son was at liberty to choose whom he pleased; but as everyone knew, sneered Dorothy, "he dares not eat or drink but as she appoints." Friends told her that he liked Doll but dared not show it, and that his mother purposely kept him away from London so that he would not see her. But the young man surprised Dorothy. Suddenly he turned up in town without his mother and visited Leicester House the very next day. A few days later, Doll was invited by his sister, her friend Anne Rich, who was married to Holland's nephew, to come to supper at Holland's lodgings at Whitehall. Devonshire was among the company, and after supper the party all went to see the Queen. After this, the whole town was talking of a marriage; Holland was confident that the Devonshires would make an address, Dorothy reported happily to her husband. Alas, the young lord vanished as quickly as he had appeared. Leicester House saw nothing more of him, and the match petered out.[28]

Dorothy stayed in London through April and May. We hear of her attending a sermon at Whitehall with her brothers. There were visits to Lady Essex and others who she hoped might help with her matchmaking. Leicester House was inundated with visitors, which led her to complain to her husband: "More company we have every day than I desire, and I think more than any other house in the town has, which is something chargeable to me but I do not know how to avoid it." The Queen had given birth to a daughter on March 17 and, after secluding herself for a month, was holding court again by Easter. Dorothy waited upon her frequently, and Henrietta Maria was charming to her. On one occasion the Queen was sitting on a low pallet, speaking so softly that Dorothy had to kneel to hear her. In this position the two women had a private chat for about a quarter of an hour, during which the Queen said many kind things about Leicester. The following day Lucy told her that the Queen had said the King was very satisfied with Lord Leicester.

Dorothy was delighted to report these expressions of royal favor to her husband, but she wondered why the King was most satisfied with him when the French treaty was going badly. Leicester might be deceived in believing the King really wanted the treaty concluded. It seemed to her that whenever Leicester made headway with the negotiations, the Secretary of State Sir John Coke criticized him for overstepping his instructions. Dorothy showed more astuteness in divining the King's intentions than his courtiers did. Although a draft treaty had been signed in February 1637, there was growing evidence that neither side was prepared to ratify it. As Dorothy suspected,

Leicester was engaged in yet another of King Charles's hopeless diplomatic missions.

She was now complaining a good deal to her husband about his extravagance. Money was in short supply at court, she wrote, and everyone, including her brothers, wondered why he could not live within his allowance. The ambassadors at this court lived far more modestly than he. No one except Sir John Finet, the Master of Ceremonies, ever had a meal at their expense. King Charles praised the foreign diplomats for this and certainly did not care how little Leicester spent on entertaining in France. Moreover, Dorothy was eager to pay back the £1,000 she had borrowed for him, as well as the loan for which her brother Algernon had stood guarantor. "The interest money doth undo us," she wrote with some asperity. Here was Dorothy at her most tactless, and touchy Leicester took umbrage. "I perceive my advice to thriftiness did not receive much welcome," she replied.[29] Dorothy's carping on his spending, albeit well merited, put a strain on the marriage, one that could not be resolved in the bedchamber.

In the middle of June, Dorothy left London with her unbetrothed daughter and returned to Penshurst, still "grieving" that "our poor Doll is sought by none."[30] Amid all the poetizing at the Caroline court, her matronly virtues did not go unsung. Of Lady Leicester, Edmund Waller wrote: "Nor call her mother, who so well does prove / One breast may hold both chastity and love." Such praise did not improve the poet's chances with "Sacharissa."

In July both Harry and Lucy visited Penshurst. They brought word that there might be a chance for Leicester to become Secretary of State. Gossip had it that Secretary Coke was getting tired and that his post might soon be vacant. Dorothy grasped at the idea. She detested Sir John Coke—the "old man," as she called him—because he would not allow Leicester's claims for extraordinary expenses. "It shall be part of my litany," she once told Holland, "to deliver all my friends from embassies till Secretary Coke be laid down in peace."[31] Harry claimed that he had laid the groundwork with the Queen, suggesting that she had more or less promised that Leicester would succeed Coke. (In his letters to his brother-in-law in Paris, Harry took all the credit so that Lucy's part remains obscure. Dorothy suspected that it had been minimal.) Success depended on keeping the plan secret, Harry explained. The King did not like such matters to proceed without his knowledge: "Nothing would destroy the design so much as that." The Queen would handle it in her own way at the proper moment. Harry returned to court, leaving a very hopeful sister at Penshurst.

Alas, in September Harry wrote that "Mercurius" (Dorothy's false friend Walter Montagu) had tattled to the King. "Our master loves not to hear other people give what is only fit for him," Harry wrote. Dorothy refused to give up. Convinced that the Queen could still bring her doting husband around, Dorothy drafted a letter to Henrietta Maria, setting out the case for Leicester in the strongest terms. She sent it to Harry to deliver. Her uncourtierlike language shocked Harry. "I would have had it changed to a more mild style, where there was such a difference of persons," he wrote his brother-in-law, but Dorothy would not change a word. Reluctantly, he brought the letter to the Queen, excusing his sister's presumption as the strong feelings of "a kind wife."[32]

LUCY A WEALTHY

WIDOW

DURING HIS VISIT to England in 1636, the Lord Deputy of Ireland commissioned the court painter Sir Anthony Van Dyck to paint two portraits of him in the black armor he wore for ceremonial occasions in Ireland, one full-length, the other three-quarter-length. The latter, which Wentworth referred to as "the short one," was for Lady Carlisle, and immediately on his return to Ireland he instructed his agent, William Railton, to have it carefully set in the frame he had chosen. It was to be left at Sir Anthony's until Railton knew where Lady Carlisle wanted it delivered. Lucy had promised to reciprocate with a Van Dyck portrait of herself, and Railton was told to make sure that her Ladyship's portrait would be shipped with the rest of his goods to Ireland.[1]

Of the numerous portraits Van Dyck painted of Lucy, the gift portrait for Wentworth is far and away the most beautiful. From her youthful appearance it was painted three or four years earlier, probably soon after Van Dyck came to England from the Netherlands in 1632. It is the portrait of a slim, graceful figure in a magnificent satin gown. The artist has caught the sex appeal of this woman who enslaved so many men. In his recent biography of Van Dyck, Robin

Blake perfectly describes the charm of the painting and its sitter: "Lady Carlisle draws aside a hanging to reveal the shadowed room within. Casting a glance towards the spectator and with arched eyebrows and a sly, sexy smile, she seductively invites you to follow her into the dark."[2] It is significant that it was this seductive portrait that Lucy chose to give to Wentworth.

Sometime after the exchange of portraits with Wentworth, Lucy posed with Dorothy for a double portrait by Van Dyck. Now at Sudeley Castle in Cheltenham, the painting shows the sisters seated in a garden. Lucy is elegantly gowned in silver-blue satin with bare shoulders; Dorothy is in a matronly brownish-purple gown, her shoulders covered by a stole. Lucy is pointing to a wall fountain from which water flows into a basin. This iconography is said to symbolize tears of grief at the absence of their husbands—in Dorothy's case, Leicester's long but temporary absence in France; in Lucy's, the finality of death. It has been suggested that Lady Carlisle commissioned the painting "in response to questions about the propriety of her relationship with Thomas Wentworth."[3] However, the fact that the painting was hung at Penshurst indicates that the commission came from Dorothy.[4]

In the double portrait, Dorothy is seen to have a long, thin face with a long, thin nose. Lucy looks little different than she does in the gift portrait for Wentworth. Van Dyck painted another portrait of Lucy that probably shows her as she actually looked around 1637. She is dressed in a rich burnt orange gown, with a fur tippet or stole; there is a hint of a double chin. But time was passing—she was thirty-eight, after all—and the portrait with the tippet was painted when she was already the Dowager Countess.

Where other women faded from view when their husbands died, Lucy enjoyed her greatest prestige in the years after Carlisle's death. Having fashioned herself into an independent courtier, she had avoided the pitfalls of widowhood. Her new inherited wealth and close friendships with the Earl of Holland and the Lord Deputy of Ireland enhanced her importance immeasurably. It did no harm also that Algernon, with whom she was very close, was playing an increasingly active role in court politics. Under the tenth Earl of Northumberland, all the stigma attached to the Percy name had been erased. The youthful earl was one of the greatest magnates in England and a foremost court lord. (His two portraits by Van Dyck permit us to see the aristocratic hauteur that so awed Northumberland's contemporaries.) To hear the Secretary of State Sir Francis Windebank thanking Northumberland for the privilege of delivering a letter to Lady Carlisle gives us an inkling of the status of the brother and sister. "I hold it a great honour vouchsafed me by your giving me that occasion to kiss her hands and to make profession of my devotions to your most noble house," he fawned. Bishop Brian Duppa, who became the Prince of Wales's tutor in 1637, later recalled Lady Carlisle as "a great lady waited on by all the great persons of the court."[5]

It was at this triumphant stage of her life that Sir Tobie Mathew wrote his famous "Character of the Countess of Carlisle." These "pictures drawn in black and white," as he liked to call them, were his claim to wit. Unfortunately, they evoked laughter more often at him than with him. While in Spain in 1623, he had "drawn" a picture of the Infanta—"the foolishest thing that ever you saw," Buckingham and Prince Charles had written King James. After finishing the Countess of Carlisle's character, he ventured one on Queen Henrietta Maria that was "held a ridiculous piece." His word picture of Lucy, however, was thought very clever and earned him a grudging place in Sir John Suckling's "A Session of the Poets":

> Toby Mathew (pox on't! how came he there?)
> Was busily whispering in some-body i th'ear
> When he had the honour to be named i' the Court.
> But sir, you may thank my Lady Carlisle for 't;
>
> For
> Had not her Character furnished you out
> With something of handsome, without all doubt
> You and your sorry lady these had been
> In the number of those that were not to come in.

Knowing that the Lord Deputy liked to see the latest satires and verses, the Reverend George Garrard sent him a copy.[6] Wentworth would not have been pleased to see his admired friend described as a "sorry lady." Suckling was unique among the court poets in disparaging Lady Carlisle.

No one knew the Countess of Carlisle better than Sir Tobie. She was his patroness and, after the Earl of Portland's death in 1633, his protector. Tobie Mathew was a man who needed protection at the English court. In the first place, he was a Jesuit, some said a priest, in a country where such were banned. More than that, his effeminate manner made him a figure of amusement to some. Others, like Suckling, were openly disdainful of him. Now in his sixties, Sir Tobie found a safe harbor with Lucy. He was never far from her side—dining, supping, beaming at her witticisms, and tendering his own. Everyone knew where to find him. "You may hear of Sir Tobie Mathew at my Lady of Carlisle's," Leicester informed Hawkins in a postscript.

It has been suggested that the Countess of Carlisle was seeking to form a rival salon to the Queen's at her house in the Strand.[7] There is no foundation for this supposition. In the first place, Lucy, like her brother Harry and her cousin Holland, was a member of the Queen's set, barring those periods when Lady Denbigh was in the ascendancy, at which time Lucy, in her excessive pride, withdrew from the Queen's court. Moreover, to tempt the courtiers away from Henrietta Maria, Lucy would have had to provide the kind of entertainment she herself despised. Queen Henrietta Maria was even more in love with masquing than her mother-in-law had been, and, encouraged by the King, she always had a masque in progress. For her part, Lucy had disliked masquing since her humiliating experience as a bride, when King James and Queen Anne had forbidden her to stage the masque of the Amazons. Nevertheless, while the Cavalier poets who buzzed around the Queen Bee were not habitués of Lady Carlisle's gatherings in the Strand, they nevertheless lavished almost as much praise upon her as they did upon the Queen. Rather than competing with the Queen, Lucy's gatherings may be said to have been the anteroom to Henrietta Maria's salon for aspiring dramatists and poets. A well-phrased tribute to Lady Carlisle could have served as a letter of recommendation to the royal patron.

Waller, Carew, Sir William Davenant, and lesser poets such as William Habington all paid tribute to Lucy's beauty and charm, but a college don and occasional playwright named William Cartwright extolled her intelligence and influence as well in his "Panegyric to the Countess of Carlisle":

> You appear a Court, and are no less
> Than a whole Presence, or throng'd glorious Press;
> No one can ere mistake you. 'Tis alone
> Your lot, where e'r you come to be still known.
> Your Power's its own Witness: you appear
> By some new Conquest, still that you are There.

That the poet most in vogue in Paris found his way to Lady Carlisle's house in the Strand on a visit to London is not surprising. Vincent Voiture, worldly and charming, was the lion of the leading Parisian salon of the day, that of the Marquise de Rambouillet. Though he found Lady Carlisle to be as beautiful as he had heard, the celebrated French poet detected an underlying "poison" in her charms, and did not hesitate to say so in a poem. Lucy also made less than a good impression on another French visitor, this one a politician, the Comte de Brienne, who conceded her beauty but was not impressed with her intelligence. In this light, Lucy may not have measured up to the standards set by the "bluestocking" Madame de Rambouillet.[8]

But it was not poets who dominated Lucy's gatherings. Since her first emergence at court, she had sought out the power brokers. The talk at her salon was of court politics. (Had this subject not always fascinated her?) While Lucy expressed her opinion of people often unkindly (apparently uncowed by the disgrace she had brought upon herself by her disparagement of Châteauneuf), she added little to the substance of the important discussions, according to Tobie Mathew. She was wise enough to know her limitations.

Not only was Sir Tobie the majordomo of her salon, but he was also her jester, as the following story (related by Conway to Went-worth) illustrates. One day Sir Tobie was expatiating on the delicious-ness of a cup of chocolate. Imported from the Spanish overseas dominions, chocolate was as yet almost unknown in England, but Sir Tobie had often enjoyed it during his travels in Spain. After hearing him praise the strange concoction, Lady Carlisle expressed the desire to taste it. Shortly afterward, he arrived at her chamber with some chocolate and with much bustle made up a cupful. He poured out half for himself, drank it, and then (Conway chuckled) "liked it so well that he drank up the rest," and Lady Carlisle "had no share but in the laughter."[9]

The "Character of the Countess of Carlisle," which passed around the court in manuscript, made him her laureate as well.[10] But it was a panegyric only on the surface. Those who read it carefully would have seen that Tobie Mathew was slyly getting back at his pa-tron for her laughter when he drank all the chocolate, for all the times she cut him with her rapier wit, for the "prithee, Sir Tobie do this and Sir Tobie do that." It is the picture of a powerful courtier through the eyes of a hanger-on. Years of attendance on her had taught him what lay under Lady Carlisle's famous civility. He was ob-viously speaking from experience when he described her as an un-grateful friend. She would give you a gracious reception one day and scorn you the next. Her very occasional acts of gratitude were no more than "cold charity." Those near her were taken for granted, and she would do more for total strangers. (How this must have rankled, for he calls it "her greatest injustice.") In short, the more you obliged her, the less she valued you. But the subtle Sir Tobie was a master of euphemism and equivoque. "She has as much Sense and Gratitude for the actions of friendship, as so extreme a Beauty will give her leave to entertain." And again, "She is of too high a mind and dignity, not only to seek, but almost to wish, the friendship of any Creature."

Despite suave reference to her "unnumbered perfections," the character portrays Lady Carlisle as self-centered, vain, and lacking in tenderness. Cold and passionless, she could not love anyone. (Sir Tobie's equivoque: "She hath too great a heart to have naturally any strong inclination to others.") Choleric by nature, she controlled herself, not out of concern for those around her but because a show of temper was beneath her dignity. She was merciless in her satire, "discovering that which we strive most to conceal, our imperfections and errors." Because of her egotism, her conversation went "by way of compulsion towards herself." Mathew confirmed that she was of "a cheerful nature." According to him, she had been told by her physicians that she was inclined to be melancholy. "This opinion of theirs," he wrote, "proved to be the best remedy for it, by the mirth which she expressed at it." She could suffer no condition but "plenty and glory," failing which she would retire out of sight. Her ambition was strong but undirected, because there was nothing left for her to desire. If Sir Tobie's character of Henrietta Maria was in the same vein, no wonder the Queen called it "an ungentil libel."

Reading this character analysis of Lucy, we begin to better understand Dorothy's complaints about her. Yet offsetting Lucy's self-centeredness that her sister so disliked was her strong family feeling. She "extremely loves" her brothers and sister, Mathew wrote, mainly because the same blood ran in their veins as in hers. For that reason, she also loved their children; but she cared little for more distant relatives because they had too little common heredity with her to share in her excellencies.

The fact that Lucy did not quash the "Character" (at the end of her life she allowed it to be published) indicates that she saw in it only what she wanted to see: she was without equal in beauty and wit, that "the Majesty of her person teaches Reverence," "she hath a grace and facility in her expressions . . . that refines the Language," and all the other outrageous compliments by which Sir Tobie disguised his criticism.

A side of Lucy that did not appear in the character was her stinginess. In contrast to the prodigality that marked her life with Carlisle, Lucy lived "thriftily" in her widowhood, according to her sister. Having inherited a fortune, she was very cautious about spending it. "I learn frugality from those that are rich and have none to care for,"[11]

Dorothy remarked snidely to Leicester, apparently as disapproving of her sister's thriftiness as of her husband's extravagance. The only thing on which Lucy spent lavishly was jewelry, and that was an investment as well as an adornment. She saved money wherever possible. In February 1637, while Dorothy was still in the country, she was put out to hear that Lucy was stabling her horses and keeping her servants at Leicester House without even asking her. Indeed, both Lucy and Harry used Leicester House as an inn in Dorothy's absence. But Dorothy did Lucy an injustice when she told Leicester that her wealthy sister "gives nothing that I hear of," because a month later, in April 1637, Lucy made her a most generous gift of £500 out of her profit from the Irish wine customs.[12]

Apart from a pension of £2,000 a year, Lucy's principal income came from the Irish grants she had inherited from her husband. Although a widow (a feme sole, in legal terminology) could administer her own estate technically, it was customary for her male relatives to act as her trustees. In accordance with Lucy's wishes, Lord Wentworth became her trustee along with her two brothers.[13] Wentworth managed her Irish interests and acted as her financial adviser. Much of his correspondence with her, although couched in gallant terms, was really about money.

Lucy's Irish wine customs grant dated back to the previous reign. King James had prodigally granted away from the Crown its traditional revenue from customs duties—"farming out" the customs, as it was called. In return, the customs farmers paid the King an annual rent or a percentage of the profits. James had farmed out all the customs duties on goods imported into Ireland and had assigned the wine duties from the Irish farm to the Earl of Carlisle. This was just part of the generous patronage James had given his old favorite. As well, Carlisle had been granted the profitable licensing of wine and aqua vitae in Ireland. The wine customs grant and the licensing of beverages had all passed to Lucy on his death.

In addition, Carlisle had bequeathed her his lands in County Wicklow, known as the Birnes Country. A large strip of land along the east coast not far from Dublin, the Birnes Country included the manor of Newcastle and comprised some eighty thousand acres, of which the arable land was worked by freeholders. Carlisle had purchased the manor and received a patent for the rest shortly after Charles ascended the throne. Subsequently, the patent was rescinded and only later partly restored. Since then, Irish officials had been making difficulties about "finding" the title to the land. (This was a standard tactic to wear down the patentee so that he would relinquish his claim to the officials at well below value.) Establishing title to the Birnes Country, Wentworth told Lucy, "had troubled my Lord all his life and holds the same for us after his death."[14] Wentworth had urged Carlisle to sell his grant to the Crown, and just before his death Carlisle had agreed to do so for £15,000. Nevertheless, he died without surrendering the grant, and it turned out that he had assigned his interest in the Birnes Country to his kinsmen, Sir James Hay and Archibald Hay, to whom he was deeply in debt. Lucy's trustees now found themselves engaged in a wrangle with the Hays; but in the meantime she was receiving a very nice income from the encumbered lands.

From the moment Lucy came into possession of her inheritance, Wentworth strongly advised her to give up her Irish grants, promising that with the money he would buy her new land. In taking this position he had a double purpose; as he told his friend Archbishop Laud, he wanted to fetch the grants back to the Crown and also to serve her Ladyship.[15]

After Charles dissolved the parliament of 1629, he had to find his revenues in other ways. Wentworth had dedicated himself to putting the shaky royal finances on a firm foundation, and to this end he was trying to restore to the Crown all the lucrative sources of income James and Charles had granted away. Since coming to Ireland he had bought in most of the Irish farm for the King. This was noble enough in purpose to suit even the righteous, unvenal Archbishop Laud. But what was little known was that the Lord Deputy had secured a quarter interest for himself in the customs farm.[16] For, admittedly, he had a third purpose: to enrich himself during his office in Ireland. Happily for King Charles, Wentworth's private purpose was not incompatible with serving the royal interest. As between Lucy and the King, Wentworth maintained a delicate balancing act. But the truth was that his dual role as Lady Carlisle's trustee and the King's agent put him in a conflict of interest.

During Wentworth's visit to England in 1636, he had talked to Lucy about surrendering the wine customs grant. She was not averse if he could find her other investments yielding an equal revenue. Her other caveat was that he should not go ahead with the sale unless she was satisfied. Wentworth thought he had her convinced; but when he returned to Ireland she had second thoughts. She sweetly informed him that certain people were telling her that the grant was worth more than Wentworth said and that he was advising her to sell it too cheaply. According to these unnamed persons, her grant was worth £20,000, and they were even suggesting that the Lord Deputy was not giving her all her profits from the customs, which, they said, should amount to £2,000 a year. Wentworth was outraged at this attempt to discredit him in Lucy's eyes. On December 12, he wrote her an agitated letter. Where did "these gentlemen" get the figure of £2,000 per annum? For the past thirteen years the profit had never exceeded £1,000 to £1,300 a year; he sent her a certification from the customs officers to prove it. As for their total value of £20,000, her brother the Earl of Northumberland, as one of her trustees, should demand "to hear the reasons of those who value it so highly." Suspecting that it was the Hays, Wentworth explained to Lucy how it was to their advantage if she kept the grant. They could make a claim for payment of her late husband's debts against her profits from the wine customs. And if she died before the term of the lease expired, they could recover their money from her executors. "As long as you keep this lease there is hope for your creditors," he told her bluntly.[17]

Though he may have undervalued the grant in the King's interest, he was quickly proven right about the Hays. In March 1637, they petitioned the Lord Treasurer for payment of their loans out of the money Lucy received from the wine customs. It seemed that Carlisle had also assigned his share of the customs to his creditor cousins. The Lord Treasurer granted them a warrant, but the customs farmers refused to pay, saying that the late earl had given assignments to a number of other creditors who were clamoring to be paid out of the customs.[18] So far the Hays were blocked, but their continuing attempts on her income from the wine customs made Lucy more amenable to surrendering the grant. On April 28, Northumberland wrote Wentworth that he had spoken with his sister about parting with her Irish customs. Although some people were telling her the price was too low, she was "resolved to be governed by your Lordship." However, canny Lucy was not ready to let the wine customs go at any price Wentworth might set. "She believes," continued Northumberland, "that if she part with them under eight years' purchase [a price equal to eight years' income], she lets them go at a much under-value." As far as he was concerned, he would be very glad if she were "well rid of them, and that the money were employed as your Lordship proposed." Wentworth replied that he would do his utmost for Lucy's profit, both in drawing up the contract with the Crown and in putting her money in land. He assured Northumberland that he would "never give my consent that my Ladyship part with her interest till my conscience be satisfied the offer be brought up to the very uttermost value," but he asserted that eight years' purchase was too high. Moreover, the buyer (the King) was not eager. It would seem that Wentworth was weighting the balance in favor of the King in these negotiations, a suspicion strengthed by his telling Secretary of State Coke that Lady Carlisle's wine customs grant could be bought in for seven years' purchase.[19]

The same underlying conflict of interest cropped up in the matter of Lucy's landholdings. Wentworth was trying to convince her that her best course was to sell the Birnes lands to the Crown. In an alarmist letter dated April 17, he outlined the difficulty he was having in settling "the Birnes business." Although they both knew that her late husband had intended the money to go to her, the "plain truth" was that there was a defect in the grant, and, worse than that, the estate clearly belonged to the new earl as the heir at common law. This could bring in question the sizable payments already made to her. However, he could reassure her in one respect. Even if her stepson discovered that the

Birnes Country was his by right, he would never be able to secure title "without me." Moreover, if the land reverted to the Crown, the Hays and the other creditors "will be turned to grass," which he imagined would not make her sorry. Knowing Lucy's indiscretion, Wentworth cautioned her not once but twice to keep this information to herself. In raising the defect as a reason for disposing of the grant, Wentworth was not being candid with Lucy. He had used the same argument to talk Carlisle into selling. He had known for years that the title to the land could be "found," or proved, at any time.[20]

By the end of 1637, Wentworth, with Lucy's approval, had struck a bargain with King Charles to buy back the wine customs grant for the Crown. On December 1, Charles issued an order to the Lord Deputy "to pay the Dowager Countess of Carlisle £16,000 in compensation for the surrender of her share in the profits of the wine impost in Ireland."[21] Nevertheless, the transaction did not go through at this time. Northumberland may have been the stumbling block, because six months later Wentworth was urging Lucy not to let her brother "depart from the conditions or break off the bargain."[22] As it turned out, the delay in consummating the sale was very much to Lucy's advantage. Receipts from the Irish customs were rising spectacularly, thanks to the increase in trade owing to Wentworth's efficient administration of the economy. In 1638 Lucy's profit from the wine customs was £5,000—a hefty increase over what she had formerly received.[23]

Meanwhile Wentworth was looking for land to buy for her with the proceeds from a sale of the Irish wine customs—and getting in a lot of trouble for it. As he ruefully told Archbishop Laud, people thought he was buying land for himself, and it was "raising one great dust about me." No Lord Deputy of Ireland had ever had more enemies than Thomas Wentworth. His fearless and high-handed methods had deprived many great persons of their spoils, and, at the same time, rumor had it that he was lining his own pockets. Now his "calumniators" were trying to turn the King against him, he told Laud, by claiming that "I purchase all before me."[24] Despite his injured tone, Wentworth was indeed acquiring land for himself through purchase and grant; he had just bought ten thousand acres in Cosha near the Birnes Country, a rough, wooded terrain where he built himself a hunting lodge that he named Fairwood.[25]

He went there often for relaxation, and many of his letters to Lucy were written from Fairwood Park at Cosha. Recalling the wonderful days when they rode over the downs together at Nonsuch, he dreamed of having her visit him. Cosha, he wrote her in the summer of 1638, was "a wild and melancholy place," but her conversation would render it as pleasant and healthy a situation as any he had ever seen—"I mean for two or three months in the summer." The woods and rocks of Cosha evoked the romantic in Wentworth. His most high-flown sentiments were written to Lucy from there. With his wife and children in Dublin, his thoughts dwelled on Lucy. Indeed, he projected them onto the very place itself. "So long as I am here," he once wrote her, "even these barbarous rocks, mountains, and habitations are able to think as much honour of your Ladyship as the fairest pastures, deepest meadows, and most frequented cities of the world."[26]

While Wentworth could only dream of Lucy's charming presence, his archenemy Holland was with her every day. The two men had detested each other for years, and now they were rivals over Lucy. She wanted to bring them together, and to please her, Holland wrote a conciliatory letter to Wentworth in September 1637. But their mutual devotion to "that excellent person" was not sufficient to turn them into friends. Conway confided to Wentworth that Holland was no more his friend than in the past, but requested him not to tell Lady Carlisle that he had said so.[27]

Lucy's continuing influence over Holland was legendary at court. Among his patronage appointments, Holland was Chief Justice in Eyre; this gave him power to levy fines on landowners who he determined were making illegal use of the royal forests. The revival of this obsolete statute was not working out too well, according to Conway: "This business of the forests is getting Holland many enemies and little money for the King," he wrote Wentworth. In 1637 Holland levied a huge fine of £20,000 on the Earl of Salisbury. This was as much as it cost Salisbury to maintain his opulent lifestyle for several years, and it led to a great quarrel between the two nobles. To resolve the matter to his father-in-law's satisfaction, Northumberland got Lucy to speak to Holland. Since "her dog" could refuse her nothing, the fine against Salisbury was remitted.[28]

Indeed, Lucy was such a mover and shaker at court that even Archbishop Laud acknowledged that he was "beholden to her." As the enemy par excellence of the papists who surrounded the Queen, Laud was persona non grata with Henrietta Maria. Nevertheless, disturbed by the number of conversions to Roman Catholicism among the aristocracy in the autumn of 1637, he felt he had to speak to the Queen. Despite the King's assurance that he would find her "very reasonable," the Archbishop was sure he would not get a favorable hearing unless Lady Carlisle smoothed the way for him. So he asked the Lord Deputy if he thought her Ladyship would help him. Wentworth replied that he was confident she would, if it lay in her power. And he gave his friend his assessment of Lucy. "I judge her Ladyship very considerable," he wrote Laud, "for she is often in place, and is extremely well skilled to speak with advantage and spirit for those friends she professeth unto, which will not be many."[29]

Wentworth knew whereof he spoke. Lucy expended her influence and powers of persuasion on his behalf as she had for no one else, and he turned to her repeatedly. For instance, when he refused to give captaincies in the Irish horse troops to Henrietta Maria's favorites, he looked to Lucy to handle the strong-willed Queen. (Wentworth bitterly resented Henrietta Maria's "meddling" in Irish appointments— she should leave such matters to the King and himself, he told Lucy.)[30] Lucy was his goodwill ambassador at the English court. His letters to her are full of gratitude for all she was doing for him.

eleven

FAMILY AFFAIRS

ON DECEMBER 6, 1637, Lady Northumberland, not yet thirty, lay on her deathbed at Syon House, her blond hair fanned out on the pillow, her lovely face covered with the pustules and craters of small-pox. She had had the last rites that morning. In a far corner of the room, Sir Theodore Mayerne and Dr. Matthew Lister were holding a consultation. With a sinking heart, Lord Northumberland observed them shaking their heads. As he held his wife's cold hand, it took a supreme effort of will to contain the tears welling up in his eyes. His beloved Anne, whom he had married for love against his father's wishes, was being taken from him. At the foot of the bed stood her father. Lord Salisbury made no attempt to control his grief but wept audibly. A shudder agitated the delicate frame on the bed, then the dreaded sound, and Anne was gone. The Reverend George Garrard led the bereaved husband from the room.

As soon as Dorothy heard the news, she rushed to Syon House to comfort her brother. The Earl of Northumberland gave way to his grief in a manner that surprised Garrard, who, together with Lord Conway, never left his side. "Passion hath the least outward power [over him] of any man I know," Garrard wrote Wentworth, "yet in this it had got on him a great mastery." While Northumberland had followed his father's advice to the letter and governed his wife and family with great strictness ("No man was more absolutely obeyed" in his household than he was, according to a contemporary), the death of his wife left him utterly devastated. Dorothy was not surprised. She once told Leicester that, despite a coldness in her brother's manner, "there is more truth and fidelity in him than in a thousand Hollands and as many Henry Percies." The dead woman's grief-stricken father, the Earl of Salisbury, kept repeating over and over that he wanted to die himself.

The two earls, however, were at odds on the type of funeral for their dear Anne. Northumberland wanted an expensive funeral with all the trappings, but Salisbury was against it. So the body was embalmed and sent by barge to Petworth, where it was interred in the Percy crypt. After the funeral, Northumberland went to London to stay with Lucy. She would cheer him up more than Dorothy could.[1]

Lucy had recently moved into Salisbury House, one of the stately mansions on the Strand whose gardens ran down to the Thames. Salisbury House had been built by the present earl's father in 1602, when he was Queen Elizabeth's principal minister. But times had changed, and most of the great houses on the Strand had been broken up into apartments. The Cecil mansion had been divided into Great Salisbury House and Little Salisbury House; Lucy rented the latter. The Percys and the Cecils were united not only through marriages but also through Lucy's friendships with the Cecil ladies. If Lucy could be said to have any close female friend, it was Elizabeth Howard (née Cecil), Countess of Berkshire. Dorothy was a little jealous of Lady Berkshire, although she pretended otherwise, for Lucy spent a good deal of time at Charlton, the Berkshires' country house in Wiltshire, and was virtually a member of the family. In April 1637, when the eldest son married a Roman Catholic and the parents were "in great affliction," Lucy was there with the Cecil ladies, "all highly incensed against the young lord."[2]

There was "much ado about Papists" both at court and in the country. A papal legate named George Con had come to England from the Vatican in the autumn of 1636. Exuding suavity and charm, he had made himself the darling of society. The Queen adored him, and he was received in the finest houses. Of course, he knew enough to become an admirer of the Countess of Carlisle, and, being in fashion, he qualified for her friendship. They were seen together frequently. She brought him to dine at Leicester House with Dorothy. His success in making converts among the ladies had earned him a very bad name among the Puritan-minded nobility. The King was greatly opposed to these society conversions, as was Laud, who hated the papists every bit as much as he hated the Puritans. Because she defended Con in conversation, Lucy was accused of being a papist by some. But, as Con told Cardinal Barberini, there was nothing to it because "Lady Carlisle has no religion but her own complexion."[3] Sir Tobie Mathew also disagreed with those who said she was likely to change her religion, because that would be admitting she had formerly lived in ignorance.

Much of the hysteria about popery was generated by fear that Archbishop Laud was leading England back to Rome. Had his critics been able to read his diary they would have known that nothing would have been more hateful to him. Nevertheless, it was true that Laud loved the ceremonial ways of the Old Faith, as was evident in his "innovations," such as a railed-off communion table, kneeling and genuflections by the laity, and clergy in rich, embroidered copes. Moreover, under Laud's High Church doctrines, the episcopacy, like the Catholic bishops, claimed to hold their miters in apostolic succession, while the only authority the Puritans recognized was the Scriptures.

Although resentment of the Laudian church merely simmered in England, Charles's attempt to foist it upon Presbyterian Scotland caused an explosion. The spark that set it off was King Charles's order to the Scottish bishops to use a revised form of the English Book of Common Prayer. The new prayer book promulgated all Laud's innovations in ceremony and vestments, and these were anathema to a people who followed the severe Calvinism adopted by John Knox in the sixteenth century. Moreover, the Scots generally regarded the bishops imposed on them by King Charles as the instrument of English domination. The Presbyterian church, the Kirk, sought to replace the official Episcopal church in Scotland with its own system of governance by assemblies of elders, or presbyters, chosen by the people.

In July 1637, when Laud's new Book of Common Prayer, with its "Catholic" liturgy, was read out in Edinburgh Cathedral, the people rioted. The dean was pelted with sticks and stones and the bishop's robe was torn to shreds before he could escape the crowd. The same outcry greeted its reading in all the Scottish churches.

Strange to say, the riot in Scotland over the Book of Common Prayer was almost completely ignored in England. A lawyer named Edward Hyde, later to be the Earl of Clarendon and the historian of the Rebellion and the Civil Wars in England, marveled at the lack of interest. Although the whole kingdom avidly read about events in Germany or Poland in the "corantos" or gazettes, hardly a word about Scotland appeared in the weekly newsletters sent to paying customers abroad or in the provinces. Neither was it discussed at the Privy Council. The King referred the whole matter to the Marquess of Hamilton, whose qualifications for bringing an end to the civil disorder rested on his being Scotland's greatest landlord, albeit an absentee one.

By the winter of 1638, however, discontent in Scotland had turned into a rebellion. Almost unanimously, the Scottish people had signed a National Covenant abolishing the episcopate and rejecting all the innovations introduced in Laud's prayer book. The bishops were afraid for their lives. Recalling his father's saying "No bishops, no king," Charles faced up to the inevitable war. As a first step, he put his council in the picture. No one at court could now claim ignorance; nevertheless, the lack of concern continued, courtiers preferring to pursue their usual scramble for patronage.

The Scottish troubles did not yet impinge on Lucy's life. Of greater interest to her was the arrival in May 1638 of the Duchesse de Chevreuse. Marie de Chevreuse never traveled simply for pleasure, and the nature of her business was soon an open secret. A leader of the French nobility that opposed Cardinal Richelieu, she was in the pay of Spain and, in fact, came to England directly from that country. She brought with her the tentative project of a marriage between the King of Spain's son and Princess Mary, the King of England's eldest daughter, then seven years of age.[4]

The prospect of a Spanish match appealed to Charles as much as it had to his father, especially under the present circumstances, when he might need Spanish gold to wage war against his disobedient Scottish subjects. For this reason, Madame de Chevreuse was shown every courtesy. Although the wife of the French ambassador stood in Henrietta Maria's presence, Madame de Chevreuse was given a tabouret, or little stool, to sit on as if she were a visiting queen. Trying to explain "the matter of the tabouret" to Richelieu's satisfaction kept the Earl of Leicester busy for months at Paris.[5]

His diplomacy was further put to the test by the presence in England of Marie de Medici, Henrietta Maria's mother. Following a failed coup against Richelieu in 1630, she had been exiled from France by her son, Louis XIII. She had spent most of her exile as a discontented and unwanted guest of the Spanish governor at Brussels. Having worn out her welcome in the Spanish Netherlands, she and her bedraggled courtiers had moved on to The Hague and from there to England. Charles could hardly turn away his wife's mother, who was nothing more than a refugee in reality. Her presence in England, however, further complicated Anglo-French relations. The Queen Mother and the Duchesse de Chevreuse, despite a common enemy in Richelieu, were constantly conniving against each other, disproving the maxim that politics make bedfellows, strange or otherwise.

Actually, as all the court knew, the French duchess had found a most congenial bedfellow. Being a lady who could not go to bed alone (Cardinal de Retz said of her that she had to love someone), Madame de Chevreuse had immediately taken up with her former lover the Earl of Holland. Surprisingly, their flagrant affair did not evoke Henrietta Maria's famous scowl that could empty a room. The gay little queen, older and more sophisticated now, no longer expected her dashing favorites, men like Holland and Henry Percy, to be monogamous or celibate. As with the ideal of chivalric love in the medieval courts, platonic love at the court of Charles I was honored more in the breach than in reality. This was reflected in court poets such as Suckling, Thomas Carew, and Sir Richard Lovelace, in whose love poems sexual innuendo lay barely hidden under the high-flying, saccharine sentiment.

To Dorothy, Lucy made fun of the Duchess's love of intrigue, but she listened enthralled to her tales of the dangerous liaisons, secret negotiations, and derring-do that filled Marie's life. For her part, the French duchess was charmed with Lady Carlisle. In fact, Holland was quite put out to find his lady friends preferring each other's company to his. From Marie, Lucy heard the inside story of the downfall of the Marquis de Châteauneuf, the French ambassador who had almost ruined her career at court. For her own purposes, Madame de Chevreuse had inspired "a fatal passion" in the dignified diplomat. Mad about his temptress, he had joined her cabal against Richelieu. The Cardinal had discovered his treachery and imprisoned him in the fortress at Angoulême, where he languished for years.[6] With such delicious news from abroad, Lucy gave little thought to the Scottish threat on England's doorstep.

Family aggrandizement and court rivalries continued to occupy her mind. The Percy family had received great honor with Northumberland's appointment as Lord High Admiral in March 1638. Since Buckingham's death, the Admiralty had been in commission (administered by a committee), and the King simply appointed an admiral of the fleet each summer; Northumberland himself had been put in command for the past two summers. Holland had been angling for the permanent post for a decade, and when he lost out he was furious. With tongue in cheek, Conway reported to Wentworth that Holland had gone off in a huff to his estate at Kensington, called a council of his petticoat cabinet, and put the question: Should he bear his disappointment patiently or publish his resentments? With his habitual contempt for Holland, Wentworth replied that this dashing of his hopes should give the Earl more leisure to write a Character and to visit Madame de Chevreuse. The Queen and Lady Carlisle were also making great sport over poor Holland's disappointment.[7]

Actually, Northumberland was a very poor choice. Since his wife's death he had been sick most of the time, and by midsummer he had still not taken out the fleet.

Lucy's financial affairs also claimed her attention far more than the rebellion in Scotland. The sale of her Irish wine customs was still not through by the summer of 1638, despite Wentworth's eagerness to have it done with. However, at the beginning of June, Lucy finally surrendered her patent to the Birnes Country to the Crown, as Wentworth had been urging. The price, £15,000, was "really and bonafide paid,"[8] but Lucy may have had to share it with her stepson, for a later survey indicated that the land was conveyed by the second Earl of Carlisle, his wife, the Dowager Countess (Lucy), and the trustees. In any event, Lucy received at least £8,000 "down upon the nail," to use Wentworth's expression. Although he was acting as her trustee, the money appeared to be for him. He remarked sarcastically to King Charles that this would give "those noble friends I have near Your Majesty" the opportunity to "report me for a mighty good man, that is, in the phrase of the City, for a mighty rich man."[9] In fact, the honest broker was well rewarded. From his recovered Irish lands, Charles granted Wentworth the choice parts: the manor of Newcastle and a newly created manor of Wicklow, both yielding a good rent. Nevertheless, Wentworth had still made a good bargain for the Crown, and he pressed on with his plan to redeem the Carlisle grants. He advised Charles to buy out the second earl's interest in the West Indies, "as not indeed fit to rest in the hands of any subject."[10]

As he had promised her, Wentworth purchased other land for Lucy with the money realized from the Birnes Country sale. In County Monaghan in Ulster, he bought her the leases for the lands of Upper Trough and Glaslough from Sir Robert Parkhurst, a London alderman with considerable Irish holdings. To hold the leases in trust for Lucy, he put them in the names of two of his reliable underlings, Captain William Billingsley and Sir Philip Percival, clerk of the Irish Court of Wards and Liveries. He also took a twenty-two-year lease for her, in Percival's name, of Shillelagh in County Wicklow, which abutted his own property of Cosha.[11]

The Shillelagh lease, purchased with £4,000 of Lucy's money, is a striking illustration of the legal nonentity of women, and their help-less reliance on the good faith of their male trustees. Though en-dorsed "a copy of my Lady Carlisle's lease," the document on its face states that Sir Philip Percival bought the lease from one Calcott Chambre. There is no mention that Percival is holding the lease in trust for Lady Carlisle. Moreover, she did not get physical possession of the document. No wonder she was to have great difficulty estab-lishing her right to Shillelagh in years to come.

Having made these land purchases for her, Wentworth wrote Lucy at the end of July 1638 that it was an "absolute necessity" that she name her heirs. Only she knew for whom she intended her lands in the event of her death. Was it "my Lord Admiral, Mr. Percy, or my Lady of Leicester?" Cagey about her wealth, Lucy refused to make her intentions clear. Simply convey the land to me and my heirs with-out naming any other person, she instructed Wentworth. That "will give me a power of disposing of it as I please and tis that I wish, not being willing to tie myself any way." That would keep Harry attentive and Dorothy hospitable! Wentworth replied that her wishes would be "perfectly obeyed in the estating of your lands."[12]

WHILE LUCY WAS RIDING over the downs at Nonsuch and Al-gernon was convalescing at Petworth or Syon, Dorothy was spending her summer at Penshurst, weighed down with her customary respon-sibilities. Repairs had to be made on the estate—some of the cot-tages were "near falling down," she told Leicester—and many things had to be done about the house. All this cost money, and Leicester's out-of-line expenses were swallowing up the rents. Moreover, noth-ing had come in of the £900 due from the Norfolk lands that Leices-ter had inherited in 1637 from a distant relative. Absence had not made Dorothy and Robert fonder. In fact, their loving relationship had been eroding over the two years they had been apart. Dorothy's criticism of his spending and her well-meant advice on just about everything had antagonized Leicester to the point that in late 1638 he wrote her flatly "not to trouble herself with anything that concerned him." As if this were possible with the family finances and the administration of the estate all on her shoulders! In reply to his "unkind expression" Dorothy wrote:

> Though you are pleased to give me much of your affection and to desire mine, yet will you not allow me the liberty of a friend, which I am sure may be prejudicial to you, but if you have me to say nothing but what I am sure agrees with your humour, I can conform myself to it; and had I not an extraordinary passion for you, I should have brought myself to that complaisance long since. But I do so tenderly consider what concerns you as I can hardly keep myself from telling you such things as to my knowledge are prejudicial to you, but will endeavour it no more than I have done, for I am weary of angering you.[13]

A less controversial subject was the beds, silver, and other household goods that Leicester had purchased in France for Penshurst and the London town house. French luxury goods were famous. One could get far better things there than in England, Dorothy told her husband. French fabrics, above all, were superior to English. Among the things Dorothy most appreciated was a yellow damask bed, which "if it please God to bless our endeavours, may come seasonal for Doll."

Poor Doll! Beautiful as she was, at twenty-one she was still unmarried. Eligible men were being picked off rapidly. Rakish Lord Lovelace had just been betrothed. In the autumn of 1638, Dorothy made a final push to capture the Earl of Devonshire for her daughter. Through Lucy she enlisted the aid of the Queen and her favourite equerry, Sir Henry Jermyn. The Queen could easily make the match if she would only talk to Lady Devonshire, Dorothy grumbled, but despite Henrietta Maria's promises, she had not yet done anything. Dorothy recruited anyone who had any influence with the Devonshires. Their cousin the Earl of Newcastle had been very much on side for a while. But then he had written "a foolish letter" to Lucy, who, characteristically, had laughed at it and shown it to everyone. He learned of this, of course, and since then had turned "very cold."[14]

In Paris, Leicester was doing his best to line up a husband for Doll. He was ideally placed to do so since all the young English lords making the grand tour paid their respects at the English embassy. A few years earlier he thought he had a good prospect in William Russell, the fourth Earl of Bedford's son and heir; but as it turned out Russell was in love with the vivacious and pretty daughter of the infamous Lady Somerset and had married her on his return from the Continent. Leicester had put himself out to an extreme degree for the Earl of Devonshire when that most desirable of husband material had been in Paris. At the present juncture, another very eligible young man was on the scene: Lord Henry Spencer, who, at nineteen, was already in possession of his title as a baron and in two years would come into his fortune. But Leicester had discovered that the youth was pining for Elizabeth Cecil, the Earl of Salisbury's second daughter and the sister of the dead Countess of Northumberland. The Cecil girl was also Doll's principal rival for Devonshire. Dorothy agreed that it would be hard work to divert Spencer. He was known to be so infatuated with the Cecil girl that he had been unwilling to leave England.[15] If she did not get Devonshire, she would most certainly get young Henry Spencer.

With all her problems, Dorothy did not mention the King's troubles in her letters until December 1638, when she reported to Paris that the payment of all pensions had been suspended until the Scottish affairs were settled. The King was making plans to march against the rebellious Scots, and, according to Northumberland, the royal coffers were never emptier. Dorothy wondered how Lucy would react to having her pension stopped. Not surprisingly, Lucy complained to Wentworth, but all he did was commiserate. Holland did more. As a New Year's gift he presented Lucy with a diamond bracelet that cost him £1,500. Even the Queen did not get anything as valuable that year, except from the King. Lucy was more in favor with the Queen than she had been for a long time. Henrietta Maria appointed her and Lady Denbigh collectors for a special contribution from the ladies of the realm toward the Scottish expedition.

As war with Scotland came closer, Wentworth was increasingly keen on settling the business of Lucy's wine customs. In February

1639, he wrote Northumberland that although profits were at their best this past year, he feared they would not see such a good year again in a hurry. With the uncertainty ahead, he wanted to complete the sale of the grant while the Irish customs were still "in repute and credit." "A word from your Lordship to the Irish committee would end the business," he told Northumberland.[16] In April the Commission on Irish Affairs was still considering the contract for the King's purchase of Lady Carlisle's wine customs. Aware that Northumberland was not pressing the matter, Wentworth advised Lucy to go to the commission with her brother and speak to the commissioners herself. She should let them know that she was willing to accommodate the King by surrendering her grant, but she should insist on a fair price.[17]

BY THE SPRING of 1639, the mustering of an army to do battle with the rebellious Scots had begun. The Earl of Arundel was named General-in-Chief and the Earl of Essex, General of the Army. Holland was in his glory. Through the Queen's influence, he had been made General of the Horse. The Earl of Northumberland, however, was ordered to remain in London. With a real war at hand, the command of the fleet had been given to the inexperienced Marquess of Hamilton. The Lord High Admiral was given a far more important charge, in the King's opinion if not his own. Bringing the Queen to Northumberland, His Majesty said, "This is my jewel and I entrust her to you."[18]

Troops and the money to pay them were now Charles's overwhelming concern. He sent letters to the Lord Lieutenants, commanding them to come to York with a specified number of horse and foot from their counties. Letters in the name of the King went out to knights and squires across the country, asking for contributions. Nineteen contributed, twenty-one promised but did not pay up, and hundreds did not even reply to the letter. Ultimately, however, Charles was able to gather an army of 19,614 foot soldiers and 3,260 cavalry.[19] Among the nobility who answered the call for troops was Harry Percy, who brought a regiment of 867 infantry.

Charles planned to lead his army himself into battle. On March 27, the anniversary of his coronation, he left for York; with him in his coach were the Earl of Holland and the Duke of Lennox.

The war went badly for him from the start. Scottish royalists were easily beaten by the rebel Covenanters, and "like Job's messengers," couriers brought news to York that even the strongly royalist city of Aberdeen had fallen. Charles now sent Lord Hamilton into Scotland with three thousand cavalry to subdue the rebels. He himself moved up to Berwick on the River Tweed, which bordered on Scotland. He sincerely hoped that Hamilton would stop the Covenanters' army before it crossed the river because he simply had no confidence in his own army.

From his tent, Charles observed the troops bivouacked in the camp at Berwick. They were a sad lot of raw conscripts. Not only were they untrained, but they were undisciplined. He listened to the shouting and swearing from the camp with enormous distaste. His officers reported that the men were shooting at them. He had to believe this when one day he found a bullet hole in his own tent.[20] Charles at Berwick was no Henry V at Agincourt. Not only would he not rally his men with inspiring speeches, but he dared not go among the mutinous fellows.

As it happened, the frightened Hamilton did not have to engage the Scottish forces. The Scottish general stayed on his side of the Tweed and sent word to Charles that he wished to negotiate a truce. An insultingly small delegation of Scots arrived at Charles's tent at Berwick with conditions he abhorred—namely, that Presbyterianism be the official religion of Scotland. Charles was no less determined to impose the Anglican form of Protestantism on his Scottish subjects. It was a standoff.

HOW UNIMPORTANT EVENTS across the Channel were to Charles and his ministers was obvious from the caliber of English diplomacy. Totally unrealistic and utterly hopeless, it gave the men conducting it such malaise that all begged for their recall. As the ambassador to Spain put it, his role was "no more but to hear and advertise."

With the Anglo-French treaty out of the question, Leicester too wanted to vacate his post. As it happened, there was renewed hope that he could become Secretary of State. Sir John Coke, to whom he had reported all his years abroad, was nearing eighty. There was much talk of his retirement—a retirement, truth to tell, which the old gentleman was being hustled into by overeager candidates for his position. Sir John Temple was Leicester's advocate at this juncture. Temple, a minor officeholder in the royal service, was an old friend of Dorothy's and Robert's. His father had been secretary to both their famous uncles—Sir Philip Sidney and the Earl of Essex, Queen Elizabeth's favorite. Because of this tie, Leicester had given the living of Penshurst to Temple's brother-in-law, the Reverend Henry Hammond. On their frequent visits to the rectory, Sir John and his wife spent a good deal of time at the manor house with Dorothy. The previous November, Lady Temple had died at her brother's house. During her long, lingering illness, Dorothy was kindness itself. Temple was filled with gratitude, and when he returned to court was resolved to do his utmost to help the Earl and his "incomparable lady."[21] He was soon aware of the jockeying for the secretaryship and urged Dorothy to come up to London to plan strategy. From Temple we learn that Dorothy had established a faction at court, having enlisted her friends and relatives in her husband's cause. On February 7, 1639, Temple wrote Leicester: "I hope it [the secretaryship] may be happily accomplished by that Party and Strength her Ladyship can draw together here."[22] Coke's biographer certainly viewed Dorothy as a pernicious influence in the old secretary's downfall: "Historians do not agree in their assessment of the ambition of the earl of Leicester, but there is no doubt about the glaring ambition of his wife. She saw her husband's embassy as a stepping-stone to higher things—to Coke's Secretaryship."[23]

Temple set out to convince Leicester that it was the proper time for him to move in. If he neglected this opportunity, Temple wrote, some inferior person would get the position. England needed "able men" to carry it through "the shocks and violent concussions" likely to ensue. Leicester heeded the call and, pleading "urgent private business," applied for leave of absence. Northumberland informed his brother-in-law that the King had "stuck" a little at the request but finally agreed after some cajoling by the Queen.[24] Leicester obtained two months' leave, and the Lord High Admiral sent a ship to bring him over.

The "private business" concerned not only Leicester's own future but Doll's as well. At last he had procured a prospective husband for her—nineteen-year-old Henry Spencer. The elusive Devonshire had become betrothed to Elizabeth Cecil. In March they were married, leaving young Spencer in Paris to swallow his disappointment and look elsewhere for a bride. Seizing the opportunity, Leicester proposed his own daughter. Aided by an exquisite painting of Doll by Van Dyck, which Dorothy had just sent over to Paris, he found Spencer a most willing suitor. Devonshire's marriage created much less disappointment at Penshurst than might have been supposed, considering Dorothy's three years of unremitting efforts to capture him for her daughter. So far as Doll was concerned, she suffered a far greater sense of loss over the sister than over the brother. Anne Rich had died a few months earlier following a short illness. Doll was so distraught over her friend's death that Waller wrote a poem about her "tears and sorrow-wounded soul." Dorothy shed no tears over Devonshire but waited in happy anticipation for Henry Spencer, back from his grand tour, to come to pay suit to Doll.

After all their years of separation, Dorothy and Robert had no time to get reacquainted. Leicester no sooner arrived in London than the King commanded him to join the nobility at York. Charles thanked him fulsomely for his wise and conscientious service abroad and informed him that he was appointing him to the Privy Council, but sadly there was no mention of the post of Secretary of State, and Leicester was ordered to return to his ambassadorial post. On reflection, Leicester felt that he had been a little too forward in advising the King to accommodate his differences with the Scots. In May

Leicester was back in London, and soon afterward at Penshurst, where he assumed the gratifying role of father of the bride.

The couple had met and fallen in love at first sight. They had a good deal in common. Both were serious young people who wanted the same things in life: to live at Althorp, the Spencers' ancestral home in Northamptonshire, to look after the tenantry, and to raise a family. Studious and intelligent, they earnestly discussed books and life as they strolled along the avenue of beeches in Penshurst's park. By early June they were betrothed. Dorothy and Robert were delighted with the match. And so were their close friends, particularly Lord Mandeville, who sent a messenger with his good wishes as soon as he heard the news. Their old friend had had a special fondness for Doll since her childhood—his mock chivalric wooing of her was a family joke. Thanking Mandeville for his congratulatory message, Leicester wrote that nothing "could more confirm me in my opinion of my daughter's good fortune than your approbation of her choice." He was particularly glad that the young couple would be living in the vicinity of Lord and Lady Mandeville. He told his Puritan friend that while he himself was a "reprobate," he understood that young Spencer's ancestors had inclined to the Puritan "brotherhood." Unless he was very much deceived in his prospective son-in-law, he said happily, "he is like to prove both a good husband and a good man."[25] The groom's mother was as pleased about the match as the bride's parents were. Since her son was still a minor, she joined with him in a petition to the Court of Wards to have his lands released "in view of his marriage agreed upon with Lady Dorothy Sidney."[26] Leicester meanwhile was instructing Hawkins to get the necessary documents signed by the Keeper of the Privy Seal before the end of term. It all worked out, and on July 11, 1639, Dorothy and Robert saw their "dear Doll" married to a suitable young man who adored her.

The wedding at Penshurst was a great affair attended by many guests. The marriage ceremony was performed according to the Book of Common Prayer by the Reverend Henry Hammond. Leicester, usually glum, was in a joyful mood as he gave the bride away. When the ceremony ended with the newly wedded couple exchanging a kiss, Lucy and Dorothy embraced each other with tears of happiness running down their cheeks. Everyone present was taking pleasure in this perfect union. Even the disappointed suitor, Edmund Waller, graciously told the twenty-two-year-old bride that she was as freshly beautiful as when he wrote his famous lines to "Sacharissa" some half a dozen years before, and, on request, he recited them: "Go, lovely Rose! / Tell her that wastes her time and me / That now she knows / When I resemble her to thee / How sweet and fair she seems to be." (After what he called "the common joy at Penshurst," Waller wrote a letter to Doll's sister in which, tongue in cheek, he wished on Doll "the first curse imposed on womankind—the pains of becoming a mother!")[27]

It was a glorious midsummer day, and after the ceremony the guests strolled through the gardens, then in full bloom, and plucked cherries and peaches from the trees in the famous orchards. A Lucullan feast of viands grown and raised on the estate, thanks to Dorothy's overseeing, was mightily enjoyed by the company. For the moment, the perilous times that lay ahead were far from their thoughts.

All the nobility had come home from the north, for the war was quickly over. After bivouacking outside Berwick with his forces for some weeks, Charles had signed a treaty with the Scots on June 14 and disbanded his army. None but the most optimistic thought that the treaty of Berwick was anything but a truce. Charles had hardly taught the rebels a lesson. Indeed, the one encounter with the Scots at Duns near Berwick had been a fiasco. The Earl of Holland, magnificently accoutered with a gleaming breastplate and richly laced breeches with a knot at the knees, had remained stationary with his crack cavalry troop, gaping at the small company of Scots while the horses pawed the ground impatiently. Convinced that he was outnumbered, he turned around and galloped back to camp. Notwithstanding his "shameful retreat,"[28] Holland was at the wedding in all his finery, glorying in the title of general.

After the wedding Leicester returned to France, taking twelve-year-old Robin with him. Dorothy was to join him with her elder girls

Lucy and Anne, and Lord and Lady Spencer, as soon as arrangements could be made. Many things had to be done first. The newlyweds had to pay visits to Henry's uncle, the Earl of Southampton, at his country seat, and of course to his mother at Althorp in Northamptonshire. Meanwhile Dorothy had her retainers looking out for six fine coach horses to take with her to France. She also wanted to give the City merchants who did business in France enough advance notice of her departure so that they could present her with gifts, if so inclined. "If they expect more courtesies from my lord, I think they will be content to oblige me," she told Hawkins.[29] Most important were the handing over of the estate business to Hawkins and the instructions to the governess who was to take charge of the four little girls during her absence. Then there was the packing up of household stuff for two families. They were moving into an unfurnished house because, shortly before coming to England, Leicester had been forced to leave the Hôtel des Ambassadeurs, where he had been lodging at the French government's expense since his arrival. So Dorothy was taking beds, stools, chairs, tapestries, rush mats, Turkey carpets, linens, and her sedan chair from Penshurst. The Spencers had eleven trunks. There was also a box of books, which Leicester had ordered, on the Scottish nobility, on Charles's Scottish coronation in 1633, and on the holding of a Scottish parliament—a scholar's response to the war with Scotland!

On September 12, the goods were shipped from the port of London, bound for Rouen. Shortly afterward, Dorothy and her family set out for Dover, stopping to spend the night at Canterbury with Leicester's sister Barbara, Lady Strangford. The next day they boarded the *Antelope,* which Northumberland had commanded his vice admiral to have ready for them.[30] The Channel crossing was calm all the way, a mercy since her Ladyship was pregnant—not the bride, but the bride's mother, yet again.

Dorothy arrived in Paris to find Robert installed in a magnificent residence right next door to the palace of the Louvre, for which he was paying the exceedingly high rent of 480 pistoles per annum. Some time before her arrival, Leicester had written to King Charles virtually demanding an increase in his allowance in order to furnish the embassy in a "decent manner." Had Dorothy been there, she might have stopped him from sending this foolish letter, for, as she had warned him more than once, the King had no desire for his envoys to put on a show for the host country. Wishing his diplomats to spend as little as possible, the King was antagonized by the pretensions of his ambassador extraordinary to France. The Queen relayed the King's displeasure to Northumberland, who wrote Dorothy that Charles had showed such "adverseness to paying for the hiring and furnishing of your house as I should not advise the pressing it further; for their Majesties being at this time very intent upon saving, it would certainly receive a denial."[31]

Leicester's extravagance may have been one of the reasons he did not become Secretary of State when Coke was turned out of office some months later. In an encoded letter to Leicester on November 21, 1639, Northumberland dashed his brother-in-law's hopes: "I was much surprised to understand how peremptorily the King refused the Queen's [request] to make you secretary. What the reason should be I cannot imagine, except it proceed from the Archbishop who certainly wished not your Preferment; but I hope we may hereafter prevail, though we have failed at this time."[32]

After three years of intense lobbying, Leicester had failed to win either of the positions he so coveted.

A NOBLE AND INTELLIGENT

FRIENDSHIP

LUCY HAD NO SOONER said good-bye to Dorothy than she found herself welcoming Wentworth. The Lord Deputy arrived in London on September 21, 1639, and it was as if they had last met three days before and not three years. Their unspoken mutual benefit pact, sweetened by letters of compliment, had cemented their friendship. With Lady Wentworth safely tucked away in Dublin, Lucy assumed the role of the Lord Deputy's dearest friend and confidante. Wentworth told Lucy in confidence that King Charles had sent him a handwritten note at the end of July, commanding him to come over—only a crippling attack of gout had stopped him from answering the call at once. Charles had ordered him not to reveal that he had been summoned but to find some private reason for his trip to England.[1] This posed no problem. As a result of Wentworth's heavy-handed housecleaning in Ireland, he was plaintiff or defendant in half a dozen suits before the Privy Council and the Star Chamber.

Charles had turned to Wentworth in desperation. The Scots were as intransigent as they had been before the truce at Berwick. A renewal of the war was inevitable, and meanwhile the Exchequer was empty. All his counselors had turned out to be slender reeds. Holland with his white satin suits and foppish manners was no wartime general, nor was Hamilton, who was indecisive and divided in his loyalties between England and Scotland. Northumberland had a sound head but an unsound body; at every crisis he took to his bed. Pembroke and the others had no advice to offer. On the other hand, Charles had complete confidence in Wentworth. He had done a first-rate job in Ireland, setting up a workable administration and increasing royal revenues substantially. He was the only adviser the King could count on.

Wentworth was received at Whitehall like a conquering hero. He radiated power. As he strode down the palace corridors, shoulders hunched and head thrust forward, the courtiers bowed and fawned. He lived like a king in Ireland and had taken on kingly ways. The country house he was building in County Kildare had greater frontage than the Earl of Salisbury's Hatfield. And at Dublin he held court in a manner to rival Whitehall.

Lucy preened herself in the company of this powerful man who so obviously admired her. He would do anything for her and sought every means to please her. Knowing how eager she was for the advancement of her family, he confided that while in England he expected to be made Lord Treasurer, and then he would urge the King to appoint Leicester to succeed him as Lord Deputy. One day he asked her how old her nephew Viscount Lisle was. When she told him that Philip was twenty, he said the King was raising three thousand cavalry, and, if she wished, he would make the boy a colonel. Exhilarated by her power over the man of the hour, Lucy boasted to her sister and brother-in-law that she could guarantee them Wentworth's utmost assistance: "He intends great kindness and service to you and all your family."[2]

Soon after his arrival, Lucy told Wentworth that she was in need of money. With pensions going unpaid, she was dependent upon her Irish income. In letter after letter to Sir George Radcliffe, his longtime friend and lawyer whom he had made principal secretary in Ireland, Wentworth tried to expedite Lucy's payments from the Irish wine customs. She herself had discovered that some £999 was owing her for the year 1635, and she was claiming this in addition to her current profits. It will be recalled that Sir James Hay, Carlisle's agent in Ireland, had advised Lucy that Wentworth was undervaluing the profits from the customs. Wentworth had vigorously denied it, accusing Sir James of malice. It appeared that Lucy had been shortchanged after all, and Wentworth clearly wanted to make amends. He directed Radcliffe to see if the money had been paid into the Exchequer, and if it had, to find some way of reimbursing Lady Carlisle, "it being most justly due to her ladyship." This was an admission that he had been remiss as her trustee. Since the money had not gone into his pocket, it was either negligence or, more likely, an attempt to cheapen the price the King would have to pay to buy in her grant. Now it was Lucy's best interests that were uppermost in Wentworth's mind.

Being in London gave him the opportunity to "settle the business" of the wine customs once and for all. The settlement differed from the original 1637 contract under which the grant was to be bought in by the Crown. Instead, Lucy would transfer title to the King (by way of a conveyance) but continue to receive the profits from the wine impost for the remaining eight years of the grant. She would covenant to pay the King £2,000 per annum until the grant expired. Radcliffe expressed some disapproval of the transaction. "I do well understand you," Wentworth replied. He would also have preferred to have the grant bought in outright, "but that must not move me to wrong my Lady, or injure [?] the trust her Ladyship reposes in me." Meanwhile, £4,000 from the wine customs was due Lucy immediately, to be issued out of the Irish revenues. Wentworth dispatched a letter of authorization from the King for the Lord Justices of Ireland and the necessary warrants for the Vice-Treasurer. He pressed Radcliffe to "speedily" send over the money for her Ladyship's use.[3]

Alas, Lucy's happy reunion with Wentworth was spoiled when word came from France in October that Dorothy was seriously ill. Lucy was frantic with worry. All her love for her sister and her dependence on her, going back to their childhood days at Syon House, welled up. "It is not possible for me to express the trouble I have suffered for my sister's indisposition," she wrote Leicester. She begged him for a detailed report of Dorothy's condition. She could scarcely contain herself from rushing over to Paris, but then decided it would be more sensible to wait for word. A week later, Dorothy's condition was unchanged. Lucy's only consolation was that her sister was reportedly cheerful—a good sign since cheerfulness was "not her humour." Northumberland was as worried as Lucy, declaring to Leicester that his sister's recovery was the thing in the world he most earnestly desired. (Harry was at Bath, taking the waters for a sore arm acquired on the tennis court. No letter on his sister's illness has survived.) By the end of the month, Leicester was able to reassure them that Dorothy was out of danger and on the road to recovery.[4]

While Dorothy was ill, Lucy could think of nothing else, but now the tense political situation thrust itself upon her. "The Scotch business grows worse every day," she wrote Dorothy on November 7, 1639, and on November 21, she reported that there was "great expectation of war." Using the cipher that Leicester had sent her (replacing names with agreed-upon numbers), she passed on all the inside information that she had gleaned: Northumberland was to be offered command of the King's forces; the Lord Deputy was going to Ireland to bring over an army of ten thousand, and it would not cost the King a penny. She had been told in confidence (she wrote on December 5) that a parliament would be called to raise subsidies for the war, but they must keep this secret until they heard it from others. She revealed things about the Queen that would have caused whispered conferences between Dorothy and Robert in the privacy of their bedchamber. Lucy had overheard the Queen use "strange, violent persuasions to the King, such as must make us ill with France, which were a strange action in the condition we are in." (Under the combined influence of her mother and her friend Marie de Chevreuse, Henrietta Maria had conceived a great dislike of Richelieu and was, at the moment, strongly opposed to her brother's regime.) Lucy hinted at a relationship between the Queen and her bland Master of the Horse, Sir Henry Jermyn. "There are some things that I scarce dare write you," she told Dorothy. Did her sister understand her ciphered letters, she inquired. Was there a danger they would be intercepted? "My heart would not conceal anything from you, so much it loves and trusts you."[5]

One thing that disturbed her was that their brother Algernon did not see eye to eye with Wentworth. Following the failure of his talks with the Scottish commissioners in December, Wentworth concluded that it was too late for the neutrality he had always urged upon the King, and he was now counseling war. Northumberland, also a member of the newly appointed Council of War, disapproved of Wentworth's hawkish policies. As strongly as Wentworth argued his point of view, Northumberland could not be persuaded. Moreover, while Wentworth was for the King, right or wrong, Northumberland's latent animosity to the monarchy surfaced. When Wentworth instituted a collection among the nobility for the war, setting a good example with a contribution of £20,000, Northumberland gave only £5,000. "The reason I do so," he wrote Leicester, "is that I believe the King would not expect more from me whose House hath in these latter ages received little or no assistance from the Crown."[6] Let those who had made fortunes through royal favor or held beneficial places make the big contributions, he commented with obvious disgruntlement to his brother-in-law.

On December 19, Lucy was pleased to report that Northumberland and Wentworth were getting along much better, and she took the credit herself for the reconciliation. She had made them be friends, she exulted to her sister. Meanwhile, regrettably, it looked as if Wentworth would not be leaving his post so soon. He had been promoted, with the grand new title of Lord Lieutenant of Ireland. But Dorothy and her husband could be assured that when he did step down, he would see that Leicester got his place.

It was probably disappointment over the lord deputyship that made Leicester write a mean-spirited letter to Lucy, accusing her of taking more interest in Wentworth than in her own kith and kin. Lucy replied that she hoped she had misunderstood his heavily ciphered letter, but if Leicester thought it a fault in her to express friendship to the Lord Lieutenant, then she was "very guilty, not having omitted anything that I could imagine for his service." Indeed, if she had done otherwise, Leicester could expect her to fail him too. "For if I could be so ungrateful to a person so extremely deserving from me, it were neither just nor safe for any other person to trust me."[7] She could not see how her friendship with Wentworth could be a disservice to him, she told Leicester, with more than a touch of asperity.

It is hard to reconcile the writer of this letter with Sir Tobie Mathew's "Character of the Countess of Carlisle." Wentworth brought out the best in Lucy. Of a sardonic humor himself, he was, nevertheless, above the kind of character assassination indulged in by her circle at court. And Lucy responded with a similar high-mindedness when she was with him. Her letter to Leicester revealed the fires of compassion and loyalty that Tobie Mathew had suspected lay banked in her nature "like suppressed flames."

Her loyalty was not misplaced. Wentworth was doing everything he could to get her money for her. When it was not forthcoming from Ireland as "speedily" as he had hoped, he deducted a portion from her last rent payment to the Crown for the wine customs and consigned it back to her. Through this and other "shifts," he managed to obtain about a thousand pounds for Lucy out of the tight English revenues, but "the rest must be made up" from Ireland as soon as possible, Radcliffe was told. Even if construction work on Dublin Castle had to be delayed, Lady Carlisle must be paid: "Let the buildings stay, in the name of God till Spring," he ordered Radcliffe.[8]

At the beginning of January, Lucy informed her sister that Wentworth was to be created an earl. The impressive ceremony took place in the Presence Chamber at Whitehall on January 12, 1640. Preceded by heralds, Thomas Wentworth was presented to their Majesties by five earls. First came Newcastle, carrying on his arm the upper robe, then Cleveland bearing the sword, next Clare with the coronet, finally Northumberland and Hamilton (in his English creation as the Earl of Cambridge) flanking Wentworth on either side. As Secretary of State Sir Francis Windebank read out the patent, Wentworth was robed, his sword girt to him, and the coronet placed on his head by each earl in turn. When the ceremony ended, the new Earl of Strafford, accompanied by the other earls, withdrew from the chamber to the sound of drums and trumpets.[9]

This was the realization of Wentworth's dream. He had begged

Charles for an earldom—on his knees, in fact, when he had come over in 1636—and now with the kingdom on the edge of disaster he had received it. Sadly, an earldom in Charles's court in 1640 did not mean what it had in the past. Perhaps that was why Lucy made only passing reference to it. The foundations of Lucy's world—a world founded on royal favor—were beginning to crumble. No longer did the courtiers seem eager to ingratiate themselves with the King and Queen. That season, when the royal masques were staged, the room was almost empty. "Though they speak of making His Majesty happy," Lucy wrote Dorothy, "there is yet little appearance of it." She was impatient for her sister's return. "There are few things can make me happy, and your company is the principal."[10] Lucy's growing pessimism was not shared by Strafford. The new earl sincerely believed that kingship based on divine right could not fall.

IF STRAFFORD HAD dropped into a tavern and listened to the talk swirling around him, he would not have been so certain.

Opposition to Charles's personal rule had become vocal, even violent. While the King's arbitrary methods of taxing the people continued to be a source of discontent, it was the religious issue that lit the fire. The Bishops' War, as the war with the Scots was called, was about to be renewed. The idea of fighting Protestants—and those his own natural subjects—was turning the ordinary Englishman against the King, especially since the perception was that he was relaxing the antipapal laws to please his Catholic queen. In this climate of suspicion and distrust, there was widespread opposition to Archbishop Laud's insistence on "popish" ritual in the churches, such as bowing to the altar or kneeling to receive the sacrament. Another abuse in the popular mind was the High Commission, the religious counterpart to the Star Chamber, where ministers who questioned the Laudian reforms were fined, deprived of their livings, and excommunicated. Posters vilifying Laud were appearing all over London. One day a riotous mob attacked the Archbishop's palace at Lambeth, but Laud had sufficiently fortified the place (as he said, he had cannons as well as canons), and the attackers turned around and departed.

With an Irish appointment out of the question for the time being, the Leicesters revived the idea of Robert replacing Secretary of State Coke. In February the old man was dismissed, made the scapegoat for the disgraceful conduct of the war with Scotland the previous year. Northumberland poured cold water on the Leicesters' hopes, and the newly minted Earl of Strafford regretfully informed Lucy that Leicester had little chance. When Sir Henry Vane got the post, Strafford was almost as disappointed as Leicester, for the new secretary—"a bustling, subtle, forward courtier"[11]—was no friend to him. Still hoping to oblige Lucy and her family, Strafford was casting about for some other plum for Leicester. He floated the idea of Leicester succeeding Sir Francis Cottington as Master of the Court of Wards. Cottington had been indisposed a good deal recently, and Strafford insisted that he was dying of consumption. The plan died a lot sooner than Cottington.

Everything at court now centered on the expedition against Scotland. Northumberland was named Commander-in-Chief. (Clarendon would later say that Strafford had ceded the command in the hope of binding the Lord High Admiral closer to the King's cause.) To pay for the war effort (estimated by Northumberland at no less than a million pounds a year),[12] Charles had no other recourse than to call Parliament. Strafford, the proponent of this distasteful expedient, was to make a flying visit to Ireland, hold a parliament there to raise an army, returning in time for an English parliament in mid-April. Yet, in the midst of all his stress, Strafford did not forget Lucy's business. One suspects that in her sweet, tactful way, she made sure of it. He instructed Radcliffe to prepare an order for payment of "that £999 demanded by my Lady Carlisle" so that the money would be ready when he came over.[13]

Before Strafford left for Ireland, Lucy arranged for him to lease Leicester House. Toward the end of February, she and Northumberland took him on a tour of inspection, and he liked the place very well. Dorothy and Leicester welcomed the extra income. Like all of

Charles's diplomats, Leicester was still not getting his allowances from England. In the present penury, it was far beyond Hawkins's power to get any money for his master, and indeed the Earl was borrowing from his agent and his relatives. Even Northumberland was coming up against a stone wall when he pressed for Leicester's payments. The truth was, he told his brother-in-law, that there was "not a groat in the Exchequer."[14]

In spite of criticizing Lucy's friendship with Strafford, Leicester had no compunction about asking for his help. Hawkins was instructed to hold off soliciting for money until the Lord Lieutenant returned from Ireland. "I think he will assist me," Leicester told his agent.[15]

When the new tenant of Leicester House wanted two new beds, Lucy asked her sister to purchase them in Paris. These beds were to cause a royal row between Dorothy and Robert. Dorothy used her "best care" in having them made up, "one of green wrought velvet lined with satin, garnished with gold and silver, the other of red damask garnished with silk." With the twelve chairs and six stools for each bed, which Dorothy said was "just the number that is used here to all good beds," they came to £446 sterling. Strafford paid Hawkins promptly, but the agent used the money to pay off one of Leicester's most pressing debts. When Dorothy heard of it, she flew into a passion, screaming at her husband that she had engaged her credit for those beds and that she was being importuned to death by her creditors. Chastened, Leicester hurriedly wrote Hawkins that if he had not yet paid over the money, he must send it at once "for the use to which it was designed."[16] In March Dorothy had given birth to yet another girl in "a rich bed of crimson velvet," purchased by Leicester for her lying-in. Having her eleventh child at the age of forty-one, when she herself was about to become a grandmother (Doll was pregnant), had clearly not improved Dorothy's temper.

Lucy was also confined to her bedchamber in March, with a bad attack of her chronic stomach trouble. For months she had been complaining to Dorothy about stomach pain, vomiting, and heavy menstrual bleeding, but she had kept going for Strafford's sake.

While he was in Ireland, she gave way to her illness, dousing herself with physic and other nostrums. Her brother Algernon understood how miserable she felt and would have come to see her had he not been ill himself. There was precious little sympathy from Harry, however. On April 9, he wrote the Leicesters that their sister was much better and would be completely well if she would stick to any one course of treatment. On April 16, the patient herself wrote that she planned to take a little air for the first time since she fell ill. She also informed them that "the Parliament has begun this day so strangely as I find everybody despairs of any good that can come from it."[17]

Strafford was still not back when Parliament—the first since 1629—convened on April 15. He had left Ireland on April 3 with a severe case of dysentery, crossed the Irish Sea in a gale, and collapsed at Chester. Bedridden at the coastal town for a week with "gout, late seasickness, and continuing looseness," by force of will he dictated a blizzard of letters to his secretaries. Not least of his concerns was Lucy's money. To Radcliffe he wrote: "Send me the accounts, how they stand betwixt my Lady Carlisle and me . . . so as thereby I may particularly understand what I have to pay unto her Ladyship, and see the same may be performed accordingly." He knew full well that "something may be expected from me as soon as I come to London."[18]

On April 18, Strafford arrived at London, too late to manage the parliamentary session effectively. Lucy's foreboding had not been for nothing. The session was a replay of the parliament of 1629. The Commons, under the leadership of John Pym, a veteran of the parliaments of the 1620s and a prime mover of the Petition of Right, refused to grant supply for the war before their grievances were heard. Charles played his part by dissolving it before three weeks were out. At the Privy Council, Strafford lost control to Sir Henry Vane and, in the end, voted in favor of dissolving Parliament as being the King's will. Not Northumberland. He spoke out against dissolution and, as Lucy told Dorothy, did not seem to care that the King and Queen were displeased with him. "It grieves my soul," he wrote Leicester a few days after dissolution, "to be involved in these councils; and the sense I have of the miseries that are likely to ensue, is held by some a disaffection in me."[19]

In the general fear and foreboding at court, Lucy was astonished at Strafford's optimism. "My Lord Lieutenant is the only person I hear hopeful of the King's affairs," she wrote Dorothy. It seemed to her that everything was on his shoulders. He was so busy that she hesitated to remind him of his promise to find employment for Leicester. But he brought it up himself, she was pleased to tell her sister. Busy as he was, he was acting as Leicester's advocate with Laud and the King and Queen.

Some of Strafford's other activities pleased her less. There was some negotiation with the Spaniards that he would not tell her about, and when she asked he always denied it. Yet people saw the Spanish agent going in and out of Leicester House. She expressed her worries to Dorothy. "They say we shall have money from them, which our people extremely apprehends." It was only too true. Strafford was attempting to negotiate a loan from Spain, and under very unfavorable terms at that. To use money from Catholic Spain to fight their Scottish brethren was a damnable thing to most Englishmen. Lucy understood the anti-Spanish sentiment in England much better than Strafford did.

In June Strafford had a relapse and lay dangerously ill at Leicester House. The grossly fat royal physician Sir Theodore Mayerne huffed and puffed up the stairs daily to weaken the patient with more bloodletting. Outside the house, an angry mob armed with stones shouted and threatened. "Black Tom," as they called Strafford, was immensely unpopular with the London apprentices, hundreds of whom worked in the wool and cloth trades in the capital. All over England, the Earl of Strafford was held to blame for the dissolution of Parliament and the impending renewal of war with the Scots. When the King, left without supply by the Short Parliament, seized the bullion in the mint deposited by merchants and goldsmiths—an action condemned by Northumberland as "the most mischievous thing"—Strafford was falsely blamed for it.

In the London taverns, the talk was that Strafford would bring over an Irish army of papists, some said to fight the Scots; others darkly hinted the forces would be used to preserve the King's tyranny in England. Rumors that he would be accused of treason were so persistent that Lucy reluctantly brought up the subject with him. He was now sufficiently convalescent to take a little air in the garden, and Lucy would walk beside his sedan chair "on the high gravel walk," worriedly discussing this dread possibility. He scoffed at the rumors. "My Lord Deputy is still confident he cannot be accused of treason," she wrote Leicester on July 7.[20]

In this same letter, Lucy answered another accusation from her brother-in-law that she was favoring her friend over her family. It seemed that some visiting Englishmen had commented to him about his sister-in-law's close connection with the Lord Lieutenant. No doubt egged on by Dorothy, who was forever grumbling that her sister did not use her influence for their good, he wrote Lucy another carping letter. She replied that she could "not yet find how your believing that my excessive considerations of others should make me negligent of your service," but this time she was more conciliatory, assuring Leicester that his concerns came first with her. No matter what Dorothy thought, Lucy's strongest loyalty was to her family.

It was this strong family feeling that impelled Northumberland to overcome his distaste for mixing in the affairs of Charles's faltering government and to busy himself, finally, with Lucy's Irish grants. In spite of Strafford's repeated pleas, he had done nothing to quicken the sale of her wine customs—it had been left to Strafford to conclude that business. The matter of her grant to license wines and aqua vitae in Ireland still remained. In the face of riots against the government in England—"so general a defection in this kingdom hath not been known in the memory of any,"[21] he wrote Leicester in June 1640—Northumberland was worried that prerogative grants might soon not be worth the paper they were written on. He sprang into action, presenting the Commission on Irish Affairs with a "scheme" for the purchase of his sister's grant, which was readily accepted by the commissioners. On July 19, the King, then at Hampton Court, gave his approval and ordered that "the necessary sums" (£7,200) be paid into Northumberland's hands. Lucy's grant had been unloaded none too soon. A year later the grant was worthless because, as the Irish Lord Justices informed Secretary Vane, liquor was being sold throughout Ireland without a license.[22] Thanks to her brother's scheme, Lucy received some money for surrendering her licensing grant. It cannot have been much, for she was now in real financial straits, according to Strafford. "You must take care that the moneys for my Lady Carlisle be paid to her at London this term," he impressed upon Radcliffe, "for she have need of it."[23]

The Earl of Northumberland did not show equal dispatch in carrying out his responsibilities as commander-in-chief of the King's forces as he had just shown in his sister's affairs. In July the army commanders were leading their pressed soldiers northward, but the Commander-in-Chief remained behind at Syon House, observing dispassionately to his brother-in-law that the troops that did not desert would be readier to draw their swords against their officers than against the Scots.[24] In fact, there was a series of mutinies among the troops levied in Essex, Hertfordshire, Warwickshire, and Dorset. An Essex company killed their lieutenant on a rumor that he was a papist, while some from Dorset (as it was reported to the Privy Council) "in a most barbarous and inhumane manner dragged [an officer] through the streets, and after hanged up his dead body."[25]

In August, after successive fits of ague (a common sweating fever), Lucy was nursing herself back to health at Tunbridge Wells. We see an example of the flatterers who swarmed around her at the spas. Sir Kenelm Digby, an ambitious courtier who had managed to get himself appointed as the Queen's envoy to the Pope, was taking the waters before setting out for Rome. Sir Kenelm was delighted to find the Countess of Carlisle there for (as he expressed it to Sir Tobie Mathew) "the eminency of her condition maketh her able to sow blessings everywhere she passeth." She was most gracious to him, and he was flattered to be able to walk and talk with her. Hoping to consolidate this new intimacy, he asked Sir Tobie to convey his thanks to Lady Carlisle for her favor at the Wells, as she was so eminent he dared not tell her himself. "I have ever esteemed this brave lady above all others our climate may brag of," he declared with questionable sincerity. But if self-interest guided his pen, Sir Kenelm was clearly charmed by Lucy: "So much sweetness and civility as she is mistress of, mingled with all other excellencies, I never yet met with in any besides herself."[26]

While Lucy was at the spa, she received news that the Earl of Northumberland was very ill. She left at once for Syon House, where she found Algernon feverish, attended by Sir Theodore Mayerne and another court physician. Harry was there as well, and brother and sister waited anxiously for the fever to break. In a few days the doctors reassured them that the Earl was out of danger; though very weak, he was on the mend. Harry, meanwhile, was occupied with raising a second cavalry troop at his own expense to serve with the royal horse guards. It was a measure of King Charles's respect for the Earl of Northumberland that he took time out from his war counsels to pay a visit to the patient at Syon House. Though he could not offer his own services, Northumberland informed Charles that he was sponsoring two troops under his nephew Lord Lisle for His Majesty's horse guards.[27]

Northumberland could not have chosen a more inauspicious moment to fall ill. The Scots were on the march. With the commander-in-chief out of action, the King surprised his Privy Council by announcing that he would go in person to hearten his troops. At this the Earl of Holland made the most astute remark of his career: what the soldiers wanted was their pay, he said, and the King's presence would not provide that. When all was said and done, Strafford was the only person to replace Northumberland, and although he had never fully recovered from his winter illness and was now suffering a bad case of the stone, he undertook the task of leading the army. Traveling in great pain, he arrived at York just behind the King. Meanwhile, the Scots had crossed the Tweed into England. Under strict orders from Charles, Strafford stayed in his sickbed while his trusted friend Lord Conway was easily routed in a skirmish at Newburn and abandoned the important city of Newcastle without a struggle.

Strafford's command was undermined from the beginning. The English had no heart for this fight. A dozen Puritan peers, among them the Earls of Bedford, Essex, and Warwick, who throughout the years of Charles's personal rule had shunned the court, signed a petition asking for a parliament. (Indicative of the esprit de corps at York, Harry Percy and his nephew Lord Lisle were fighting over precedence for their troops.)

How to pay for the renewed war against Scotland was Charles's problem. The Spanish loan had not materialized. Word was coming in from the regional lord lieutenants that the sheriffs and constables could not raise the trained bands (the militia) without money. (The response from the Privy Council was that at a time of invasion, every man was expected to serve at his own charge.) An appeal by Henrietta Maria to the Catholic aristocracy produced little in the way of contributions and increased the antipapist hysteria.

In feudal style, Charles summoned the nobility to come to York for a Great Council of Peers "to perform the services due for their tenure."[28] The peers answered this archaic call for fealty in such numbers that the harried Master of Ceremonies, Sir John Finet, could not find a single earl in London to act as escort for the Danish ambassadors. The only place at York that could hold such a crowd was the dean's house, which stood beside the Gothic church of Yorkminster. There, on September 24, Charles, seated on a thronelike chair under a canopy of state, addressed the nobles. "An army of rebels was lodged within this kingdom,"[29] he said, and what advice did their Lordships have for him? Their advice was to sign an armistice with the Scots and to summon Parliament. Charles had already accepted the inevitable, and Hawkins, who happened to be at York on September 24, wrote the Earl of Leicester that the writs for a parliament had been issued that day.

On November 3, Lucy attended the opening of Parliament in the old palace of Westminster. She had dressed for the occasion in a fashionable velvet gown, modestly filling in the low-cut bodice with an inset of muslin and covering her shoulders with a cape against the damp cold of the stone hall. As always, Lady Carlisle looked magnifi-

The most High and Mighty Monarch IAMES by the grace of God King of Great Brittaine, France, and Ireland. Borne the 19 of Iune. 1566.

The most excellent Princesse ANNE Queene of Great Brittaine. France. and Ireland. Borne the 12 of October. 1574.

Are to be sold at the whit horse in pater noster Alley by Iohn Sudbury and George Humble

King James I and Queen Anne

COURTESY OF THE STAPLETON COLLECTION/
BRIDGEMAN ART LIBRARY INTERNATIONAL

Anne of Denmark by Paul Van Somer

James Hay, First Earl of Carlisle

COURTESY OF THE NATIONAL PORTRAIT
GALLERY, LONDON

*George Villiers, First Duke of
Buckingham by Daniel Mytens*

COURTESY OF CHRISTIE'S IMAGES/
THE BRIDGEMAN ART LIBRARY INTERNATIONAL

Lucy Percy, Countess of Carlisle by Van Dyck

Dorothy Percy, Countess of Leicester by Van Dyck

Henry Rich, First Earl of Holland by Daniel Mytens

COURTESY OF THE NATIONAL PORTRAIT
GALLERY, LONDON

*Thomas Wentworth, First Earl
of Strafford by Van Dyck*

COURTESY OF THE NATIONAL PORTRAIT
GALLERY, LONDON

King Charles I and his family c. 1632 by Van Dyck

Algernon Percy, Tenth Earl of Northumberland by Van Dyck

COLLECTION OF THE DUKE OF NORTHUMBERLAND,

ALNWICK CASTLE

Oliver Cromwell
by Robert Walker

COURTESY OF THE NATIONAL

PORTRAIT GALLERY, LONDON

cent, but the double chin that had just been hinted at in her last Van Dyck portrait was now unmistakable.

Whereas for the opening of Parliament in April, the King had ridden through the London streets in the royal coach to display himself to the populace in the black velvet and ermine robes of state and wearing his crown, this time he avoided the eyes of the public by going by barge the short distance from Whitehall to Westminster. He was met at Westminster Stairs by the Lords in a body, who escorted him first to Westminster Abbey for prayer and then to the House of Lords, where he took his seat on the throne. Crowned and in the robes of state, Charles emanated the aura of majesty, but Lucy sensed a lack of confidence in him that she had not seen since his youth.

The King began his address to the assembled Lords and Commons with the stark statement that the honor and safety of the kingdom was at stake. He admitted that the war against the Scots had so far been a failure. The Scottish army was sitting in Newcastle, and he warned that unless Parliament voted supply for the war, the English army would have to be disbanded before it could put the rebels out of England. He told Parliament that a loan from the City of London was enough to maintain the army for only two months. If the parliamentarians would grant him adequate supply, he promised to "satisfy their just grievances" and to "concur so heartily and clearly with them that all the world would see his good intentions."[30] Lucy feared that this blanket promise would be taken as a sign of weakness. The King then stated that Lord Keeper Sir John Finch would give an account of events since Parliament had last met in April. Not only did this very nervous official not help the King's cause, but Lucy thought he gave the worst speech she had ever heard. Writing to the Earl of Leicester after the opening, she reported that the King's speech was very well received—"with much reason, for he made them great promises."[31] But any initial spirit of cooperation between King and Parliament soon evaporated.

The temper of the parliament that convened in November 1640 was one of sullen hostility to the royal government. The King's party was sadly outnumbered in the Commons. Men known to be in opposition to the court had been returned over Charles's handpicked candidates. One after another, the members read out petitions from their constituents, complaining of arbitrary punishments inflicted by the Star Chamber and the High Commission. Overwhelmingly Puritan, they opposed Laud's changes to church doctrine and liturgy. Like most of their countrymen, they were opposed to the weakening of penalties against English Catholics. To a man, they were firmly opposed to Charles's personal rule financed by extraparliamentary measures such as ship money, forced loans, and the sale of monopolies.

These knights and squires, most of whom had trained as lawyers or had spent at least one semester at Oxford or Cambridge, could rise to oratorical heights. Sir John Colepeper, member for Kent, fulminated against monopolies, calling them "a Nest of Wasps or swarm of Vermin which have over-crept the Land: these like the frogs of Egypt, have gotten possession of our Dwellings, they sup in our Cup, they dip in our Dish, they sit by our Fire, we find them in the Wash-House and Powdering-Tub, they share with the Butler in his Box; they have marked and sealed us from Head to Foot, they will not abate us a Pin: These are the leaches that have sucked the Common-wealth so hard, that it is almost become hectical [feverish as with a consumption]."[32]

In the upper house, the Puritan lords were equally opposed to Charles. Many kept strict households in their vast country houses where Scripture was their guide, and they abominated Laud's changes, which had their tenants bowing and kneeling before the altar in their village churches. There were secular concerns as well. Some lords felt hampered in their exploitation of the Americas by Charles's pro-Spanish foreign policy, constrained by his forest laws, and pinched by substantial fines in the Star Chamber. In both the upper and lower houses, virtually all were opposed to the war with the Scots, and Strafford was blamed for it.

On the eve of his journey south to certain impeachment, Strafford sent an earnest appeal to Radcliffe: "For love of Christ, take order that all the money due to my Lady Carlisle be paid before Christmas, for a nobler nor more intelligent friendship did I never meet with in my life."[33] But Lucy was not to get her money. Within days of Strafford's impeachment, the English parliament sent for Sir George Radcliffe and charged him with high treason too, thereby silencing Strafford's key witness.

A king who believed he ruled by divine right, a parliament in revolt against his autocratic rule, a disaffected nobility, the Puritans' detestation of the Laudian Church of England, a widespread fear of Catholicism among the common people, an unpopular war with the Scots—all of these forces and factions would coalesce in an explosion that would rock England to its foundations.

STRAFFORD'S TRIAL

AND EXECUTION

LUCY WAS SICK IN BED, nursing a fever, when she heard the dreadful news that the Earl of Strafford had been accused of high treason and was now in custody. She had expected that he would come back from the north to a dangerously hostile parliament, but she was unprepared for the suddenness of the attack.

Having ridden hard all night, Strafford had taken his seat in the House of Lords that morning. After a few hours, he had left to consult with the King nearby at Whitehall. Their discussion was interrupted by a breathless man who had come to warn Strafford that a delegation from the Commons was going to the Lords to ask for his impeachment. At this, Strafford had rushed back to Westminster Hall. But John Pym, the spokesman for the Commons, had already laid the charge of treason before the Lords. Strafford was ordered to wait outside while the Lords considered the charge. After ten minutes of standing in the lobby with a group from the Commons, who kept their hats on to show their disrespect for him, he was recalled to the House of Lords and ordered to kneel while the Earl of Manchester read out the charge of treason. Strafford's request to speak was denied, and he was informed that he would hear the articles of impeachment in due course. When he attempted to enter his own coach, he was held back by the Black Rod—the principal usher of the House of Lords—who informed him that he was under house arrest and would be staying with him at his lodgings.[1]

Strafford's impeachment was largely the work of one man: John Pym. Now close to sixty, Pym was a devout Puritan lawyer who had been a very active member of Parliament since James's reign; in fact, he had been a manager of the abortive attempt to impeach the Duke of Buckingham in 1627. In those years, he and Wentworth (not yet Earl of Strafford) had fought side by side against Charles's determination to override the law. Wentworth's desertion to the King's side in 1629 undoubtedly influenced Pym's relentless attack on him in 1640.

Over the years when Parliament was suspended, Pym had been treasurer of the Providence Island Company, of which the Earl of Holland was governor. This employment had brought him into close association with Holland and his brother, the second Earl of Warwick, as well as other great Puritan lords involved in the overseas venture. Now with Parliament once more in session, Pym was able to use that connection as a conduit to the upper house. In the lower house, he resumed his lifelong fight to bring the King under the laws of Parliament. To accomplish this, Pym sincerely believed that the Earl of Strafford, the dangerous champion of the divine right of kings, had to be destroyed.

While Pym fleshed out the charge, Strafford remained a prisoner in the house of the Black Rod, his request for bail refused. The Earl was to be tried by his peers, and on November 25, he was brought before the Lords to hear the articles of impeachment. Lucy was among the spectators who listened to the long list of allegations. It was alleged that he had intended to subvert the fundamental laws of the kingdom and introduce a tyrannical form of government. He was accused of assuming royal power over the King's subjects in England and Ireland, of enriching himself at the expense of the royal revenues, of encouraging papists, of stirring up enmity between England and Scotland, of incurring dishonorable defeats at Newburn and

Newcastle, and of incensing the King against parliaments. Pym left it open to add other charges.[2]

After the reading of the articles, Strafford spoke. He asked for time to consider the charges and for leave to consult counsel and call witnesses—no more than a prisoner's right to natural justice. Lucy, not an unbiased spectator, raved about his speech and bearing to the Leicesters. Everyone had been filled with wonder, she said; indeed, she had never heard "so great and so general a commendation of any action." Moreover, he was sincerely confident that he would over-come all the accusations. She had never seen him discomposed for one minute, she told her relatives. Yet when he was taken away in a closed coach, this time to the Tower of London, he left a dejected woman sitting with the other gorgeously clad courtiers. "So much am I distracted with my own thoughts," she wrote her brother-in-law, that she could not attend to anybody's business but Leicester's own.[3]

In the fluid political situation, Lucy and her brothers were still trying to get another appointment for Leicester. "Some advantage should fall to him out of all the changes," was how Northumberland put it. They were not agreed, however, on which potential vacancy was the most desirable. Northumberland favored the lord deputy-ship while Harry liked secretary of state; Lucy's first choice was lord treasurer, but since that was unlikely, she preferred secretary over lord deputy because that would give her Dorothy's company in En-gland.[4] Northumberland was not going to court these days but was keeping to his house. He had rented the Earl of Newport's mansion in St. Martin's Parish because it was near Leicester House, and there Lucy went to discuss their strategy regarding Leicester. She scolded her brother gently, telling him that he would have to take a more ac-tive part if they were to succeed. She also informed him that Holland was secretly after the lord deputyship for himself, although she thought him "the unlikeliest in the kingdom" to get it, since he was in disfavor with both their Majesties.[5] She herself, she was happy to say, was very much in the Queen's good graces and therefore able to assist the business.

Harry, as usual, was striving to appear as important as his elder siblings. In his letters to Leicester, he tried to cut Lucy out, urging his brother-in-law to make him his exclusive agent with the Queen. It was no wonder that Dorothy, in disgust, complained to Lucy of the "divisions among their friends."

No matter who approached her, Henrietta Maria was always very well disposed toward Leicester. She was at this time trying to enlist as many friends for the King as she could. But despite his need for supporters, Charles was extraordinarily averse to any promotion for his ambassador to France—even with all the Queen's blandishments. Only Algernon could bring the King around, Lucy told Dorothy. The King would do anything to secure him to his service, but their brother was "so backward in engaging himself at this time" that he was of little help to Leicester.[6] She suggested that Dorothy urge Algernon to show more interest in the King's service but not to let him know the suggestion came from her. Lucy also told her sister that Leicester's greatest well-wisher was the Lord Lieutenant. She knew as a fact that he was pressing the King to name his successor, for if people saw that he would not be kept in the royal service, it might be some advantage to his defense and would certainly accord with his private desires.

On her visits to the Tower, Lucy found Strafford unvaryingly cheerful. "My Lord Lieutenant's confidence does daily increase," she told Dorothy.[7] But his good spirits no longer reassured her, because she realized that the man was fearless. As Christmas drew near, she became more and more depressed. "We shall know no more of my Lord Lieutenant's business till after Christmas," she wrote Dorothy on December 17, "which gives me great pains, for uncertainties and doubts are very unpleasant to me where I am so much concerned as I am in all his Lordship's interest." Indeed, she took it "so much to heart" that she had made herself sick. She had been in bed for a week, she informed her sister, but was feeling a little better now after the doctor came and let blood.

Dorothy's reponse was heartless. She accused Lucy of preferring Strafford to her own brother Northumberland, which elicited a frantic denial. With a shock, Lucy realized that Dorothy was prejudiced against Strafford. In this greatest sorrow of her life, she was to have no support from her sister. As for Northumberland, he was clearly indifferent to Strafford's fate. Of her family, only Harry remained staunch to their once-great friend.

Even in her despair, Lucy did not lose her consuming interest in finery. With Dorothy in Paris, she could not resist the opportunity to acquire the latest fashions. A portrait of Doll had just arrived, and Lucy was taken with her dress. She would be much obliged, she wrote Dorothy in mid-December, "if you would command me a petticoat and bodice of the fashion of my Lady Spencer's picture." It did not have to be green satin like Doll's; Dorothy could use her own discretion as to color and material, but Lucy was eager for a similar dress "for I must consider the fashion."[8]

Dorothy was pregnant again. And seemingly Doll had inherited her mother's high fertility, for she was already expecting her second child. Notwithstanding their condition, the ladies of the English embassy participated in all the seasonal merrymaking, and Dorothy gave Lucy a full report. "We are so glad to hear some of your gallantries," Lucy replied, adding that she had never seen a London Christmas with so little going on. People talked of nothing but miseries. There were none of the customary masques, theatricals, or dances. "It is a charity to divert us," she told her sister.[9]

Parliament was on a witch hunt. Strafford's impeachment had been followed by Laud's and Lord Keeper Finch's. Like Secretary Windebank, Finch fled to the Continent. The bishops were next; popular fury was such that they were hunted through the streets, and insults and even stones were hurled at them. As Hawkins told Leicester, "every day begets new accusations." Charles was desperately trying to mollify his outraged subjects. In the new year, there was talk of a major government shuffle. Members of the opposition group were to be given some of the highest positions in the kingdom. The meddling queen tried to buy Pym off by offering him the chancellorship of the Exchequer but was turned down with a wry smile. If the Queen and Northumberland, working together, could not get either the lord deputyship or secretary of state for Leicester in the present state of affairs, "there must be a curse upon us," Lucy declared to Dorothy.

Meanwhile the Leicesters were growing impatient with their "influential" relatives and their promises. At the beginning of 1641, they enlisted the help of sycophantic Sir John Temple who was still in London, waiting to take up his appointment as Master of the Rolls in Ireland. On January 1, Leicester set the project in motion with a letter to Temple. The target was the Queen's favorite, Sir Henry Jermyn. Temple was to bribe Jermyn to support Leicester's candidacy for the lord deputyship. Temple replied approvingly that the Earl was "now absolutely fallen upon the right way for compassing his designs." Barring intervention by Parliament, the Queen would make all the new state appointments: her power over the King was so great that those around him were "fain to use some artifice to conceal it." And Jermyn's influence over the Queen was known to everyone at court. Jermyn, in turn, "took counsel" only with his secretary, Robert Long. Temple would work through Long, "of whom he is as confident as of himself, and so may the Earl of Leicester be likewise."[10]

While dealing through the King's friends, Leicester was also mending his fences on the parliamentary side by writing to Viscount Mandeville—probably under Dorothy's prodding. Her hardheaded approach was manifest in the entire scheme to bypass their well-meaning courtier relatives. Leicester was chronically irresolute. Like many intellectuals, he was too analytical; he saw the pros and cons of every action and so took none. Dorothy, on the other hand, was adversarial by nature and thrust straight ahead to her goal without a backward glance. Around the turn of the year, Leicester wrote at least two letters to Mandeville, professing his sympathies for the Puritans and stating that he wanted "to live in the good opinion of the brethren."[11]

Temple reported that Jermyn was pleased with the Earl's proposal, but the latter would have to name the specific amount of the "present." Robert Long impressed upon Temple that he had never seen Jermyn do anything without money. He informed Temple that Sir Henry Vane also wanted the deputyship and was ready to pay for it. On January 21, Temple wrote Leicester with obvious trepidation that to forestall Jermyn's closing with Vane, he had been forced to make an offer of £4,000. Leicester was coldly furious, informing him that he would never pay so much money. But Temple was wise in the ways of the court. Through Long he negotiated a deal with Jermyn whereby Leicester would guarantee him an equivalent amount in patronage when he became Lord Deputy of Ireland. It would be up to Leicester whether he wanted to honor this commitment, of course, wily Temple told him.[12]

Lucy and her brothers knew nothing about Temple's commission except that he was earnestly trying to help Leicester. After the new appointments were made, with once again with nothing for Leicester, Lucy and Harry regarded his "business" as "desperate." Still, no successor to Strafford had been named. Holland's bid for the deputyship was out in the open, and some of the parliamentary leaders were about to petition the King on his behalf. Temple was pleased to report that Lady Carlisle was zealously working to cross her old admirer Holland.

On January 30, Strafford was brought to the House of Lords to hear the detailed charges against him. Out of pity he was allowed a stool to sit on. If strangers were moved, seeing the ravages that two months in a damp prison had wrought in his appearance, Lucy's distress can only be imagined. She was "so distracted" that it took her a week before she could pick up her pen and write to her sister. She reported that the Lord Lieutenant was still superbly confident, "with much reason, both from his own innocence and the weakness of his charge." His strength of character simply amazed her. "To see him, you would not believe he had ever been happier," she told Dorothy in wonderment.[13]

In fact, Strafford was feeling relieved. Notwithstanding all Pym's best efforts, the ninety-one pages of charges did not contain a single one that constituted high treason. There were serious accusations certainly, particularly the claim that he had raised an army in Ireland to enforce King Charles's prerogative in England, but in Strafford's opinion, none were capital crimes, and he returned to the Tower to draft his response—ever optimistic.[14] On February 24, when he was brought to deliver his answer, he was in such good spirits that, waiting for the Lords to call him in, he passed the time drawing caricatures—no doubt of his accusers. He had rebuttals for all nine general and twenty-eight specific accusations, above all stressing that he never advised using the Irish army against the English but simply intended "to reduce the Scots to their obedience."[15] For Pym and his friends, the opportunity given the prisoner to answer the charges against him was just a formality, and plans for the trial began at once.

Henrietta Maria had now become Strafford's champion. Although the opposition clothed their intentions in declarations of allegiance, the attack on Strafford was in fact an attack on the King. Charles knew it, and Henrietta Maria (whose antipathy to Wentworth it had been Lucy's task to soften) belatedly realized that the fallen statesman was the royal family's mainstay. From her experience of the venality of the English courtiers, she believed she could buy off his enemies. In the dark of night she held rendezvous with those she regarded as "the most wicked," meeting them all alone at the back stairs of the palace and leading them up by torchlight to a vacant apartment of one of her ladies-in-waiting. In later years she would admit that she made few converts.[16] Lucy could not have failed to know about the Queen's intrigues. She was extremely close to Henrietta Maria at this time, and even if she had not discovered these nocturnal meetings for herself, the indiscreet queen would have told her. According to Clarendon, knowing Lucy's great concern for Strafford, the King and Queen included her in all their anxious discussions on how to save him.

Lucy would also have known about the army plot that Harry was hatching with some other daring officers. It all began when Parliament allocated an enormous sum to pay off the Scottish army squatting in the north of England, while leaving the English army unpaid. Harry had gone into debt raising a troop for the Scottish war, and so had other commanders of his acquaintance; they met to air their discontent in Harry's chamber at court. While they were in their cups, the idea was born of taking control of the northern army and bringing it to London to save Strafford. Each conspirator brought in others until the group included the court poets Suckling and Davenant; George Goring, the son of Lucy's old admirer; Sir Henry Jermyn; and that same Captain Billingsley in whose name Strafford had put one of Lucy's Irish leases. Even in such a clandestine operation, quarrels over precedence erupted, and these proved fatal to the undertaking. When the others refused to let Goring be Commander-in-Chief, he revealed the embryonic plot to Pym's friends.[17] Pym filed it away for future use.

While Strafford's future was looking dim to everyone but himself, Temple's negotiations on Leicester's behalf were at last proceeding very satisfactorily. Jermyn was only waiting until "the Earl of Strafford's business be despatched," Temple reported on March 4. He cautioned that Jermyn's name must never be mentioned in connection with the appointment lest it prejudice Parliament against Leicester. Nor his own name, for that matter. The Lord Admiral and Lady Carlisle must have all the honor of it.

ON MARCH 22, 1641, Strafford's trial began in the awesome setting of Westminster Hall, whose great raftered ceiling soared above the scaffolding erected to seat the public. At the far end of the hall was the throne with a chair placed beside it for the Prince of Wales; but the King had been requested to stay out of sight in one of two enclosed "closets" built for the occasion for the royal family. In front of the raised dais with its empty throne, the Earl of Arundel, the Lord High Steward, was seated on the green woolsack, presiding over the trial in his most lordly manner. In front of him were the great officers of state, the judges in their scarlet robes, the black-gowned clerks huddled around their table (among them John Rushworth, whose transcribed shorthand notes would provide an official daily record of the trial), and, to the side, the peers of the realm in ermine-lined red velvet. All these sat as on a stage, facing the bar covered in green baize. Standing at the bar were a dozen members of the Commons, led by John Pym, who were to conduct the prosecution. A table had been set out for the prisoner at the bar, who was constantly attended by the Lord Lieutenant of the Tower. Behind Strafford sat his four secretaries, who handed him papers as he required them, and behind them his lawyers at a long table piled with tomes.[18]

For such a "glorious assembly" the decorum was remarkably bad. A Scottish commissioner, who attended daily, reported home that the spectators in the galleries ate throughout the proceedings, "not just confections but flesh and bread, bottles of beer and wine going thick from mouth to mouth without cups, and all this in the King's eye." Some people even urinated through the scaffolding.[19]

Half hidden by a tapestry in one of the enclosed boxes, the Queen and her ladies, among them Lucy, attended every day, taking copious notes that they discussed in the evening. Unfortunately none of Lucy's letters about the trial have survived; however, from those of the period leading up to the trial we can safely surmise that her distress was intense. Just looking at her friend would have been enough to move her to tears. She had not seen Strafford since the end of January because only his lawyers, his doctor, and a few servants were permitted to visit.[20] Strafford had turned into an old man in the Tower, bent and gray-faced, wearing a snug little cap to keep out the cold. But if he was broken in body, his mind was as sharp as ever. He defended himself, as the Queen said, "with dauntless spirit and irrepressible wit."[21] All those who were not his sworn enemies were struck by his courage and greatness of mind. "Truly his Lordship carries himself very gallantly," Temple reported to Leicester. To Pym, impatient to be done with the business, Strafford's able rebuttals were simply "impertinent exceptions."

How Lucy's heart must have pounded when the prosecution moved on to the charge that the Lord Lieutenant had enriched himself in Ireland at the expense of King Charles and his subjects. She had reason to fear that she would be questioned when, on Monday, March 29, the matter of her own Glaslough lands inadvertently came up. Strafford had testified that he had referred all land claims to the courts, and to disprove this the prosecution he cited the case of Viscount Baltinglas. This Irish peer had owned the estate of Glaslough and had mortgaged it to Sir Robert Parkhurst. A dispute had arisen, and Parkhurst had petitioned the Lord Lieutenant to determine possession. The prosecution charged that not only had Strafford heard the case, but after deciding it in Parkhurst's favor and dispossessing Lord Baltinglas, he had leased the land for himself. Strafford acknowledged that he had bought the lease from Sir Robert Parkhurst; however, it was not for himself "but in trust for a Noble Person."[22] By not naming Lady Carlisle, he gallantly protected her from being called as a witness. Two days later, he was even more protective during an inquisitionlike examination concerning his profits from the Irish customs.

Strafford was looking very bad. The prosecution was making a strong case that he had engrossed the profits from the customs while serving as the country's highest official; moreover, that he enhanced his profits by raising the tariffs, to the great distress of the native population. When the prosecution stated that the Earl of Carlisle had surrendered his grant to the King in 1633 and accused Strafford of getting his hands on the wine customs as well, he could easily have refuted the charge. He did not tell them that the grant had continued to be held by Lady Carlisle and that she had enjoyed the profits virtually to the present time. If Lucy was grateful to her friend for not involving her in these horrendous proceedings, she may have been less appreciative of his care of her when she heard Sir James Hay's testimony.

Sir James had been called to testify as to the profits from the wine customs. Stating that Lord Carlisle had sent him to Ireland as his agent in 1635, he produced an account for that year prepared by the auditor for Ireland. This showed that the profits from the wine customs, after the King's rent was deducted, amounted to £2,387—a far cry from the £1,388 Lucy had received from Strafford.[23] This was not news to her; it was obviously from Hay that she had learned about the £999 outstanding from 1635. Yet hearing the auditor's account read out baldly in the court, it would have been natural to feel some bitterness that Strafford, her trustee, had knowingly undervalued the grant when she first inherited it—especially since it looked as if she would never see her rightful profits now.

April 5 was a day of high drama, when witnesses were examined on the most serious of the charges. The great question was whether, at a meeting of the Privy Council on May 5, 1640, the Earl of Strafford had advised using the Irish army to subdue the Scots or the English. With a little prompting, the Secretary of State, Sir Henry Vane, recalled that it was the latter. His testimony was refuted by all the lords who had attended the council meeting in question.[24] Seeing the weakness of Vane's testimony, Pym tried to buttress it with what was clearly manufactured evidence. In the Commons a few days later, he produced a piece of paper that, he said, contained a copy of Vane's minutes of the fateful council meeting, given to him by Vane's son. Sir Henry Vane the Younger, one of the most radical parliamentarians, immediately jumped up to corroborate Pym's statement. He declared that he had made the copy without his father's knowledge and that the original minutes had later been burned. Pym acknowledged that the piece of paper he held in his hand was his own copy of young Vane's copy, which he had destroyed after transcribing it. Carefully emphasizing the damning words supposedly spoken by Strafford to the King, Pym read aloud: "You have an army in Ireland you may employ *here* to reduce *this kingdom*."[25] From the reaction it was clear that the Commons was prepared to find Strafford guilty of treason on the doubtful evidence of a copy of a copy.

On April 10, at Westminster Hall, Strafford summed up his defense in a brilliantly logical speech that would have convinced any listener with an open mind. He had little trouble discrediting Vane, whom he called "a single witness disavowed by all the rest." He maintained that none of his actions in Ireland or England could be stretched to constitute a treasonable offense under statute or common law. Was he to be punished by a law that did not yet exist? Ominously, he warned his fellow peers of setting a dangerous precedent: "Beware that you do not awake these sleeping lions by the raking up of some neglected, some moth-eaten records—they may sometime tear you and your posterity in pieces."

Strafford's peroration was a defense of the royal prerogative, but with qualification. The prerogative was a necessary reserve power for extraordinary occasions—"the laws must have place at all other times." The best way to nourish both the rights of the subject and the royal prerogative was by "the frequent use of parliaments." To sum up his philosophy of governance, he declared that "the happiness of a kingdom consists in the just poise of the King's prerogative and the subject's liberty and that things should never be well till these went hand and hand together."[26] (It must be said that his political philosophy was not borne out by his practice in fourteen years of public life.) At the end, when he spoke of his children, he had to stop for weeping.

It was beginning to look as if Strafford would be acquitted despite "the universal hatred" for him. Having foreseen just such an eventuality, Pym was steering a bill of attainder through the lower house. If the prisoner could not be found guilty under the laws of the land, he would be voted guilty by an act of Parliament. "Nothing will satisfy the House of Commons but his head," Sir John Temple reported to the Earl of Leicester. On April 21, the bill of attainder passed the Commons and was sent up to the Lords.

In the midst of these terrifying events, Lucy was called upon to perform what must have seemed a travesty of her old duties as Lady of the Bedchamber. To appease the Puritans, Charles had arranged a Protestant marriage for his eldest daughter, Mary, a child of ten, with the fifteen-year-old son of the Prince of Orange. On April 27, the young Prince William arrived in England for the wedding. Although the celebrations were muted, there was dancing and masquing, and, thanks to Dorothy's purchases for her, Lucy was in the height of Parisian fashion. On May 2, the festivities culminated in the marriage ceremony. The royal wedding was a macabre event haunted by the ghost in the Tower.

The time had come for Pym to use the younger Goring's revelation of the foolhardy and ineffectual conspiracy of Harry Percy and the other commanders. On May 3, Pym informed the House of Commons that a plot was afoot to bring the army from the north to "overawe" Parliament, take over the Tower, and effect the Earl of Strafford's escape—all this in conjunction with a French invasion by sea.[27] He named no names, except to say that the conspirators were people close to the Queen. Jermyn, Suckling, and Davenant fled to the Continent safely, but Harry Percy was recognized at Dover and beaten within an inch of his life. Suffering a badly injured leg, he dragged himself back to London to his brother's house.[28]

Northumberland had by now defected from the King's party and become a Pym supporter. Lucy had slowly come to realize where his sympathies lay. At first she had thought that only illness was keeping him away from the court. Then she began to see that he was actually avoiding it. By January he was murmuring about giving up his army command. Because Lucy's correspondence with Dorothy ceased in early February 1641, we do not know what strains Northumberland's change of loyalties placed on the relationships among the sisters and brothers. Temple's letters show, however, that the family maintained a united front in their efforts to secure a lucrative post for Leicester. And it is significant that Harry, in his hour of need, sought sanctuary with his brother.

Somehow, Pym and his friends learned that Northumberland was harboring his brother. No doubt they threatened to reveal the whereabouts of the injured conspirator. Northumberland may even have gone along with them out of conviction. In any event, by some means they got him to persuade his brother to write a letter of confession to Parliament, exposing the plot and the plotters. Pym agreed that Northumberland could withhold the letter until Harry could make his escape. On May 5, it was read out in the Commons and a resolution was passed charging Harry Percy, Jermyn, and Suckling with treason. Later that day, Northumberland, in his capacity as Lord High Admiral, grimly signed a writ for the "strict stopping of the ports" and the arrest of his brother and his fellow conspirators.[29]

Panic and fear gripped the easily excitable London mob. As the House of Lords deliberated on the bill of attainder, thousands of shouting people milled around Westminster demanding Strafford's death, inflamed by news of the army plot to save him. On May 7, the bill passed the Lords. It was generally thought that it would stop there, that the King would never assent to it. Indeed, he had told Parliament on May 1 that he could not in good conscience do so. But on May 10, after agonies of indecision, fears for his queen's safety (an angry mob had gathered under her windows), and a letter from Strafford releasing him from his promises, Charles signed the attainder. The following day he sent the eleven-year-old Prince of Wales to the House of Lords with a fruitless appeal for life imprisonment instead of death for Strafford.

On May 12, 1641, hours before daylight, the stands erected on Tower Hill to seat thousands of spectators were already filled. Thousands more were standing, some of the more adroit scrambling onto piles of lumber or large rocks for a better view. There was an air of festivity, as if the crowd had come to see a coronation. When the black-hooded executioner mounted the scaffold at the top of the hill and began adjusting the position of the block, an anticipatory buzzing ran through the enormous crowd. This became a hush when they sighted the Earl of Strafford approaching with his brothers, his chaplains, a guard of soldiers, and his servants. He himself was walking between his cousin the Earl of Cleveland and an Irish archbishop. The crowd receded to allow a pathway for them. One spectator observed that Strafford carried himself "more like a general at the head of an army than a condemned man." His behavior on the scaffold was as edifying as Lucy and his other admiring friends would have expected. In a clear, modulated voice that carried far, he said he submitted to the judgment "with a quiet and contented mind." Although it was his "ill hap to be misconstrued," he said he had never done anything but that which aimed at the prosperity of the King and his people. He questioned whether "the beginnings of the people's happiness should be written in letters of blood," and he expressed the hope that "no one drop of my blood rise up in judgment against them." His courage never flagged. He took off his doublet "as cheerfully," he told those around him, "as if I were going to bed." Refusing a handkerchief for his eyes, he laid his head on the block. With one stroke the executioner beheaded him.[30]

SEVERAL DAYS BEFORE the execution, Leicester had quietly come over to England. Although he asserted in his journal that he had been summoned by the King, he had in fact come without leave at Temple's instigation. With "Strafford's business despatched," Temple had written, the Irish appointment would soon be filled, and if Leicester was not on the spot, someone else might extort it from the harassed King. But Jermyn had kept his part of the bargain after all.

Charles had agreed to appoint Leicester. Besides, Charles realized that Leicester would be acceptable to Parliament as Northumberland's brother-in-law and Lisle's father (Philip was now a warm supporter of Pym). A week after Strafford's execution, the King named the Earl of Leicester Lord Lieutenant of Ireland—"the greatest employment of this kingdom," exulted Temple.

From Paris Dorothy sent a surprisingly lukewarm letter of congratulations to her husband: "According to my weak devotion I have given God my humble thanks for the satisfaction that you have received, and I shall not omit to present my best prayers for a blessing upon all your proceedings, and that this new honour may bring to you an increase of all that is called happiness." Possibly she realized that it was too late to be happy in Charles's service. Moreover, she was extremely uncomfortable in this late pregnancy. "Till God will be pleased to deliver me from that great pain and danger, I cannot rejoice at anything for my own sake."[31] Harry's situation naturally disturbed her also. He had just arrived at Calais, she informed her husband, and she asked him to communicate the news to her brother and sister.

Poor Harry had landed in France in a dreadful state. He had not had time to recover before fleeing England, and for weeks he was immobilized at Calais with his badly injured leg. At last he was able to move, and on July 22, he arrived at Paris. Dorothy welcomed him with open arms and, seeing him "very weak and indisposed," immediately began looking after him. But the next morning a messenger arrived posthaste from Dieppe with a letter from her husband, ordering her not to receive Harry into the house.[32] Even for an independent woman like Dorothy, an authoritative order from the husband was to be obeyed. She was forced to turn her own brother away from her door. The King's troubles with his subjects had at last shattered the family solidarity of the Percys.

LUCY CHANGES HER

GALLANT

OVER THE SUMMER of 1641, Parliament was busy paring down King Charles's powers. Under Pym's guiding hand, legislation was passed to require the summoning of Parliament every three years, to prevent the dissolution of the present parliament without its consent, to abolish the Star Chamber and the High Commission, and to end ship-money levies and the forest laws. A bill was also introduced to abolish church government by bishops "root and branch," but it was premature for such a radical motion. The King's every move was blocked. At loggerheads with his English parliament, Charles placed his hopes on winning over his Scottish parliament, and in August he left for Scotland. Henrietta Maria took up residence at Oatlands in Surrey, the lovely dower manor of English queens.

It was while the King was in Scotland that Lucy did an extraordinary thing. After mourning the Earl of Strafford for several months, she became a bosom friend of John Pym, the pudgy little man of sixty who seemed to have no life outside the committee room and whose skill at managing Parliament had brought her dearest friend to the executioner's block. A disgusted royalist sneered that Lady Carlisle "had now changed her gallant from Strafford to Mr. Pym."[1] Edward Hyde (the future Lord Clarendon), who was still a member of Pym's inner councils at this time, attributed Lady Carlisle's turning coat to disillusionment with the King and Queen. "After she had for a short time murmured for the death of the Earl of Strafford," he would later write, "she renounced all future devotion for those who would, but could not, protect him, and applied herself to and courted all those who murdered him, with all possible condescensions."[2] Lucy may well have asked herself why she should give her fidelity to a king and queen who could not even save their most loyal subject. Besides, she saw the King at too close quarters: wrongheaded, ineffectual, ruled by a wife who was sadly wanting in judgment.

But was Lucy also disillusioned with the friend she had so trusted? Under Strafford's trusteeship, the substantial Irish holdings she had inherited from Carlisle had melted away. Partly it was the troubled times; the empty Irish and English Exchequers could not be squeezed to pay out the £16,000 she was supposed to receive for surrendering her wine customs grant—she was fortunate to have got even £1,000. But there were no rents coming in from Ireland either. In fact, her Irish lands were in jeopardy. Viscount Baltinglas was petitioning the English parliament to recover the Glaslough estate, and an Irish peer named Lord Brabazon was making claims on Shillelagh.[3] Strafford had died, leaving Lucy with nothing to prove her right to the leases that he had purchased with her money from the sale of her inherited lands. At the time, he had given her to understand that the proper documents had been drawn up to verify that the leases were held in trust for her. Now she needed those documents. Time and again she asked William Railton, the Wentworth family's London agent, to get these "writings" for her.[4] He promised to do his best, but, so far, she had not received them. For these worthless leases she had given up her valuable inherited lands! Strafford had talked her into selling the vast tract of the Birnes Country to the King by telling her that the title was defective, yet it had been perfected quickly enough once she surrendered the grant. And while he had got her a fair price, she now knew that he had personally profited to the tune of several thousand pounds a year in rents from the two manors in the Birnes Country that the King had regranted to him. Indeed, a modern historian has written, "It is not unreasonable to suggest that this incident of the Birnes Country may have had something to do with the famous transfer of Lucy Carlisle's platonic affections from Strafford to Pym."[5] In retrospect, Lucy may have felt that she had less reason to be grateful to her dead friend than she had supposed. Among her new friends there was no dearth of people to tell her that Strafford had been unworthy of her trust. One of these was Sir John Clotworthy, an old enemy of Strafford's from Ireland, for whom Pym and his friends had found a safe seat in the English Commons, where he had seconded Pym's campaign against Strafford.[6]

The Queen was unaware of Lady Carlisle's desertion. In fact, Henrietta Maria believed that Lucy was on her side and that she was getting valuable intelligence about the King's enemies from her favorite lady-in-waiting. One September day in 1641, Lucy arrived at Oatlands with a paper that she said she had obtained from Viscount Mandeville, a leader of the parliamentary opposition. Secretary of State Edward Nicholas thought it useful enough to the royal cause to have it published.[7] At the time she brought this paper to the Queen, Lucy was already in daily contact with Mandeville and Pym. In Edward Hyde's opinion, they were using her as a conduit to the impressionable and talkative queen.

Lady Carlisle was ideal for their purposes. Henrietta Maria trusted her, not only because of her long years in the royal service but because of the "eminent and constant affection" she had shown the Earl of Strafford during his impeachment. And Lucy was not reticent about the Queen in her conversations with her new allies. As Hyde put it, she "communicated all she knew, and more, of the natures and dispositions of the King and Queen."[8] Pym was able to extract from Lucy a psychological portrait of the little queen who wielded such power over her husband. A master at manipulation, in the great game he was playing to change the government of England, Pym moved people like pawns. At will he could summon up a mob of apprentices from the London workshops to demand the measures he was trying to push through Parliament. By means of Lady Carlisle, he sent the Queen messages that stirred up her excitable nature. Foreseeing her reaction, he planned his next move.

It was likely at Viscount Mandeville's house in Chelsea that Lucy became so friendly with John Pym. There, a cabal of opposition lords met regularly with Pym and his lieutenants in the Commons to plan their parliamentary strategy.[9] Among them were some of the greatest peers of the realm. Several were privy councillors appointed during Strafford's trial, when King Charles still hoped to win them over; the Earl of Essex had been named Lord Chamberlain as late as July 1641. Essex, Warwick, Holland, and Newport were Lucy's first cousins. Mandeville (who was to become Earl of Manchester in 1642 on his father's death) was her cousin by marriage. As treasurer of the Providence Island Company, Pym had known these Puritan lords for years. There is little doubt that Lucy was brought into the cabal by the Earl of Holland. Lucy had drifted away from Holland after Strafford returned to England in the autumn of 1639. The two men were on the worst possible terms, and, with all her savoir faire, she had been unable to maintain a friendship with both. But now, with Strafford gone, she fell back on Holland. In this new phase of their friendship, they were on more equal ground. Lucy was in her forty-second year, and Holland was over fifty. He no longer wrote poetry to her, and she no longer "made sport" of him. The gallantry of the past was replaced by a "strict friendship" that would carry the pair into dangerous waters in the turbulent years ahead.

Holland had been disaffected from the King for a year or more. Indeed, in April 1640, Archbishop Laud was advised that while the Earl of Warwick was the visible head of the Puritan party, his brother Holland was the invisible head.[10] Had Holland not been a younger son with an insatiable desire for luxurious living, he would have joined his brother and the other Puritan lords in the political wilderness during the 1630s. By blood ties, business interests, and religion he belonged with them. When there was nothing more to be gained from the royal service, he deserted.

At Henrietta Maria's urging, Charles made one last effort to retain Holland. Before leaving for Scotland he appointed him Lord General of His Majesty's Forces beyond the Trent River. As the war with the Scots was over—peace was signed on September 2, 1641— this glorious title entailed no more than disbanding the northern army. After his return from the north, Holland all but ignored the Queen and consorted with "those Lords who were against the bishops and the Book of Common Prayer."[11] Not only did Holland attend the meetings at Lord Mandeville's, but he frequently played host to Pym and his friends at his beautiful country house in Kensington.

Political intrigue had always fascinated Lucy. She had played a considerable role in court politics by cultivating great men. Now Pym was the great man of the hour. Through him she was at the center of momentous events. Canny Pym had found a natural *intriguante* in the Countess of Carlisle. Whether there was a sexual side to Lucy's relationship with John Pym is doubtful. But his personal influence over her can be inferred from the manner in which she assimilated his Puritan ways. We do not hear of Holland "condescending" to attend a sermon by one of Pym's favorite fire-and-brimstone preachers. Yet Lady Carlisle "became such a she-saint that she frequented their sermons and took notes."[12]

It was in this "fashion" that Dorothy found her sister when she returned from France in October 1641. Leicester had gone back to Paris to take formal leave of the French court and to bring his family home. Before leaving France, Dorothy had stocked up on luxury goods suitable to their anticipated viceregal splendor in Ireland, most notably a rich and costly coach.[13] Showing off her magnificent purchases to a soberly dressed Lucy, Dorothy may have thought with some satisfaction that their roles had been reversed. Here she was, the country wife, dazzling the great court lady with the latest things from Paris.

Leicester expected that on the King's return from Scotland, he would get his orders to take up his post as Lord Lieutenant of Ireland. In the meantime, he had to be in London to attend the Privy Council and the Committee on Irish Affairs, so Dorothy settled the family into Leicester House. Doll and Henry Spencer had left France in June and spent the summer with their two babies at Althorp, his family home in Northamptonshire. To Dorothy's delight, in the autumn they came up from the country to join the family at Leicester House in order for Henry, now twenty-one, to take his seat in the House of Lords. Dorothy did not need grandchildren to have a baby in the house. Her latest, born that summer, was a boy christened

Henry—a Percy name but also a compliment to a beloved son-in-law. This child, who was to be her last, was as dear to Dorothy as her first-born. Golden-haired and smiling, he brought joy into the family life, which, all too often, was made discordant by the parents' arguments.

During the three years they had been parted, the personality traits that had caused temporary rifts between husband and wife in the past had grown more pronounced. Naturally assertive, Dorothy had turned into a strong, no-nonsense, controlling woman. Her always limited powers of conciliation had rusted, and she no longer troubled to save her husband's feelings. For his part, Leicester had always had a tendency to withdraw into isolation. Living a bachelor's existence in Paris for so many years, he found it difficult to readjust to married life. Frustrated by his aloofness, Dorothy had become more aggressive and demanding during her two years in France. Now, back in England, the tensions between them erupted into more quarrels about money.

The Leicesters' financial arrangements were like those of total strangers. Certainly, it was unusual between spouses that when Dorothy borrowed money from her husband she had to pay him interest, and he, in turn, had to pay her for his keep as if he were staying at an inn. Hawkins was once again delivering the rent money to Dorothy. Leicester would later complain that she did not pay interest on his debts, so that his indebtedness grew "as it proved very near to my undoing."[14] Nevertheless, he did nothing about it at the time but, typically, allowed his resentment to fester in his mind.

Suddenly, Leicester had more to worry about than his business accounts with his wife. He received word that the Irish Catholics had risen against the Protestant English settlers. It had been the policy of both Elizabeth and James to "colonize" Ireland with English families, granting them large plantations that had displaced the native Irish. The Irish Rebellion of 1641 was an attempt to take advantage of King Charles's problems at home. A conspiracy to take over Dublin Castle and seize the armaments had been uncovered in time, but in northern Ireland the rebels were attacking castles and government arsenals. Rumors were rampant of burning and plundering and of atrocities against Protestants. Leicester immediately informed the Privy Council, which went in a body to the Commons. On center stage for once,

Leicester informed the members of Parliament of the bloody events in Ireland. Sounding purposeful and decisive, he declared that men and money must be sent at once "to save Ireland, for the safety of England depends upon it."[15] Laying aside the Grand Remonstrance—a comprehensive attack on the royal prerogative and the episcopacy that Pym was steering through the House at this time—the Commons passed a series of resolutions dealing with the Irish business. These included an urgent request to the Lord Lieutenant to name officers and to hasten over to Ireland himself with all due diligence.

After his hard-hitting speech to the Commons, Leicester subsided into his habitual indecisiveness, and when an ordinance was passed by both houses directing him to levy volunteers in England "to secure Dublin and the English Pale," he dithered, questioning whether he could raise troops without the King's warrant. This led the Commons to take a further bite out of the prerogative, declaring that an ordinance of Lords and Commons was sufficient in itself.[16]

Dorothy had none of her husband's difficulties over divided loyalties. She threw herself into Lucy's faction with gusto. Indeed, Hyde thought her "equally active and tempestuous" as her sister. According to him, she "drew the principal persons who were most obnoxious to the Court, and to whom the Court was most obnoxious, to a constant conversation at Leicester House."[17] In Dorothy's wainscoted withdrawing room, the talk was allowed to roam freely, with no respect for persons, and bordered more than a little on lèse-majesté. Lucy appears to have introduced Pym into Dorothy's salon, for when Dorothy went to Penshurst in the summer, Pym kept in touch with her by letter.[18] How did Leicester feel about his wife's nest of anti-royalists under his roof? Hyde believed it was very disagreeable to the Earl's "nature and prudence." Arguing against this, however, were Leicester's continuing close friendships with Northumberland, Mandeville, and Pembroke, all of whom were openly opposed to the King.

Meanwhile, Lucy continued to carry Pym's planted stories to the Queen. Unlike most messengers bearing bad news, she was received with open arms. Poor Henrietta Maria closed her mind to any doubts she may have had about Lucy; there were so few people she could trust any more, as she said to Secretary Nicholas.[19] It may well have been Lucy who brought her the sinister report about a meeting at Holland House where, during a discussion of the many plots and conspiracies of the day, the Earl of Newport was said to have advocated seizing the Queen and her children. Not long before this, Henrietta Maria had received a most disturbing visit from the Earl of Holland. Her erstwhile courtier informed her that because of "the Jesuits and other dangerous persons" in her house, Parliament wanted the instant removal of the Prince of Wales and Prince James, the Duke of York, to their own palace of Richmond. The Queen gained a reprieve by saying that the princes were at Oatlands to celebrate their sister's birthday.[20] However, the report of Newport's remark, on top of Holland's visit, had her badly frightened.

The story about the Earl of Newport was one of the many tales of woe that Henrietta Maria had to tell her husband when he finally returned from Scotland at the end of November. The Irish Rebellion had fueled anti-Catholic sentiment in the country. Both in and out of Parliament, it was focused on the Queen. Many Puritans honestly believed that she was the center of "a malignant party" that intended to bring back Roman Catholicism and to destroy the liberty of the English people. Rumor had it that she and her clique had actually incited the Catholic rising in Ireland. Mobs of London apprentices roved around Westminster shouting the catchphrase "Down with papists and popery."

At Christmastime an enormous crowd, armed with staves and other crude weapons, assembled outside Westminster and Whitehall Palace to protest the King's replacement of the Puritan Lieutenant of the Tower with one of his own most trusted veterans, one Captain Lunsford. Storming into Westminster Abbey, they threatened to pull down the organ. They were so threatening that the militia had to be called out. Only when word spread among the crowd that the King had revoked Lunsford's appointment was a riot averted. From then on, Charles had a guard put on the palace around the clock.

There were no revelries at Whitehall this Christmas. Inside the palace the Queen could not shut out the sound of the tumultuous crowd. With her protruding teeth and nervous gestures, she was like a cornered mouse when Lady Carlisle, plump and sleek, arrived one day during Christmas week with horrible news. Pym's party intended to accuse Her Majesty of high treason, she confided to the Queen. It was true that there was some private talk of her impeachment, but Hyde was certain that it "was imparted to her upon design."[21] Lucy was undoubtedly sent by Pym to frighten the Queen into some precipitate and foolish action.

Pym was anxious to bring matters to a head. King Charles was winning over some of the moderates in Parliament with assurances that he had no intention of deviating from the religion and liberties of Queen Elizabeth's reign. Moreover, the extremist demands in the Grand Remonstrance had alienated some of Pym's worthiest supporters. Edward Hyde, for example, had gone over to the royalist side. Another was Sir John Colepeper, who had made the colorful speech against monopolies in 1640.

With Lucy's help, Pym played on the Queen's fears with the desired result. Frightened out of her wits, Henrietta Maria urged Charles to impeach her enemies before they could impeach her. The purported threat against his wife galvanized the King into action. On January 3, 1642, he sent his Attorney General to the House of Lords to accuse Viscount Mandeville and five members of the Commons of high treason. The five were the worst troublemakers: John Pym, Denzil Holles, John Hampden, William Stroud, and Sir Arthur Haselrig. The charges centered on "a traitorous endeavour" to deprive the King of his rightful power and to alienate his subjects. Simultaneously, the Sergeant-at-Arms, quaking in his boots, asked the Speaker of the House to render up the five members at the King's command.

Parliament stonewalled the King. The Lords coolly struck a committee to "examine precedents," and the Commons sent respectful word to the palace that since their privileges were involved, they would require time to consider the matter. Not only did Parliament refuse to obey the King, but it countermanded a royal order to seal the trunks and papers in Pym's and Holles's lodgings.[22]

AS WE HAVE SEEN, Lucy was not above putting her ear to the door when the King and Queen were having a private discussion. The day after Parliament refused to render up the five members, she heard them arguing. Placing her hands on her silk skirt to stop the rustling, she tiptoed to the door and eavesdropped. Henrietta Maria was railing at her husband for allowing the parliamentary leaders to defy him. She threatened to leave him if he did not go to the Commons and "pull these rogues out by their ears."[23] Charles seemed reluctant, offering sound reasons why it was a dangerous course to take, but Henrietta Maria was in such a temper that Charles finally agreed. He would go to Parliament with a small guard that afternoon.[24]

Without a moment's hesitation, Lucy betrayed her royal masters. She sent a warning to Pym that the King was coming to Parliament in person to arrest him and the other four members that day. That was in the late morning. Shortly after noon, Lucy entered the Queen's private chamber to find her alone, silent and unmoving as a statue, staring at the watch in her hand. The minutes ticked by. All of a sudden, Henrietta Maria became her effervescent self. "Rejoice with me," she exclaimed to Lucy, "at this hour the King is, as I have reason to hope, master of his realm, for Pym and his confederates are arrested before now."[25]

The Queen's joy was premature. Before Charles and his guard of soldiers arrived at Westminster, an army officer burst in and informed the House that the King was on his way with several hundred soldiers. "Whereupon," recorded John Rushworth, the parliamentary clerk, "a certain Member of the House" jumped up and announced that he had received "private intimation from the Countess of Carlisle that endeavours would be used this day to apprehend the five Members."[26] The five men hurriedly departed. Forewarned by Lucy, they had planned their escape. At Westminster Stairs a boat was waiting to waft them down the river to the City, where friends were on hand to give them sanctuary.

Moments later the door of the House was thrown open and the King, gesturing to the soldiers to remain outside, entered with his nephew. Walking toward the Speaker's chair, he cast a glance at the empty bench where Pym normally sat. Taking the chair from the Speaker, he asked the Commons to render up the five members he had impeached. Then, looking around the room and not seeing any of them, he sadly observed that "the birds were flown." The House was in an uproar. As he walked out, the members shouted insultingly, "Privilege! Privilege!"

The King's coup had failed, largely because of Lucy. Certainly the five members of Parliament gave her full credit. Sir Arthur Haselrig later expressed "his thanks to God that through the timely notice given by the kindness of that great lady, the Lady Carlisle, bloodshed had been prevented." Bulstrode Whitelocke, present in the House during these dramatic events, confirmed in his *Memorials* that Lady Carlisle was regarded as a heroine by the parliamentarians:

> And divers imagined that if the five members had not received a secret notice from a great court lady, their friend (who over-heard some discourse of this intended action, and thereof gave timely notice to those gentlemen) whereby they got out of the House just before the King came: otherwise, it was believed, that if the King had found them there, and called in his guards to have seized them, the members of the House would have endeavoured the defence of them, which might have proved a very unhappy and bad business.[27]

To royalist supporters, the Countess of Carlisle at last stood revealed as a spy and a traitor. It was, of course, the end of her long service at court. Unaware of Lucy's eavesdropping, Henrietta Maria blamed herself entirely for her *malheureuse indiscrétion* in confiding in her, the more so as the King never uttered a word of reproach.[28]

King Charles felt he could no longer stay in London. The City was in a veritable state of mutiny, boldly harboring the five fugitives. On January 10, 1642, Charles quietly left Whitehall with his family and slipped down the river to Hampton Court. He had commanded his First Groom of the Bedchamber and the Lord Chamberlain to accompany them, but Holland and Essex refused point-blank to do their duty.[29]

PART THREE

THE

FORTUNES

OF

WAR

MOURNING A BELOVED

SOLDIER

IN LATE AUGUST 1642, a great stave with its fluttering banner was planted outside the walls of Nottingham Castle in the north of England. Charles had raised his standard, and the war between King and Parliament had begun. Dorothy, who was at Penshurst in the south, was not afraid for her household. "But who can tell what may happen," she wrote Hawkins, "for our miserable divisions, in my opinion, are more like to increase than conclude."[1] Her husband and son-in-law were among the lords attending the King at the raising of the standard at Nottingham Castle.[2] Both had been late in declaring their colors. While some peers and Commons members had gone over to the King when Parliament introduced a bill giving itself the right to raise a militia, the Earl of Leicester and Baron Spencer had continued to attend the parliamentary sessions. It was only in July that the Lord Lieutenant-elect of Ireland joined the King. Doll's husband had remained an active member of the Commons through the winter and spring, but in the summer, when every man had to choose sides, with a heavy heart and little inclination, young Henry Spencer followed his uncle the Earl of Southampton to royalist headquarters at York. He volunteered for the King's bodyguard—a cavalry troop of wealthy young noblemen and gentlemen, one of whom estimated that together they were worth £100,000 a year.³ Fighting for the King was the lesser of two evils, Henry told Doll, since he would rather be hanged than fight on the Parliament side.⁴

Doll was at Penshurst with her babies, awaiting her third child. Sweet-natured as ever, she never complained, but she lived for Henry's letters. It was such a comfort for Dorothy to have her there with her dear little girl, whom they all called Poppet, and baby Robert, sharing the nursery with Dorothy's own babies, Frances and Henry. A little over a year old, Henry already gave promise of extraordinarily good looks. Like Doll, he had the best features of both sides of the family, having been exempted from the long, narrow face of the Sidneys and from his mother's thin, pointed nose, inherited from the Percys. The war would certainly touch Dorothy's older sons. She supposed they would have to join the royalist army, considering their father's position. As she wrote to Hawkins unenthusiastically, she did not see how her son Philip could avoid going to the King.

With her husband and son-in-law serving the King, Dorothy and her household were regarded as royalists. In truth, her heart was with the parliamentarians. She encouraged Pym's letters: "Mr. Pime [sic] need not fear the miscarriage of his letters to me," she informed Hawkins, "for they have not opened any one of mine since I left London."⁵ In doing so she felt no disloyalty to her husband, because she knew that only self-interest kept Leicester in attendance upon the King. Day after day he waited upon Charles, pleading for permission to take up his post in Ireland, but he was always put off. Dorothy began to despair of ever being the chatelaine of Dublin Castle. This did not make her any more zealous for the royalist cause. Moreover, most of her family and friends were on Parliament's side. Her cousin the Earl of Essex was Commander-in-Chief of the parliamentary forces, and her friend the Earl of Manchester (Viscount Mandeville) was in command of one of Essex's foot regiments. Of all of them, of course, her brother Algernon had the greatest influence on her. When thirty-two peers left the House of Lords and went to York, Northumberland did not budge. No longer Lord High Admiral—Charles had dismissed him in a very bitter letter—he sat on the Committee of Public Safety that was attempting to govern the country without the King and the Great Seal. Parliamentary politics agreed with him as the royal administration never had. He was in excellent health and was about to remarry. His wife-to-be was the daughter of the Earl of Suffolk. As part of her dowry, she was bringing with her her family's magnificent London mansion in the Strand.

Lucy was as involved as ever in her intrigues. She would arrive at Penshurst full of mysterious hints of secret plans and conferences with Holland. But more often she talked about her problems with her Irish property. Lord Baltinglas and Lord Brabazon were pursuing their claims to her Glaslough and Shillelagh lands in the English parliament, and although she had been pressing the Wentworths' agent in London, William Railton, for months to get her the documents she needed to prove her ownership, she still had not got them. No doubt it was Dorothy who suggested she enlist the aid of Sir John Temple. The Leicesters' devoted friend had assumed his duties as Master of the Rolls in Ireland and was living in Dublin. Getting no satisfaction from Railton, Lucy sent word to Temple to procure the documents for her from Sir George Wentworth, Strafford's brother and chief executor. In due course, Temple wrote back to say that he had pressed for them on numerous occasions but had been unsuccessful. All George Wentworth could find, which he passed on to Temple, were some useless papers regarding the Birnes Country, which Lucy had long since surrendered to the Crown.[6]

At this time, Lucy's nephew Philip, Lord Lisle, was in Ireland fighting the rebels, and at the end of May 1642, he and Temple called upon Sir Philip Percival. The only thing Percival could tell them was that when Strafford gave him the money to purchase the Glaslough and Shillelagh leases, he had indicated verbally that they were in trust for the Countess of Carlisle. Percival showed them the lease for Shillelagh. It was in his name without any reference to the trusteeship. (With the Irish Rebellion raging, it is doubtful if either the Strafford heir or Percival was receiving any rents from these lands; Percival's own rent roll was drastically reduced.) He assured his visitors that he would make over the leases to Lady Carlisle "if her Ladyship obtains license of the House and consent of Lord Strafford's trustees."[7] The best Temple and Lisle could do was to obtain a note from Percival setting out what he had told them.

Sir George Radcliffe's release from prison in the autumn of 1642 gave Lucy some hope. On October 13, 1642, she wrote Railton asking him to speak to Radcliffe for her. The letter was subtly threatening. As usual, she put her demands in the mouths of others—an understandable circumlocution considering the legal powerlessness of women. People were telling her, she wrote, that she was never going to see those writings, and they were pressing her "to take some other way for the getting of them." But it would be extremely against her own desires "if ever I do one act or have a thought, but to serve all creatures that had any relation to my Lord of Strafford."[8]

While Lucy was waiting impatiently for this "writing," she received several letters from Leicester, who was waiting just as impatiently for his orders to go to Ireland. There could have been few things more uncongenial to a private person like Leicester than following the King and his army. But follow them he had, from York to Nottingham. In September, from the camp at Nottingham, he sent Lucy several letters in which the classical balance of his sentences mimicked his own inhibiting faculty of seeing both sides of every question:

> The Parliament bids me go presently, the King commands me to stay till he despatch me. The supplies of the one and the authority of the other are equally necessary. I know not how to obtain them both, and am likely to have neither; for now they are at such extremes as to please the one is scarce possible, unless the other be opposed. I cannot expect the Parliament should supply me, because it is not confident of me; and as little reason is there to think that the King will authorize me, for he is as little confident.[9]

He had always thought himself an honest man, he said, but here he was, suspected and distrusted by both sides.

Why did Leicester cry on Lucy's shoulder? It is likely that he hoped his sister-in-law would show his letters to her parliamentary friends. Shortly afterward in a letter to Northumberland, he mentioned that he had written "to some particular friends, in hope that thereby the Truth might be known, and myself rightly understood." The letter to Northumberland was an attempt to justify his prolonged stay at court and was intended for the eyes of Parliament: "You may communicate it to the House of Peers, as in your judgment and favour to me you shall think fit." He explained that he had gone to Nottingham because he was told that there he would get his orders. But despite "perpetually soliciting to be despatched" he still did not have the King's leave to go to Ireland. He then went on to declare that he was "as innocent as a new-born child" in a controversial matter over some horses. It seemed that Parliament had allocated funds to buy several hundred draft horses for the Irish service. These were at Chester waiting to be shipped for Ireland when Charles commandeered them to pull his munition wagons. Parliament was incensed, and Leicester was clearly afraid that he would be blamed. He wanted the parliamentarians to know that not only had he objected, but he had actually countermanded the King's orders, to no avail. Northumberland presented this letter to the House of Lords, and it was subsequently printed by order of Parliament.[10] Those who read it might well have thought the subject matter metaphorically apt, for Lord Leicester was clearly trying to ride two horses at once.

Meanwhile at Penshurst, the women waited for their men. Doll felt the loneliness and pain of a soldier's wife. She would sit by the hour at the difficult task of deciphering Henry's coded letters. For Dorothy it was a prolongation of the years of separation. Once again she had the responsibility of running the estate and getting in the rents. As her letters to Hawkins show, one of her problems was deciding which of the creditors should be paid out of the dwindling rent roll. In one instance Dorothy gave priority to her own sex. Leicester House was under repair, and the workmen were going unpaid. Authorizing Hawkins to distribute £100 that she was able to spare from her meager resources, she wrote: "Let the poor clamourous women be satisfied and do the best you can to give them all some contentment with this money."[11]

Henry was on the march with the King. From Nottingham they marched west to Derby, Stafford, and Leicester, and on to Shrewsbury. At the county seats and major towns, Charles made fine, noble addresses to the inhabitants, who readily contributed money and plate to his campaign. The local gentry raised troops so that by the time they reached Shrewsbury, Henry was able to report that King Charles had six thousand foot, fifteen hundred dragoons, and above two thousand horse. The life of a Cavalier (the popular name for the King's troops, while the parliamentary troops were known as Roundheads) held no charms for Henry. He was disgusted with the jostling for position and the "bandy discourse" more suitable to a drawing room, he said, than a military camp. If there was any way out with honor, he would take it, he wrote Doll from Shrewsbury. But there was no way out, and not only did he hazard his life for King Charles, but he gave £2,000 to the war chest.[12]

It was a camp divided into militants and moderates. Prominent in the King's councils was the war party headed by George, Baron Digby, his father, the Earl of Bristol, and Charles's nephew, Prince Rupert. Rupert, the second son of Elizabeth of Bohemia, had arrived at Nottingham covered with glory from the Dutch campaigns. He at once began the work of shaping the King's supporters into a fighting force. He was famous above all for his daring cavalry charges; Henry and the rest of the horse guards were quickly instructed in this dangerous maneuver. Rupert had come to fight, and fight he would; but the Digbys, father and son, had more selfish reasons for promoting the war. They were on Parliament's list of delinquents; in the event of an accommodation, they would lose their estates. Most of this militant faction consisted of the Queen's courtiers, and since she was vengefully opposed to anything but Parliament's unconditional surrender, these men worked against any peace negotiations. Henrietta Maria had gone to Holland in February to pawn the Crown jewels to raise money for the royalist army. Henry heard (and passed it on to Penshurst) that she was coming back to England to stop the King from making peace. Charles was totally under her influence, and until she returned he was deaf to all advice. Henry loathed the Queen's party, which he never called anything else but "the Papists."

Henry belonged to the group of moderates in the royalist camp. Led by his uncle the Earl of Southampton and Lucius Cary, Viscount Falkland, they were urging Charles to reach an accommodation with Parliament before it was too late. Although the two lords had been treated with scant respect when they went to Westminster with some propositions from Charles, Henry remained convinced that the way was still open for a treaty with Parliament—and he told the King so personally. He found Charles "very much averse to peace," which he attributed to the pernicious influence of the Queen and her party. His letters became increasingly gloomy. The enemy he feared was not so much Essex, then on the march with a large army, but the Queen's party. If the royalists won, he told Doll (and he knew how this would grieve her), they would have to leave England, because the papists would make life insupportable for those like him who had opposed them. Already the moderates were receiving threats from these warmongers.

As the royalist army marched south to Birmingham, the soldiers assumed they were on the way to London. This was the one bright spot for Henry, because from London, he assured his pregnant wife, "by the Grace of God I will come to Penshurst, where I hope to see you past all your pains." But Doll's hopes were raised for nothing, because the royalist forces did not reach London. After a bloody and inconclusive battle at Edgehill (where Henry and the other volunteer guardsmen, eager to dispel their reputation as show troops only, went dashing in the vanguard against the enemy's pikes and muskets),[13] the royalists were turned aside by superior forces near London and retreated to Oxford, where Charles established his headquarters. In November, when Doll went into labor and gave birth to a daughter, Henry was not with her to hold her hand. Instead, he was at Oxford, chafing at the bit that held him honor-bound at Charles's wartime court.

In spite of the war, there was some good news for the women at Penshurst. Leicester had finally received permission to go to Ireland. November found him at Chester, waiting to take ship. Unfortunately, he was still there weeks later. First of all sickness, then adverse winds detained him. In vain did his sons, fighting the Irish rebels, urge him to come quickly. Leicester nursed his illness and stared moodily at the rough sea, forgetting the old adage that he who hesitates is lost. In December he was ordered by the King to return to Oxford.[14] No reason was given, but Charles was known to have been very offended by Leicester's printed letter to Northumberland about the horses.

At Oxford, the embittered Leicester took rooms in Queen's College. The cloistered and spired university city, where he had studied in his youth, was his perfect habitat, but the times were wrong. The quadrangles were filled with quarreling Cavaliers, and the colleges were overrun with women who had come to join their fighting menfolk. Flirtations and intrigues flourished. When not in the field, Prince Rupert set an example for "indulging his pleasures."[15] The atmosphere at this wartime court was even more uncongenial for Henry than for Leicester, who, after all, could spend his days in the libraries. As a member of the nobility, Henry was quartered in St. Aldgate's Parish so as to be near the King's lodgings at Christ Church college. Virtually all the houses in Oxford had been requisitioned and were abominably overcrowded. Nevertheless, room was found for Henry's four servants. In January 1643, he was sent home to Northamptonshire to recruit troops. He did such a good job in what was actually parliamentary territory that it was said of him that he "mustered and trained half the county."[16] In the course of this duty, he managed to pay a short visit to his wife at Penshurst.

For Doll and Henry in the winter of 1643, it would have meant a bittersweet renewal of lovemaking, admiring the new baby together, and playing with the toddlers. Poppet, the eldest, was at the baby-talk stage. On his return to Oxford, Henry would write with mock gravity that he regretted he could not correspond with the young lady, but he was not learned enough in her own language. Dorothy was almost as pleased to see Henry as Doll herself. She loved this young man who was the answer to her prayers for this special daughter. Often impatient and scolding with her own husband and children, Dorothy was quite tamed by young Spencer. He took a fond and bantering tone with his formidable mother-in-law, teasing her for her refusal to accept compliments gracefully. Dorothy basked in the transitory happiness of the young couple. All too soon Henry was saying good-bye to his wife, his mother-in-law, and "the little ladies," as he called his numerous sisters-in-law.[17]

Henry was back at Oxford when the Earl of Northumberland arrived in February at the head of a parliamentary delegation bringing propositions for a treaty. The delegation found Charles polite but intransigent. Confident of victory in the field and knowing that his wife, who was expected in England momentarily, would never approve, he rejected the harsh conditions for peace laid down by Parliament. In March Northumberland was again dispatched to Oxford, this time to see if he could arrange a truce based on the disbandment of both armies. Having experienced the wartime shortages at royalist headquarters, Northumberland wisely brought his own furniture, his own food, and wine from his excellent cellar at Syon House. Bulstrode Whitelocke, one of the parliamentary commissioners who accompanied him, recorded that the Earl "provided sumptuously for his colleagues and himself" and that "the King came in for his share of the good things which he did not disdain to accept."[18] Even Northumberland's best burgundy could not smooth the way for a truce, though according to Whitelocke they did at one point reach an agreement that the Queen's party sabotaged overnight.

Henrietta Maria had just arrived in England, bringing with her much-needed money and arms. From York, where she was under the protection of the Earl of Newcastle, the royalist general in the north, she commanded her husband not to disband under peril of losing her. "If you make a peace, and disband your army before there is an end of this perpetual parliament," she wrote Charles, "I am absolutely resolved to go to France, not being willing to fall again into the hands of those people, being well assured that, if the power remains with them, it will not be well for me in England."[19] Thinking only of herself, she used her excessive influence over the King to make a truce impossible. Charles refused to disband his army, and on April 15, Parliament recalled its commissioners. The collapse of the treaty negotiatious at Oxford was a terrible disappointment to the moderates at court, to no one more than Henry Spencer.

In June, however, Henry had exciting news to report to Doll. King Charles had made him an earl. Doll, pregnant again from their short reunion in January, was now the Countess of Sunderland. Not only that, but Henry was making plans to have her join him at Oxford as soon as he could find a suitable house. This was no easy matter because evacuees from parliament-held districts were pouring into the garrison town. In other news from Oxford, Harry Percy had returned from the Continent and was fighting for the King at the head of his own regiment.

The fortunes of war were favoring the royalists. The Earl of Newcastle had won the north with a decisive victory over the parliamentary generals Ferdinand, Baron Fairfax, and his son, Sir Thomas Fairfax. In the west of England, the royalist Sir Ralph Hopton had defeated Sir William Waller and his Roundheads. In the raids and skirmishes around Oxford, Prince Rupert's cavalry were a terror to the opposing forces. Fighting beside Rupert at Chalgrove Field on June 18, Harry Percy's regiment distinguished itself, falling on the flank of the enemy and "putting the reserve of the rebels to flight."[20] It was partly in recognition of this feat that Charles created Harry Baron Percy of Alnwick. On July 13, Henrietta Maria made a triumphal entry into Oxford. Henceforth the battle cry of the Cavaliers was "God for Queen Mary." Meanwhile at Westminster, Pym was ailing and seemed to have lost his touch. Parliament was divided, with extremists undermining Pym's management and Essex's conduct of the war.

At this juncture, the Civil War was being fought on Dorothy's doorstep. Kent was in Parliament's territory, but popular sentiment was for the King, and, encouraged by events, a royalist uprising began in nearby Tunbridge and Sevenoaks on July 18. Dorothy had reason to be thankful that Penshurst was regarded as a royalist household, for once-respectful townsfolk were plundering the great houses belonging to parliamentary families. For a week the looting and rioting continued, until the rising was put down by a parliamentary force. One sad result for Dorothy was that the indispensable Henry Hammond, the rector of Penshurst Church, a known royalist, was forced to flee to Oxford.

On July 25, the very day the Kentish uprising ended, royalist forces under Prince Rupert enjoyed a stunning victory in the surrender of Bristol, giving the King control of the second-largest port in England and four ships that were in the harbor—a welcome return of a portion of his navy that had been taken over by Parliament at the beginning of the war. Henry, the new Earl of Sunderland, fought bravely in the storming of Bristol and was eagerly anticipating the attack on London to end the war. But to Henry's extreme disappointment, Charles suddenly changed his plans and began a siege of Gloucester. Wearily, Henry set out to join him.

Instead of storming the city, as at Bristol, a plan that had resulted in heavy casualties, the strategy at Gloucester was to mine the wall and effect entry through the breach. While the engineers were digging a gallery to carry the mine to the wall, the soldiers burrowed into trenches, firing upon any of the besieged who dared to sally forth. From the trenches before Gloucester, Henry wrote Doll a letter full of longing for her. The arrival of her letters "put all the inconveniences of this siege out of my thoughts," he told her. Yet on the whole he did not mind the trenches, despite the noise of guns and drums and the cries of the wounded. There was good company, and he preferred it to the loneliness of the little cottage where he was billeted. How he envied those who got permission to go to their own houses, "but I hope ere long you will let me have your company and Poppet's, the thought of which to me is most pleasant, and passionately desired," sighed the homesick young soldier.[21]

In this letter, dated August 25, 1643, he noted the defection from the parliamentary side of the Earls of Holland, Bedford, and Clare. Many of those nobles who had originally opposed the King most actively were now having second thoughts. The peace party in the House of Lords included not only the three defectors but Salisbury, Pembroke, Rutland, and (it was rumored) even Northumberland.[22] Although bound by the harsh terms laid down by Parliament in the Oxford Propositions, Northumberland had been personally inclined to grant concessions to Charles. In the summer of 1643, Holland was so convinced that the royalists would win the war that he openly advocated a peace plan that was a virtual capitulation to Charles. Over-confident as always, he promised to induce his cousin Essex to turn over the parliamentary army to the royalists. When this harebrained scheme failed and the Commons voted down renewing peace negotiations, Holland, with Bedford and Clare, went over to the King. At the time that Henry was writing his letter to Doll, the three earls were expected at Oxford any day. The young lord who had sacrificed so much for the royal cause viewed these latecomers with a jaundiced eye. Without doubt they would get a better reception than they deserved, he wrote with contempt.

As it happened, he was proved wrong. No fatted calf was killed for the return of the prodigals. Holland and the others were received at Oxford with icy coldness. Henry reported to Penshurst that he had never seen the King "use anybody with more neglect" than Holland.[23] Even though he attended the King at court and camp, Holland did not get back his old offices. Charles complained that his former first Groom of the Bedchamber showed no remorse for his perfidy, and Henrietta Maria was dead set against him. After a few months, convinced that nothing was to be gained, Holland deserted the King for the second time and turned himself in to a parliamentary garrison, whence he was taken under guard to London. While under examination by a parliamentary committee, he issued a public declaration stating that he had gone over to the King in the belief that he was the ideal person to persuade Charles to listen to Parliament's just demands. But finding that his counsel was not heeded, he had speedily returned to Parliament like a stream that overflows its banks but soon reverts to its proper channel (as he put it). With a hodgepodge of maritime and nautical similes (for this was the Man Who Would Be Lord High Admiral), Holland cleverly made his peace with Parliament.[24]

Although Henry had been confident in August that Gloucester would fall as Bristol had fallen, the arrival of Essex's army on September 5 forced Charles to raise the siege. The momentum of the royalist victories was broken. Charles did not bother to hide his depression from his supporters. Henry too was aware that the time lost was of critical importance. "I am afraid our sitting down before Gloucester has hindered us from making an end of the war this year," he wrote

Doll from Oxford on September 16. Taking advantage of a lull in the fighting, he was back at Oxford for a few days. He reported to his wife that he had called on her father, and he gave her the latest news from the various battlefronts. Doll was always at the center of his thoughts. He was trying very hard to find a house good enough to bring her to after the birth of the baby. He mentioned with satisfaction that he had "taken the best care about my economical." In fact, he had made his will, named his trustees, and provided a generous jointure for his wife. The letter is relaxed in tone, as if the writer was enjoying a respite. But it was only for a moment. If the King did not come to Oxford in the next few days, "I shall not fail to return to the army."[25]

A few days later, on hearing that Charles was in pursuit of Essex's southbound army, he rode out to join his master. Prince Rupert had dashed ahead and blocked the London road at Newbury. On the night of September 19, the body of the royalist army caught up with Rupert's cavalry. Early the following day, Essex's troops advanced upon the royalists. All day long a fierce battle raged on the outskirts of Newbury. Some of the officers of the royal cavalry were so contemptuous of the London trained bands, who made up the bulk of Essex's infantry, that they rode into battle without body armor. Henry was too sensible a young man for such bravado, and we can picture him galloping onto the field in the steel cuirass he is wearing in Robert Walker's portrait, his long, brown curls flying behind him. He charged the enemy repeatedly until a cannon shot felled him. Unfortunately, he did not die immediately but lay in agony for some hours. He stayed conscious to the end, and his family and friends were told by witnesses that he expressed his "satisfaction of conscience that he had entered upon this action," resigning his soul into the hands of God "with pious ejaculations."[26]

THERE WAS A LOUD BANGING at the door of Penshurst. A footman from Leicester was asking to speak to John Sudbury, the house chaplain. The servants knew that it was terrible news, and an eerie silence fell on the house. When the chaplain appeared, the footman handed him a letter that the Earl of Leicester wanted him to deliver immediately to Lady Leicester. But Doll had heard the knocking on the door. Who was it? she asked the first servant she encountered. Reluctantly, the man told her that it was a footman with a letter from her father. Was it not addressed to her mother or herself, she asked? He said he understood that his Lordship's instructions were to hand it to Mr. Sudbury. Rigid with fear, she waylaid the chaplain. At first he would only say that Lord Falkland had been killed. But this did not satisfy her, and (as Sudbury related to Leicester in a long, moving letter)[27] he was "forced" to tell her that Lord Sunderland was wounded. Doll gave way to "a great passion of grief," the greater because she feared he had not told her everything. She begged him for the truth and would not be diverted by religious platitudes. At last the chaplain was able to break away and go to Lady Leicester's chamber.

When Dorothy heard his news, she fell into "the greatest passion" that Sudbury had ever seen and fainted dead away. Sudbury and her maids brought her around. As she lay groaning, they made her see that she must get a grip on herself so that she could go to comfort Doll. Finally, Dorothy recovered herself and, supported by Sudbury, went to her daughter. Clasping her in her arms, she broke the news. Doll cried out so loudly that even the stable hands heard her. After some time, Dorothy managed to quiet her hysterical daughter. In his letter to the Earl of Leicester, Sudbury wrote that her Ladyship had spoken "such comfortable words to her and in so affectionate a manner, as I am confident it was not possible for any divine or orator, with all their study and premeditation, to have been able in so short a time to have charmed so great a grief so well." Needless to say, he added, neither of their Ladyships had much rest that night.

In a brief note that Dorothy sent back with the footman, she described their daughter's state. "Doll thinks of nothing but her great loss, which I confess to be beyond expression," she told her husband. As for herself, she could not find words to express "the grief of my poor heart." Although she had buried a baby daughter—the first Lucy—Dorothy was more deeply affected by Henry's death than by any other. It was "far beyond anything" she had ever suffered, she confessed to her husband. To see her "dear child" with her great belly, hugging her three fatherless babies, was almost more than Dorothy could bear. But despite her sorrow, the next day, while Doll lay prostrate in her grief, Dorothy took hold of her late son-in-law's financial affairs. Calling in Sudbury and some of the servants as witnesses, she opened a black box containing his papers so that Sudbury could note them down for Leicester and the other trustees. In a businesslike account to her husband, Dorothy dealt with the wardship of the eldest son and the liquidation of debts and legacies. From time to time, she had to rouse Doll to ask her some questions. But it was not easy to get answers because Doll had not troubled her head about finances. Indeed, Dorothy told her husband, Henry had recently sent a document that would have made "a good addition to his wife's fortune," but Doll had neglected to sign it.[28]

Probably her father, rather than her mother, afforded Doll her greatest consolation. From Oxford he wrote her a letter stoical in tone but permeated with his deep love for her. In essence, he was counseling her against giving way to her grief. There was no purpose advising her not to grieve, he wrote, and it was not his intention; but knowing her "tender and sensible nature," and the love she had felt for her husband, he was afraid she was in danger of "the vanity of bemoaning that which hath no remedy." She must bear in mind that her husband had suffered when anything troubled her. Would she now act in a way that would cause him pain if he could see her? She must govern herself for his sake and take care of "those pledges of your mutual friendship and affection," especially the unborn one.

> I know you lived happily, and so as nobody but yourself could measure the contentment of it. I rejoiced at it, and did thank God for making me one of the means of procuring it for you. That now is past, and I will not flatter you so much as to say I think you can ever be so happy in this life again; but this comfort you owe me, that I may see you bear this change and this misfortune patiently.[29]

It was a letter that Doll would have unfolded countless times in the privacy of her bedchamber, away from her mother's less sensitively expressed concern for her.

The two women took it for granted that the body would be transported to Althorp for burial in the Spencer family chapel. What they did not yet know was that Henry's corpse had been rifled by some of the enemy's soldiers, and that when Leicester managed to recover it, it was not fit for Christian burial. He sent only the heart to Althorp.[30] The horrors of war had penetrated Penshurst with a vengeance.

FOR THE PRESENT, the tragedy had taken Dorothy's mind off a most worrisome problem. In April 1643, Parliament had passed an ordinance for sequestrating the estates of "notorious delinquents." Any local committee, or two members thereof, could label a landowner a delinquent and seize his estate. As in all revolutions, it was a time for settling scores and for getting one's hands on one's neighbor's property. Someone—Dorothy did not know who—had got a sequestration order against the Earl of Leicester. Everyone at Tunbridge, the county seat, denied having anything to do with it; nevertheless, the Penshurst tenants had already been forbidden to pay their rents to the estate manager. If the order were not quickly revoked, it could prove "very prejudicial to us," Dorothy wrote Hawkins.[31] At any moment heavy-booted Roundheads could march in and seize the manor. Dorothy had appealed to Parliament against the order on the grounds that the Earl of Leicester was not a delinquent, that his appointment as Lord Lieutenant of Ireland had been approved by both houses, and that he was not shirking his duty but remained at Oxford by the King's command. Her best hope, however, was that she was Northumberland's sister and the mother of Lord Lisle and Algernon Sidney, both red-hot Parliament men.

Dorothy must have been struck by the truth of the old adage that bad luck comes in threes, because shortly after the dire events of September, the King dismissed Leicester from his office as Lord Lieutenant of Ireland. No reason was given. Leicester wrote the Queen an unwise letter, insisting on an explanation.[32] He told her he "could not imagine" what he had done, but surely he could have deduced that his loyalty was suspect. His conduct had been ambivalent, to say the least; witness the letter to Northumberland that Parliament had printed. Moreover, he remained on the friendliest of terms with Northumberland, and his own sons were on Parliament's side. But there was another reason, which the King did not disclose even to his closest adviser, Edward Hyde. Charles was planning to bring over an Irish army to help subdue the parliamentary forces—the very thing that Strafford had been accused of. Leicester was apt to be unenthusiastic about dispatching Irish Catholic clansmen to fight Protestant Englishmen, so Charles replaced him with the Earl of Ormonde, his loyal general in Ireland, to whom he had entrusted the plan for sending over the Irish army. The Leicesters' dream of being viceroy and vicereine of Ireland was over. The "rich coach" that Dorothy had purchased in France for riding about Dublin in state was put up for sale, "never used," at £300.[33] Leicester remained at Oxford for several months more, making himself even more unpopular by refusing to sign a letter, drafted by Lord Digby and his clique, which attempted to dissuade the Scots from crossing the border again, this time as Parliament's ally.

Pym, visibly wasting away with cancer of the bowel, had rendered Parliament one final service by forging an alliance with the Scottish Covenanters. On September 25, 1643, 25 peers and 288 members of the Commons signed the Solemn League and Covenant, committing Parliament to replace the Church of England with the Presbyterian form of church government. In return, the Scottish commissioners agreed to lend military support to the parliamentary forces fighting the royalists. Meanwhile, parliamentary fortunes were rising. Excise taxes were levied to raise money for the army (in the name of the King, to fight the King), and the Earl of Manchester's second-in-command, Lieutenant-General Oliver Cromwell, was creating well-disciplined troops who went into battle inspired by the belief that they were fighting for the Almighty. In January 1644, the Scots made good their promise to the English parliament, sending an army through the snow across the border. In the early spring, a parliamentary army marched up to join the Scots. The Earl of Newcastle and his outnumbered royalist forces had to withstand a siege at York by two armies.

Despite the insistent calls upon him from all fronts, Prince Rupert galloped to the rescue. Through a brilliant diversionary tactic, Rupert was able to relieve York, but by the time the good news reached Oxford, Rupert and the northern royalists had been decisively defeated at Marston Moor by Cromwell, who surprised them with a preemptive strike. Newcastle decided he had had enough. Having given upwards of a million pounds and the best years of his life to the royal cause, he abandoned his post and sailed away to Hamburg. Two weeks later, the demoralized town of York surrendered, and northern England was lost to the King.

The battle of Marston Moor touched the family at Penshurst. Young Algernon was severely wounded fighting for Parliament and narrowly escaped being taken prisoner. Compensating for the disaster at Marston Moor, the royalists were doing well in the south. In June Charles's forces wiped out Sir William Waller's army at the battle of Cropredy Bridge.

At the same time as Charles lost the north and Newcastle's invaluable services, he was also deprived of his adored wife. "The Queen," observed the royalist Sir Philip Warwick, "was ever more forward than stout." A month earlier, when bad news started coming in from the north, she hurriedly left Oxford for Bath, complaining of discomfort related to pregnancy. After taking the waters, she went on to Exeter to have her baby. Charles, frantic with worry from her letters, begged Sir Theodore Mayerne to go to her. Most reluctantly, the old doctor heaved his bulk into the royal coach and traveled through hostile country to Exeter. Arrived at the Queen's bedside, he unsympathetically diagnosed her complaints as simple hysteria. Actually, Henrietta Maria had reason for alarm, because the Earl of Essex was marching toward Exeter, bent on taking her prisoner. On June 16, 1644, she was delivered of a daughter, and as soon as she was able to rise from her childbed, she fled to France on a Dutch ship.[34] Had she not panicked, however, Henrietta Maria would have been safe from capture. In July her husband's forces drove Essex into royalist Cornwall, where he was forced to capitulate, leaving his troops and making his escape by sea.

In June 1644, Leicester left Oxford and returned to Penshurst. It was still his, thanks to swift and effective action by Dorothy. As a result of her appeal, strongly supported at Westminster by Northumberland, Parliament had lifted the sequestration order.[35] Leicester was happy to find his "dear Doll" and her family staying at Penshurst. The infant Henry, born two weeks after his father's death, touched his heart immediately and turned the somber Leicester into the fondest of grandfathers.

There were many stormy scenes, however, between husband and wife. The physical attraction that had bound them together for so many years had evaporated. Dorothy was forty-six, harassed and worried by the responsibility of managing the estate with a civil war going on. What rents came in went to her, yet they were hardly enough. Many of the fine old trees in Sidney's Coppice had to be cut down and sold as timber to the ironmaster. When Leicester requested money for his running expenses, Dorothy was impatient and short with him. "My wife had it all and would not part with one penny," he recorded bitterly in the "Diary of Events" he compiled in 1650. In fact, grumbled Leicester, when the Norfolk rents stopped coming in, he had to find an additional £400 to compensate Dorothy, or she would "no longer keep house." She silenced all his complaints by threatening to turn the running of the household over to him. This, of course, sent him in retreat to his study. He even thought of breaking up the marriage, "but being loathe to dissolve my family as a thing dishonorable and prejudicial to my children, gave way to her unreasonableness."[36]

sixteen

SECRET CABALS AT THE HOUSE OF
THE COUNTESS OF CARLISLE

AFTER PYM'S DEATH in December 1643, a sharp division arose on the parliamentary side. On the one hand were the peers and the members of the Commons who stood by the agreement with the Scots to make Presbyterianism the state religion in England. On the other were the Independents, not so numerous in Parliament but increasingly influential in the army. The army would have nothing to do with any state religion, and fanatical sects of all stripes were represented in its ranks. The English Presbyterians, led by Denzil Holles in the Commons and the Earl of Essex in the Lords, wanted to negotiate peace with the King. Oliver Cromwell and Sir Henry Vane the Younger, leaders of the rising Independent party, were distrustful of Charles and aimed to beat him into total submission. To achieve his ends, the ambitious Cromwell set out to train an army of men of lowly origin imbued with religious fervor, which became known as the New Model Army, and to get rid of his superiors, Generals Manchester and Essex.

The Civil War had been the making of Oliver Cromwell. He came from a Puritan family who, in his generation, were simple farmers. For a short time he attended Cambridge University, where he was remembered as "one of the chief matchmakers and players of football, cudgels, or any other boisterous sport or game . . . more famous for his exercises in the fields than in the schools."[1]

He settled down to farming and raising a family, but sometime in the 1630s, he experienced a religious conversion that gave him the reputation locally as a godly man. The county sent him to Parliament in 1628 and again in 1640. A backbencher in the early days of what was to become the Long Parliament, through serving on committees the tall, ruddy-faced rustic in "a suit of plain cloth which seemed to have been made by an ill country tailor" (as a fellow member described his dress) emerged from obscurity as a radical reformer. He was taken up by Pym in the Commons and the opposition peers in the Lords. When Charles declared war on Parliament, Cromwell raised a cavalry troop in his home county of Huntingdonshire and, with no military training, immediately showed himself to be a brilliant army commander. From all accounts, he exulted in fighting, laughing uproariously as he rode into the fray.[2] In January 1644, the Earl of Manchester promoted Cromwell to lieutenant general under his command. Before the year was out, however, each man wanted to get rid of the other. Manchester heard on good authority that Cromwell was talking openly against the nobility, saying "that he hoped to live to see never a nobleman in England."[3] For his part, Cromwell regarded the parliamentary generals, Manchester and Essex, as crypto-royalists. In the end, Cromwell was instrumental in sidelining the two. Sir Thomas Fairfax, who had been fighting on Parliament's side, was named Lord General of the New Model Army, and Cromwell his General of the Horse.

The division between the English Presbyterians and the Independents continued outside Parliament. Demagogic lay preachers seconded the Independents, stirring up a populist reaction, while a small but influential group of aristocrats were secretly conspiring with Denzil Holles to make peace with the King and destroy the Independents. The leader of this group was the ever-opportunistic Earl of Holland, who, because of his defection to the royalists the year before, was banned from taking his seat in the Lords.[4] Holland had had time to recover from his pique over his poor reception at Oxford. He was now heart and soul for preserving the monarchy. Actually, he had not been entirely insincere in his public recantation, when he announced that he had gone over to the King to mediate a peace. Though unacceptable to both sides, Holland had proved to be ahead of his time. As the war went on, it was gradually dawning on many members of the nobility that they could not afford the luxury of supporting constitutional and religious reforms. With the rise of the fanatical Independents, it began to look as if reform might not stop short of the destruction of the monarchy. If the King were deposed, many among the aristocracy feared they would be swept away with him.

In the opinion of Holland, Essex, and Manchester, Charles would have to make concessions, but he must not be decisively defeated. Their line of thinking was not shared by all their own class. Although Northumberland had been in sympathy with the peace lords in 1643, their failure at that time and the growing power of Vane and Cromwell had convinced him that the militant Independents would be the winning party. Having reached this conclusion, the Earl of Northumberland cast in his lot with the new order, lending it his illustrious name. Not only was he associated with the war party in Parliament, but in 1644 he agreed to serve with Vane and Cromwell on the Council of the Two Kingdoms—the executive committee that conducted the war from Derby House, a government office building in Westminster.[5]

The peace party had no more ardent supporter than Lady Carlisle. Why had Lucy chosen to follow Holland rather than her own brother? Perhaps it was simply that wartime England was too dreary for her. Time had dulled her anger over the sacrifice of Strafford, and she could look back with nostalgia on the elegant life at court. Moreover, neither Vane nor Cromwell attempted to enlist her courtier's graces as Pym had done. At Holland's urging, she joined in a secret scheme to aid the King.

The scheme was based on an alliance between the Scots and the English Presbyterians. The idea was to persuade Charles to accept Presbyterianism in return for the support of the Scottish army, and then King, Scots, and English Presbyterians would overwhelm the

Independent faction. The crux of the scheme was to win over the Scots and get Charles to make religious concessions.[6] Lucy showed the same zeal for Holland's and Holles's schemes as she had earlier shown for Pym's. Dr. George Bate, a physician who knew her, diagnosed her conduct as the efforts of an aging beauty to remain on center stage. Where once she commanded admiration for her personal charms, she now set out to impress the world with her cleverness.[7] Contemporaries spoke of her as "Sempronia"—the "busy stateswoman" of Ben Jonson's *Cataline*.

All Lucy's famous tact and exquisite amiability were put into service to win supporters for the scheme. Her London house was the meeting place where persons of diverse interests were brought together, ostensibly for the pleasures of her dinner table. One day the guest of honor was the Chancellor of Scotland, the Earl of Loudon, a leader of the opposition to Charles's policies in Scotland, who had come to England at this time as an envoy from the Scottish parliament. To please his hostess, without making any real commitment, he "solemnly declared that he had come to assist in settling a peace, and not for the purpose of ruining the King of Great Britain, nor royalty." In any event, Lucy felt sure that she had "penetrated into his real designs." On another day, four lords of the upper house were at her table. To keep the peerage from defecting to the Independents, as her brother Algernon had done, Lucy wined and dined many of them. Enjoying the fine dining, which was becoming rare in war-torn England, their Lordships swore that they wanted nothing more than "the re-establishment of the person and the affairs of the King."[8] Her exalted position served as cover for these secret activities. Later, when Denzil Holles was charged by the army with "the contrivance of secret cabals at the house of the Countess of Carlisle," his explanation was that he simply went to pay his respects to "a person of so great honour and desert."[9]

Another great lady involved in Holland's schemes was the Dowager Countess of Devonshire, who had caused Dorothy such aggravation during Doll's marriageable years. "A rich and magnificent lady who lived long in the greatest state,"[10] she could trace her ancestry back to Robert the Bruce and often did. The Countess, as Dorothy had found to her own disadvantage, was a most sagacious and prudent lady. In her early widowhood she had fought and won thirty lawsuits to disencumber her son's inheritance. Prudence and sagacity continued to govern her conduct: she was known to spend her mornings in devotions, household affairs, and minute examination of the account books. She entertained lavishly, even during the war, at her elegant town house in Bishopsgate Street. According to her sycophantic biographer, she "never affected the title of a Wit; carried no snares in her tongue, nor counterfeited friendship, maintained no paradoxes or imperious disputes, never spoke evil of anyone and would not listen to others who did."[11] As we have seen, Dorothy's view of her was that she was "full of civility, craft, and coldness."

Unlike Lucy and Holland, Lady Devonshire had never flirted with the parliamentary side, nor had her sons. Her elder son's estate had been sequestrated, and the younger, General Charles Cavendish, had been killed fighting for the King. She remained staunchly royalist through all her troubles and chided Holland like a schoolmistress for his former disloyalty to the King. She had the poor man apologizing over and over for his past "crimes." Even with all her firmness of character, it is doubtful that she dared criticize Lucy for her temporary defection. The two strong-willed countesses remained friendly co-conspirators.

Lady Devonshire's Scottish connections were extremely useful in making the alliance with the Scots that was the cornerstone of the scheme. Because of their growing distrust of Vane and the Independents, the Scottish commissioners in London were receptive to the overtures of the English Presbyterians. They saw eye to eye on church government in England, and both groups desired to buttress Essex and Manchester against Cromwell. In the autumn of 1644, Scottish support seemed assured. All depended now on Charles's readiness to adopt Presbyterianism. Holles had managed to sound out the King privately while on a parliamentary delegation to Oxford in October. As most people did with Charles, Holles misinterpreted his polite silence for acquiescence. In fact, Charles was adamantly opposed to giving up the Church of England. Buoyed up by his own successes in the southeast and by the Earl of Montrose's victories over the Covenanters in Scotland, he was in no mood to make concessions. Moreover, with the English Presbyterians at odds with the Independents, and the parliamentary generals fighting among themselves, he was smugly confident that he could divide and conquer. Thus optimistic, Charles was angry with some of his courtiers at Oxford, who (he wrote Henrietta Maria at Paris) were "strangely impatient for peace." They were urging him to go to London on the shaky ground that his presence there would bring Parliament back to obedience. "Among this persuasion," Charles told his wife, "Percy [Lucy's brother Harry] is one of the chief."[12]

There can be no doubt that the peace party at Oxford was aware of the schemes brewing in London. It was well known that Lady Carlisle passed everything on to her brother Harry. (Lucy and Holland sometimes employed young women in their families as couriers. Holland sent intelligence to Oxford by his daughter, Isabelle Thynne, and Lucy sent a list of London royalists to the King with a niece, who was discovered on the way by the Roundheads and narrowly escaped arrest.)[13] To implement their scheme, Lucy and Holland needed people around the King, and they clearly concerted their plans with Harry. But Charles suspected that there was a conspiracy to get him to London against his will. He banished Henry Wilmot, the victor of Cropredy Bridge, and Harry, realizing that he was next, resigned his commission as general in charge of ordinance.

With Harry out of commission, Lucy and Holland looked in another direction for an advocate with the King. A new French envoy, Monsieur de Sabran, had recently arrived in England. One of his first moves was to get in touch with Holland and Lady Carlisle, who were regarded as old friends of France. He informed them that Cardinal Mazarin had sent him to mediate a peace between King Charles and Parliament because, like his predecessor Richelieu, Mazarin was afraid that England might set a bad example to the French people by becoming a republic. So far Sabran's mission was compatible with their own aims. However, the French diplomat did not share their belief that the Scottish alliance was the way to achieve peace. In fact, his instructions were to oppose Presbyterianism for England, it being obvious that the intolerance of the Scottish church would bode ill for English Catholics. Despite this basic difference, Lucy and Holland decided that Sabran was their man. Another set of peace negotiations was in the offing, put forward by Parliament. If Charles dismissed them out of hand, it would destroy the peace party that they were so painstakingly constructing at Lucy's admirable dinners.

The French diplomat had access to the King. He had accompanied Charles on his summer marches, and he and his secretary had passes to go to the King's headquarters at Oxford. The plan was to get Sabran to influence Charles to consider Parliament's terms or, at least, to make them a basis for discussion. In November arrangements were made for Sabran to meet secretly with Holles at Lady Carlisle's house.[14]

Sabran advised his superior at Paris, the Comte de Brienne, about the secret conferences at Lady Carlisle's. De Brienne, who was acquainted with Lucy from earlier missions to the English court, was hardly complimentary to her in his reply: "The lady, at whose house you assembled, formerly piqued herself on her great beauty and her great talents; years must have carried off the one, but I doubt they have acquired for her the latter of these qualities."[15]

WHEN TREATY NEGOTIATIONS with Parliament opened at Uxbridge in January 1645, compromise was the furthest thing from Charles's mind. From France, emotional letters arrived from Henrietta Maria, dwelling on Parliament's animosity to her and her religion. In equally emotional letters, Charles assured her that he could not live without her and would only make a peace that would "invite thy return."[16] Three years of war had taught him nothing. His commissioners were instructed not to yield on the issues of the episcopacy and the militia, but "to make sure that the Peace once settled, all things shall return into their Ancient Channels." Trusting in the old standbys of the stick and the carrot, he authorized his commissioners to promise patronage to the parliamentary leaders and "in private discourses to put them in mind that they were arrant rebels and that their end must be damnation."[17]

As chances of a treaty receded, the court at Oxford was buzzing with rumors of a plot to take the fifteen-year-old Prince of Wales to London to mediate between his father and the members of Parliament. Charles was furious. Believing Harry Percy to be the ringleader, he first arrested him and then ordered him to leave Oxford. Harry soon joined Wilmot at Henrietta Maria's court of exiles at Saint Germain-en-Laye, a few miles from Paris.

Harry's escape to the Continent was in the best tradition of the dashing Cavalier. On his way to the coast, he was captured by Sir William Waller and Cromwell. Among his party was a soldier with a pretty face who aroused Cromwell's suspicions. To confirm them, he asked the soldier to sing, which "he" did (as Waller recorded) "with such a daintiness that Cromwell scrupled not to say to Lord Percy that being a warrior he did wisely to be accompanied by Amazons."[18] After this exchange, the parliamentary generals had a good laugh and let him go with his female companion. Whether Harry was shamefaced or not, it is a safe conjecture that Dorothy would have been mortified when she heard the story and Lucy would have found it hilarious.

Meanwhile, Holland and Lucy were very dissatisfied with Sabran. His brand of mediation without a Scottish alliance had proved toothless. After a visit to Oxford in March, Sabran came back predicting doom for the King. Since he was given to "speaking rashly of his negotiations" in front of Lucy's other guests, his defeatist attitude was doing their cause no good.[19] Through their contacts at the French court, Holland and Lucy succeeded in getting him replaced by Jean de Montereul, who had been the French agent in London just before the war. But by the time Montereul arrived in July 1645, the King had already lost the war.

THE DECISIVE BATTLE took place on a mile-wide field near the village of Naseby in Northamptonshire. At ten o'clock on the morning of June 14, 1645, the two armies were drawn up in battle formation, each cavalry and infantry regiment forming a neat square. In the center of the battle line, King Charles's infantry division faced the troops of General Thomas Fairfax and the seasoned veteran Major General Philip Skippon. On the right wing, Sir Marmaduke Langdale and the Newark Horse looked across at the cavalry of the formidable Cromwell. (According to a Roundhead colonel in the field with him, Cromwell was seized by a fit of laughter just before the battle began, a sound that, reaching the ears of the Cavaliers, no doubt had a psychological effect.) On the left wing, the King's nephews Rupert and Maurice, sons of the Queen of Bohemia, disdainfully eyed Colonel Henry Ireton's country bumpkins on horseback. To the sound of trumpet and fife, both armies moved forward, the royalists shouting "God for Queen Mary," the Parliament troops roaring a rousing "God our strength." Prince Rupert chased Ireton's cavalry off the field in the mad dash that was his specialty. In this whirlwind attack, Ireton had his horse shot under him, his thigh run through with a pike, and his face struck with a halbert, and he was taken prisoner, although he managed to escape. Skippon was also badly wounded by Charles's musketeers, but when Fairfax told him to retire from the field, "the old man answered he would not stir so long as a man would stand." Cromwell's Ironsides, as his crack cavalry were known, in hand-to-hand combat forced Langdale's troops to flee, then, turning on the unprotected flank of the main body of royalist infantry, slashed through their ranks. Attempting to stem the stream of his retreating cavalry, King Charles called out vainly, "One charge more and we recover the day." In a few hours the New Model Army had routed the royalist troops, taking four thousand prisoners and all the enemies' artillery and supply wagons. Fairfax claimed six hundred dead on the King's side and less than a hundred on his own.[20]

Unknown to Charles, he had suffered another loss that would have serious consequences. Among the booty taken by the New Model Army was a trunk with his private papers, among them letters to and from Henrietta Maria that his enemies would later use to incriminate him as a traitor to his people.

Cromwell gleefully attributed the victory at Naseby to "the hand of God," but his God-fearing soldiers had pursued and slaughtered the fleeing royalists, gratuitously slashing the faces of their female camp followers.[21]

The Civil War had ended. Cromwell's New Model Army was simply mopping up the remains of the royalist forces.

The Independents were triumphant. Some were even talking of forcing the King to abdicate in favor of his six-year-old son, Henry, Duke of Gloucester, and making Northumberland Protector; Parliament had recently appointed the Earl guardian of the royal children. Even more disturbing for the representative of French absolutism were the republican and democratic ideas freely expressed in the burgeoning popular press, freed from royal censorship. Montereul immediately took up with Holland and the Countesses of Carlisle and Devonshire. An extremely civil and cultivated diplomat—he had served his apprenticeship as secretary to a Roman cardinal—not the least of his attributes was his "*agréable, divertissante et complaisante*" table talk. At Lady Carlisle's dinner table, Montereul listened attentively as his hosts outlined the position of the English Presbyterians. Lucy and Holland had expected to find a partisan in him and they were not disappointed. In a report to Mazarin, Montereul praised their "zeal and courage" and particularly commended Lady Carlisle for doing "her duty to her king and country [without] considering what she owes to the ties of blood and the interests of her brother [Northumberland]."[22]

Holland and his ladies were having second thoughts about the King coming to London. Their present plan—the very one for which Harry Percy had been banished—was to have the Prince of Wales ("who was not yet odious to the people") come to Parliament to act as mediator. Regarding this plan as foolhardy, Montereul was able to bring them back to the idea of salvaging the monarchy by inducing Charles to accept Presbyterianism. Since a Presbyterian monarchy was better than no monarchy at all, Mazarin gave Montereul the go-ahead but warned that Henrietta Maria's opposition would be the stumbling block. Montereul arranged for Sir Robert Moray, a Scot who had served in the French army and was highly regarded at the

French court, to go secretly to France to win her over.[23] At first (as Harry wrote Lucy from Saint-Germain) the Queen would not listen to the Scottish envoy, telling him bluntly that the Scots and the English Presbyterians together "could not have a power equal to that of the Independents."[24] Only after Mazarin made her see the essential republicanism of the Independent party would she agree to advise her husband to accept Presbyterianism. But the sacrifice of his religion was the one thing Charles would not do for her. As the disastrous year of 1645 came to an end, he was ready for desperate courses. He offered to go to London personally to negotiate a treaty with Parliament.

In late December, Montereul reported to Mazarin that "Holland and his friends now agree it is dangerous for the King to come to London." In their opinion, the only course open to the King (and Montereul concurred) was "to make a dash for the Scottish army." The startling idea of the English monarch giving himself up to the Scots was duly authorized by Mazarin, and Montereul sounded out the Scottish commissioners in London. What guarantees would they give if the King voluntarily went over to their army in the north of England? They were profuse with their promises. The King would be received with honor, he would enjoy perfect security, no one would force his conscience, and the Scots would assure his prerogative if the English parliament tried to remove it.[25] The coterie at Lady Carlisle's were just as forthcoming with their promises. When King Charles was safe with the Scottish army, they assured Montereul, there would be no trouble at all in getting the English Presbyterians and the City of London to declare for him. Quite reassured, one cold January day Montereul journeyed to Oxford and unfolded the plan to the King.

Charles's proposals for a personal treaty had been rebuffed by Parliament, and he had been informed that should he come to London he would not be admitted to Westminster. He knew it was only a matter of time until Oxford was taken and he was captured. So he listened to a proposition that would have been unthinkable a few months earlier. The loyal Sir Philip Warwick was present at the discussions where "Mr. Montreville [sic] averred it in his master's name that if the King would put himself into the hands of the Scots, he should be there safe both in person, honour and conscience."[26] It was this assurance, Warwick stated in his memoirs, that decided Charles to go along with the idea. On a wet spring evening, he stole away from Oxford in disguise, accompanied only by his Groom of the Bedchamber, John Ashburnham, and a minister named Hudson.

On May 5, 1646, King Charles rode into the camp of the Scottish army. He was taken to Newcastle, where he became a virtual prisoner. The Scottish army commanders immediately disavowed any undertakings made by their commissioners in London.[27] Ashburnham was sent away, and although Hudson was allowed to remain, the King was badgered without cease by Presbyterian divines to sign the repugnant Covenant. Even his wish that the young Duke of York be allowed to join him was denied. His next affliction was a set of "impudent" proposals from the London parliament that his hosts tried to force upon him with such insistence that by comparison (he wrote Ashburnham) the pressure over the Covenant "was but slight insinuations."[28] When the abject Montereul arrived at Newcastle on July 9, he found the King utterly hopeless. Indeed, that very day Charles had written to Ashburnham at Saint-Germain that he was "lost" if he did not escape to France before the end of August. "Take heed that I be not believed too late," he warned.[29] Montereul explained how he had been misled by the Scottish commissioners in London but could find no words to express his dismay. The perfidious Scots had cozened them all—King Charles, Mazarin, and himself and the Earl of Holland's circle of English Presbyterians. Montereul left somewhat consoled by the King's assurance that he did not blame him. As Charles wrote his wife, he blamed Mazarin, not Montereul, for inducing him to throw himself into the arms of the Scots.[30]

Charles was a chess player, and to help while away the time, he played the game a good deal in captivity. Of an ironic turn of mind, he could not help thinking, as he played, that in England's great game of chess, the king had become a pawn. The Scottish army was using its royal prisoner to bargain with the English parliament for its back pay. At the beginning of 1647, the Scots sold him for half the arrears, amounting to £200,000. When the thirty-six carts of gold reached Newcastle, the Scottish army handed over its monarch to the parliamentary commissioners and marched home.[31] Within a few weeks Charles was taken to Holdenby House in Northamptonshire, where the new French ambassador, Monsieur Pomponne de Bellièvre, found him "guarded with great severity although enough ceremony." Charles was under such close restraint that his guards watched him even at his private prayers.[32]

The English Presbyterian leaders, Warwick and Manchester, were as keen as Holland and Lady Carlisle on coming to an agreement with the King while he was in the hands of a parliament controlled by their party. For reasons of his own—perhaps not least an avuncular feeling for the royal children in his care—Northumberland joined the would-be peacemakers. They had drafted a four-point proposal that they wanted Charles to send to Parliament as his own. It called for him to agree to Presbyterianism for three years and parliamentary control of the militia for ten; he was to declare that the Irish were rebels and to confirm the appointments made by Parliament under its own Great Seal. If Charles would send this message, the English Presbyterians would do their utmost to enable him to come to London to negotiate a settlement with Parliament. As with the earlier schemes, the English Presbyterians were working with France. Referring the proposal to his superiors, Bellièvre pointed out that it contained some very hard conditions, but given the King's perilous state he thought it was the only course.[33]

Throughout February 1647, Bellièvre was in daily conference with Holland and Lady Carlisle. Their main concern was to get the King out of custody. As Bellièvre told his superiors, the worst thing was for the English people to become accustomed to seeing him in prison. Early in March, Charles's assent to the plan came by a circuitous route. In a letter to Bellièvre, Mazarin said he had been informed by Henrietta Maria's confidant Sir Henry Jermyn that King Charles would agree to the four points, provided that the Earl of Northumberland would promise to support him in Parliament. Lady Carlisle was to write the Queen if her brother would engage himself to do this.[34] But by this time, Parliament was facing a crisis.

Parliament and the army had been heading into a confrontation for months. The war was over, and both houses had voted to disband the New Model Army. It was like trying to cage a tiger. Officers and soldiers, brimming with confidence, refused disbandment until their arrears were paid. When Parliament reacted with niggardly offers and sanctions against those who petitioned for their pay, the army turned into a formidable enemy.

At the beginning of June, rumors were circulating that the army might seize the King. Lucy and her friends panicked. This would destroy all their plans. On June 2, Bellièvre reported that he was being pressed by "the Presbyterians of the Lower House, the Scots here, the Counts of Warwick and Holland, the Countesses of Devonshire and Carlisle" to write to King Charles, imploring him on their behalf "to do everything possible to avoid falling into the hands of the army." "They say," Bellièvre wrote without conviction, "that his Majesty should escape from Holdenby and come to London where they have assurances from the principal people in the City that they want the King . . . His Majesty should come with despatch and go to the mayor's, then to Parliament accompanied by the mayor and all the City, and after a few words on the good of the realm they do not doubt he will be able to install himself happily at Whitehall." They had no proposals, however, as to how the King was to escape from Holdenby, nor could they give any assurance of success. Bellièvre concluded by saying that with "such a dangerous and uncertain business," he himself had no advice to give.[35]

It is doubtful that Charles ever received this counsel of desperation. That same Wednesday, June 3, 1647, a cavalry detachment of some five hundred men from General Fairfax's army, under Cromwell's orders, clattered into the courtyard of Holdenby House. The parliamentary guard refused to fight his old companions-in-arms, and the low-ranking officer in charge, one Cornet Joyce, strode unannounced into the King's bedchamber. He woke him rudely and ordered him to get dressed because he was taking him to other quarters. The King asked him on what authority he was acting. Gesturing toward the troops that could be seen out the window, Cornet Joyce replied, "On that authority."

It looked like checkmate and game. With the King a prisoner of the army, Holland, Lady Carlisle, and Lady Devonshire retired from political intrigue for the moment. Northumberland, quite in character, reverted to the pro-army faction, which began its own negotiations for a settlement with the King.

seventeen

"I WOULD RATHER SERVE THE PRINCE THAN LIVE"

THOSE YEARS WHILE Lucy was deep in political intrigue, Dorothy was living privately in the bosom of her family under the shadow of the Civil War. Leicester had retired completely from the public arena, thoroughly disapproving of everything that was done by both sides. When Northumberland tried to get him to resume his seat in the House of Lords, he declined. However, there was considerable satisfaction in the Sidney household when, in 1646, Parliament appointed the eldest son, Philip, Viscount Lisle, to his father's old post of Lord Lieutenant of Ireland.

The marriages and careers of her children were Dorothy's main concern. In 1645 the alliance with the Cecils that had begun with Northumberland's first marriage was cemented when Philip married Catherine Cecil, the second-youngest of the Earl of Salisbury's daughters. The effect of the war on aristocratic finances was indicated by Catherine's dowry. While Salisbury had given £12,000 with Anne when she married Northumberland in 1628 and £10,000 when Elizabeth married Devonshire in 1639, he gave only £6,000 with Catherine.[1] Still, it was a gratifying alliance so far as the Leicesters were concerned. On January 24, 1647, the two families rejoiced together at Salisbury House at the christening of the young couple's

first son. Although Salisbury seconded Northumberland in supporting the Independents while Lucy was a prominent supporter of the
English Presbyterians, all quaffed their wine together, united by family sentiment. A week later Philip left for Ireland, accompanied by his
brother Algernon, whom he had appointed Governor of Dublin. But
Philip was known to be a creature of Cromwell's, and he was not in
Ireland four months before the Presbyterian faction in Parliament
had him recalled with his brother.[2] This was simply a temporary setback. As ardent supporters of Cromwell, both were rising young men.

Robin, Dorothy's third son, was following in the footsteps of his
father and grandfather. After completing his exercises at a French
academy, he went to Holland, where, through his father's influence,
he became colonel of an English regiment in the Dutch service. Doll
was still living with her parents. Regarded as a paragon of piety, charity, and perfect maternity, she was placed on a pedestal by everyone
around her—a living statue of a virtuous matron. It was taken for
granted that she would never remarry but would carry the torch for
her gallant husband forever. As for the other girls, negotiations were
in hand to marry Lucy to the son of a well-to-do baronet, although
the Leicesters did not think much of the father's honesty. But Lucy
was twenty-two and a husband had to be found. There was no talk of
marriage for twenty-one-year-old Anne. This patient young woman
seems to have been earmarked to look after the parents in their old
age. Three of the other girls, Mary, Elizabeth, and Frances, were
showing telltale signs of tuberculosis. Their gentle, dry coughing was
a familiar sound in the house. The prettiest of the girls (always ex-
cepting the peerless beauty of the eldest) was Isabella. Flighty and
fun-loving, at thirteen she was a charmer. She already had an admirer,
her first cousin Viscount Strangford, a boy of about her own age who
came to live with his uncle's family in the summer of 1646.

Dorothy had been most eager for this wealthy orphan to become
Leicester's ward. The boy's father, the unsavory rake who had run off
with Barbara Sidney in 1619, had died shortly after his son's birth in
1634. At that time Leicester's sister had begged him to take the wardship, but the Earl had refused; instead, one Sir Thomas Fotherley had
become the boy's guardian. In 1642 Lady Strangford died. Leicester

was then at Oxford, and Dorothy wrote him that she understood from a reliable source that the boy's estate was worth some £4,000 a year, "the rents I believe as well paid as any in England." She was very upset to think that a stranger had the disposal of such a fortune and urged Leicester to ask the King to remove Fotherley and give the wardship of his nephew to him. "I do not know how you can hope for the like opportunity of obtaining such a benefit," she told her husband.[3] Leicester, who possessed a finer conscience than his wife, felt he should sound out the present guardian first. He found Fotherley loath to part with the wardship, and the latter drove such a hard bargain that Leicester dropped the matter. Then, in February 1646, Parliament abolished wardship along with all other vestiges of the royal prerogative. Although there was still money in it for the guardian, free use of the income from the estate was now a thing of the past.

When next approached, Fotherley was more amenable, especially since the Earl's letter included an invitation for him and his wife to accompany young Strangford on a visit to Penshurst.[4] By coincidence, Fotherley had been employed by Dorothy's father for many years as receiver general for the Percy estates in the north of England.[5] Possibly from profits made while in this employment, Fotherley had gone on to become a landed gentleman and member of Parliament. In 1640 he had been knighted. Dorothy had not seen him since he was a liveried servant in her family, but with young Strangford's fortune at stake, she would have been as gracious as she knew how. In the pleasant surroundings and in an atmosphere of flattering intimacy with the Earl and the Countess, Fotherley agreed to let the youth remain with his uncle and to provide the Earl with an annual allowance of £1,000 out of the boy's estate to care for him. As was to be expected, young Strangford's allowance led to fresh quarrels between Dorothy and Robert. She insisted on having £900 of it to help defray household expenses, and in retaliation Leicester took the Warwickshire rents away from her. He claimed this was but the barest compensation, because "the troubles" had reduced those rents "to little more than £100 per annum."[6]

Every Michaelmas, "with much ado and more unreasonable wrangling," husband and wife worked out a financial agreement for the coming year. It was a time for the other members of the family to stay clear. Leicester was very bitter about Dorothy's avariciousness, as he perceived it. He complained in his diary that she engrossed all the income while leaving him with much of the expenses. Justly or unjustly, he complained that out of the £100 remaining to him of Strangford's allowance, he had to pay the wages of the youth's servants and other charges. Certain things in particular riled him. For instance, when he asked Dorothy to pawn a few small jewels so he could send Robin to Holland, she refused "with anger and scorn, wondering, as she said, that I would desire them of her." And there was the time that Lord Salisbury's son was drinking the waters at Tunbridge Wells, and Leicester invited him to stay at Penshurst instead of lying at some farmer's house. Dorothy exacted £100 from her husband on that account. All this, of course, is Leicester's version.[7]

Unfortunately, Dorothy did not record her side of the story, but undoubtedly she felt justified in taking control of the family's much reduced income in order to run Penshurst and Leicester House. As she knew only too well, Leicester had no money sense, and so far as she was concerned, he could do without a boxful of books every few weeks in these times of austerity.

Despite the expense of living in London, the family spent every winter at Leicester House, where Lucy was a regular visitor. With her news and her anecdotes, she cheered up her morose sister and brother-in-law. She had lost nothing of her malicious sense of humor in the prevailing religiosity and made sport of the famous preachers of the day, as she had once done of the courtiers. Her stories were often racy, which shocked the prim and proper Dorothy, but Leicester loved them, the racier the better. One tale amused him so much that he recorded it in his diary for February 7, 1646:

> Lady Carlile told my wife and me this story. Mr. Sedgwick, minister of the Covent Garden and of great credit among the Presbyters, being in his study, his wife came to him for a booke or to ask him some question. But he desyring to give her some other entertainment, fell to dally and to play with her. She finding how

he was disposed, spake to him to stay till night which then grew neare, for it was evening, but he went on with his purpose. Then she said to him, If you have a minde to do that, stay till anon, when we shall be in bed. To which he answerd, Yes, now and anon two. It hapned that a maide was at the doore and, looking through the keyhole, spyde and heard what they did and sayd, which she having told again it came to the knowledge of the Countess of Peterborough, who at that time had some dislike to Sedgwick, and sent [some]one to him to desyre him to send her his new booke lately printed and called *Now and Anon two,* referring to the words aforesaid. How he tooke it I know not, for there ends the story. But he is said to be a sensuall and voluptuous man.[8]

The Earl and Countess were doing little entertaining in these years, but on January 20, 1648, they celebrated the marriage of their daughter Lucy to John Pelham with a fine entertainment for their friends. It was the last occasion for merriment that Leicester House was to witness for some time, for England was moving swiftly into the Second Civil War.

KING CHARLES WAS determined to escape from Hampton Court. Although the conditions of his captivity were not severe, he suspected that he might be poisoned. In late-night conversations with his longtime Groom of the Bedchamber, John Ashburnham, and Sir John Berkeley, Charles planned his escape route. The first stage went well. He walked down the palace back stairs unimpeded and, under cover of night, joined his friends. Unfortunately, no decision had been reached beforehand as to where he should go once he successfully escaped. Each man recommended a different destination. Finally, Charles agreed with Ashburnham to seek sanctuary at Carisbrooke Castle on the Isle of Wight. Leaving the King at the house of the Earl of Southampton, Ashburnham and Berkeley journeyed to the Isle of Wight to sound out the governor of the castle,

Colonel Robert Hammond. Hammond, a former colonel in the New Model Army, agreed to receive the King.[9] By voluntarily walking into captivity at Carisbrooke Castle, Charles had made the worst possible decision.

In Parliament power seesawed between the Presbyterians and the Independents. With the latter in control in January 1648, parliamentary orders were issued to Colonel Hammond to dismiss the King's servants and to keep him within the castle walls. (On hearing that Charles's imperturbability had for once deserted him, Leicester wrote in his journal that it was no wonder, "being reduced from three kingdoms to three rooms in a poor castle.") In the House of Commons Cromwell was ranting against monarchical government. Army officers were talking freely of bringing the King to trial. In the face of the King's peril, royalists had formed an alliance with the Presbyterian party to rescue Charles and the monarchy. All over the country, groups of royalists were meeting secretly, accumulating arms and ammunition in preparation for a nationwide rising. Charles had made a secret treaty with the Scots, and in Scotland Hamilton (now Duke of Hamilton) and his brother, the Earl of Lanark, were raising an army to march into England to join forces with the English royalists. At Saint-Germain, the Prince of Wales was eager to get to Scotland to take up arms for his father but was frustrated by the politics of his mother's court.[10] It must be said that there were reasons for the rising that had nothing to do with fealty to King Charles. Though the Independent party was led by landed gentry such as Oliver Cromwell and his son-in-law, Henry Ireton, many of the rank and file were Anabaptists, Levellers, and other radicals who wanted to abolish private property. Fear of losing what they had was driving the privileged classes into the royalist camp or even out of the country. In the winter of 1648, there was a positive exodus of wealth to the Continent, the price of gold shot up, and ordinary people were saying that "some of our great masters intend to fly from us and leave us in the lurch."[11] In February Northumberland was making no secret of his intention to go to France. He did not go, but a large shipment of his goods was stayed on its way to Holland.

At the center of the royalist plot in London were the Earl of Holland and Lady Carlisle. Holland had managed to get the Prince of Wales to name him general for the projected uprising, and he was busy commissioning officers right and left. But shortage of money for arms was a real problem. The war had blown away all the pensions and sinecures Holland had long enjoyed as a royal favorite. Lucy was another financial casualty of the war. Cut off from her Irish income, she was on the verge of actual poverty. Nevertheless, she pawned her pearl necklace for £1,500 to equip Holland's troops.[12] Lady Devonshire was also active in "these glorious designs," to use her biographer's grandiloquent phrase. Although living in the country at Ampthill, her brother's estate, she was in continual correspondence with the English and Scottish royalists. In addition, Lucy and Holland were cheered and encouraged by the reappearance of an old friend. Many of the exiles had quietly returned to England from the Continent to rally to King Charles. Among the returning royalists was George Goring—Holland's dear old crony and Lucy's lifelong admirer.

Charles had no more loyal subject than George Goring. "Had I millions of crowns or scores of sons," he had written his wife from abroad, "the King and his cause should have them all."[13] In 1644 Charles had repaid Goring's devotion by raising him to the peerage as Earl of Norwich—a title that had become extinct with the death of Carlisle's first father-in-law, Edward Denny. During the First Civil War, Charles had employed Goring as his special ambassador, first to France and then to The Hague. Now he was back in England to give his life if necessary for his king.

These old courtiers were involved in a dangerous business. People more discreet than Lucy and Holland would have had difficulty concealing their activities; in their case, with their habitual indiscretion, it was an impossibility. In March it was rumored that the Earl of Manchester, the Earl of Holland, and the Countess of Carlisle were going to Spa "to avoid the storm they have just cause to fear."[14] In fact, Holland had taken the precaution of obtaining a pass to go to Spa. Suspected by Cromwell and the Independents, Holland and Lucy nevertheless remained in England.

In spite of the danger, Lucy threw herself recklessly into the royalist plot. She conducted Holland's correspondence with the Hamiltons in Scotland and was in constant touch with the Queen's court at Saint-Germain. (Though Henrietta Maria appeared to be completely reconciled with Lucy, at this very moment she was pouring the story of Lady Carlisle's perfidy into the sympathetic ear of Madame de Motteville.) Lucy was in fact the clearinghouse for correspondence among the foreign and domestic conspirators. The Queen's letters to the King were sent to Lucy, who forwarded them by various couriers, and the King ordered that his letters to the Queen be sent under cover to Lady Carlisle because he did not trust the postmaster.[15] Charles, the Prince of Wales, now a smooth, frenchified eighteen-year-old, wrote Lucy letters full of gratitude and praise, which she undoubtedly showed to everyone.

In fund-raising she was indefatigable, begging and borrowing money from wealthy London aldermen and the impoverished aristocracy. To raise money in the City, she worked hand in glove with a merchant named Lowe.[16] She may have recruited him, or, as some said, he may have "taken pains to insinuate himself" into the royalists' inner circle. In any case, he had gained their confidence. The royalists were banking on the City, which appeared to be swinging over to the King, and Lowe's good connections in London were an asset to the cause. He was particularly trusted by the Presbyterian faction. But Edward Hyde, then on the Continent with the Prince of Wales, thought the garrulous and gregarious Lowe a poor risk, wondering that any "sober man could be imposed upon by him."[17]

Some of the money raised by Lucy and Lowe went toward helping Charles escape from Carisbrooke Castle. As his imprisonment became increasingly harsh and began to look like a life sentence, Charles made a number of attempts to escape. These were engineered by a motley group of mainly little people: his few remaining retainers, some of the servants in the castle, royalists on the Isle of Wight, and a handful of others based in London. One of the principal conspirators was Captain Silus Titus, a guard sent by Parliament who had defected to the King. Another was Jane Whorwood, an independent young woman whose flaming red hair suited her fiery nature. Jane Whorwood undertook dangerous courier missions for the royal cause, and for weeks on end kept a ship ready to transport Charles to Holland. Sir Henry Firebrace was another key figure in the attempted escapes. Firebrace had been a Page of the Bedchamber before the war and continued to serve his master in captivity.[18]

In late March, a plan was hatched for Charles to make his escape by sawing off the bars in his window. The plan foundered, however, when Charles found he could not squeeze his shoulders through. After this latest failed attempt, Firebrace, Titus, and several others were dismissed by Parliament; Colonel Hammond had received full particulars about their part in the conspiracy from Cromwell and the Derby House committee. "Intelligence came to the hands of a very considerable person," Cromwell wrote Hammond, "that the King attempted to get out of his window, and that he had a cord of silk with him, whereby to slip down; but his breast was so big, the bar would not give him passage."[19] Clearly, an informer had infiltrated the King's inner circle. There was much finger-pointing among the conspirators, and Lucy and Lowe did not escape suspicion. Mrs. Whorwood suspected Lowe, and Firebrace distrusted Lucy, reminding the King that the Lady Carlisle had "proved faulty." Nevertheless, Charles persisted in trusting her. "I think she wishes now well to me," he replied in code, although he granted that her first loyalty was to "546, 493"—no doubt her brother Northumberland.[20]

At this time Northumberland, although a member of the Derby House committee, was holding clandestine meetings with the royalist plotters. "Northumberland and other lords are now much of your part," Alexander Fraser, a Scottish doctor living in London, reported to the Earl of Lanark.[21] But the Derby House committee's secret correspondence with Hammond reveals that Northumberland himself signed some of the letters informing the governor of his royal prisoner's escape plans. On March 13, 1648, Northumberland had sent Hammond advance notice of the escape planned for later that month, and had advised him that two of his own men were involved.[22] Charles's correspondence passed through Lucy's hands, and as she could never resist showing private letters, it is a distinct possibility that she showed the Isle of Wight correspondence to her brother. So Lucy may have betrayed the King again, perhaps unwittingly, for, like Dr. Fraser, she may have regarded Northumberland as a partisan of the King's cause at this time. Yet no one was more familiar with Northumberland's change of loyalties than Lucy. She and her co-conspirators knew how provoked he had been in February by the revelation of a royalist attempt to spirit Prince James, the Duke of York, to Scotland or Holland. He had wanted to give up his guardianship of the royal children after that, but the House of Commons would not let him. When the young duke actually made his escape to Holland two months later, the royalist plotters rightly suspected that the angry Northumberland had turned back to Cromwell and the Independents.

By April Lucy and the English royalists were deeply discouraged by the Hamiltons' inaction. A Scottish royalist in London scolded the Earl of Lanark: "Your Cavalier and Presbyterian friends are all perishing or languishing in expectation of your help, and unless your assistance prove opportune in money as well as in the army, it is to be feared you will spare your purse to spend your blood." Lanark blamed the delay on obstructionist tactics by the Marquess of Argyle, the head of the rival Campbell clan, but in the meantime the Hamilton brothers' failure to march into England with their army of ten thousand men, as promised, was causing divisions and desertions among English royalists. In particular, Lanark's outspoken Scottish correspondent warned him to make haste or he could not count on the influential Northumberland, whose "unconstant mind" made him unpredictable. The writer added that "Lady Carlisle is yours heartily."[23]

By May the Hamiltons' "patient friends" in England were tired of waiting and began the uprising without them. In the north, royalist forces took Berwick and Carlisle. In Wales, a pocket of resistance at Pembroke Castle turned into a full-fledged royalist insurrection. In Kent, a spontaneous rising took the London organizers by surprise. Loyal Kentish gentry were swarming to a series of rendezvous, ready at a word to march on London. At this point, Holland attempted to take control of the situation, dispatching some of his commissioned officers to Kent. When his old crony Norwich volunteered to be general, he filled out a commission for him on the spot. The "pleasant and genial" Norwich was a poor choice for a general in the field. He was by nature a conciliator, and in trying to please everyone he showed himself unsuited to command. The royalist cause received an unforeseen advantage ("a call from Heaven," in Hyde's words) when, simultaneously with the Kentish rising, a mutiny broke out among the sailors on the dozen or so ships lying in the Kentish Downs, waiting to go out on summer patrol duty. Putting their officers ashore, the common seamen of the fleet declared for King Charles and sailed for Holland to put themselves under the command of the youthful Duke of York.[24]

Quite apart from the spontaneous mutiny, negotiations had been under way in London with Captain William Batten, who had just been replaced as vice admiral of the parliamentary fleet. The royalists were trying to win him over to their side with as much of the fleet as he could command. Should he agree to join the Stuart cause, the plan was for him and his loyal seamen "to fetch the King from the Isle of Wight." The taciturn Batten, already disaffected with Parliament, was prepared to "adventure his life and his fortune in the business," but first he wanted some form of written engagement from Scotland.

The agent who had negotiated with Batten asked the Earl of Lanark to send the required paper at once, under cover of a letter to Lady Carlisle. She was fully conversant with the affair, he told Lanark, and receiving the paper "from her hand Captain Batten will esteem highly of it."[25] But Lucy waited and waited, and still the paper for Batten did not arrive from Scotland. Neither did the Hamiltons' army. Meanwhile the rising in Kent under Norwich's generalship had been put down by Fairfax. Faithful old Norwich had then moved into Essex and was now under siege with his troops at Colchester. Pembroke Castle had been captured by Cromwell, and Berwick and Carlisle could not hold out much longer. An abortive escape attempt by the King had further damaged the cause. Some of the most active of the King's party had been imprisoned, while others had fled to the

Continent, finding England "too hot" for them. Holland was complaining of being let down on all sides.

In spite of the urgency, the Hamiltons had not yet sent the paper for Batten, so Lucy and Lowe decided to take matters into their own hands. On June 24, they forged a letter from the Hamiltons "to speed Batten on his way." After the deed was done, Lucy wrote a contrite letter to the Earl of Lanark, confessing that she had "committed a greater fault than my last."[26] (We are left wondering what her former indiscretion was.) However, she had no need to apologize for the result. Captain Batten came over to the royalist side, bringing with him several ships including the *Constant Warwick,* "one of the best frigates the Parliament had built."[27] At the same time as Batten sailed into the Dutch port of Helvoetsluys, the Prince of Wales arrived from France to take command of the "revolted fleet." Writing to the Prince of Wales on July 14, Lucy took full credit for winning Batten over, suggesting that the captain's "interest and power with people who may be useful" made him a most desirable catch.[28] The Prince clearly agreed with her, for he knighted Batten and made him rear admiral of his fleet.

In the meantime, Holland had at long last taken to the field, spurred into action by the incessant demands of the young daredevil Cavaliers. With these officers and a levy of untrained men, Holland set out on July 4 to relieve Colchester, taking a roundabout route through Surrey in the hope that many more would rally to his standard. But as Norwich had found out, the ordinary Englishman was indifferent to the Stuart cause and the number of recruits was negligible. On July 7, Holland's forces were attacked near Kingston by a parliamentary regiment and routed; pursued by the Roundheads, the retreating remnant was decisively defeated at St. Neot's in Huntingdonshire on July 10. Holland himself did not see action. He had gone ahead to Kingston to provide quarters for the troops and was taken prisoner at his inn, caught with his boots off. It was another inglorious battle for Holland.[29]

Lucy's dismay at this disaster can be imagined. With Holland under house arrest in his ancestral castle of Warwick, it was up to her to deal with the aftermath. Writing to the Prince of Wales, Lucy acknowledged that the expedition to relieve Colchester had been undertaken without sufficient caution, but she asked him to judge people "from their intentions, not from their success."[30]

As Holland's co-conspirator, Lucy was in great danger. A woman in a man's world, she may have longed for a protector at times. Lady Norwich had just died, and perhaps Lucy began to look on old George as a possible husband. The Dowager Countess of Lindsey certainly thought so.[31] But Norwich was still holding out at Colchester in the wettest summer in living memory, facing disgruntled troops and imminent starvation when all the horses were eaten. Despite any qualms she may have felt in the dark of night, Lucy showed no signs of flagging. In fact, after Holland's arrest, Lucy was recognized by the royalists as "the person that hath the authority."[32] The Prince of Wales and his council had given her sole authority to levy funds and to make disbursements in the Prince's name. She was so trusted that the Prince's secretary sent her blank checks "for Colchester to do what she will, for the rest he leaves it to her discretion."[33] Strict orders were issued to the gentleman making collections for the fleet that any monies received were to be paid to Lady Carlisle and to her only. In his own hand, the Prince declared how much he owed "to her endeavours and more to her affections daily expressed to the King and himself." Lucy replied in the courtier's language: she would "rather serve the Prince than live," she wrote young Charles.[34]

It was near the middle of July when the Duke of Hamilton finally crossed the border with an army of ten thousand men. The Argyle clan and the politically powerful Presbyterian ministers had foiled his plans to enlist the battle-seasoned Covenanters' army, so his troops were mainly crofters on his own lands or those of the lairds under Hamilton influence. Marching in the van of the troops, the Duke of Hamilton made a glorious appearance with "trumpeters before him, all in scarlet cloaks full of silver lace, and a life-guard of Scotch-men, all very proper and well-clothed, with standards and equipage like a Prince."[35] But for the rest, he did not conduct himself like a general.

Instead, he led his troops in such a lackadaisical manner that he was suspected of having some ulterior purpose.

While Cromwell was marching north with his psalm-singing veterans to meet the Scots, the Prince of Wales put to sea. By the end of July, his fleet was lying in the Kentish Downs, blockading the Thames. Hammond and the Derby House committee worried that he had come to rescue his father from the Isle of Wight. The royalists, however, took it for granted that he was simply marking time before joining Hamilton and the Scottish army. Among the crowd of Cavaliers aboard the Prince's flagship, the *Constant Reformation,* was Harry Percy.[36] Indeed, Lord Percy was a leading member of the Prince's clique. Here again the family connection was at work, with Harry and Lucy reinforcing each other in the Prince's esteem.

A rather peculiar set of circumstances provided Lucy with the ideal opportunity for communicating with the Prince of Wales while his ship lay in the Downs. En route to England, the Prince's fleet had captured an English ship bound for Rotterdam, carrying a cargo of cloth belonging to the Company of Merchant Adventurers. Delighted with such easy pickings, on entering the Thames the fleet took a number of other merchant ships, including one belonging to the East India Company. In the City there was great consternation over this disruption of commerce and the financial loss. The City asked Parliament's permission to negotiate the release of the ships. Surprisingly, Parliament quietly allowed commissioners to board the Prince's flagship. Mr. Lowe "with wonderful address" got himself appointed a commissioner.[37] Since he could come and go freely to the fleet, Lowe was the perfect go-between for carrying Lucy's messages to the Prince. In her letter of introduction, she stated that "the bearer has been so faithful a servant to the King your father and his interest that I cannot refuse the recommending of him to Your Highness's favour."[38] Anyone vouched for by Lady Carlisle was good enough for Prince Charles.

Through Lowe, Lucy kept young Charles informed of "the condition of affairs in England." More than that, she offered advice that Edward Hyde regarded as pernicious. In his opinion, Lady Carlisle and Holland had all along given the royalists false hopes of the support they could expect from the City of London. Now, cautioned by Lucy and Lowe not to alienate the City, which they assured him was inclined to the King, the Prince released the cloth ship for a fraction of its value. At the same time, he gave written assignments to certain lenders to the Crown to reimburse them out of the proceeds from the sale of the other prize ships. According to Hyde, one of those favored was Lucy, who was to be repaid for the £1,500 she had raised by pawning her necklace, "upon the sale of a ship that was laden with sugar, and was then conceived to be worth above six or seven thousand pounds."[39] And she probably received the money, for Harry was "a very importunate solicitor" on his sister's behalf. By assigning the prize goods to individuals, the Prince of Wales was left without money to pay or provision his fleet. The sailors became very discontented, forgetting their recent vows of loyalty and obedience to the King, and when the Prince of Wales sailed back to Holland, chased by Parliament's new fleet under the Earl of Warwick, many of his seamen defected.[40]

The Prince had pulled up anchor because by the beginning of September 1648, the royal cause was hopelessly lost. On August 19, after three days of fierce fighting, Cromwell, with half the number of troops, defeated the Scots and the North Country royalists at the battle of Preston. Hamilton fled but was taken prisoner. His army was so scattered that Leicester, following events from Kent, heard that there were not twenty men together anywhere. No longer able to expect relief from the Scots, Norwich rendered up Colchester to General Thomas Fairfax on August 27. Norwich was taken prisoner, and the other two royalist generals were executed on the spot. Back at The Hague, the Prince and his council finished up the paperwork by sending Lucy "blank acquittances with particular sums" for those who had financially supported the King's lost war.[41]

THE SECOND CIVIL WAR had not left Penshurst unscathed. Roundhead troops, quartered nearby at Sevenoaks, harassed the household and treated the Earl of Leicester with "incivility and affront." But Northumberland was always there to stand up for the family, and on September 28, the committee at Derby House issued orders to the officer in charge to cease such conduct forthwith.[42]

The household had other troubles. During the summer their daughter Mary had succumbed to consumption, and while mourning their loss, Dorothy and Leicester were vexed by a lawsuit brought against the Earl in the Court of Chancery by formerly trusted associates. Not only that, but Leicester was involved in some well-bred wrangling over his daughter-in-law Catherine's jointure and dowry payments with Lord Salisbury. Northumberland was mediating the latter dispute. The squabbling between Dorothy and Leicester was getting even more acrimonious. Leicester argued that with one daughter married and another dead, Dorothy's allowance should be reduced, but she would not hear of it. Nevertheless, at Michaelmas, when it came time to settle their "contract" for the coming year, he successfully beat her down from £900 to £700 of the £1,000 per annum that his nephew paid to live with them.[43]

Young Strangford himself was a cause of dissension. Though only fifteen, the precocious lad had asked for his cousin Isabella's hand, and Dorothy, whose greatest aim was to make advantageous marriages for her children, was completely in favor of his suit. Leicester disapproved because of the close blood relationship and also because he had his doubts about his nephew's character. But with Doll and his son Algernon seconding Dorothy, he agreed much against his will to the betrothal, imposing the conditions that the young couple wait a year to wed and that they continue to live at Penshurst until Strangford came of age.[44]

While Dorothy's mind was bounded by family life, Leicester pored over the flood of new books and pamphlets from the now uncensored presses, following in detail the momentous events that were unfolding in the autumn of 1648. These periodicals were fiercely partisan. Indeed, it was a war of words. No doubt because of the King's perilous situation, the royalist press was very active, publishing a succession of short-lived periodicals with *Mercurius* in the title.

Some antimonarchical papers were also called *Mercurius,* so that a reader paying his penny might find he was reading propaganda for the other side. The most scurrilous antimonarchical journalist was Marchmont Nedham, who edited or wrote for a number of periodicals. *Perfect Occurrences,* a weekly paper edited by a disreputable forger named Henry Walker writing under the pseudonym of Luke Harruney, was nothing more than a mouthpiece for Cromwell. For straightforward domestic news, there were diurnals, published daily. Leicester undoubtedly subscribed to *The Moderate Intelligencer,* which covered foreign news.

In September a parliamentary delegation hurried to the Isle of Wight in a last-ditch effort to reach agreement with the King before the army usurped Parliament's power. For weeks the commissioners (Northumberland among them) urged Charles to conclude a treaty quickly. Charles made some grudging concessions, and at the end of November the commissioners returned to London with a treaty. But time had run out. On December 2, a bitter, blustery night, a large company of soldiers landed on the Isle of Wight. The following day they took the King to Hurst Castle, a foreboding pile little better than a dungeon. There, the last of his well-wishers among his Parliament-appointed attendants, James Harrington (future author of *The Commonwealth of Oceana*), was summarily removed. Before Harrington left, Charles managed to pass a letter to him for Sir Henry Firebrace. The smuggled note requested Firebrace to forward the King's best wishes to his friends Captain Titus, Lady Carlisle, and Jane Whorwood.[45] A gentleman to the last, Charles had sent them thank-you notes.

The outraged House of Commons voted to censure the army's seizure of the King. But on the same day that Charles was hurried off to Hurst Castle, General Fairfax's army marched to London and took up its quarters at Whitehall and St. James's Palace. On December 6, when the members came to the House, they found the doorway barred by Colonel Thomas Pride and his musketeers. Consulting a list of names supplied by his superiors, the colonel separated out some hundred members who were excluded or taken into custody.

Among those sent to prison was Sir John Clotworthy, Pym's old follower and Lucy's friend. The sixty or so members left sitting after Pride's Purge were dyed-in-the-wool republicans. Just before Christmas the King was moved to Windsor Castle, but the familiar comforts there were akin to the condemned prisoner's last meal. Before the year was out, the Rump Parliament (as it was now called) brought in an ordinance for the trial of Charles Stuart, charging him with high treason for waging war upon his subjects.

For some time Northumberland had not been attending the House of Lords (in fact, only five or six peers were sitting regularly), but at this critical juncture he returned with half a dozen other lords to do his utmost to stop the trial. Very much to the point as always, he argued that since treason was a crime against the King, the King could not be tried for treason against himself. Under Northumberland's leadership, the House of Lords refused to pass the ordinance for the King's trial. The Commons proceeded anyway, appointing a commission under the presidency of John Bradshaw, a respectable barrister recently named Chief Justice of Chester, to act as the King's judges. More illustrious lawyers had declined the honor.[46]

At this time the family at Penshurst was surprised by the unexpected arrival of Philip and Algernon, who stayed for a week.[47] Although both had been named to the commission to try the King, Dorothy's sons did not have the stomach for regicide.

The decision to try the King for treason was made by the strongman of the hour, Oliver Cromwell. Initially reluctant to put him on trial for his life, Cromwell had ultimately agreed with the army radicals that Charles was "a man of blood" who must die, and monarchy with him. While supposedly listening to peace overtures from Parliament and the army, Charles had incited a second bloody civil war and secretly negotiated with the Scots to invade England. In Cromwell's mind, Charles had proved himself incorrigibly untrustworthy, and so long as he lived, England was in danger of returning under the yoke of his absolute rule. Waging war against his people was the charge against him, but, taking the long view, the divine right of kings was on trial. It would happen in different circumstances, but with the same results, in France in the eighteenth century and in Russia in the twentieth.

ON JANUARY 20, the King's trial began in Westminster Hall before sixty-seven undistinguished men sitting as a High Court of Justice. Charles was brought in under guard and took his seat on a red
velvet chair placed within a partitioned box at the bar that had been
specially constructed for the trial. To his right were the prosecution
lawyers. The left section was vacant because he was not allowed any
counsel. Keeping his hat on to show his disdain, Charles cast "a stern
look" around him at the galleries filled with friends and relatives of
the commissioners, and at the great pushing crowd behind his box
kept back by guards with halberds; finally he directed his unwavering
gaze to the body of grim-faced men who were to be his judges. Prominent in the front row with Lord President Bradshaw were Cromwell
and his son-in-law, Henry Ireton.

When the chief prosecutor, John Cook, stood up to speak, the
King tapped him reprovingly on his shoulder with his silver-headed
cane, as he would a servant who was out of line. For an instant, Cook
hesitated. Impatiently, Lord President Bradshaw ordered him to read
out the charge. "As the author of all the cruel and bloody wars," Cook
intoned, "Charles Stuart, the King, was guilty of treason." Charles inquired by what authority he was being tried. In the name of the Parliament, Bradshaw told him. With a wry expression, Charles replied
that to his knowledge Parliament consisted of the Lords, the Commons, and the King, and he saw no Lords present. Despite Bradshaw's insistence, Charles refused to plead guilty or not guilty until,
as he said, he was convinced of the court's lawful authority. It was his
duty to defend the people, and "if power without law may make
laws . . . I do not know what subject he is in England that can be sure
of his life or anything that he calls his own." The exasperated Bradshaw informed him that if he did not plead, he would be assumed
guilty.

Notwithstanding the King's contemptuous refusal to answer the
charges against him, yea or nay, the proceedings continued for two
more days. One session was taken up with the clerk reading in a mono-
tone the sworn depositions of thirty-five witnesses, all humble folk,

among them an ironmonger, a shoemaker, and a barber surgeon, who had either seen the King raise his standard at Nottingham (one deponent, a painter, said he had painted the standard pole himself) or observed him leading his troops into battle. When Charles attempted to give his reasons for his actions, the Lord President cut him off, declaring that as a prisoner, he could speak only when authorized to do so by the court. *"I am not an ordinary prisoner,"* Charles thundered, losing his composure. Strange to say, his stammer had disappeared during his trial.

On January 27, 1649, the Lord President pronounced the High Court's decision. "Charles Stuart, as a tyrant, traitor, murderer, and a public enemy to the good people of this nation, shall be put to death by severing of his head from his body." Escorted by the guards, Charles was hurried out of the hall. Sneering soldiers blew tobacco smoke in his face as he passed them.[48]

It was widely known that Cromwell had to resort to threats to get the signatures on the death warrant. In one case, he held the wrist of a reluctant signatory and guided his hand to spell out his name.[49]

On January 30, 1649, a multitude of people were milling around Whitehall. They had come to see the King beheaded. The scaffold had been constructed so as to adjoin the classical facade of Inigo Jones's Banqueting House, and at the appointed hour Charles stepped out of one of the long windows. He was accompanied by the Duke of Richmond, the Earl of Southampton, his chosen spiritual adviser Bishop William Juxon, and Colonel Francis Hacker; the latter had been his keeper throughout the trial and had signed the warrant for the executioner.

At last Charles was able to have his say, although only those on the scaffold could hear him. Declaring his innocence, he claimed it was Parliament, not he, who began the war, but God's judgment upon him was just, because he had allowed an unjust sentence (meaning the death penalty for Strafford) to take effect. He forgave everyone, as Bishop Juxon could bear witness, but speaking from his wounded soul he called himself "the martyr of the people." In due course, the English people would grant him this title. With the final comment that he was going from a corruptible to an incorruptible kingdom, he turned to the executioner. "I shall say but very short prayers, and then thrust out my hands." That would be the signal for the ax to fall. Stuffing his flowing locks into a white nightcap handed him by the bishop, he lay down and put his head on the block. At the agreed-upon signal, the executioner at one blow cut off his head. Charles's courageous demeanor instantly became the stuff of legend.[50]

THE NEXT FEW DAYS after the King's execution witnessed a constitutional revolution. As well as formally abolishing the office of King, the Rump Parliament voted to abolish the House of Lords. Any peers who wished to do so could stand for election to the single house. (To Leicester's scorn, both his cousin the Earl of Pembroke and the Earl of Salisbury took their seats as "cheerful Commoners.")[51] Vesting all legislative power in itself, the unicameral parliament established an executive Council of State, composed of a maximum of forty members with a president, that met at Derby House. The Leicesters and their connections were well represented on the Derby House committee. Their son Philip, Lord Lisle, was appointed a member, as were Pembroke and Salisbury. There were a few other peers, but the greater part of the committee was composed of regicides.[52]

In February Lucy received a letter from the Prince of Wales (now proclaimed Charles II by the Scottish parliament). The letter came from The Hague and was dated two days before his father's execution. Charles wrote that he was "truly sensible" of her kindness to his father and himself. He explained that he would write her more often if he were not afraid that his letters exposed her to danger. However, he "could not forbear to take notice" of Lord Northumberland's support for his father in the House of Lords and prayed Lady Carlisle to tell her brother so. He promised that if it was ever in his power, he would make "such real acknowledgment thereof both to him and to her that she shall have cause to believe that he is truly and unchangeably, Her very affectionate Friend."[53]

As gracious as this letter was, it is unlikely that it afforded Lucy much comfort. By the time she received it, Holland and Norwich were on trial, along with the Duke of Hamilton, Baron Arthur Capel, and Sir John Owen, for instigating the Second Civil War. In the autumn, when Parliament was dominated by the Presbyterian faction, it had looked as if they would simply be banished; but when Cromwell and the Independents regained control, their fate was sealed. As in King Charles's case, a special High Court of Justice under Bradshaw was constituted. The trial of the lords began in Westminster Hall on February 10. In spite of desperate behind-the-scenes efforts to save their lives, on March 6, 1649, they were condemned to death by beheading.

All the condemned men petitioned Parliament for mercy. Hamilton's and Capel's petitions were denied with little debate by the majority, and Sir John Owen was unexpectedly reprieved; but in Holland's and Norwich's cases, the suspense was almost unbearable. The debate over Holland lasted from eleven in the morning until seven at night; when the vote was taken there were thirty for him and thirty-one against. When Norwich's petition was voted upon, one of the naysayers was out of the chamber, so the yeas and nays being equal, the Speaker cast the deciding vote. In the charged atmosphere, Speaker William Lenthall gravely pronounced his vote in the prisoner's favor. Thus by a single vote each, Holland's life was lost and Norwich's saved. In March the three unlucky lords were beheaded in Palace Yard in Westminster. Hoping for a last-minute reprieve, both Hamilton and Holland made long, rambling speeches on the scaffold.[54] Among all his high-sounding sentiments, Holland surprised his listeners by declaring that Lady Devonshire would have to believe in his sincerity now, and he seemed to derive comfort from the thought.

Throughout these dreadful days, Lucy was staying with Dorothy at Leicester House. Doll's five-year-old son Harry was dying (probably of consumption), and on Wednesday, March 14, "the sweet boy," so beloved by the family, breathed his last. The house was in deep mourning when, on the following day, there was a loud knock on the door and there stood Colonel Thomas Harrison with a guard of soldiers. Known as one of Cromwell's most fanatical colonels, Harrison was the usual escort for important political prisoners. It was he who had escorted King Charles from castle to castle during his last days. When Lucy heard who it was, she knew he had come for her and quickly ran to her room. On being told that Lady Carlisle had retired, Colonel Harrison demanded that she come down at once. When she appeared in the hall, he read out a warrant for her arrest. The women were alone. Leicester was still in the country. Dorothy ran to Lucy and tried to speak to her, but she was shoved aside by the soldiers.[55]

Lucy was taken under guard to the Council of State at Derby House, where she was examined. One suspects that her nephew Viscount Lisle and her friend the Earl of Salisbury would have made it their business to be absent for her examination. Instead, strange and hostile faces confronted her, among them General Cromwell's leathery countenance with the prominent nose and the large wart over his eyebrow. She was informed that she had been arrested on suspicion of treason. (Much of the evidence against her had come to light during the trial of Holland and the others.) After a harrowing examination, which she had to undergo without benefit of counsel, she was taken back to her own lodgings by the same uncouth guards who had brought her. For five days she was kept closely guarded under house arrest. One day her house was searched and her papers taken away. Another day a committee came from the Council of State and questioned her for hours. Then on March 21, she was taken to the Tower. The Lieutenant of the Tower was handed a warrant from the Council of State, ordering him to keep Lady Carlisle a close prisoner.[56]

The Countess of Devonshire narrowly missed a similar fate. She too was under suspicion, and, in fact, an armed guard was dispatched to her brother's country house to bring her up to London. By luck, the goldsmith with whom she did her banking got wind of her imminent arrest from his friends in the government and bribed a member of the Council of State, "whose narrow fortunes rendered him greedy enough of money," and the case against Lady Devonshire was dropped.[57] The Countess of Carlisle's imprisonment was on everyone's lips. Some said that the Council of State meant to put her to death; others maintained that her brother the Earl of Northumberland would save her by giving his undertaking that she would no longer "play the stateswoman."[58]

The Commonwealth of Ladies, a salacious lampoon on royalist noblewomen published in 1649, made capital out of Lady Carlisle's misfortunes:

> This is a Lady indeed, that seven years since took saile with Presbytery, being charged in the *Fore-deck* by Master *Hollis,* in the *Poop* by Master *Pym,* whilst she clapt my Lord of *Holland* under hatches. And this was a lucky *Supply* at that time, because *Toby Matthewes* and *Wat Montague* were both *fled for Religion.* About 3 years since, being weary with that *faction,* she revived a correspondence upon the *Royall accompt;* among the rest with divers *foreine Ambassadors,* especially *Mons. Believerey,* till she was put in the *Tower,* where she now pines away for want of *fresh-Cod* and knoweth not which way to lead her *Nags* to water, since the *State* hath cut off all her *pipes* of intelligence.[59]

Mercifully, proud Lucy would not have seen this scatological attack on her as she endured the long, painful days in the Tower of London.

PART FOUR

A

NEW ORDER

eighteen

IN THE TOWER

AS HER DAYS IN THE TOWER dragged on, Lucy's mind inevitably returned to her childhood visits to her father and to the time in her early womanhood when he kept her with him to try to prevent her marriage. Then her stern father had enjoyed the liberty of the Tower, strutting, cane in hand, on the ramparts or in the gardens. Through lavish bribery of the warders (who had wept to see him leave) he had converted the Martin Tower into his own private castle with every convenience, including a laboratory for his experiments. Lucy's comfortless existence in the Tower, in contrast, was more like Strafford's. Little had she dreamed when she visited that courageous man in his cold, damp quarters, where the gloom of night never lifted, that one day she would be confined in similar circumstances. Held as a close prisoner, she was not permitted to step outside for a breath of fresh air. The few faithful servants she had with her in her captivity bartered with the warders for her necessities. With some money at her disposal, however, Lucy was still living in relative luxury, compared with some royalists whose estates had been sequestrated and, having no ready cash, were literally starving to death in prison.

Apart from her servants and warders, the only living creatures she saw were four members of the Council of State who had been appointed to examine her—Thomas Scot, John Lisle, Colonel Edmund Ludlow, and a Mr. Holland.[1] All were regicides. She was usually questioned by Scot, the head of intelligence for the new Commonwealth. His presence on the committee indicated the seriousness with which the government viewed Lady Carlisle's activities in the royalist uprising. Beleaguered by questions she could answer only by incriminating others, Lucy was no longer the great lady but a helpless prisoner.

On more than one occasion, Lucy was shown the rack. A royalist newsletter reported that she was terrified at the sight of the great wooden wheel that pulled the victim's bones apart as easily as a chicken's, and implored her jailers, "Do not hurt me for I am only a woman and cannot endure pain, I will confess whatsoever you have me."[2] In view of her overweening pride and her courage in plots past and future, these words seem out of character, and, in fact, another source asserts that Lady Carlisle remained staunch under questioning.[3] In any case, her warders were bluffing her. The rack and the torture chamber known as the Room of Little Ease had been abolished along with the Star Chamber in 1641. But Lucy's health, always uncertain, was breaking under the strain of the harsh conditions and constant interrogation, and she petitioned the Council of State to lighten the conditions of her imprisonment.[4]

Meanwhile, the outside world had no idea what was happening to her. "I hear no more of the Lady Carlisle what shall become of her, I hope she will save her life," the Dowager Countess of Lindsey wrote her cousin Lord Montagu on April 12, 1649. She added that she hoped Lucy Carlisle would live to get a husband since her best prospect, Lord Norwich, was rumored to be marrying Lady Kingsmill.[5] (The diarist John Evelyn heard this rumor too and passed it on to his father-in-law, Sir Richard Browne, in France.) Although Norwich did not marry Lady Kingsmill, he was not to provide a safe haven for Lucy. On his release from Windsor Castle in May, he left England to join Charles on the Continent and did not return until just before the Restoration.

On April 11, the Council of State ordered the committee dealing with "Lady Carlisle's business" to bring in its report. For one reason or another, the report was deferred from session to session, and it was not until April 21 that the council got around to considering it. On April 24, Thomas Scot was instructed to report to the House on the Countess of Carlisle's case with all speed. Until Parliament's pleasure was known, she was to remain in the Tower. Nevertheless, her petition had been favorably received, and on April 26, the Council of State directed the Lieutenant of the Tower "to permit the Countess of Carlisle to take the air and see her friends within the Tower, in his presence or that of his Deputy."[6]

Attempts by the family to get her liberty enlarged still further met with no success. The charges against her were extremely serious; there is reason to believe that it was only her sex that saved her from execution along with Holland. One suspects that her nephew Lisle could have done more to at least ease the conditions of her imprisonment. He was a leading member of the Council of State, sitting on dozens of important committees. He was also the bosom friend of the influential parliamentarian Sir Henry Vane the Younger and a close associate of Cromwell. But Lisle was averse to soliciting personal favors, and he was certainly fainthearted so far as his aunt was concerned. Unfortunately, at this juncture Northumberland was in the political wilderness. He had made no secret of his disdain for the regicide government and was living in retirement on his estates.

While Northumberland could do nothing for the one sister, he was in a position to oblige the other. Along with his withdrawal from all public affairs under the new Commonwealth government, Northumberland was giving up the guardianship of the royal children. In early April he requested the Council of State "to relieve him of the expense and responsibility" of their charge. But when he told Dorothy what he had done, she indicated that she would be glad enough to take over the care of the children. That the government allowed £3,000 a year for their maintenance was undoubtedly an inducement. Northumberland immediately wrote the younger Vane recommending his sister the Countess of Leicester as the children's guardian. "You know her so well," he told this family friend, "that I am confident you believe she will as much intend the good education of the children as any person that can be employed about them, and for her good affections to the Parliament, I think none that know anything of her will doubt them."[7] The appointment was confirmed, and on June 14, 1649, Dorothy brought nine-year-old Prince Henry, Duke of Gloucester, and fourteen-year-old Princess Elizabeth to Penshurst.

Dorothy was under strict orders from Parliament not to treat the children like royalty. They were to be simply Harry and Betty, and to be treated the same as her own children and grandchildren. To the extent that Gloucester took his lessons with her son Henry and her grandson Robert, Dorothy abided by this injunction. But for the rest (and despite Northumberland's assurance to Vane that Dorothy was a good republican), she created a little court for the royal children. She sent to Whitehall for a loan of furniture and plate, and in due course there arrived velvet bedsteads fringed with gold and silver, jewel-toned Turkey carpets, and a treasure trove of silver—dishes and plates, porringers and candle cups, candlesticks, snuffers, basins, ewers, and a warming pan. Dorothy set up a separate table for the royal lodgers, where they were waited upon by their own retainers (they had brought an establishment of ten or eleven servants), and their bedsteads and carpets were placed in the largest of the bedchambers.[8]

They were sweet children. The Duke was no different from other little boys his own age, preferring the playing field to the classroom and, according to the tutor Mr. Lovell, finding Latin particularly "painful." Princess Elizabeth was the image of her father, with the same innate dignity. She wrung Dorothy's heart when, in her quiet manner, she described the last meeting she and her brother had with their father. Indeed, she had written it all down so that she would not forget a word. It was the day before his execution.

The Earl of Northumberland had brought the children from Syon House to St. James's Palace. The King had greeted them tenderly, embracing them both, and then, taking Elizabeth's hands, he had spoken to her very solemnly. He told her she was not to grieve for him, because he was dying a glorious death for the laws and the religion of the land. He gave her a message for her mother, which he made her repeat very carefully: she was to tell the Queen that his thoughts had never strayed from her and that his love for her would be the same to the last. While she wept uncontrollably, he tried to console her, saying that they would all be happy again and that God would restore the throne to her brother Charles. Above all, he made her promise never to give up the Church of England, and he prescribed some books against popery that she was to read. Then he took her little brother on his lap and said, "Sweetheart, now will they cut off thy father's head, and perhaps make thee a king, but mark what I say, you must not be a king as long as your brothers Charles and James live." Choking with emotion, Elizabeth told how her brother, though only nine years old, had replied, "I will be torn in pieces first."[9]

The royal children settled in very well at Penshurst. The young duke had his playmates, and Princess Elizabeth, so mature for her fourteen years, soon became fast friends with Frances and the older Sidney girls. Not surprisingly, the young princess developed a schoolgirl crush on Doll. Dorothy, who was always sympathetic to lonely young people (we recall her kindness to poor Anne Hay, Carlisle's neglected daughter), created a real home for these illustrious but unfortunate children. Alone among the numerous family at Penshurst, the master was unhappy about the royal visitors. He complained to Dorothy that their presence would increase his expenses in "fuel, wasting of household stuff," and so on, that he would have "less liberty in his own house," and that he would "be obliged to attendance which would be troublesome" to him. Dorothy soon discovered that all this grumbling was simply a preamble to a further reduction in her allowances. Coming to the point, Leicester argued that £3,000 a year was "a great accession of means" to her, well beyond what she would have to spend on the children's upkeep. Truly, he "thought it strange" that he should have "almost nothing for all expenses, debts, interest money, charges at law, etc." while she should have "near £7,000 a year to keep this family." Therefore, he ventured, it was only "reasonable to abate a great part" of the £700 she was getting for Lord Strangford.

Dorothy was singularly unmoved by all her husband's arguments and, predictably, began to "rant and scold." But Leicester had re-

solved to take off £400 a year from his wife's share of Strangford's allowances, come what may. Wearily but triumphantly he recorded in
his diary that "this caused a huge storm in the house, but I persisted
in it."[10]

SUMMER IN THE TOWER was a double penance for Lucy. She had
always spent her summers in the country. How she missed the fresh
air of Penshurst! In September Lisle informed his family that Lady
Carlisle's servants had appeared before the Council of State to try to
"obtain leave for her to go sometimes with the Lieutenant to take the
country air." But this attempt (he wrote) received the same answer
"which all our other motions have done, that the business must be reported to the House before they enlarged her liberty."[11] In his opinion, little could be gained for her at the present time. Indeed, the
delay in proceeding with her case was wearing Lucy down. Although
in August the Council of State again directed Scot to report to the
House regarding the Dowager Countess of Carlisle, she heard nothing further for months.

It is not surprising that Lady Carlisle's case was in abeyance, because the new Commonwealth was undergoing tremendous difficulties. The obstreperous Irish had risen in support of Charles II, and in
July Cromwell had gone to Ireland to put down the rebellion. He had
done so by a brutal massacre of the Irish garrisons at Drogheda and
Wexford. But Ireland was only one source of trouble. In the winter of
1650, the new government was fearful of yet another invasion from
the troublesome Scots. To lessen the danger from within, the House
ordered "all delinquents and papists" out of London. Since the Council of State was empowered to decide which delinquents should be
proceeded against and which released and pardoned, Lisle offered a
glimmer of hope for his aunt. This might "open a door for my Lady
Carlisle," he wrote the family.[12] Still nothing happened, and it was not
until March 1650 that Lucy's case again came up before the Council.

The papers taken from her house were to be examined, and the
Lieutenant of the Tower was summoned to attend. This caused great

trepidation among her relatives. Were there incriminating letters from Dorothy or Northumberland among the papers? Happily, Lisle was able to allay their fears. Scot had assured him that there were no letters from either Lord Northumberland or Lady Leicester and, in fact, "whatsoever there is of only private concernment shall be concealed." In the bedchamber of Lucy's maid, however, the officers had found a cipher that appeared to be for corresponding with Lord Jermyn in Paris. If this proved to be so, it did not bode well for his aunt.[13]

Meanwhile, despite her perilous situation, the incorrigible Lucy had become involved in another conspiracy. Once again a plot was afoot to rise for the King—this time for King Charles II. It was a complicated operation involving the English Presbyterians and Cavaliers, royalists abroad, and the Scots. The plan called for Charles to lead a Scottish army into England where he would be joined by a powerful force of supporters from across the country. On June 24, 1650, Charles duly landed in Scotland. That same month a royalist agent on the Continent, one Thomas Coke, was sent to England to coordinate plans with the London Presbyterians.

That Lucy, confined in the Tower for her part in the royalist rising of 1648, was fearlessly engaged in the plot to restore the Stuarts two years later shows that intrigue was in her blood. Nor was it difficult for her to acquire intelligence and pass it along to her brother Harry on the Continent. Security at the Tower was far from tight. The warders had their price for everything, and their paid services included spiriting confidential letters in and out of prison. We can visualize Lucy in her prison chamber, holding a newly arrived letter in front of the fire until the secret message, written in a special water that only became visible when warmed, emerged. This fluid was widely used by conspirators. Thomas Coke confessed that he had "a little glass of the same water in my study at Gray's Inn."[14] Although in 1650 the Council of State was unaware of her clandestine activities, her case was further postponed, so for a second summer Lucy remained in the fetid air of the Tower.

The tense political situation in 1650 also had its effect on

Dorothy's household. The first sign that something was stirring was a visit to Penshurst in August by the Speaker of the House, William Lenthall. He arrived at dinnertime and, seeing the royal children dining apart from the family, expressed his great displeasure to Lady Leicester. What was the reason for this special treatment? Had she not been ordered to treat them no differently than her own children? If he expected a docile answer, he was most certainly taken aback. Fixing him with a haughty stare worthy of her brother Northumberland, Dorothy replied defiantly that she would never allow any member of her household to sit at the table with the King's children.[15]

The next thing the Leicesters knew, an official notice arrived from Parliament informing them that the children were to be removed from Penshurst. They were instructed to get them ready for Anthony Mildmay, who had been assigned by Thomas Harrison, now Major General Harrison, to escort "Henry Stuart and Lady Elizabeth" to Carisbrooke Castle on the Isle of Wight. Lady Leicester was ordered to pack up all the plate, hangings, and other stuff belonging to the Commonwealth, for transport to London. Dorothy may have thought that it was her impolitic response to Lenthall that was the cause of the children's removal, but she would have been wrong. With Charles in Scotland and James in Holland, the shaky Commonwealth government thought it prudent to get their young brother out of the country so he would not become a rallying point for royalist activity. Princess Elizabeth too was regarded as a potential threat by the regicide government. The frail young girl was acquiring a reputation as a virtual saint. "Miraculous reports" were circulating among royalists at home and abroad "of her virtues and abilities, of her piety and adherence to all her Father's principles."[16]

It was a terrible wrench for the children. They had been happy at Penshurst with Lady Leicester and her family, and now they were to be taken away. Dorothy and Doll were especially worried about the Princess being kept in that bleak, drafty castle where her father had been imprisoned. Of recent months she had become increasingly pale and wan and had spent many days just lying down in her bedchamber. Delicate to begin with, in all probability she had contracted consumption at Penshurst, for seventeen-year-old Elizabeth Sidney was in the highly contagious, final stages of the disease. Before leaving Penshurst, Princess Elizabeth entrusted two pieces of jewelry to the Earl and Countess of Leicester for safekeeping. One was a very valuable pearl necklace given to her by Prince William of Orange at the time of his marriage to her elder sister, Mary. The other was a diamond necklace. In case she should die, she said, the pearl necklace was to go to her sister, but the Countess of Leicester should have the diamond necklace because of her great kindness to her and her brother. At the same time, she left some trinkets with Doll as keepsakes.[17]

Dorothy had little time to regret the loss of the children and the guardianship, with its perquisites and allowances. The allotted year had run out, and Isabella and young Strangford were clamoring to be married, undeterred by the fact that poor sister Elizabeth was dying. She was suffering greatly, with constant pain in her stomach, but bore it all with angelic patience, sustained by her deep religious convictions. For the imminent events of marriage and death in the family, the Leicesters required an Anglican clergyman to administer the sacraments. Parliament had outlawed the Church of England: bishops were abolished, church lands were sold, and using the Book of Common Prayer for the rites of baptism, marriage, and burial was made a criminal offense. Many Anglican priests and ministers had been deprived of their livings. Parliament had usurped the Earl of Leicester's right to name the rector of Penshurst Church,[18] and the family at the great house would have nothing to do with the parliamentary appointee. (The village church itself, so dear to Dorothy, had been sadly desecrated by zealous Puritans, the stone heads of the statues knocked off and the furniture and vessels destroyed.)[19] Fortunately, the vicar in the nearby village of Leigh was willing to risk conducting the services according to the outlawed rites of the Church of England.

On August 22, the Reverend Robert Antrobus married Isabella Sidney to her cousin Viscount Strangford in the chapel at Penshurst—to the joy of her mother and the misgivings of her father. On October 7, he buried Elizabeth Sidney, to the infinite sorrow of both parents. As portrayed in Leicester's journal, this young woman was a model daughter. Though he had seen little of her while she was growing up, since his return to Penshurst five years earlier they had grown very close. Her "heavenly disposition" provided a refuge from his stormy life with her mother. In the last months of her life, he had spent many hours sitting by her bedside while they talked of God and the efficacy of prayer. Half an hour before her death, she held his hand and told him she would pray for him. The heartbroken father recorded in his journal that Elizabeth died with "such a divine assurance of her future happiness that she left the world with more joy than if she had gone to be married to the greatest Prince on the earth."[20]

The family at Penshurst soon learned of the death of another young Elizabeth. Early in September, word came from Mr. Lovell, who had left Penshurst to become the Duke of Gloucester's tutor, that Princess Elizabeth had passed away soon after arriving at Carisbrooke Castle. His former employers lost no time in preparing a declaration for Lovell to sign, to the effect that on her deathbed the Princess had confirmed her intention of bequeathing the diamond necklace to the Leicesters.[21] With Lovell's signature on the document, Dorothy assumed the necklace was hers. Accordingly, she made no mention of it to Anthony Mildmay, who advised the parliamentary revenue committee that all that remained in her Ladyship's hands were some damask linen tablecloths and napkins. When the matter came to light a year later, Cromwell and Parliament demanded that the jewelry be handed over to the state, and Dorothy entered upon a wrangle with the authorities that was unresolved at her death.[22]

On September 3, 1650, the Lord General Cromwell defeated the Scottish army at Dunbar in Scotland, killing three thousand Scots and taking ten thousand prisoners. Cromwell claimed a loss of not more than thirty soldiers on the English side. This resounding victory inspired the Commonwealth leaders with new confidence, and the Council of State settled down to its normal business, including the matter of political prisoners in the Tower. On September 19,

Thomas Scot was ordered to make his report on the papers discovered at Lady Carlisle's house. Perhaps to oblige his friend Lord Lisle, Scot's report was sufficiently benign that on September 25 orders were issued to release the Countess of Carlisle, "prisoner in the Tower," for two months "for the benefit of her health," on her own recognizance. She was required to reside twenty miles outside London and to post a bail of £10,000. Considering that other prisoners were bailed on recognizances of £1,000 or £2,000, the amount of her bail was extraordinarily high. It would seem to reflect the council's recognition of Lady Carlisle's legendary mischief making, as well as her relationship to the wealthy Earl of Northumberland. In the meantime, until her bail was ready, she was to have the liberty of the Tower.[23]

It is likely that the Glaslough estate was put up as security for her bail. She had succeeded in getting back this part of her Irish lands at least. Sir Philip Percival had died in 1647. Shortly before her arrest in 1649, she sent his son and heir, John Percival, then a student at Cambridge, a copy of the note her nephew Lisle and Sir John Temple had obtained from Sir Percival in 1642. This was the note acknowledging that, on Strafford's instructions, he had bought the Glaslough and Shillelagh lands in trust for the Countess of Carlisle. On the strength of this note, Lucy asked John Percival to assign over the leases to her. Encouraged by his mother, Percival sent the note to the second Earl of Strafford, then living in exile at Caen in Normandy. He himself knew nothing about the business, John Percival wrote, "but of the Lady's nobleness he had such a high value that he is sure she would claim nothing but what she conceives to be her own." The young earl asked the advice of his uncle and trustee, Sir George Wentworth. Wentworth was not satisfied to have his nephew drop all claims to the Shillelagh lease; no doubt some confusion existed because of the first Earl of Strafford's own land acquisitions around Shillelagh. But in June 1650, while Lucy was still in prison, Sir George sent a declaration to John Percival, giving him clearance to convey the Glaslough lease to Lady Carlisle "without fear of question from the Earl of Strafford or any other." Accordingly, John Percival took the necessary legal steps. At long last, Lucy acquired possession of the Glaslough lands that Strafford had purchased with her money in 1638.[24]

ON OCTOBER 1, 1650, Lucy walked out of the Tower a free woman for two months. Her ordeal had certainly affected her health, yet her spirit was unbroken. Optimistic by nature, she was confident that she would find some way out of returning to the Tower. Her intention was to go to Dorothy at Penshurst (just the thought of the country air made her feel better), but for a day or two she rested at Leicester House. On the day she was leaving for the country, she received a visit from Colonel Henry Cromwell, the Lord General's brother.[25] Perhaps this was simply a courtesy call, or, more likely, he had come to remind her that her recognizance required her to behave herself and "to do nothing prejudicial to the present government."

The reunion of the sisters was rendered even more emotional because it occurred in the shadow of Elizabeth Sidney's death. Ironically, Lucy's imprisonment had begun with a death in Dorothy's family, and she had come out of prison just in time for another. In all probability, the sisters had not seen each other since the dreadful day of Lucy's arrest, because up to her final hours in the Tower, Lucy had been under close restraint and had had no visitors. Dorothy was shocked by the ravages that a year and a half in prison had wrought in her sister's appearance. For her part, Lucy found Dorothy not only in mourning but in a deteriorating marriage and bemoaning the fact that Doll, after all their years together, had recently gone to live on her own at Althorp with her young family and her sister Anne.[26] In their mutual need, the aging sisters clung to each other as closely as in their childhood. Once again it was the two of them against the world.

In November, pleading ill health, Lucy asked for an extension of her leave, which was granted for a further three months.[27] At the end of that period, the Council of State allowed "the Countess of Carlisle liberty to continue in the country upon her bond in the same sums and former condition of her recognizance for three months longer."[28] But in March 1651, the royalist agent Thomas Coke was taken prisoner by the Commonwealth government and turned informer. Among the hundreds of people he implicated in the plot was Lucy. In his confession to the Council of State in April 1651, Coke declared: "The ladies looked upon as active in the Presbyterian design are the Lady Carlisle and the Lady Peterborough, the former, though in prison, yet kept weekly correspondence by ciphers till the King went into Scotland, with her brother, the Lord Percy, who always acquainted the King therewith, and sometimes me, with his intelligence."[29]

Sir Edward Nicholas, a royalist living in exile at The Hague, left no doubt that Coke's revelations were true. Writing to Edward Hyde on May 3, 1651, Nicholas lamented:

The King's business and friends in England are totally ruined by the many discoveries lately made there by what Mr. Tho. Cooke hath [it is said] voluntarily discovered. He, being a perfect and prudent Presbyterian, was [it seems] held fittest to be intrusted with the secrets of all His Majesty's designs and friends in England, which he hath so fully and clearly made known to his old friend Bradshaw as it is said there are not less than 2000 noblemen and gentlemen of quality imprisoned and under restraint there at present.[30]

To another royalist correspondent, Nicholas described the Coke affair as the worst misfortune to befall Charles "since the horrid murder of his blessed father, it being like to prove the ruin of most of His Majesty's best affected subjects in England."[31] In his revelations, Coke ungallantly named not only Lady Carlisle and Lady Peterborough but also that other inveterate plotter the Countess of Devonshire, whose house in Bishopsgate served as a meeting place while Lady Carlisle was in prison.

For some reason, the Council of State did not see fit to put Lucy back in the Tower. In June, following a report from Thomas Scot, she was granted an indefinite extension of leave on good behavior, on condition that she not travel more than five miles from Penshurst without Parliament's permission. Even the discovery of her correspondence with Charles II while Prince of Wales, which was taken at the battle of Worcester in September 1651 by Cromwell's victorious forces, did not cause her recommittal. In March 1652, Lucy was officially freed and her bail bonds discharged.[32] Apparently the Council of State had decided that Lady Carlisle, aging and ill, no longer posed a security threat to the Commonwealth.

A DYSFUNCTIONAL

FAMILY

IN THE SUMMER OF 1652, Doll surprised everyone by remarrying. Dorothy was in favor of her remarriage—or at least not opposed to it, apparently, since she held the wedding at Penshurst—but Leicester strongly disapproved of his daughter's choice. The bridegroom, Robert Smythe, was the grandson of the wealthy widow of Sir Thomas Smythe whom his father had married shortly before his death. The aftermath of that match had been some unpleasant litigation. Leicester's sister Barbara's marriage to the heir of the Smythe fortune, the first Viscount Strangford, had been far from happy, and now Isabella's marriage with their son seemed destined for trouble. Allying the Sidney pedigree with Smythe money had always turned out badly, in Leicester's opinion. John Evelyn, drinking the waters at Tunbridge Wells, just happened to drop in at Penshurst on the day of the wedding. He found it "full of company on the marriage of my old fellow collegiate, Mr. Robert Smith, who married my Lady Dorothy Sidney, widow of the Earl of Sunderland."[1] Among the wedding party milling on the lawns that fine summer day, the father of the bride was conspicuously absent, having chosen (as he noted in his journal) to remain in London.[2]

Poor Doll was coming in for a good deal of criticism over her re-marriage. Her very perfections had consecrated her to eternal single-ness, like some vestal virgin. Her remarriage certainly disillusioned William Temple for one. The son of the Leicesters' old family friend Sir John Temple, William had adored Doll as a schoolboy. When his idol stepped off her pedestal and made this unexceptional second marriage, he was keenly disappointed. He wrote his fiancée, Dorothy Osborne, that the Countess of Sunderland would have "gained by keeping herself a widow." Dorothy Osborne, then at Tunbridge Wells, was astonished by the marriage. "Who would ever have dreamt Mr. Smythe should have had my Lady Sunderland," she wrote William. It was not that she thought him not good enough for Lady Sunderland, but that she thought her Ladyship regarded herself as too good for him. She passed on a bit of gossip about Lady Sunderland making the rounds at the Wells: "I think I shall never forgive her one thing she said of him, which was that she married him out of pity. It was the pitifullest saying that ever I heard, and made him so contemptible that I should not have married him for that reason." Indeed, if Dorothy Osborne can be believed, Doll was very condescending to-ward her new husband, receiving his respectful approaches "like a gracious princess." "They say 'tis worth going twenty miles to see it," the caustic young woman informed her fiancé.[3]

Leicester came to accept Doll's marriage, but at the end of De-cember 1652, he had a serious quarrel with his eldest son, Philip, that ended in a more or less permanent estrangement. There had been trouble brewing between the two for years. Lisle complained that his father never omitted an opportunity to reproach him. It is true that Leicester often made snide comments, sneering at Lisle's "fre-quent use of 'God Willing' and 'as God pleases' and other cant ex-pressions of the times." While Leicester continued to be a lukewarm royalist, Lisle was ever more devoted to the republican cause. But it was not Lisle's close association with Cromwell and the Common-wealth government that aggravated Leicester; it was his failure to use his position for the family's advancement. This reluctance on Lisle's part came to the fore when Leicester's cousin the Earl of

Pembroke died in 1650. Leicester wanted Lisle to obtain part of his deceased cousin's estate for him, but instead some colonel got it. When Leicester complained to his son that he had neglected the family's interests, Lisle replied that he never asked for gifts from Parliament, "and it was exceedingly contrary to my disposition to solicit such a thing." In Leicester's eyes, this branded him both unfilial and a fool.[4]

On this ill-fated winter day at Penshurst, perhaps goaded by Leicester's sarcasm, Lisle struck his father. Leicester's anger spurts from the pages of his journal like blood from a wound: "The Lord Lisle most unnecessarily and causelessly, undutifully and impiously, defied and affronted me, and not only so but assaulted and struck me in my own house."[5] There was no forgiveness in Leicester's heart, and the bad relations between father and son made life more difficult for Dorothy, the more so as she was raising Philip's two older children, because his wife had died in childbirth in August 1652.[6]

As if her husband's break with her eldest son were not enough, shortly afterward, Dorothy found herself cut off from her daughter Isabella. Strangford had taken up with dissolute companions and, early in 1653, though still not of age, had left Penshurst with his wife and rented lodgings in Covent Garden. On the advice of his tavern companions and a litigious lawyer, he was now suing his father-in-law in the Court of Chancery. Though he had not asked for a dowry at the time of his marriage, now suddenly he was threatening that if he did not get a large one, he would renege on the jointure he had settled on Isabella. He was also claiming repayment of most of the £1,000 per annum that the Leicesters had received for his keep for all the years he lived with them. He demanded an accounting and the return of the signed document that enabled Leicester to collect his rents during his minority. Henceforth, he would collect his own rents, he informed his father-in-law.[7]

Leicester's response to these unwarranted demands was one of cold resentment. Dorothy, however, wrote a stinging rebuke to her ungrateful son-in-law. She had little time to write, she told him, but "in short" he was "abased," and she would not give "five pounds" for all that he would get "by these violent courses." She went on to castigate him for alienating her daughter: "You have made an unpleasant separation between your wife and me, but I hope you will recompense it to us both in giving her all the contentment you can." Clearly, the ardent lover had turned into a bad husband. Dorothy's heart was sore for her child. "I am much assured of her kindness to you," she continued, "and I think her deserving other ways, yet will she not by her merit be protected from injuries, if you give up your judgment to the dispose of low mean people that serve nothing but their own interest." She ended her scolding by saying that "except you drive me from it, I will continue to love and serve you."[8] Unfortunately, the youth did not mend his ways. He was drinking heavily with boon companions whom Leicester scorned as no better than "cheating knaves, half-witted and half mad."[9]

The quarrel was out in the open. Strangford calumniated his in-laws all over London, and in self-defense Leicester had "to let the world see you deal ill with me."[10] Things came to a head in September 1653, when Strangford served notice to his tenants that their Michaelmas rents would be collected by his own agents, and he forbade them to pay a cent to the Earl of Leicester's agents.[11]

Leicester was furious and decided to go up to London to see a lawyer. But on the eve of his departure, he and Dorothy had a violent quarrel. It started out as the usual row, with Dorothy ranting and railing at her husband about something that displeased her. Suddenly Leicester, who was seldom heard to raise his voice when his wife berated him, began shouting at her in a terrifying manner that he would not stand for her unreasonableness any longer. The crash of cabinets and Dorothy's cries indicated that he was ransacking her room. Leicester had exploded and run amok after a lifetime of quietly tolerating Dorothy's domestic tyranny. Before leaving Penshurst for London, he dismissed all the servants and left Dorothy "to digest it" as best she could.[12] Arrived at London, he went directly to Leicester House, where he continued his rampage, ordering the houseful of relatives, dependents, and hangers-on to get out. Among those staying there was his sister-in-law. Not choosing to wait for further abuse, Lucy wasted no time in gathering her things together and was the first to flee the house. Leicester—that most reserved and private of gentlemen—had created a public scandal.

Describing his descent on Leicester House to her favorite nephew Lord Bruce, Lady Devonshire (who had a firsthand account from Lucy) remarked that "the infinite divisions and distractions of that family are not imaginable."[13] She could not describe them all since they were as numerous as the many people reportedly living in the house. Dorothy Osborne was frankly relishing the gossip. "Is it possible what they say that my Lord Leicester and my Lady are in great disorder, and that after forty years patience he has now taken up the cudgels and resolves to venture for mastery?" she asked William Temple in amusement.[14]

With Leicester House no longer available, Lucy had to make new living arrangements. Little Salisbury House, where she had resided before her imprisonment, was occupied by two of the Cecil daughters and their families, so Lucy rented herself a fine lodging at Covent Garden.[15] (Built in the 1630s by the Earl of Bedford, Covent Garden was the first of London's squares.) Thanks to the honesty and goodwill of John Percival, she had recovered all her Irish property and could live in comfort.

The recovery of the Shillelagh property had come about in the following way. The previous winter, while Lucy was staying with Dorothy at Leicester House, Sir John Clotworthy had come to pay his respects to her. As a leading parliamentary Presbyterian, he too had suffered imprisonment for several years. They passed a pleasant hour or two talking about mutual friends, no doubt agreeing that if John Pym were still alive, he would have joined them in prison, for the first wave of reformers had become Oliver Cromwell's victims. In the course of their reminiscences, the name of the late Sir Philip Percival came up. Sir John was related to the Percivals, and Lucy took the opportunity to show him Sir Philip's note acknowledging that he held Irish lands in trust for her. Explaining that the younger Percival had turned over the greater part of the trust to her some years earlier, she consulted her visitor as to how she could obtain possession of the rest. Charmed and flattered, Sir John offered to help. He advised her to draw up the proper legal document, "confidently" assuring her that John Percival would concur in anything she suggested. He himself would write to his young kinsman.[16]

Lucy acted quickly on Sir John's advice. She had a declaration of trust drawn up for John Percival's seal and signature and dictated an accompanying letter. The letter stated that his father was her trustee for the lease of the lands called Shillelagh, bought with £4,000 of her money from Calcott Chambre for a twenty-two-year term. The truth of the trust was manifested in his father's note of May 30, 1642, a copy of which she had formerly sent him. He had already assigned her the Glaslough lease mentioned in the note. But now with the Shillelagh lease nearing the end of its term, "and to prevent the total loss of the future profits and thereby of the £4,000 given for the same," she was asking him to sign the deed declaring this trust; the legal interest would remain with him until she desired an assignment. To these formal documents she added a pretty little note in her own scrawl:

> Sir
>
> I have already found the effects of your Justice, in the most considerable part of your father's trust, so as I do with much confidence make you this demand, both as I know you to be very civil, and obliging, and as I am assured by many, that what I now ask, will never be refused, by those, from whom I expect less favor, this opinions, and many more, that I have taken in your advantage, make me here particularly,
>
> > Your faithful servant
> > Lucy Carlile[17]

Dorothy had a friend, Robert Worsley, who shuttled between England and Ireland, and on his next journey he took Lucy's documents to John Percival in Dublin. In addition, Worsley brought Sir John Clotworthy's letter urging Percival to "relinquish the trust to its rightful proprietors." He also presented the young man with a letter from his mother. "You must do what is just, honest and honourable towards Lady Carlisle," Lady Percival instructed her son, "by which you will do her Ladyship but right, and yourself more."[18] John Percival was only too eager to please Lady Carlisle (although he had the declaration redrafted to indemnify himself against any claims for rents or arrears of rents),[19] and in due course Lucy got possession of the Shillelagh lease. Owing to Strafford's carelessness as her trustee, his execution, and the Civil Wars, it had taken fifteen years.

While her new lodgings were being prepared, Lucy decided to stay as a paying guest with the delightful Carlile family at Richmond. She had known Lodovic Carlile (no relation to her late husband) as a not very successful playwright at court. His wife, Joan, was an artist—equally unsuccessful. Before the Civil Wars, they had got along on Lodovic's sinecure as Keeper of the Deer at Richmond Park, where they lived in the lodge. Surprisingly, the Commonwealth government had allowed them to stay on at the lodge, and they managed to subsist by taking in lodgers. Petersham Lodge, just inside Richmond Park, was a very comfortable, genteel boardinghouse patronized mainly by royalist society. The Carliles supplied everything but linen, and one satisfied guest remarked that staying there was like being in one's own house. The Carliles treated each "new set of sojourners" like a house party; they planned picnics in the park and took their guests visiting the many noble houses in and about Richmond.[20]

Richmond had always been a favorite spot with the nobility. Famous for its good country air, it had the advantage of proximity to London. In 1650 Lady Devonshire purchased Roehampton, one of the finest of the estates at Richmond; its original owner, the Earl of Portland, had lavished a fortune on it. Here she presided in the same state as she did at Devonshire House in London. On October 11, 1653, she had a visit from Lady Carlisle, who came to tell her that she was to be her neighbor.[21] During Lucy's stay at Petersham Lodge, the two old friends spent much time together, making the social rounds. Among those whom they called upon was Bishop Brian Duppa, living in retirement in a modest house at the foot of the hill. The bishop was so depressed about the abolition of the episcopacy and the fate of the Anglican clergymen ejected from their livings that he had no heart for gallivanting. But he was no match for the commanding countesses, who took it upon themselves to draw him out of his seclusion. Half pleased and half annoyed, the elderly prelate wrote a benefactor: "I am for the present in the midst of two very noble neighbours, my Lady Devonshire at Row-Hampton, and my Lady Carlile at Petersham, who will not suffer me to be so much a hermit as otherwise I would be."[22]

Bishop Duppa had known Lady Carlisle well in the late 1630s, when he was tutor to Charles, then the Prince of Wales. He was astonished to see "this great lady formerly waited on by all the great persons of the court" taking pleasure in the simple joys of country life. One day he found her sitting alone on the seat at the top of Richmond Hill, gazing down on the lovely view of the winding Thames. During his ascent he had been meditating upon "the uncertainty and vanity of worldly things," and, sitting down beside her, he could not resist sermonizing on this theme with "that great lady" who had experienced both the heights and the depths of fortune. He was gratified to find her a willing listener (clearly Lucy had not lost her charm), and the good bishop returned to his home convinced that Lady Carlisle was "enjoying herself more in this retiredness than in all her former vanities."[23] If Bishop Duppa was right, it was the fulfillment of Sir Tobie Mathew's prophecy that should Lady Carlisle ever fall from her eminent position, she would go "to the other extreme of retiredness" and live in obscurity.

But Dorothy Osborne would have thought the bishop laughably gullible. In her opinion, Lady Carlisle was a worldling of the most insincere kind. "All she aims at," Dorothy wrote her fiancé, "is to go beyond everybody in compliment." Dubbing her "the most extraordinary person in the kingdom," Dorothy begged William to send her a sample of Lady Carlisle's writing. When he sent her a letter (probably one that Lucy had written to his father), Dorothy was devastating. "Tis writ in the way that's now affected by all that pretend to wit and good breeding," she sneered, "only I am a little scandalized I confess that she uses that word faithful, she that never knew how to be so in her life."[24]

There were others who shared her opinion of Lady Carlisle's character. At The Hague, Sir Edward Nicholas was disturbed to learn that Charles was going to make Harry Percy his Lord Chamberlain, and he wrote Charles's chief adviser, Edward Hyde, to try to avert it. Lord Percy was not to be trusted, Nicholas said, not the least because of his relationship to Lady Carlisle: "He will discover all things that are communicated to him to his dear and virtuous sister Carlisle, who has been, through the whole story of his late Majesty's misfortunes, a very pernicious instrument, and she will assuredly discover all things to her gang of Presbyterians who have ever betrayed all they know to the ruling rebels."[25]

There was good reason for Nicholas's sarcasm. He had been Secretary of State when Lucy betrayed her royal masters by warning the five members of Parliament of their impending arrest. As a loyal servant of the Crown, he would have found her detestable. But he had a more current and personal reason for wanting to keep her and her brother away from young Charles. The royalists in exile were divided into two factions: the party of Queen Henrietta Maria and her unofficial consort Lord Jermyn, which had close links with the English Presbyterians; and the opposition group headed by Hyde, composed of Cavaliers on both sides of the Channel. These groups battled for the heart and ear of the king-in-waiting. Nicholas, a member of the Hyde faction, was certainly biased against Percy and Lady Carlisle, both of whom adhered to the Queen's party.

By the middle of November 1653, Lucy was settled in Covent Garden. True, she loved the country, but she loved city life even more and was far from forsaking worldly vanities. Although Cromwell had replaced the corrupt, self-perpetuating Rump Parliament with a convention of godly men from each county (known to an increasingly cynical population as the Reign of Saints), life for the upper classes seemed to have taken on a prewar gaiety in 1653. "All I can tell you," Lady Devonshire wrote her nephew at the end of November, "is that suppers and balls are much in request." If he wanted to be received by "the nobler society," she told him in jest, he would have to reclaim his "high flying hawk and swift tiring fox." She reported that the Earls of Warwick and Salisbury were off to Newmarket for the races, and she asked him to pass on to his wife that "the garb in the town is ladies all in scarlet, shining and glittering, as bright as any 'ante-maske.'"[26]

Though Lucy was now in her midfifties, we can picture her resplendent in a red gown—advancing age would not have stopped her from keeping up with the fashion.

But daily life was about to darken. On December 16, 1653, Oliver Cromwell was solemnly invested as the Lord Protector, and a corps of bullying major generals took over the running of the country. The new Lord Protector and his family were ensconced in solemn state at Whitehall and Hampton Court. England had a new king lacking only the name. In its first few months, the military dictatorship issued a stream of ordinances bringing back Puritanism with a vengeance. To the disgust of Warwick, Salisbury, and the other sporting lords, horse racing was among the interdicted activities. Women's fashions obediently reflected the new order. Soon Lady Devonshire was advising her nephew's wife, who was coming up to London for the season, that the times required "frugality, and that no clothes are quite out of fashion."[27]

LEICESTER HAD RETURNED to Dorothy, and their married life ground on in the familiar pattern, but the washing of the family's dirty laundry in public had left its scars. Dorothy was a proud woman, and she differed from Lucy in that there had never been a breath of scandal about her before. Nevertheless, she had gone on the offensive, broadcasting far and wide that Leicester had broken open her cabinets and taken her letters and jewels. Leicester denied it vehemently, but for weeks this had been the talk of the town. The report had spread throughout England and to the Continent—even Harry Percy heard about the fracas in France. With peace restored, Dorothy was sadder but little wiser. Leicester complained to Northumberland that his wife "demanded unreasonable things," and if she did not get them would "rail and asperse those who displeased her."[28] Dorothy was particularly sharp with her spinster daughter Anne, who had returned to Penshurst when Doll remarried. Well-meaning and kind under it all, Dorothy could have saved herself much grief if she had learned something of the courtier's art of tact from her sister.

As she grew older, Dorothy became more devout. She was given to long discussions with tutors and chaplains about the vanity and falseness of the world. In a letter to Robert Worsley, she observed that change for the better was an illusion: Parliament and the Protectorate had turned out to be as arbitrary, unjust, and tyrannical as the monarchy.[29] Perhaps some of her disillusionment had to do with the fact that Princess Elizabeth's necklace was locked up in the Exchequer instead of in Dorothy's own jewel box.

During the Protectorate, Algernon Sidney was living at home with his parents. He had retired to Penshurst in disgust when Cromwell assumed kinglike power. In fact, when the Lord General dismissed the Long Parliament in April 1653, Algernon, sitting by the Speaker, had been one of those whom Cromwell had ordered Major General Harrison to forcibly eject. Algernon spent his retirement from public affairs studying and writing about republicanism. Reading Shakespeare's tragedy *Julius Caesar*, he saw a parallel to his own times: a great general making himself a king. He conceived the idea of staging the play privately as a form of protest against Cromwell. Playacting had been banned and the theaters closed since 1642. Nevertheless, private performances by professional players, as well as amateur theatricals, were put on in the great houses. However, *Julius Caesar* had not been seen since the closing of the theaters. Algernon himself took the role of Brutus, playing Caesar's murderer with gusto. The first performances took place in the great hall at Penshurst for the family alone; had they been limited to this, there would have been no great flurry of excitement. But after the tryout in the country, Algernon moved the play to Leicester House. All the town flocked to see it and were immensely entertained. Lisle, whose loyalty to Cromwell was unimpaired, complained bitterly to his father that it was "a public affront" to the Lord Protector. Algernon had intended it to be so.[30]

"Death to the tyrant" was being proclaimed offstage as well as on. Conspiracies against the life of the Lord Protector followed one another in rapid succession. Algernon Sidney was only one of the doctrinaire republicans bitterly alienated by Cromwell's assumption of supreme power. One disillusioned fellow dogged the Protector's footsteps, armed to the teeth with a variety of weapons. Threats also came from radical groups such as the Levellers: even Major General Harrison was imprisoned for plotting with the Anabaptists against the Protector. The royalists, guided by a secret council known as the Sealed Knot, never ceased plotting. In 1655, encouraged by Charles from abroad, a group of Cavaliers attempted a rising that was nipped in the bud. Cromwell had known all about it through paid informers and (as Bishop Burnet wryly put it in his *History of His Own Time*) "had all the King's Party in a net."[31]

Lucy continued to busy herself with the royalist schemes, although she no longer played the leading role she had while Holland was alive. She was in constant touch with the Queen's party at the Louvre through Harry, and her friends at home were the English Presbyterians, who were all royalists now. Much of her activity was devoted to reconciling Charles's quarreling supporters—although her intervention was usually unsolicited. When Lord Salisbury and Denzil Holles fell out on one occasion, she convinced Holles to accept Northumberland as arbitrator, even though (as she told Salisbury rather proudly) Holles recognized the advantage Salisbury might derive from his close ties of "friendship and alliance" with her brother. She was not unaware that she had the reputation of a busybody. "Tis not from my inclination of being busy," she assured Salisbury, "but my earnest concern in all that relates to your Lordship."[32]

Lord Salisbury was a great friend to Lucy in the dark days of the Protectorate, and she was a frequent visitor to Hatfield House. Unlike his Cranborne Manor in Dorset, which had been sacked by the royalists, to whom he was "despicable" for sitting in the regicide parliament, Salisbury's great house in Hertfordshire had come through the troubles unscathed. Imposing Hatfield—with its turrets, strapwork, oriel windows, great hall, minstrels' gallery, and a clock tower like the one at her beloved Nonsuch Palace—had hardly changed since Lucy's first visits with Carlisle. She would have found life there as agreeable as ever. A disappointing heir to the brilliant Cecils who had made his family fortune, William Cecil was a simple soul at heart. He confined his Puritanism to the chapel; for the rest, he lived in luxury, enjoying his paintings, horses, falcons, and guests. His household accounts reveal that during the influenza epidemic of 1657, he traveled to London himself "to fetch my Lady Carlile down to Hatfield." In return for his hospitality, Lucy kept him informed of developments in London. Every day brought more bad news. She wished she could write "something that were pleasant," she told him in 1658, "but our world is too full of sad stories to do that for we hear of nothing but High Courts and imprisonments."[33]

Trials for treason were a regular occurrence. In the winter of 1658, the Earl of Ormonde, the last of Charles I's Irish viceroys, visited England. Suspecting that he had come to spy, Cromwell had him closely followed. On being informed that John Mordaunt, an incorrigible royalist plotter, was often seen with Ormonde, Cromwell ordered Mordaunt's arrest. His suspicions were justified. Mordaunt was indeed implicated in a plot to overthrow him. This struck hard at Lucy's immediate circle. Mordaunt was the younger son of her Presbyterian friend the doughty Dowager Countess of Peterborough, who was a cousin of Lucy's old friends the Earl and Countess of Berkshire. On April 23, 1658, Lucy wrote Salisbury (himself a cousin of Lady Berkshire) that she had been at Berkshire House to commiserate "with some of the afflicted." "They do not apprehend so much danger for Mr. Mordaunt as I do," she told Salisbury. She had arrived at Berkshire House to find Mordaunt's young wife relating in a "most delightful" manner an interview she had had that day with the Lord Protector.

Beautiful and vivacious, Elizabeth Mordaunt was widely admired as the perfect helpmate for her dauntless Cavalier. Her charm brought him supporters and funds, and she had extricated him more than once from the consequences of his rashness. Now she had gone to Cromwell to save her husband. Accustomed to influencing people, she was confident that she had completely won over the all-powerful Protector. Indeed, she informed her admiring audience, she was expecting him to wait upon her the next morning, as he had promised. In a few well-chosen words, Lucy sketched a "Character" of this young woman for Salisbury, showing her reveling in the romantic part of the loyal, courageous, and selfless wife. "I have heard a long time as all romances must have extremes of gallant and mean, so she play her part to the full," Lucy said, adding that the Protector "who understands such things so well" played up to his visitor's "romance humour" by acting the gallant.[34] It was no surprise to Lucy that not only was Mordaunt not released, but he was subjected to the same harsh treatment in the Tower that she had undergone. His imprisonment was shared by his loyal wife. In June he was tried for treason in Westminster Hall, and his life was saved by the mere margin of the President's casting vote.[35]

It is doubtful that Lucy spent much time at Penshurst. She would not have felt welcome in Leicester's house after he had turned her out with the others during his dreadful public quarrel with Dorothy in 1653. Now London society was gossiping again about the Earl and Countess of Leicester. They were said to be on the verge of a separation. The rumors were only too true. In the early winter of 1658, Leicester finally decided to leave Dorothy after forty-two years of marriage. Politely declining Northumberland's offer to arbitrate their differences, he explained how impossible his life with Dorothy had become. While acknowledging that his own temper was often out of control ("some passionate and hasty words upon great provocations peradventure have escaped me"), he assured his brother-in-law that he had paid Dorothy "all the civilities due to the Earl of Northumberland's daughter, and I have loved her better for being your sister than I could have loved any woman that was not so." Whatever little time remained to him, he told Northumberland, he "would fain pass it quietly." Therefore he was "thinking of a retreat for myself that your sister may live somewhere secure from my passions and more to her contentment."[36]

Before her husband could leave her, however, Dorothy fell mortally ill. Likely some form of cancer, her illness was described by her son Algernon as "long, languishing, and certainly incurable." Though suffering greatly, Dorothy became surprisingly mellow, her only complaint that she could not see her darling youngest son, Henry, before she died, as he was traveling on the Continent. She took great comfort in religion and the certitude of an afterlife and, when not racked with pain, lay calm and peaceful in her canopied bedstead, surrounded by her Mortlake tapestries, family portraits, and lacquered cabinets. In her new and unexpected benignity, she drew Leicester back to her. As he sat by her bedstead day after day, a semblance of their old love was rekindled.

On July 10, 1659, with her husband's permission, she made her will. She left £1,000 to Algernon and the rest to her beloved Henry. Nothing for poor Anne, the remaining unmarried daughter who nursed her in her illness. For all Leicester's complaints about Dorothy's avariciousness, she had precious little to bequeath. Clearly, the money wrested from him at each Michaelmas accounting had gone toward the management of the estate. She left some lands in Kent, which her Lord had allowed her to buy in her own name, two annuities totaling £300, and personal effects valued at £500. Still tenaciously claiming Princess Elizabeth's necklace, Dorothy listed it among her belongings.[37]

For over a year, Dorothy dragged on. Though we have no accounts to draw on, Lucy would, of course, have visited her, and we can imagine these visits by looking backward to the time when Dorothy was very ill in Paris. Lucy was so frantic then that had Dorothy not recovered fairly quickly, she would have gone to her in France. Now, Dorothy was dying. She had found serenity through religion and the revival of her husband's love, and it is a fair conjecture that it was she who comforted the sobbing Lucy rather than the other way around.

Early on the morning of August 20, 1659, Leicester was awakened with the news that his wife was dying. Hurrying to her bedside, he found her failing fast but still lucid. She took his hand and (Leicester recorded in his journal) spoke these words: "My love hath been great and constant to you and I beseech you to pardon my anger, my angry words, my passions, and whatsoever wherein I have offended you, even all my faults and failings towards you." She then turned to Anne, who was kneeling by her bedside. "Nan," she said, "I confess that I have been sometimes sharp and unkind to you, but I have always loved you well. I desire you to forgive all my passions and sharp speeches."[38] Having sought absolution from her dear ones for her human failings, Dorothy quietly expired one month past her sixty-first birthday.

It was ten days before Leicester could bring himself to write to Northumberland about his sister's death, and when he did, it was in the anguished tones of the inconsolable widower. Her passing was the greatest sorrow he had ever suffered, he told Dorothy's brother; he had lost that which he loved best in the world.[39]

It was the story of Dorothy's father all over again. Death seemed to have erased all memory of the years of marital strife; even his so recent intention to leave her was forgotten, and Leicester mourned Dorothy's passing extravagantly. Undoubtedly, a sense of guilt and remorse at his shortcomings as a husband was an element in his grief. Without Dorothy's energy and life force, Leicester became a shell of a man, alienated from his children, alone in his study overlooking the garden and the crenelated walls, perhaps straining his ears for an echo of the impatient voice that had once so disturbed his peace and quiet.

"THE OLD LADY CARLISLE IS DEAD"

DOROTHY'S DEATH CERTAINLY was a great (although expected) blow to Lucy. From early childhood, the sisters' lives had been as intertwined as the grapevines growing up the garden wall at Syon House. They were not always compatible. There had been the tensions of their middle years when Dorothy, lonely and bitter, had been unbearably provoked by Lucy's swollen self-satisfaction. But while the strong sisterly bond may have been strained, it was never broken. In 1640 Lucy could in all sincerity describe herself to Dorothy as "the person [that] loves you best, and can most joy in seeing you contented."[1] One of the most vivid pictures of the sisters is of Dorothy running to Lucy when the Roundhead colonel came to arrest her.

Looking back over their lives, it is clear that Lucy depended on Dorothy for emotional support. From her youth she had turned to her sister at every crisis of her life: when their father was attempting to stop her marriage; when she was recovering from smallpox; when she was widowed—in short, whenever her glittering life had gone awry. Penshurst had been her refuge during her years on parole, and on her release from prison, she had continued to live with Dorothy until Leicester's revolt.

Lucy was doubly bereaved in 1659. In March word came from France that Harry was dead. Though she had not seen him for years, they had kept in close touch. It was well known that in all the multifarious plots hatched in these years, Lord Percy and Lady Carlisle were collaborators, each on his or her own side of the Channel. As young Charles's Lord Chamberlain, Percy wielded considerable influence in the royalist government in exile. Much of his intelligence came from his sister in England. Harry's dying abroad created complications, so that Northumberland had to send his steward over to France to arrange matters. Since he died without leaving a will, his estate devolved upon his wealthy brother.[2]

However shaken she was by the deaths of her sister and brother within a few months of each other, Lucy's mourning was cut short by the momentous events that were developing in England and in which she again could not resist playing a part. In the autumn of 1658, Cromwell had died after a swift decline, to be succeeded by his son Richard, who proved unequal to the task of governing and was forced to step down in May 1659. Since then, confusion had reigned. Richard's last official act was to call a parliamentary election, but the resulting parliament was soon engaged in the familiar tug-of-war with the army. The effect of this jockeying for power was a breakdown of the normal processes of government. In short order, the country witnessed the dissolution of Richard's parliament, his de facto abdication, and the restoration of the Rump Parliament. Not surprisingly in these anarchical times, a royalist rising was planned for the late summer. Charles was to come over from Flanders, and Cavaliers all over England would take up arms. In the event, nothing much happened beyond John Mordaunt and his Howard cousins staging an abortive rising in Surrey. Lack of coordination and Parliament's early warning of the plot doomed the uprising to failure. Mordaunt fled to Calais, where he was soon joined by his ever-faithful Elizabeth.[3] Meanwhile General John Lambert, an ambitious former officer of Cromwell's, entered Westminster with his troops and expelled the Rump, only to have it restored within two months.

In the cold winter of 1660, people could talk of nothing but "a full and free parliament" to settle the nation. It was understood that this was the first step in restoring the monarchy. "As to his Majesty's restoration, all things and men concur," John Mordaunt wrote Hyde.[4] The question was how and when a full parliament could be called. The man who held the key was General George Monck, a "dull, heavy" fifty-year-old professional soldier who had fought in all Cromwell's wars at home and abroad. Commander-in-chief of the Scottish forces, Monck was plodding his way south in January with seven thousand seasoned troops. Monck publicly opposed reviving free elections, but he could not have helped being influenced by the mass of petitions he received in every county, begging him to recall "the old, long-interrupted parliament." On February 3, Monck's army tramped into the capital, greeted on all sides by cries for a free parliament. Monck ordered the House to admit the members excluded by Pride's Purge in 1648 (which prompted one witty lady to remark that the Rump had become a "gigot"). Bonfires were lit all over London, and a jubilant citizenry roasted hindquarters of meat in celebration of the Rump's demise. In March writs were issued for a free election, and Parliament dissolved itself. In the taverns, men were openly toasting the King's health (something only a Cavalier in his cups would have dared before this), and at the Exchange people were shouting "God Bless King Charles the Second."[5]

To bring matters to this pass, there had been a good deal of maneuvering behind the scenes by the royalists. The mastermind was Edward Hyde, Charles's Lord Chancellor. Among those Hyde sent over to England to facilitate the restoration of the monarchy was John Mordaunt, who had joined the exiles in Holland after his failed Surrey uprising. Despite his limited commission, Mordaunt had taken upon himself the authority of a plenipotentiary (nor did he discourage admirers from proclaiming that "the King would owe his crown to my Lord Mordaunt").[6] His pretensions did not go unchallenged. His letters to Hyde were full of complaints about other royalists. His particular bugbear was Lucy: "Here are so many lies every day made of me by the Lady Carlisle and her friends that it amazes me," he wrote Hyde.[7] According to Mordaunt, all her intelligence came from France, that is to say from Henrietta Maria's party, and whatever she heard she immediately passed on to her nephews, Lisle and Algernon Sidney. "She is still Sempronia," he concluded scornfully. Since Algernon was in Sweden and Lisle in sullen retirement, Lucy could hardly have revealed royalist secrets to them. There is no doubt, however, that she was still the "busy stateswoman" of Ben Jonson's *Cataline*. Unlike Hyde and Mordaunt, who trusted Charles implicitly and were tying no strings to his return to England, Lucy and her Presbyterian friends believed that conditions had to be imposed before he assumed the throne. Indeed, Lucy did not hesitate to predict that once he was crowned, Charles would break all the engagements he had made.[8]

This was Northumberland's conviction as well. He was utterly opposed to an unconditional restoration of the Stuart dynasty. He favored a monarchy but a limited one, a monarchy substantially different from the autocratic rule of Charles's father. It now became clear that this concern was behind all his juggling, from his initial support for Pym to his eleventh-hour efforts to save the life of Charles I. Suspecting that General Monck was being won over by Hyde's representatives, Northumberland assembled a small group of lords and gentry who shared his views, including the Earl of Manchester and Denzil Holles, the leaders of the Presbyterian party. Their aim was to make Charles accept the same limits on his power that they had attempted to impose on his father while the King was a prisoner on the Isle of Wight. They made no secret of their nightly meetings at Northumberland House. "I must now acquaint you with a cabal here which gives all honest men sad hours," Mordaunt warned Hyde on April 19. "The persons are Lord Northumberland and Lord Manchester, who have debauched Lord Fairfax, Mr. Holles . . . ," and numerous others. Mordaunt added that "My Lady Carlisle lays about her too."[9] Needless to say, Lucy was involved in intrigues, but hers went beyond the cabal's objective of a limited monarchy. Devoted to the interests of Queen Henrietta Maria and Lord Jermyn, Lucy was working for a restoration that would leave the Queen's party in control.

Unfortunately, the Restoration was not to be the limited monarchy that Lucy and her brother had hoped for. The English people were in no mood to wait for the Presbyterian party to negotiate terms with Charles. They had had enough of the Puritans' dreary and repressive republic. Seeing the way the tide was running, when the new parliament convened on April 26, Monck informed the members that he "could not answer for the peace either of the nation or the army" if there was any delay in sending for the King. Any conditions could wait until he came over, and Monck moved that commissioners be dispatched at once to Holland to bring back Charles. His motion was greeted with a deafening shout of approval. Elizabeth Mordaunt proudly informed Hyde that "after the House rose, most of the considerable Members came to her husband to assure him that they and their interest would follow his directions in order to the King's service."[10]

On May 8, 1660, Charles was proclaimed King at Westminster, Temple Bar, and the Royal Exchange. When he stepped ashore at Dover on May 25, he came in without conditions (to which, says Bishop Burnet, "may be well imputed all the errors of his reign").[11] It was a triumph for Hyde and those of his party such as Mordaunt and Ormonde.

Lucy and her Presbyterian friends were dejected; all their plans to limit the power of the monarchy had been totally defeated. "They have daily consultations at the Lady Carlisle's," it was reported, "and some of them have expressed that they wished things had not succeeded in this manner if the Marquess of Ormonde and Sir Edward Hyde must govern."[12] But their opposition to the new regime was short-lived. Hyde, Lord Chancellor and soon to be the Earl of Clarendon, had predicted that once Charles II was on the throne, "the Presbyterians will become as great Cavaliers as any in the pack."[13] The Presbyterian leaders proved him right. Denzil Holles happily became a baron, and Manchester was only too pleased to be named Lord Chamberlain and a privy councillor. Even Northumberland accepted the new king's unfettered power. Commanded to court, he and Leicester went with great trepidation, only to find to their relief that they were to be sworn in as privy councillors.[14] Northumberland was so grateful that he presented King Charles with some fine antique statuary.[15] Lucy herself received a windfall. With the restoration of royal property, the keepership of Nonsuch Palace was restored to her. In September she sold the office to George Lord Berkeley for £1,100.[16] The King had no such forgiveness for the regicides. Major General Harrison was hanged, drawn, and quartered. As Lucy was carried around the town in her sedan chair, she would have seen the gruesome sight of his head set on a spike beside Westminster Hall.[17]

On November 1, the Queen Mother arrived in London with her youngest daughter. People who had not seen Henrietta Maria since she went to France would not have recognized her in the "very little, plain old woman," dressed no better (Samuel Pepys observed) than any ordinary woman.[18] Lucy was cheerfully anticipating a reunion with her former mistress. Throughout the Interregnum, Lady Carlisle had served the cause of the exiled queen, and Henrietta Maria had long since forgiven her for her disloyalty at the time of the abortive arrest of the Five Members.

On November 5, Lucy was preparing for her reunion with Henrietta Maria. After a good dinner at home, she ordered her sedan chair to be brought round and began her toilette for the visit. She was cutting a piece of ribbon when she was suddenly stricken. Without speaking a word, she died about five or six o'clock. Leicester, to whom we owe the details of her sudden demise, observed that it was the anniversary of the Gunpowder Plot, for which her father had been imprisoned. A further coincidence he mentioned was that she died at the same age as her sister—sixty-one years and one month.[19]

Lucy died as she had lived, in the enjoyment of good food, fine fashions, and royal society. Her death made no impression in the new reign. "The old lady Carlisle is dead, well yesterday morning and died last night," remarked one letter writer.[20] Another, equally dispassionate, reported that "the old Countess of Carlisle died yesterday suddenly of an apoplexy."[21] Neither Pepys nor Evelyn thought to record her passing in their diaries.

Notes

See the bibliography for the full details of references cited in abbreviated form in these notes.

Prologue

1. Brenan, *House of Percy*, II, chap. 1; Chamberlain, *Letters*, I, 463; Batho, "Wizard Earl," 346.

PART ONE MONEY AND MARRIAGE

Chapter 1 Two Pretty Sisters

1. Batho, "Difficult Father-in-Law," 744.
2. Ibid., 745.
3. Hibbert, *Virgin Queen*, 259.
4. Willson, *King James VI and I*, 379.
5. Ibid., 165.
6. Brenan, *House of Percy,* II, 129.
7. Ibid., II, 93.
8. Batho, "Wizard Earl," 346.
9. Brenan, House of Percy, II, 146.
10. *Northumberland Papers*, xxiii, lv.

11. Chamberlain, *Letters*, I, 306.
12. Strickland, *Queens of England*, VII, 344.
13. Barroll, *Anna of Denmark*, 59.
14. Chamberlain, *Letters*, II, 230, 344.
15. Old St. Paul's was destroyed in the Great Fire of 1666 and replaced by Sir Christopher Wren's domed cathedral that we see today.
16. Brenan, *House of Percy*, II, 176–80.
17. Quoted in Thomson, *Women in Stuart England and America*, 162.

Chapter 2 Dorothy's Choice

1. See Strong, *Henry Prince of Wales*, 86 et seq.
2. Nichols, *Progresses*, II, 463–67.
3. Chamberlain, *Letters*, I, 381.
4. Strickland, *Queens of England*, VII, 351.
5. Chamberlain, *Letters*, I, 418, 423.
6. For the wedding and festivities, see Nichols, *Progresses*, II, 542 et seq., and Chamberlain, *Letters*, I, 423–26.
7. De Fonblanque, *House of Percy*, II, 327.
8. Batho, "Difficult Father-in-Law," 746–47.
9. Chamberlain, *Letters*, I, 436.
10. For Sir Francis Darcy's negotiations with Viscount Lisle, see *Sydney Papers*, II, 346, and *De L'Isle and Dudley MSS*, V, 222.
11. Chamberlain, *Letters*, I, 570.
12. Brenan, *House of Percy*, II, 191.
13. Clifford, *Diary*, 30.
14. Chamberlain, *Letters*, I, 624.
15. *De L'Isle and Dudley MSS*, V, 408.
16. Ibid., V, 409.

Chapter 3 Lucy's Choice

1. Brenan, *House of Percy*, II, 189.
2. In 1619 the Banqueting House burnt down and was replaced by the present Palladian-style Banqueting House built by Inigo Jones.

3. *DNB*, Hay, James, first Earl of Carlisle.

4. Chamberlain, *Letters*, II, 13. We have a firsthand description of a suit Hay took with him on his mission to France in 1616: "I saw the cloak and hose made of a very fine white beaver [a plushlike material], embroidered all over with gold and silver; the cloak, almost to the cape, within and without, having no lining but embroidery. The doublet was Cloth of Gold, embroidered so thick, that it could not be discerned, and a white beaver hat suitable, brimfull of embroidery both above and below." Wilson, *History of Great Britain*, 93.

5. Chamberlain, *Letters*, I, 554, 560; II, 30.

6. Ibid., II, 16, 41.

7. Ellis, *Letters*, 2nd ser., III, 247.

8. Chamberlain, *Letters*, II, 16, 19; Brenan, *House of Percy*, II, 172–73.

9. The Earl would have seen a variant of the new invention of the telescope, as Thomas Harriot, an astronomer who was one of his "Three Magi," was experimenting with "perspective trunks" to see Venus "horned like the moon." Batho, "Wizard Earl," 349.

10. *Northumberland Papers*, lv.

11. Chamberlain, *Letters*, II, 57.

12. Ibid., II, 85.

13. Ibid., II, 57.

14. Ibid.

15. Sainsbury, *Rubens*, 117, n.150.

16. Chamberlain, *Letters*, II, 77.

17. Ibid., II, 94.

18. *De L'Isle and Dudley MSS*, V, 411.

19. Ibid., V, 412; *Sydney Papers*, II, 350. Anne Clifford also mentioned the Penshurst house party in her diary, although her husband, the Earl of Dorset, would not permit her to attend. She wrote that her husband "hunted and lay there all night, there being my Lord Montgomery, my Lord Hay, my

Lady Lucy [whom the editor mistakes for Lucy Bedford], and a great deal of other company." Clifford, *Diary*, 90.

20. *De L'Isle and Dudley MSS*, V, 413.

21. Ibid., V, 415.

22. De Fonblanque, *House of Percy*, II, 345; Willson, *King James VI and I*, 388–89.

23. Bentley, *Jacobean and Caroline Stage*, V, 1288–89; Chamberlain, *Letters*, II, 125.

24. Chamberlain, *Letters*, II, 181.

25. Ibid., II, 168, 378; *CSPV, 1617–1619*, 281. The salary for the Master of the Wardrobe was £222 13s. 4d. Lionel Cranfield, the next Master of the Wardrobe, claimed that Hay made some £4,000 per annum through perquisites and deals with the purveyors of materials. As well as supplies for the royal household and maintenance of the palaces, costumes for masques and revels were purchased through the Wardrobe. Jones and Stallybrass, *Renaissance Clothing and the Materials*, 201.

26. *Sydney Papers*, I, 121.

27. Chamberlain, *Letters*, II, 190, 195.

28. Manchester, *Court and Society*, I, 331.

29. *Sydney Papers*, I, 121.

30. Schreiber, *First Carlisle*, 24; Carlisle Papers, 2592, folio 73.

31. Strickland, *Queens of England*, VII, 358–63.

32. Nichols, *Progresses*, III, 531. Queen Anne's funeral is described in full on pages 538–43.

33. Chamberlain, *Letters*, II, 237.

34. Ibid., II, 235.

35. Carlisle Papers, 2592, folios 97, 134.

36. *CSPD, 1619–1623*, 71.

37. Gardiner, *England and Germany*, I, 156.

38. Chamberlain, *Letters*, II, 263.

39. *Sydney Papers*, I, 121.

Chapter 4 Buckingham's Charms

1. Bergeron, *King James*, 102–103.
2. Wilson, *History of Great Britain*, 149.
3. Carlisle Papers, 2595, folio 164.
4. Baschet Transcripts, 31/3/53, folio 52, Tillières to Puysieux, 12 November 1619.
5. *Sydney Papers*, I, 126.
6. Ellis, *Letters*, 1st ser., III, 113–14.
7. Chamberlain, *Letters*, II, 294.
8. Ibid., II, 297. Buckingham's manuscript letter to the Earl of Rutland is astounding in its effrontery: Harley MSS, 1581.
9. Gardiner, *History of England*, VI, 188.
10. *CSPD, 1619–1623*, 145.
11. Chamberlain, *Letters*, II, 280, 285.
12. *CSPV, 1623–1625*, 360–61.
13. Chamberlain, *Letters*, II, 333.
14. Ibid., II, 255, 228.
15. Stoye, *English Travellers Abroad*, 289–90; Malloch, *Finch and Baines*, 37.
16. Chamberlain, *Letters*, II, 381.
17. Ibid., II, 424.

Chapter 5 Life in the Country and Life at Court

1. The list of housewifery skills is taken from Godfrey, *Home Life under the Stuarts*, 229–30.
2. *Sydney Papers*, I, 121–27.
3. Ibid., II, 354–55.
4. *CSPV, 1623–1625*, 361.
5. Schreiber, *First Carlisle*, 48.
6. Ellis, *Letters*, 1st ser., III, 140–41.
7. *CSPD, Addenda, 1580–1625*, 649–50.
8. Ibid.; Carlisle Papers, 2595, folio 191.
9. Ibid., 2595, folio 183.
10. Ibid., 2596, folio 14.
11. *De L'Isle and Dudley MSS*, V, 438–39.

12. La Rochefoucauld, *Mémoires*, II, 12–13. La Rochefoucauld mentioned "the long attachment Buckingham had for the Countess of Carlisle."

13. *Encyclopaedia Britannica* (1955), La Rochefoucauld, François de.

14. Ellis, *Letters*, 1st ser., III, 122, 196.

15. Rushworth, *Collections*, I, 199.

16. Tillières, *Mémoires*, xxvii, 100.

17. Charles, *Letters*, 40.

18. Tillières, *Mémoires*, 135; *CSPV, 1625–1626*, 494, 498.

19. Schreiber, *First Carlisle*, 97.

20. Denbigh, *Royalist Father*, 49.

21. Smuts, *Court Culture*, 194.

22. *CSPD, 1628–1629*, 81.

23. *CSPD, 1627–1628*, 381; *CSPD, 1626–1627*, 363.

24. *CSPD, Addenda, 1625–1649*, 291.

25. *CSPC, 1575–1660*, 85–86. The English Leewards consisted of the islands of St. Christopher, Nevis, Antigua, and Montserrat. Carlisle Bay commemorates Carlisle's proprietorship of the Barbados.

26. *CSPD, 1628–1629*, 81.

Chapter 6 The Queen's Favorite

1. *CSPV, 1628–1629*, 108.

2. *CSPD, 1628–1629*, 356. In his letter to Carlisle, Goring sends his "blessings to Lord Jimmie and George."

3. *CSPV, 1626–1628*, 93, 97, 107. Gautier, the French lute player, had formerly been employed by Buckingham: *Salvetti Correspondence*, 104–107.

4. *CSPD, 1628–1629*, 169, 218.

5. Ellis, *Letters*, 1st ser., III, 253.

6. D'Ewes, *Autobiography and Correspondence*, 210.

7. For an eyewitness account of Buckingham's assassination, see Ellis, *Letters*, 1st ser., III, 254–60.

8. For Buckingham's funeral, ibid., III, 263–65.

9. *CSPD, 1628–1629*, 293, 310, 343.

10. Chamberlain, *Letters*, II, 245; Clifford, *Diary*, 115.

11. *CSPD, Addenda, 1625–1649*, 298, 294.

12. *CSPD, 1628–1629*, 343. For "Noks," see 395.

13. *De L'Isle and Dudley MSS*, VI, 1–2.

14. Osborne, *Letters*, 101.

15. *CSPD, Addenda, 1625–1649*, 297.

16. Ibid., 298, 308; *CSPD, 1628–1629*, 393.

17. *CSPD, 1628–1629*, 335.

18. Ibid., 343, 378.

Chapter 7   Court Politics

1. Newton, *Colonizing Activities*, 60 et seq.

2. *CSPD, 1628–1629*, 413.

3. Ibid., 296, 391, 413.

4. Ibid., 413.

5. *CSPV, 1628–1629*, 283.

6. Ibid., 538; *CSPD, 1628–1629*, 395, 412.

7. *CSPD, 1628–1629*, 335. Carlisle had missed a wonderful opportunity in 1628 when a consortium of London merchants offered to buy the island of St. Christopher for £20,000 plus £1,000 per annum. In 1629 the Spaniards took the island, and the consortium withdrew its offer (*Buccleuch MSS*, III, 345). The English retook the island shortly afterward. For Carlisle's far from efficient proprietorship, see Dunn, *Sugar and Slaves*, 49.

8. *CSPD, 1628–1629*, 556.

9. *CSPD, 1629–1631*, 139.

10. Schreiber, *First Carlisle*, 140.

11. *CSPD, Addenda, 1625–1649*, 330; *CSPD, 1628–1629*, 558, 559.

12. *Salisbury MSS*, XXII, 242.

13. Ibid., 269.

14. *CSPD, 1628–1629*, 558.

15. Ibid., 396, 398, 405, 446, 469. Traill's letters to Carlisle and other correspondents, together with young James's unanswered letters to his father, provide an interesting account of a seventeenth-century youth's Grand Tour.

16. Ibid., 598.

17.   Finet, *Notebooks*, 69.

18.   *CSPV, 1629–1632,* 263.

19.   Ibid., 205.

20.   *Buccleuch MSS*, III, 347.

21.   *CSPV, 1629–1632,* 271, 281.

Chapter 8   Death of Carlisle

1.   *CSPD, Addenda, 1625–1649,* 367.

2.   Finet, *Notebooks,* 87–89.

3.   Mathew, *Letters.*

4.   *CSPD, 1634–1635,* 408.

5.   *CSPD, 1631–1633,* 437.

6.   *CSPD, Addenda, 1625–1649,* 382.

7.   Strafford, *Letters,* I, 218.

8.   *CSPD, 1629–1631,* 366.

9.   *CSPD, 1631–1633,* 132.

10.   Raymond, *Autobiography,* 24.

11.   *CSPD, 1631–1633,* 293–94, 322; Carlisle Papers, 2597, folio 110.

12.   Ellis, *Letters,* 2nd ser., II, 265.

13.   *CSPD, 1631–1633,* 205.

14.   Raymond, *Autobiography,* 24.

15.   Suckling, *Works.* The salacious last verse was omitted in the 1646 publication of the poet's works. According to Carlisle's biographer, Lucy "had a reputation for libertinism during these years of which even the diplomats stationed in England were aware. At the end of 1631 she may have even become involved with Holland. She unquestionably contributed a great deal to the fantasy life of more than one gentleman of the era, whatever she may have actually done with them. Yet, through all of the stories that emerged from this period, there was no hint that Carlisle ever criticized her or was not on the best of terms with her." Schreiber, *First Carlisle,* 135.

16.   Aubrey, *Brief Lives,* 287.

17.   *CSPV, 1632–1636,* 363.

18.   Howell, *Familiar Letters,* I, 317.

19. *Sydney Papers*, II, 372.

20. Lindley, *Court Masques*, 273.

21. *CSPD, 1631–1633*, 322.

22. Strafford, *Letters*, I, 85.

23. Carlisle Papers, 2597, folios 76, 108.

24. *CSPD, 1634–1635*, 229.

25. Comber, *Life of Sir Christopher Wandesford*, quoted in Brenan, *House of Percy*, II, 240.

26. Strafford, *Letters*, I, 179.

27. Carlisle Papers, 2597, folio 140.

28. Finet, *Notebooks*, 145.

29. Denbigh, *Royalist Father*, 87.

30. Burghclere, *Strafford*, I, 260.

31. *Sydney Papers*, I, 455.

32. Strafford, *Letters*, I, 120.

33. Ibid., I, 360, 363.

34. Von Ranke, *History of England*, II, 407.

35. *Nicholas Papers*, I, 293, 301; *De L'Isle and Dudley MSS*, VI, 85.

36. Strafford, *Letters*, I, 363; Burghclere, *Strafford*, I, 261.

37. Raymond, *Autobiography*, 25. The ballad that brought tears to Carlisle's eyes was "A Farewell to Arms," dedicated to Queen Elizabeth, by George Peele (1558?–1597).

38. *De L'Isle and Dudley MSS*, VI, 40; Strafford, *Letters*, I, 447.

39. Strafford Papers, XV, folio 211, Lucy to Wentworth, 7 September 1635; VIII, folio 287, Wentworth to Lucy, 14 October 1635.

40. Strafford, *Letters*, I, 479, 511, 525.

41. *CSPD, 1631–1633*, 293; *CSPV, 1632–1636*, 558.

42. *CSPV, 1632–1636*, 558.

43. Strafford Papers, VIII, folio 377, Wentworth to Lucy, 14 May 1636.

44. Wilson, *History of Great Britain*, 154.

45. Stone, *Crisis of the Aristocracy*, 260–61.

46. Schreiber, *First Carlisle*, 137.

47. *CSPD, 1635*, 420.

48. Strafford, *Letters*, I, 525; *CSPV, 1632–1636*, 558.

49. *Various Collections*, VII, 412.
50. Edmund Waller, "To the Countess of Carlisle in Mourning."

PART TWO AT THE KING'S COMMAND

Chapter 9 Dorothy a Grass Widow

1. Howell, *Familiar Letters*, I, 295.
2. *De L'Isle and Dudley MSS*, VI, xviii.
3. *Various Collections*, VII, 413.
4. *De L'Isle and Dudley MSS*, VI, 55–56, 60, 66–67, 71.
5. *Sydney Papers*, II, 450.
6. *De L'Isle and Dudley MSS*, VI, 108.
7. Ibid., VI, 86, 124.
8. De L'Isle MSS, C 95, folio 1, Sir William Crofts to Earl of Leicester, 12/2 July 1637. (The continental calendar was ten days ahead of the English calendar. Thus, July 2 in England was July 12 in France.)
9. *Sydney Papers*, II, 450.
10. Strafford, *Letters,* I, 469.
11. *Sydney Papers*, II, 451. Writing to her sister, Edmund Waller describes Doll as "she that always affected silence and retiredness": Cartwright, *Sacharissa*, 74; Aubrey, *Brief Lives*, 308.
12. Strafford, *Letters*, I, 359; *De L'Isle and Dudley MSS*, VI, 60, 93.
13. Strafford, *Letters*, II, 156.
14. *De L'Isle and Dudley MSS*, VI, 60, 64, 66; *Sydney Papers*, II, 445.
15. Carte, *James, Duke of Ormonde*, V, 220.
16. *CSPD, 1639–1640*, 186.
17. Strafford Papers, XVIII, folio 102, Lucy to Wentworth, 7 August 1638; VIII, folio 398, Wentworth to Sir James Hay, 11 December 1636.
18. *De L'Isle and Dudley MSS*, VI, 67; *Sydney Papers*, II, 455.
19. *CSPV, 1636–1639*, 148; *Various Collections*, VII, 413.
20. *De L'Isle and Dudley MSS*, VI, 70, 90.
21. Ibid., VI, 72; Strafford, *Letters*, II, 45.
22. Ibid., I, 218.

23. De L'Isle MSS, C 82/9, Dorothy to Leicester, 19 December 1636; *Sydney Papers,* II, 463.

24. *De L'Isle and Dudley MSS,* VI, 79, 83.

25. Ibid., VI, 77, 90; *Sydney Papers,* II, 455.

26. *De L'Isle and Dudley MSS,* VI, 85, 94; Strafford, *Letters,* II, 48.

27. *Sydney Papers,* II, 472, 480 et seq.

28. *De L'Isle and Dudley MSS,* VI, 89, 101, 106.

29. Ibid., VI, 87, 100, 103, 104–105.

30. Ibid., VI, 60.

31. Ibid., VI, 62.

32. *Sydney Papers,* II, 514, 516.

Chapter 10 *Lucy a Wealthy Widow*

1. Millar, *Van Dyck in England,* 67–69.

2. Blake, *Van Dyck,* 332.

3. Wheelock, Barnes, and Held, *Anthony Van Dyck,* 68, n.44.

4. The Sudeley Castle archivist, Jean Bray, kindly supplied the provenance of the double portrait of the sisters. From the collection of the Earl of Leicester at Penshurst, the painting was inherited by Lady Brownlow, who bequeathed it to Lady Yonge. The latter sold it to Horace Walpole, afterward Earl of Orford, "for nine and twenty guineas." Inherited by Earl Waldegrave, it was sold at the Strawberry Hill sale in 1842 to James Morrison for £231. It remained in the Morrison Collection at Basildon and Fonthill until finally it came to Sudeley Castle.

5. *CSPD, 1637–1638,* 366; *Duppa-Isham Correspondence,* 74.

6. Strafford, *Letters,* II, 149.

7. This is the view of Julie Sanders in "Caroline Salon Culture and Female Agency."

8. Anselment, "Countess of Carlisle." On the question of a salon to rival that of Henrietta Maria, Anselment wrote, "Though she [Lady Carlisle] did not preside over a literary salon or circle . . . she appears indeed the unrivalled focus of ambition and hope" (221).

9. Strafford, *Letters*, II, 118, 125.

10. Mathew, *Letters*. Dedication by John Donne, son of the poet, who "hopes you [Lady Carlisle] will favour us, for many years to come, with your presence here; whose absence would make such a Chasm in our Galaxie."

11. *De L'Isle and Dudley MSS*, VI, 85, 90.

12. Ibid., VI, 122; Strafford Papers, X, folio 5, Wentworth to Lucy, 15 April 1637.

13. *CSPI, 1633–1647*, 229.

14. Strafford Papers, X, folio 2, Wentworth to Lucy, 17 April 1637. See Cooper, "Fortune of Thomas Wentworth," and Ranger, "Strafford in Ireland."

15. Strafford, *Letters*, II, 106.

16. Cooper, "Fortune of Thomas Wentworth," 243–44.

17. Strafford, *Letters*, II, 76, 106; Strafford Papers, VIII, folio 395, Wentworth to Lucy, [12 December] 1636.

18. *CSPD, 1637–1638*, 11.

19. Strafford, *Letters*, II, 71, 76, 91.

20. Strafford Papers, X, folio 2, Wentworth to Lucy, 17 April 1637; Ranger, "Strafford in Ireland," 37.

21. *CSPI, 1633–1647*, 175, 229.

22. Strafford Papers, X, folio 155, Wentworth to Lucy, 25 July 1638.

23. Ibid., X, 227, Wentworth to Lucy, 28 November 1638.

24. Strafford, *Letters*, II, 106.

25. Wedgwood, *Thomas Wentworth*, 225.

26. Strafford Papers, X, folios 170, 352, Wentworth to Lucy, 31 August 1638 and 13 August 1639.

27. Strafford, *Letters*, II, 102, 125.

28. Ibid., II, 124. See Donagan, "Courtier's Progress," 326–27. For Holland's many offices, see ibid., 325.

29. Strafford, *Letters*, II, 131, 138.

30. Strafford Papers, X, folio 307, Wentworth to Lucy, 13 May 1639.

Chapter 11 Family Affairs

1. Strafford, *Letters*, II, 142.

2. Ibid., II, 73.

3. Albion, *Charles I*, 212 et seq.

4. *CSPV, 1636–1639*, 410.

5. *De L'Isle and Dudley MSS*, VI, 143–44, 147–48.

6. Campbell, *Intriguing Duchess*, 151 et seq.

7. Strafford, *Letters*, II, 156.

8. Ibid., II, 175; *Egmont MSS*, I, 222; Cooper, "Fortune of Thomas Wentworth," 242; Ranger, "Strafford in Ireland," 37–38. Ranger assumes that Carlisle received £15,000 for the surrender of the Birnes Country, but Cooper correctly states that Carlisle did not surrender the grant in his lifetime. The sale did not actually take place until two years after his death, when the money was paid to Lucy.

9. Strafford, *Letters*, II, 175.

10. Ibid.

11. *Egmont MSS*, I, 177, 494.

12. Strafford Papers, X, folio 155, Wentworth to Lucy, 25 July 1638; XVIII, folio 102, Lucy to Wentworth, 7 August 1638 [holograph], and X, folio 174; X, folio 170, Wentworth to Lucy, 31 August 1638.

13. *De L'Isle and Dudley MSS*, VI, 153–54.

14. Ibid., VI, 155.

15. Ibid.

16. Strafford, *Letters*, II, 280.

17. Strafford Papers, X, folio 301, Wentworth to Lucy, 16 April 1639.

18. *CSPD, 1638–1639*, 621.

19. Rushworth, *Collections*, III, 886, 910–15, 926–27. For an example of Charles's commands to the Lord Lieutenants, see Charles, *Letters*, 111–12.

20. Carlton, *Charles I*, 205.

21. De L'Isle MSS, C 114/1.

22. *Sydney Papers*, II, 592.

23. Young, *Servility and Service*, 254.

24. *Sydney Papers*, II, 597.

25. *Manchester MSS*, 55.

26. *CSPD, 1639,* 349.

27. Cartwright, *Sacharissa,* 74.

28. *CSPD, 1639,* 383.

29. *De L'Isle and Dudley MSS,* VI, 176.

30. *CSPD, 1639,* 504.

31. *Sydney Papers,* II, 607, 613.

32. Ibid., II, 618.

Chapter 12 *A Noble and Intelligent Friendship*

1. Strafford, *Letters,* II, 374.

2. *De L'Isle and Dudley MSS,* VI, 211.

3. Radcliffe, *Letters,* 183, 188.

4. *De L'Isle and Dudley MSS,* VI, 195; *Sydney Papers,* II, 614.

5. *De L'Isle and Dudley MSS,* VI, 201, 203, 208. For Henrietta Maria's dislike of Richelieu and French policy, see Smuts, "Puritan Followers," 26–45.

6. *Sydney Papers,* II, 629.

7. *De L'Isle and Dudley MSS,* VI, 215.

8. Radcliffe, *Letters,* 188, 194, 197.

9. Finet, *Notebooks,* 271.

10. *De L'Isle and Dudley MSS,* VI, 222.

11. *Sydney Papers,* II, 618; Warwick, *Memoirs,* 154.

12. *De L'Isle and Dudley MSS,* VI, 219.

13. Radcliffe, *Letters,* 197.

14. De L'Isle MSS, C 85/14.

15. *De L'Isle and Dudley MSS,* VI, 243.

16. Ibid., VI, 234, 287, 312.

17. Ibid., VI, 245.

18. Radcliffe, *Letters,* 198.

19. *Sydney Papers,* II, 652.

20. *De L'Isle and Dudley MSS,* VI, 262, 270, 295.

21. De L'Isle MSS, C 85/16.

22. *CSPI, 1633–1647,* 243, 299.

23. Radcliffe, *Letters,* 221.

24. *De L'Isle and Dudley MSS,* VI, 285.

25. Rushworth, *Collections*, III, 1193.

26. Bligh, *Sir Kenelm Digby*, 240–41.

27. *De L'Isle and Dudley MSS*, VI, 319, 329.

28. Rushworth, *Collections*, III, 1252.

29. Ibid., III, 1275.

30. Ibid., III, 1335.

31. *De L'Isle and Dudley MSS*, VI, 337.

32. Rushworth, *Collections*, III, 1338.

33. Radcliffe, *Letters*, 221; Wedgwood, *Thomas Wentworth*, 319.

Chapter 13 Strafford's Trial and Execution

1. Wedgwood, *Thomas Wentworth*, 316–17.

2. Rushworth, *Collections*, VIII, 8.

3. *De L'Isle and Dudley MSS*, VI, 343–44.

4. Ibid., VI, 361; De L'Isle MSS, C 85/21.

5. *De L'Isle and Dudley MSS*, VI, 346–47.

6. Ibid., VI, 351.

7. Ibid.

8. Ibid.

9. Ibid., VI, 361.

10. Ibid.

11. Manchester, *Court and Society*, I, 362.

12. *De L'Isle and Dudley MSS*, VI, 367.

13. Ibid., VI, 374.

14. Wedgwood, *Thomas Wentworth*, 326.

15. *Wynn Papers*, 271; Rushworth, *Collections*, VIII, 22–32.

16. Strickland, *Queens of England*, VIII, 60.

17. Rushworth, *Collections*, VIII, 746–48.

18. Ibid., preface; Baillie, *Letters*, I, 316 et seq. See Wencelas Hollar's etching of Strafford's trial reproduced in Wedgwood, *Thomas Wentworth*, illustration 8.

19. Baillie, *Letters*, I, 316.

20. *Buccleuch MSS*, III, 412.

21. Strickland, *Queens of England*, VIII, 60; *De L'Isle and Dudley MSS*, VI, 393.

22. Rushworth, *Collections*, VIII, 218.

23. Ibid., VIII, 242–44.

24. Baillie, *Letters*, I, 341–42; Wedgwood, *Thomas Wentworth*, 348–49; Rushworth, *Collections*, VIII, 554–55. Holland, Hamilton, and Cottington gave viva voce evidence. Northumberland pleaded illness and the court had to make do with his deposition taken the previous December, which "entirely contradicted Vane's evidence." Wedgwood, *Thomas Wentworth*, 349.

25. Wedgwood, *Thomas Wentworth*, 358.

26. Rushworth, *Collections*, VIII, 633–60.

27. Ibid., VIII, 735; Clarendon, *History*, I, 330.

28. De Fonblanque, *House of Percy*, II, 432.

29. Rushworth, *Collections*, IV, 255–57; HMC, *5th Report,* 413.

30. Ibid., VIII, 760, 762; Wedgwood, *Thomas Wentworth*, 385–89.

31. *De L'Isle and Dudley MSS*, VI, 403.

32. PRO, State Papers France, 78/111, folio 63.

Chapter 14 *Lucy Changes Her Gallant*

1. Warwick, *Memoirs,* 225.

2. Clarendon, *History,* I, 434, n.1.

3. *Egmont MSS*, I, 177.

4. Strafford Papers, XIX, folio 114, Lady Carlisle to William Railton, 13 October 1642.

5. Ranger, "Strafford in Ireland," 38.

6. Clarendon, *History*, I, 224.

7. "The Private Correspondence between King Charles I and Sir Edward Nicholas," in Evelyn, *Diary*, IV, 75.

8. Clarendon, *History*, I, 388, 434, 481.

9. Evelyn, *Diary*, IV, 76.

10. *CSPD, 1640*, 278.

11. Clarendon, *History*, I, 387–88, 434; Donagan, "A Courtier's Progress," 345–46; Forster, *Five Members,* 29.

12. Warwick, *Memoirs*, 225.

13. *De L'Isle and Dudley MSS*, VI, 404.

14. Ibid., VI, 556.

15. Rushworth, *Collections*, IV, 399.
16. Evelyn, *Diary*, IV, 119.
17. Clarendon, *History*, I, 434–35.
18. Ibid.; *De L'Isle and Dudley MSS*, VI, 412, 556.
19. Evelyn, *Diary*, IV, 118.
20. Ibid., IV, 105; Rushworth, *Collections*, IV, 463–65.
21. Clarendon, *History,* I, 555.
22. Rushworth, *Collections*, IV, 474.
23. Forster, *Arrest of the Five Members*, 138.
24. The parliamentarians received last-minute warnings that the King was on his way; contemporary sources, including Clarendon, attributed the advance warning to Lady Carlisle.
25. Madame de Motteville, quoted in Strickland, *Queens of England*, VIII, 70.
26. Rushworth, *Collections*, IV, 474.
27. Forster, *Arrest of the Five Members*, 145.
28. Strickland, *Queens of England*, VIII, 71.
29. Clarendon, *History*, I, 507.

PART THREE THE FORTUNES OF WAR

Chapter 15 Mourning a Beloved Soldier

1. *De L'Isle and Dudley MSS*, VI, 412.
2. Parliament's clerk slightingly compared the royal standard to the "City Streamers used at the Lord-Mayors Show." Rushworth, *Collections*, IV, 783.
3. Warwick, *Memoirs,* 253.
4. Cartwright, *Sacharissa*, 88.
5. *De L'Isle and Dudley MSS*, VI, 412.
6. Strafford Papers, XIX, folio 114, Lady Carlisle to William Railton, 13 October 1642.
7. HMC, *Egmont MSS*, I, 97–98, 177.
8. Strafford Papers, XIX, folio 114, Lady Carlisle to William Railton, 13 October 1642.
9. Cartwright, *Sacharissa*, 83.
10. Rushworth, *Collections*, V, 13–15.

11. *De L'Isle and Dudley MSS*, VI, 412.

12. Cartwright, *Sacharissa*, 88, 91; Ashburnham, *Narrative*, II, appendix, vi. As well as the outright gift, Sunderland also loaned the King £5,000. Cartwright, *Sacharissa*, 81.

13. Warwick, *Memoirs*, 253.

14. *De L'Isle and Dudley MSS*, VI, 413–16.

15. Warwick, *Memoirs*, 248.

16. *Portland MSS*, I, 89.

17. Cartwright, *Sacharissa*, 90, 100.

18. Whitelocke, *Memorials*, 174. For the Oxford Propositions, see Smith, "Impact on Government," 42, 45. In addition to disbandment of royalist forces, the sticking point with Charles was Parliament's demand to abolish the bishops.

19. Strickland, *Queens of England,* VIII, 80.

20. Warwick, *Memoirs*, 262.

21. Cartwright, *Sacharissa*, 94–96.

22. Crawford, *Denzil Holles*, 97.

23. Cartwright, *Sacharissa*, 99.

24. Rushworth, *Collections*, V, 367–68.

25. Cartwright, *Sacharissa*, 99, 101.

26. *De L'Isle and Dudley MSS*, VI, 435.

27. Ibid, VI, 434–35.

28. Ibid.

29. Cartwright, *Sacharissa*, 104–106.

30. Ibid., 101.

31. *De L'Isle and Dudley MSS*, VI, 436.

32. Cartwright, *Sacharissa*, 110–12.

33. *De L'Isle and Dudley MSS*, VI, 437.

34. Warwick, *Memoirs*, 297; Strickland, *Queens of England*, VIII, 85–87.

35. *Sydney Papers*, II, 130–31.

36. *De L'Isle and Dudley MSS*, VI, 557.

Chapter 16 Secret Cabals at the House of the Countess of Carlisle

1. Heath, *Flagellum*.

2. Aubrey, *Brief Lives*, ci–cii.

3. Earl of Manchester, Letter to the House of Lords, December 1644. "Quotes about Oliver Cromwell." Cromwell Association, www.olivercromwell.org/quotes2.htm.

4. On his return from Oxford, Holland was initially allowed to take his seat in the House of Lords but was shortly disabled from sitting by parliamentary ordinance: *DNB*, Rich, Henry, first Earl of Holland.

5. *DNB*, Percy, Algernon, tenth Earl of Northumberland.

6. Wedgwood, *King's War*, 386, 407, 410.

7. Forster, *Arrest of the Five Members*, 137.

8. Disraeli, *Commentaries*, III, 178–80. Disraeli quoted a letter from Sabran to de Brienne, in which the former reported on a letter he received from Lady Carlisle.

9. Crawford, *Denzil Holles*, 109.

10. *Burnet's History*, I, 29.

11. Pomfret, *Countess of Devonshire*.

12. Part of the spoils of war at the battle of Naseby was the capture by the victorious Roundheads of Charles's and Henrietta Maria's private correspondence. Parliament published a selection of the most damaging of these papers under the title *The King's Cabinet Opened*. Rushworth, *Collections*, V, 888, 892.

13. *De L'Isle and Dudley MSS*, VI, 563; *CSPV, 1642–1643*, 237.

14. Von Ranke, *History of England*, V, 475, 479; Crawford, *Denzil Holles*, 109.

15. Disraeli, *Commentaries*, III, 181.

16. Rushworth, *Collections*, V, 892.

17. "The Private Correspondence between King Charles I and Sir Edward Nicholas," in Evelyn, *Diary*, IV, 137. For the Uxbridge Propositions, see Smith, "Impact on Government," 42, 45.

18. Waller, "Recollections," 125.

19. Montereul, *Correspondence*, I, 91; Von Ranke, *History of England*, V, 479.

20. Rushworth, *Collections*, VI, 42–46 (between pages 42 and 43, there is an engraving of the battle formations, signed I. Sturt); Gentles, "Impact of the New Model Army," 87.

21. Carlton, "Impact of the Fighting," ibid., 28.
22. Montereul, *Correspondence*, I, 117.
23. Von Ranke, *History of England*, V, 484–87.
24. Montereul, *Correspondence*, I, 75.
25. Ibid., I, 89; Von Ranke, *History of England*, V, 487; Wedgwood, *King's War*, 527.
26. Warwick, *Memoirs*, 322.
27. *Hamilton Papers*, 142.
28. Charles, *Letters*, 199.
29. Ashburnham, *Narrative*, II, 141.
30. Von Ranke, *History of England*, V, 492.
31. Rushworth, *Collections*, VI, 389–90.
32. Von Ranke, *History of England*, V, 511; *Nicholas Papers*, I, 79.
33. Montereul, *Correspondence*, I, 430.
34. Von Ranke, *History of England*, V, 510, 512. King Charles appears to have offered something like these terms in an undated letter addressed to the Speaker of the House, which may or may not have been sent. Charles, *Letters*, 214–19.
35. Von Ranke, *History of England*, V, 515.

Chapter 17 *"I Would Rather Serve the Prince Than Live"*

1. Stone, *Family and Fortune*, 30.
2. *De L'Isle and Dudley MSS*, VI, 561, 566.
3. Cartwright, *Sacharissa*, 121–22.
4. *De L'Isle and Dudley MSS*, VI, 558.
5. *Northumberland Papers*. The Earl's accounts list cost of livery for Fotherley (153).
6. *De L'Isle and Dudley MSS*, VI, 558.
7. Ibid., VI, 557–58.
8. Ibid., VI, 558, 561.
9. Carlton, *Charles I*, 320–23.
10. Clarendon, *History*, IV, 292–96; *Hamilton Papers*, 150, 154.
11. Stoye, *English Travellers Abroad*, 306; *Hamilton Addenda*, 10.
12. Clarendon, *History*, IV, 318–19, 414.
13. *CSPD*, *1644*, 261.

14.   *Hamilton Addenda*, 19; Rushworth, *Collections*, VII, 100; *Hamilton Papers,* 159.

15.   Hillier, *Attempted Escapes*, 90.

16.   *DNB*, Hay, Lucy, Countess of Carlisle.

17.   Clarendon, *History*, IV, 362.

18.   For Titus, Whorwood, and Firebrace, see *DNB*.

19.   Hammond, *Letters,* 41.

20.   Hillier, *Attempted Escapes*, 89, 143, 147.

21.   *Hamilton Papers*, 171.

22.   Hammond, *Letters*, 36, 41.

22.   *Hamilton Papers,* 196.

23.   Ibid.; *Hamilton Addenda*, 18.

24.   Clarendon, *History of the Rebellion*, IV, 331–32, 343–44, 355–57.

25.   *Hamilton Papers,* 202.

26.   Ibid., 221. This letter is unsigned but from the contents it can reasonably be attributed to Lucy. In particular, the references to her associate Mr. Lowe argue for her authorship: "Mr. Loe [sic] and I were necessitated to make a letter as from your Lop and your freinds . . ." Moreover, it was Lucy, after all, who was waiting anxiously for the letter of authorization.

27.   Clarendon, *History*, IV, 341.

28.   *Pepys MSS*, 294, "A letr, dated July 14 and endorsed recd. Aug. 10, 1648. Lady Carlile's letrs. concerning Sir Will. Batten." The *Pepys MSS* contain "Ten Papers concerning [Lucy], Countess of Carlisle," taken at the battle of Worcester and reported to the Council of State on 16 April 1651, of which this one is numbered (2) in the margin.

29.   Clarendon, *History*, IV, 384–86.

30.   *Pepys MSS*, 295, "A letr. signed Carlile, supposed to be her own hand: dated July 12. Endorsed, Lady Carlile."

31.   *Buccleuch MSS*, I, 311.

32.   *Pepys MSS*, 306, "The Lady Aubigny's letter August 5, 1648."

33.   Ibid., 296, "Minutes of Orders taken by Secretary Long."

34.   Ibid., 294, "A letter without date or subscription, supposed to

be own hand-writing. Endorsed, Lady Carlile."

35.   Rushworth, *Collections,* VII, 1193.

36.   *Hamilton Papers*, 238.

37.   Rushworth, *Collections,* VII, 1214; Clarendon, *History*, IV, 362.

38.   *Pepys MSS*, 305, "Letter dated July 31 received August 2, 1648."

39.   Clarendon, *History*, IV, 414.

40.   Rushworth, *Collections*, VII, 1254.

41.   *Pepys MSS*, 307, "Sent about 25 August to my Lady Carlile."

42.   *CSPD, 1648–1649*, 292.

43.   *De L'Isle and Dudley MSS*, VI, 446–51, 558, 577.

44.   Cartwright, *Sacharissa*, 123–24.

45.   *Egerton MSS*, 1788, folio 47, cited in Carlton, *Charles I*, 341.

46.   Rushworth, *Collections*, VII, 1382, 1389.

47.   Cartwright, *Sacharissa*, 114.

48.   Rushworth, *Collections*, VII, 1395–1425.

49.   Clarendon, *History*, VI, 223.

50.   Rushworth, *Collections*, VII, 1428–30.

51.   *De L'Isle and Dudley MSS*, VI, 586.

52.   *CSPD, 1649–1650*, 6.

53.   *Pepys MSS,* 295, "Copy of a lettr. dated Hague, 28 Jan., 1649 n.style endorsed copy of the letr to my Lady Carlile."

54.   *De L'Isle and Dudley MSS*, VI, 587.

55.   Ibid.

56.   Ibid.; *CSPD, 1649–1650*, 43–44, 47, 49.

57.   Pomfret, *Countess of Devonshire*, 80.

58.   Evelyn, *Diary*, III, 37.

59.   Neville, *Newes.*

PART FOUR A NEW ORDER

Chapter 18   In the Tower

1.   *CSPD, 1649–1650*, 49, 221.

2.   Quoted in *DNB* entry on Lucy.

3.   PRO, State Papers, 5 May 1649.

4.   *CSPD, 1649–1650*, 73.

5.   *Buccleuch MSS*, I, 311; Evelyn, *Diary,* III, 37.

6. *CSPD, 1649–1650*, 43.

7. Cary, *Memorials*, II, 127, 138–39.

8. Cartwright, *Sacharissa*, 116–17.

9. Carlton, *Charles I*, 356.

10. *De L'Isle and Dudley MSS*, VI, 558.

11. Ibid., VI, 456–57.

12. Ibid., VI, 458.

13. Ibid., VI, 476.

14. *Portland MSS*, I, 585.

15. Cartwright, *Sacharissa*, 117–18.

16. *Nicholas Papers*, I, 190.

17. *De L'Isle and Dudley MSS*, VI, 484.

18. *Penshurst Church and Village*, Guide Booklet (London, 1970), 3.

19. Ibid., 13.

20. *De L'Isle and Dudley MSS*, VI, 599, 600.

21. Ibid., VI, 484.

22. "The Countess of Leicester's Case," ibid., VI, 488–91.

23. De Fonblanque, *House of Percy*, II, 405; *CSPD, 1650*, 356, 521.

24. *Egmont MSS*, I, 177, 487, 494, 515–16. Lucy's note to Percival: Addit. MSS, 46934.

25. *CSPD, 1650*, 409.

26. *De L'Isle Dudley MSS*, VI, 559.

27. *CSPD, 1650*, 465.

28. *CSPD, 1651*, 95, 255.

29. *Portland MSS*, I, 585.

30. *Nicholas Papers*, I, 237.

31. Ibid.

32. *CSPD, 1651–1652*, 167.

Chapter 19 A Dysfunctional Family

1. Evelyn, *Diary*, I, 285.

2. *De L'Isle and Dudley MSS*, VI, 613.

3. Osborne, *Letters*, 51, 54, 61.

4. *De L'Isle and Dudley MSS*, VI, 477.

5. Ibid., VI, 614.

6. Ibid.

7.   Ibid., VI, 492.

8.   De L'Isle MSS, C 130/9.

9.   Cartwright, *Sacharissa*, 147.

10. *De L'Isle and Dudley MSS*, VI, 495.

11. Ibid., VI, 492.

12. Ibid., VI, 500.

13. *Ailesbury MSS*, 158.

14. Osborne, *Letters*, 101.

15. *Duppa-Isham Correspondence*, 74.

16. *Egmont MSS*, I, 515–16.

17. Ibid.; Addit. MSS, 46934.

18. *Egmont MSS*, I, 515.

19. Addit. MSS, 46934.

20. *Duppa-Isham Correspondence*, 33.

21. *Ailesbury MSS*, 158.

22. *Duppa-Isham Correspondence*, 71.

23. Ibid., 75.

24. Osborne, *Letters*, 100, 106, 109.

25. *Cal. Clar. SP*, II, 334–35; *Nicholas Papers*, II, 65.

26. *Ailesbury MSS*, 159.

27. Ibid., 161.

28. *De L'Isle and Dudley MSS*, VI, 500; Cartwright, *Sacharissa*, 158. After Dorothy's death, Anne, seemingly destined for spinsterhood, at thirty-four eloped with the family chaplain, the Reverend Joseph Cart, vicar of Leigh. For marrying beneath her station, her father cut her off, despite her plea for forgiveness; *De L'Isle and Dudley MSS*, VI, 624. Yet it is nice to know that "poor Nan" lived happily enough in the vicarage with a loving, if lowly, husband; Cartwright, *Sacharissa*, 165–66.

29. *De L'Isle and Dudley MSS*, VI, 496.

30. Cartwright, *Sacharissa*, 143.

31. *Burnet's History*, I, 69–70.

32. *Salisbury MSS*, XXII, 437.

33. Ibid., XXII, 431, 433.

34. Ibid.; Mordaunt, *Letterbook*, xi.

35. *Sutherland MSS*, II, 152.

36. *De L'Isle and Dudley MSS*, VI, 500–501.

37. Cartwright, *Sacharissa*, 156–57.

38. Ibid., 158.

39. Ibid., 160.

Chapter 20 *"The Old Lady Carlisle Is Dead"*

1. *De L'Isle and Dudley MSS*, VI, 271.

2. *Cal.Clar. SP*, IV, 180. Lord Clarendon's papers, housed at the Bodleian Library in Oxford, have been calendared in four volumes (1869–1932). A selection of the papers themselves was printed in *State Papers Collected by Edward, Earl of Clarendon (Clar. SP)*.

3. Mordaunt, *Letterbook*, xi–xvii.

4. *Clar. SP*, III, 664.

5. Pepys, *Diary*, I, 77, 84, 86; Evelyn, *Diary*, I, 353–54.

6. *Clar. SP*, III, 685.

7. Ibid., III, 681.

8. Ibid., III, 729.

9. Ibid.

10. Ibid., III, 734. According to Evelyn and Mordaunt, "then in great favour," was selling pardons for £1,000. Evelyn, *Diary*, I, 355.

11. *Burnet's History*, I, 96.

12. Jesse, *Memoirs*, III, 211.

13. *Clar. SP*, III, 735.

14. *De L'Isle and Dudley MSS*, VI, 622.

15. Pepys, *Diary*, I, 175.

16. Dent, *Quest for Nonsuch*, 199.

17. Pepys, *Diary*, I, 241, 246.

18. Ibid., I, 269.

19. *De L'Isle and Dudley MSS*, VI, 623.

20. *Sutherland MSS*, 184.

21. Ibid., 157. Lucy was buried near her father in the Percy crypt at Petworth in Sussex.

Bibliography

ABBREVIATIONS

BL	British Library, London
DNB	*Dictionary of National Biography*
HMC	Historical Manuscripts Commission
PRO	Public Record Office

CONTEMPORARY ACCOUNTS

Addit. MSS	Additional Manuscripts collections, BL.
Ailesbury MSS	*Ailesbury Manuscripts.* HMC, 15th Report. London, 1898.
Ashburnham, *Narrative*	Ashburnham, John. *A Narrative . . . of his attendance on King Charles.* 2 vols. London, 1830.
Aubrey, *Brief Lives*	Aubrey, John. *Aubrey's Brief Lives.* Ed. Oliver Dick. London, 1958.

Baillie, *Letters*   Baillie, Robert. *Letters and Journals.*
            Ed. David Laing. Edinburgh, 1841–42.

Baschet Transcripts   Baschet Transcripts, PRO.

Buccleuch MSS   *Buccleuch Manuscripts.* HMC. Vol. I,
            London, 1899. Vol. III, London, 1926.

Burnet's History   Burnet, Gilbert. *Bishop Burnet's His-*
            tory of His Own Time. Ed. Thomas
            Burnet. 4 vols. London, 1818.

Cal.Clar. SP   *Calendar of Clarendon State Papers.*
            Eds. M. A. Ogle, W. H. Bliss, W. D.
            Macray, and F. L. Routledge. 4 vols.
            Oxford, 1869–1932.

Carlisle Papers   Carlisle Papers, Egerton MSS, BL.

Cary, *Memorials*   Cary, Henry. *Memorials of the Civil*
            War. 2 vols. London, 1842.

Chamberlain, *Letters*   Chamberlain, John. *The Letters of*
            John Chamberlain. Ed. N. E. McClure.
            2 vols. Memoirs of the American
            Philosophical Society 12. Philadel-
            phia, 1939.

Charles, *Letters*   Charles I, King of England. *The Let-*
            ters, Speeches and Proclamations of King
            Charles I. Ed. Sir Charles Petrie. Lon-
            don, 1935.

Clar. SP   *State Papers Collected by Edward, Earl*
            of Clarendon. Eds. R. Scrope and T.
            Monkhouse. 3 vols. Oxford,
            1767–1786.

Clarendon, *History*   Clarendon, Edward Hyde, Earl of.
            The History of the Rebellion and Civil

Clarendon, *History (cont'd)*   *Wars in England.* Ed. W. D. Macray. 6 vols. Oxford, 1888.

Clifford, *Diary*   Clifford, Anne. *The Diary of Anne Clifford, 1616–1619: A Critical Edition.* Ed. Katherine O. Acheson. New York and London, 1995.

Constitutional Documents   *The Constitutional Documents of the Puritan Revolution 1625–1660.* Ed. S. R. Gardiner. Oxford, 1889.

CSPC   *Calendar of State Papers, Colonial, 1574–1660.* London, 1860.

CSPD   *Calendar of State Papers, Domestic.* Volumes covering 1611–1660, London, 1858–1886.

CSPI   *Calendar of State Papers, Ireland, 1633–1647.* London, 1901.

CSPV   *Calendar of State Papers, Venetian.* Volumes covering 1615–1661, London, 1908–1931.

De L'Isle MSS   De L'Isle Manuscripts, Kent County Council Archives

De L'Isle and Dudley MSS   *De L'Isle and Dudley Manuscripts.* HMC. Vol. V, London, 1962. Vol. VI, London, 1966.

D'Ewes, *Autobiography*   D'Ewes, Simonds. *Autobiography and Correspondence of Sir Simonds D'Ewes.* Ed. J. A. Halliwell. London, 1845.

Duppa-Isham Correspondence   Duppa, Brian. *The Correspondence of Bishop Brian Duppa and Sir Justinian Isham, 1650–1660.* Ed. Sir Gyles Isham.

Aubrey, *Brief Lives (cont'd)*   Northamptonshire Record Society Publications. Northampton, 1955.

Egmont MSS   *Egmont Manuscripts.* HMC. Vol. I, pt. 1, London, 1905.

Ellis, *Letters*   Ellis, Henry, ed. *Original Letters Illustrative of English History.* 1st ser., 3 vols. London, 1825. 2nd ser., 4 vols. London, 1827.

England and Germany   *Letters . . . Illustrating the Relations Between England and Germany at the Commencement of the Thirty Years War.* Ed. S. R. Gardiner. 2 vols. Camden Society. London, 1865.

Evelyn, *Diary*   Evelyn, John. *Diary and Correspondence of John Evelyn.* Ed. William Bray. 4 vols. London, 1859.

Finet, *Notebooks*   Finet, John. *Ceremonies of Charles I: The Notebooks of John Finet, 1628–1641.* Ed. A. J. Loomie. New York, 1987.

Hamilton Addenda   *Hamilton Papers Addenda.* Ed. S. R. Gardiner. Camden Miscellany 53. Reprinted by permission of the Royal Historical Society. London, 1885.

Hamilton Papers   *Hamilton Papers.* Ed. S. R. Gardiner. Camden Society, new ser., 27. London, 1880.

Hammond, *Letters*   Hammond, Robert. *Letters between Colonel Robert Hammond . . . and the Committee of Lords and Commons at Derby House.* London, 1764.

Harley MSS   Harley Manuscripts, BL.

Heath, *Flagellum*

Heath, James. *Flagellum, or the Life and Death, Birth and Burial of Oliver Cromwell, the Late Usurper.* 2nd ed. London, 1663.

Howell, *Familiar Letters*

Howell, Joseph. *Epistolae Ho-Elianae or The Familiar Letters of James Howell.* Ed. Joseph Jacobs. 2 vols. London, 1892.

La Rochefoucauld, *Mémoires*

La Rochefoucauld, François de Marsillac, Duc de. *Mémoires du duc de la Rochefoucauld.* Eds. D. L. Gilbert and J. Gourdault. Grands Écrivains de la France. Paris, 1874.

Manchester MSS

Manchester Manuscripts. HMC, appendix to 8th Report, pt. 2. London, 1881.

Mathew, *Letters*

Mathew, Tobie. *A Collection of Letters made by Sr Tobie Mathews Kt. With a Character of the most Excellent Lady, Lucy Countess of Carleile.* London, 1660.

Montereul, *Correspondence*

Montereul, Jean de. *The Diplomatic Correspondence of Jean de Montereul and the Brothers Bellièvre.* Ed. and trans. J. G. Fotheringham. Scottish History Society. 2 vols. Edinburgh, 1898.

Mordaunt, *Letterbook*

Mordaunt, John. *Letterbook of John Viscount Mordaunt.* Ed. Mary Coate. Camden Society, 3rd ser., 69. London, 1945.

Neville, *Newes*   Neville, Henry. *Newes from the New*
                                         Exchange, or the Commonwealth of
                                         Ladies. London, 1650.

Nicholas Papers   *The Nicholas Papers: 1641–1652.* Ed.
                                         George F. Warner. Camden Society,
                                         new ser. London, 1886.

Nichols, *Progresses*   Nichols, John. *The Progresses, Pro-*
                                         cessions, and Magnificent Festivals of
                                         King James the First. 4 vols. London,
                                         1828

Northumberland MSS   *Northumberland Manuscripts.* HMC,
                                         appendix to 3rd Report. London,
                                         1872.

Northumberland Papers   Northumberland, Henry Percy, 9th
                                         Earl of. *The Household Papers of Henry*
                                         Percy, Ninth Earl of Northumberland.
                                         Ed. G. R. Batho. Camden Society, 3rd
                                         ser., 93. London, 1962.

Osborne, *Letters*   Osborne, Dorothy. *The Letters of*
                                         Dorothy Osborne. Ed. Dorothy Gar-
                                         diner. London, 1933.

Pepys, *Diary*   Pepys, Samuel. *The Diary of Samuel*
                                         Pepys. Ed. H. B. Wheatley. 8 vols.
                                         London, 1904.

Pepys MSS   *Pepys Manuscripts.* HMC. London,
                                         1911.

Portland MSS   *Portland Manuscripts.* HMC. Vol. 1.
                                         London, 1981.

Radcliffe, *Letters*   Whitaker, T. D. *Life and Letters of Sir*
                                         George Radcliffe. London, 1810.

Raymond, *Autobiography* Raymond, Thomas. *Autobiography of Thomas Raymond.* Ed. Godfrey Davies. Camden Society, 3rd ser. Vol. 28. 1917

Richelieu, *Mémoires* Richelieu, Armand du Plessis. *Mémoires.* Ed. Robert Lavollée. Paris, 1925.

Rushworth, *Collections* Rushworth, John. *Historical Collections of Private Passages of State.* 8 vols. London, 1721.

Salisbury MSS *Salisbury Manuscripts.* HMC. Vol. XXII, London, 1971.

Salvetti Correspondence *Salvetti Correspondence, Skrine Manuscripts.* HMC, appendix to 11th Report, pt. 1. London, 1887.

Strafford, *Letters* Strafford, Thomas Wentworth, Earl of. *The Earl of Strafford's Letters and Despatches.* Ed. William Knowler. 2 vols. London, 1739.

Strafford Papers Strafford Papers, Fitzwilliam MSS, Sheffield Central Library.

Sutherland MSS *Sutherland Manuscripts.* HMC, appendix to 5th Report, pt. 1. London, 1876.

Sydney Papers *Letters and Memorials of State . . . Written and Collected by Sir Henry Sydney faithfully transcribed from the Originals at Penshurst Place in Kent.* Ed. Arthur Collins. 2 vols. London, 1746.

Tillières, *Mémoires* Tillières, Léveneur de. *Mémoires inédites du Léveneur de Tillières.* Ed. M. C. Hippeau. Paris, 1863.

Various Collections	*Various Collections, Bruce Manuscript.* HMC, 7th Report. London, 1914.
Warwick, *Memoirs*	Warwick, Philip. *Memoirs of the Reigne of Charles the First.* London, 1813.
Weldon, *Court*	[Weldon, Anthony]. *The Court and Character of King James, whereunto is now added the Court of King Charles.* London, 1651.
Whitelocke, *Memorials*	Whitelocke, Bulstrode. *Memorials of English Affairs from the Beginning of the Reign of Charles the First* . . . Ed. R. H. Bulstrode. London, 1860.
Wilson, *History*	Wilson, Arthur. *History of Great Britain.* London, 1653.
Wynn Papers	*Calendar of Wynn Papers, 1515–1690.* National Library of Wales. London, 1926.

SELECTED BOOKS AND ARTICLES

Adamson, J. A. "The English Nobility and the Projected Settlement of 1647." *Historical Journal* 30 (1987): 567–602.

Albion, Gordon. *Charles I and the Court of Rome.* Louvain, 1935.

Anselment, Raymond. "The Countess of Carlisle and Caroline Praise: Convention and Reality." *Studies in Philology* 82 (Spring 1985): 212–33.

Barroll, Leeds. *Anna of Denmark, Queen of England: A Cultural Biography.* Philadelphia, 2001.

Batho, G. R. "A Difficult Father-in-Law: the Ninth Earl of Northumberland." *History Today* (November 1956): 744–51.

———. "The Wizard Earl in the Tower, 1605–1621." *History Today* (May 1956): 344–51.

Beatty, John L. *Warwick and Holland*. Denver, 1965.

Bentley, Gerald Eades. *The Jacobean and Caroline Stage*. 5 vols. Oxford, 1956.

Bergeron, David M. *King James and Letters of Homoerotic Desire*. Iowa City, 1999.

Birch, Thomas. *The Court and Times of Charles I*. 2 vols. London, 1849.

——. *The Court and Times of James I*. Ed. R. F. Williams. 2 vols. London, 1848.

Blake, Robin. *Anthony Van Dyck: A Life 1599–1641*. London, 1999.

Bligh, E. W. *Sir Kenelm Digby and His Venetia*. London, 1932.

Brenan, Gerald. *A History of the House of Percy*. Ed. W. A. Lindsay. 2 vols. London, 1902.

Burghclere, Winifred, Baroness. *Strafford*. 2 vols. London, 1931.

Campbell, Dorothy de Brissac. *The Intriguing Duchess*. New York, 1930

Carlton, Charles. *Charles I: The Personal Monarch*. London and Boston, 1983.

——. "The Impact of the Fighting." In Morrill, *English Civil War*.

Carte, Thomas. *The Life of James, Duke of Ormonde*. Oxford, 1851.

Cartwright, Julia. *Sacharissa*. London, 1893.

Cooper, J. P. "The Fortune of Thomas Wentworth, Earl of Strafford." *Economic History Review*, 2nd ser., 11 (December 1958): 227–48.

Crawford, P. *Denzil Holles, 1598–1680: A Study of His Political Career*. Royal Historical Society. London, 1979.

Davies, Godfrey. *The Early Stuarts, 1603–1660*. 2nd ed. Oxford History of England. Oxford, 1959.

De Fonblanque, E. B. *Annals of the House of Percy*. 2 vols. London, 1887.

——. *Lives of the Lords Strangford*. London and New York, 1877.

Denbigh, Cecilia Fielding, Countess of. *Royalist Father and Roundhead Son*. London, 1915.

Dent, John. *The Quest for Nonsuch*. London, 1970.

Disraeli, Isaac. *Commentaries on the Life and Reign of Charles I*. 4 vols. London, 1828–1830.

Donagan, Barbara. "A Courtier's Progress: Greed and Consistency in the Life of the Earl of Holland." *Historical Journal* 19, no. 2 (1976): 317–53.

Dunn, Richard S. *Sugar and Slaves: The Rise of the Planter Class in the English West Indies, 1624–1713*. New York, 1973.

Firebrace, C. W. *Honest Harry, Being the Biography of Sir Henry Firebrace*. London, 1932.

Forster, John. *Arrest of the Five Members by Charles the First*. London, 1860.

Gardiner, S. R. *History of England from the Accession of James I to the Outbreak of the Civil War, 1603–1642*. 10 vols. London, 1883–84.

Gentles, Ian. "The Impact of the New Model Army." In Morrill, *English Civil War*.

Godfrey, Elizabeth. *Home Life under the Stuarts*. London, 1925.

Hamilton, Elizabeth. *Henrietta Maria*. New York, 1976.

Hibbert, Christopher. *The Virgin Queen: The Personal History of Elizabeth I*. London, 1990.

Hillier, G. *A Narrative of Attempted Escapes of Charles I*. London, 1852.

Hull, Felix. "Sidney of Penshurst: Robert 2nd Earl of Leicester." *Archaeologica Cantiana* 3 (1993): 43–56.

Jesse, J. H. *Memoirs of the Court of England*. Boston, 1901.

Jones, A. R., and P. Stallybrass. *Renaissance Clothing and the Materials of Memory*. Cambridge, 2000.

Kearney, H. F. *Strafford in Ireland 1633–1641: A Study in Absolutism*. Manchester, 1959.

Lee, Patricia-Ann. "Lucy Percy, Countess of Carlisle 1599–1660." In *Research Guide to European Historical Biography, 1450 to the Present*, vol. 3, pp. 1599–1608. 4 vols. Washington, 1992.

Lindley, David. *Court Masques: Jacobean and Caroline Entertainments, 1605–1640*. Oxford, 1995.

Lockyer, Roger. *Buckingham: The Life and Political Career of George Villiers, First Duke of Buckingham, 1592–1628*. London, 1981.

Malloch, A. *Finch and Baines: A Seventeenth Century Friendship*. Cambridge, 1917.

Manchester, William Montagu, Duke of. *Court and Society from Elizabeth to Anne*. 2 vols. London, 1864.

Millar, Oliver. *Van Dyck in England*. Exhibition catalog, National Portrait Gallery. London, 1982.

Morrill, John, ed. *The Impact of the English Civil War*. London, 1991.

Newton, A. P. *The Colonizing Activities of the English Puritans*. New Haven, 1914.

Peck, Linda Levy. *Court Patronage and Corruption in Early Stuart England.* London, 1991.

Pomfret, Thomas. *Life of the Countess of Devonshire.* London, 1685.

Ranger, T. "Strafford in Ireland: A Revaluation." *Past and Present* 20 (April 1961): 26–45.

Sainsbury, W. N., ed. *Original Unpublished Papers Illustrative of the Life of Sir Peter Paul Rubens.* London, 1859.

Sanders, Julie. "Caroline Salon Culture and Female Agency: The Countess of Carlisle, Henrietta Maria and Public Theatre." *Theatre Journal* 52 (December 2000): 449–64.

Schreiber, Roy. *The First Carlisle: Sir James Hay, First Earl of Carlisle as Courtier, Diplomat, and Entrepreneur, 1580–1636.* Transactions of the American Philosophical Society. Vol. 74, pt. 7. Philadelphia, 1984.

Smith, David L. "The Impact on Government." In Morrill, *English Civil War.*

Smuts, R. M. *Court Culture and the Origins of a Royalist Tradition in Early Stuart England.* Philadelphia, 1987.

———. "The Puritan Followers of Henrietta Maria in the 1630's." *English Historical Review* 93 (1978): 26–45.

Stone, Lawrence. *The Crisis of the Aristocracy.* Abridged ed. Oxford, 1967.

———. *Family and Fortune: Studies in Aristocratic Finance in the Sixteenth and Seventeenth Centuries.* Oxford, 1973.

Stoye, J. W. *English Travellers Abroad 1604–1667.* London, 1952.

Strickland, Agnes. *Lives of the Queens of England.* 12 vols. Philadelphia, 1860.

Strong, Roy. *Henry Prince of Wales and England's Lost Renaissance.* London, 1986.

Suckling, John. *The Works of Sir John Suckling.* Ed. Thomas Clayton. Oxford, 1971.

Thomson, Roger. *Women in Stuart England and America.* London, 1974.

Von Ranke, L. *A History of England Principally in the Seventeenth Century.* 6 vols. Oxford, 1875.

Waller, Edmund. *The Poems of Edmund Waller.* Ed. G. Thorn Drury. London and New York, 1893.

Waller, William. "Recollections," in *The Poetry of Anna Matilda.* London, 1788.

Wedgwood, C. V. *The King's War*. London, 1958.

——. *Thomas Wentworth, First Earl of Strafford, 1593–1641: A Revaluation*. London, 1961.

Wheelock, Arthur K., Jr., Susan J. Barnes, and Julius Held. *Anthony Van Dyck*. New York, 1990.

Willson, David H. *King James VI and I*. London, 1956.

Young, M. *Servility and Service: The Life and Work of Sir John Coke*. London, 1985.

Index